From Unipolar to Tripolar World

About the Author

Arvind Virmani, b. 1949, is PhD in Economics from Harvard University, USA (1975). His thesis supervisor was Nobel Laureate Professor Kenneth Arrow. The author is presently Executive Director, International Monetary Fund, Washington.

Dr. Virmani has been Chief Economic Advisor, Department of Economic Affairs, Ministry of Finance; Principle Advisor, Planning Commission; Director & Chief Executive, Indian Council for Research on International Economic Relations (ICRIER) and Member, Telecom Regulatory Authority of India (TRAI).

He has extensive experience of the financial sector having served as Chairman, Board of Trustees of SBI Mutual Fund, and Director on the Boards of LIC, Punjab National Bank and Allahabad Bank, and Trustee of Unit Trust of India. He was a member of the Appellate Tribunal for SEBI Act. He chaired the Working Group on Public Debt Management (middle office) and Inter-ministerial Group on Customs Duty Reform.

His areas of policy research include: macroeconomics, growth, international trade, tariffs, credit markets, and international relations and global security. Among his books are: *Accelerating Growth and Poverty Reduction: A Policy Framework for India's Development* (Academic Foundation, 2004), *Propelling India from Socialist Stagnation to Global Power,* Vols. I and II (Academic Foundation, 2006) and *The Sudoku of India's Growth* (BS Books, 2009).

From Unipolar to Tripolar World

Multipolar Transition Paradox

ARVIND VIRMANI

ACADEMIC FOUNDATION
NEW DELHI

ACADEMIC FOUNDATION

First published in 2010
by

ACADEMIC FOUNDATION
4772-73 / 23 Bharat Ram Road, (23 Ansari Road),
Darya Ganj, New Delhi - 110 002 (India).
Phones : 23245001 / 02 / 03 / 04.
Fax : +91-11-23245005.
E-mail : books@academicfoundation.com
www. academicfoundation.com

Cataloging in Publication Data--DK
Courtesy: D.K. Agencies (P) Ltd. <docinfo@dkagencies.com>

Virmani, Arvind, 1949-
From unipolar to tripolar world : multipolar transition paradox / Arvind Virmani.
p. cm.
ISBN 13: 9788171887996
ISBN 10: 8171887996

1. International economic relations. 2. Economic geography. 3. Power (Social sciences) 4. India--Foreign economic relations. I. Title.

DDC 330.9 22

Typeset by Italics India, New Delhi.
Printed and bound in India.

Contents

List of Tables and Figures

Tables

Figures

Overview

The first two chapters summarise from somewhat different perspectives the analysis done by the author, during 2004-05 and 2005-06, on the economic foundations of a nation's global power. The focus of much of this analysis is on Nation States, rather than regional groupings. Chapter 1 presents the current situation and makes forecasts about the future. The appendix outlines the analytical basis of our measurement of power. A more detailed discussion is left to a subsequent chapter. Chapter 2 puts the information into a historical continental/regional perspective. It also focuses on the contrast between the perspectives arising from the distribution of States (or virtual states) by the size of their economy with that arising from a measure of their power potential. It also introduces the concept of strategic technology and its role in determining a State's overall global power. Chapter 3 spells out in greater detail the concepts and measurement of power potential and overall power (developed by the author during 2004, 2005). Compared to earlier measures of national power, this analysis is grounded in accepted economic concepts such as that of the aggregate production function and information asymmetries arising from monopoly of strategic technology. The simplicity and power of this concept is then illustrated by applying it power structures since the 18th century. Chapter 4, analysis the emerging power structure and draws out its implications for India's relations with other powers, particularly the USA. Chapter 5 examines in greater detail the past and future economic counters of the Asia-Pacific and South Asian regions and its impact on global strategic architecture. It provides a definition of a regional power and a regional VIP and uses this to select countries that may play a role in the new global order. It also compares the regional economic weight of different continents and the large countries in that continent.

It is not essential to read chapters 1 to 5 sequentially as they are relatively self-contained and can be read independently. This however, entails some overlap and duplication for those reading the chapters sequentially. There is however an increase in the width and depth of the material from one chapter to the next, which hopefully is sufficient to repay the inconvenience of some repetition.

Chapters 6 analyses the strengths and weakness of China's economy and draws out some lessons for other economies. Chapter 7 examines India-China trade and the possibilities for cooperation between the two economies. Chapter 8 carries out a detailed analysis of the proliferation of nuclear materials and technology from the Nuclear Weapons States (NWS), as defined in the NPT, and their NNWS partners. It exposes the almost incredible story of Pakistan's Euro-Chinese bomb and the role played by the USA, because of its short sighted focus on immediate problems and the consequent neglect of its long term enlightened national interest.

Chapter 9 uses the revised estimates of GDP at PPP based on the new UN 2005 system and the developments in the World economy since 2006 to re-evaluate the projections made in earlier chapters. It confirms that the World will move gradually from a unipolar power structure to a tripolar one, though over a longer time frame than envisioned earlier. It also analyses in greater detail the evolution of the global power structure over the next decade or so till it becomes bipolar. This reveals a paradox. The transition is characterised by a multipolar interregnum grounded in the multiple-dimensions of power and the new constraints arising from a globalised World economy, society and polity. It brings to bear the insights of institutional economics to reflect on global institutions such as the UN Security Council and how they must evolve to reflect the emerging global order. It ends by making comprehensive recommendations for enhancing India's internal and external security in the face of old and new challenges and opportunities.

1 Evolution of World Economy and Global Power

This chapter brings out some basic facts about the global economy and relative economic power. It then projects them into the future. These mean scenarios are then used to draw certain conclusions about the evolution of global power. The appendix explains the basis for the definition of economic power.

We start with the basic economics of comparison, which is the size of an economy measured by its GDP at purchasing power parity (PPP). Next we examine the two simple arithmetic components of GDP, namely population and per capita income. We show how this has been changing with globalisation and policy reform. That is, we analyse the relationship between globalisation, policy reform and growth (very briefly). A forecast of population and per capita GDP is combined to obtain a forecast GDP. This forms the basis for drawing implications about global power. Before we do that, however, it is useful to look at what may be called the Conventional Wisdom (CW).[1] Conventional Wisdom, which is still widely prevalent with perhaps 90-95 per cent of analysts still believing it. So, the scenario presented in this chapter and the implications drawn from it are unconventional. These are, one, that the world economy is multipolar, and will remain so, and two, that global structure will go from being unipolar at the end of the 20th century to tripolar by the middle of the 21st century.

GDP at PPP

Figure 1.1 depicts the 20 largest country's share of world GDP at purchasing power parity in 2003, ordered from the largest to the smallest. It is useful to note that the largest country, USA had about

---

1. We always liked this word which has coined by *Newsweek* many years ago.

21.1 per cent of world GDP. China at the 2nd position with about 12 per cent of world GDP was about half the size of the US economy. Japan (7 per cent) and India (5.7 per cent) were about half the size of China and quarter that of the USA. Then come the other rich countries, Germany, France, UK, Italy, etc.

Figure 1.1

Country Shares of World GDP at Purchasing Power Parity (PPP)

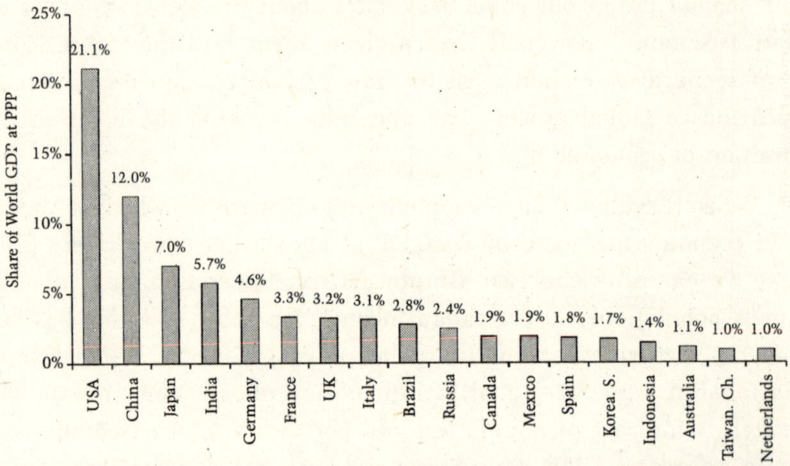

GDP in very simple arithmetic terms is the multiplication of the population with the per capita income. So, we have looked at the world GDP and then we go on to look at the two components of GDP and finally we will draw some implications. If we look at the world population share (Figure 1.2), the picture is quite different. The two countries with the largest shares of world population are China and India, each about 20 per cent of world population. The USA in this case is one-fifth the size of the largest country. That is one important point. The second point is that on the right of the USA is a country which is often missed, Indonesia, which is actually the fourth-largest in the world. Next come Brazil and Russia, which have been mentioned a lot and this is one of the reasons why they are mentioned a lot, because they come next (5th and 6th). But Indonesia, which is more populous, has been missed in many of these discussions, and it is going to be important. This may not however happen in the next 25 years, but later.

So that is one of the reasons why it is not been focused on actively. Further to the right we see mostly the rich countries and then there is a sharp drop off, very-very small proportions to the right.

Figure 1.2

Country Share of World Population

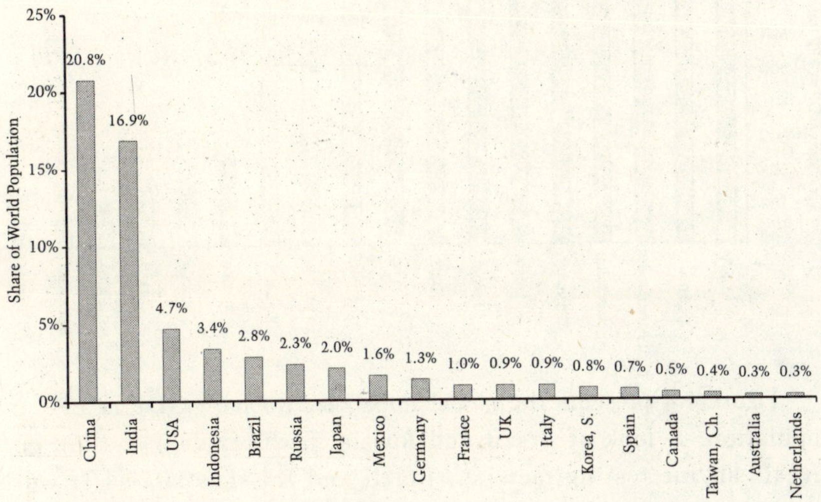

Figure 1.3 focuses on the country-wise per capita GDP. The same set of countries, which we have seen in the earlier figures are presented here also. However, they are now ordered/placed as per the per capita income at PPP. Therefore, once again USA the richest country is at the top. USA is placed at 100 per cent and the per capita GDP of other countries is shown as a ratio to the USA. From here on, most of the things we discuss will be as a ratio to the US. Most of the rich countries like Canada, the Netherlands, Australia, Germany etc., are at 80 per cent of the per captia income of the USA. China (13 per cent), Indonesia (9 per cent) and India (8 per cent) are placed at the bottom. This has two implications. One is of course, the obvious one that we are a relatively poor country; among the large countries we are actually the poorest. But the other side of this coin is the potential for catching-up, which is the basis of our future projections. The point, to be noted is that Indonesia again is in the reckoning and it also has a huge potential.

Figure 1.3

Catch-up Growth Potential

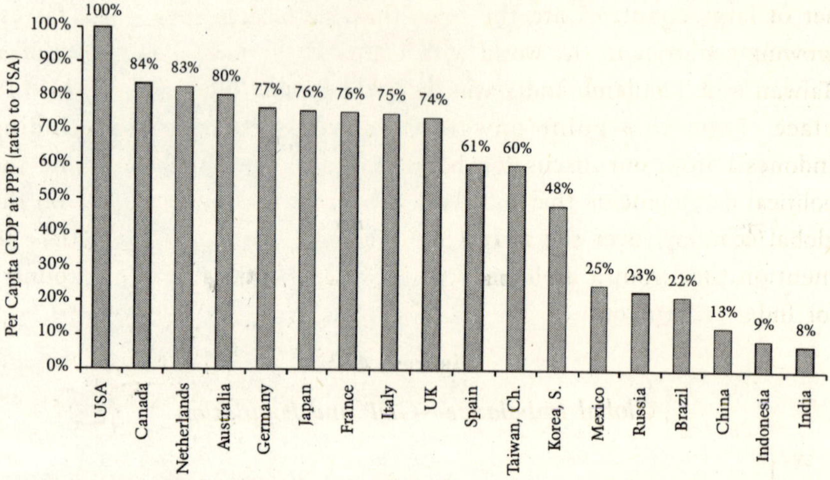

Figure 1.4 presents the global imbalance for both GDP at PPP and population. A look at Brazil and Russia in the middle of the figure reveals an interesting fact i.e., Brazil and Russia's shares of world population and world GDP are almost identical. And this is what leads into one of our conclusions that in the case of these two countries, there is not much of a gap. The US is once again at the top with a very large positive gap. China and India however have very large negative gaps. This comes out very clearly in Figure 1.5 also where the gap between world GDP share and world population share is presented. The rich countries—USA, Japan, Germany, France, UK and Italy—are the countries with the largest positive gaps, and the countries with the largest negative gap are India, China and Indonesia. However, it is our assertion that these gaps are going to narrow over this century and much of this is going to happen over the next 50 years. The appropriate question to ask is, why it will happen now when these gaps have actually existed since the Industrial Revolution. These gaps opened up during the Industrial Revolution in the 17th century and have existed for centuries. So, it is obvious that these gaps would not be easy to close. But the reason why we assert that they will be closed is evidenced in

Table 1.1. It can be seen from the table that over the last 25 years, the countries that have the largest negative gaps (Figure 1.5) from among the set of large countries are the ones that have been among the fastest growing countries in the world with China at the top followed by Korea, Taiwan and Thailand. India was at 9th place and Indonesia at the 11th place. From this point onwards, we will, however, be excluding Indonesia from our discussion because due to the Asian crisis and the political developments that followed, it will not have a big impact on the global economy over the next 15-20 years. However, we would like to mention that from a diplomacy perspective it is an important country for India to focus on.

Figure 1.4

Global Imbalance—GDP and Population

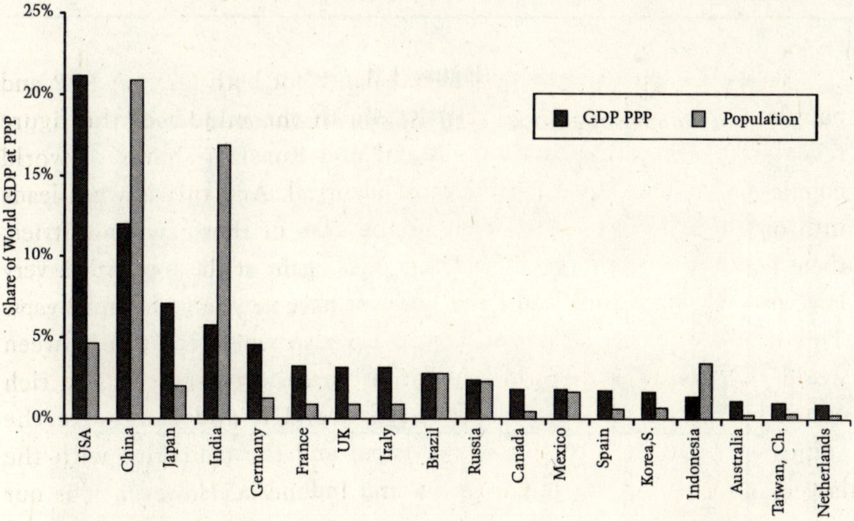

The current picture of the GDP shares, population shares, the gaps and how they have been closing, provides the basis for future projection, which was the primary purpose of our analysis. We do this by reversing the process. We start by looking at the population projections, then at the per capita income projections and finally put them together into the GDP projection. We conclude by tracing out what that implies for the global economy.

Table 1.1

Real Per Capita GDP Growth—1980 to 2003

Economy	*Rank*	*Average*
China, Pr.	1	8.2
Korea, Rep.	2	5.6
Taiwan, China	3	5.3
Thailand	4	4.7
Vietnam	5	4.6
Ireland	6	4.5
Singapore	7	4.2
Hong Kong	8	3.9
India	9	3.7
Luxembourg	10	3.7
Indonesia	11	3.6
Malaysia	12	3.6

Figure 1.5

Global Imbalance; GDP Share—Population Share

Figure 1.6 shows the share of world population as projected by the UN. The first thing to notice is that the relative population share is going to invert over the next 50 years. The inversion point is somewhere around 2035. There is a slightly revised projection which has come out since we made these projections but that does not matter. It does not

change it substantively, actually it just brings the transition point where India's population goes above China a little earlier, which is now around 2030. Basically, India's and China's population will be around the same over the next 50 years. The second thing to note is that the US share of world population remains almost the same. You can see that it remains just below the 5 per cent line in all three periods shown. The third much more important point that has recently started appearing in the reports is that Japan and Russia have more or less the same share in the world population. But as we go further in the projection, there is a dramatic change in their share of the population—each shows a decline of about 25 per cent. This is a very important factor as far as the future of Russia is concerned; this is going to have a big impact on Russia's position in the world in future. And then there are the rich countries, mostly European countries, Germany and others, which will also have declining shares of world population. Recall that the GDP of the US was the largest, even though its population was and is the third-largest. The most important thing to be noted is that China and India only have to have one-fifth the per capita income of the US to equal it in size. So, the first important point that emerges is that China and India have the capability of equalling the US economy in size, because they only need to catch up to one-fifth of US per capita income. The second point which appears from this population perspective is that there is really no other country which can equal the US without exceeding its per capita income. Though obvious, this is an important point to note because leaving aside Indonesia, the other countries are just too small. The per capita income would have to be far in excess of the US to equal the US economy in size.

Therefore, in my view, the above discussion clearly shows that only tripolarity is possible in terms of nation-states; remember, we are talking about nation-states only, which is what we have presented. India is currently a low income country, so there is a big scope for catch-up and in our judgement that is going to happen. China is currently a lower middle income country so the scope is slightly less, but it will also catch up. Consequently, the key issue is going to be the trends in growth of per capita GDP in these two countries, over the next 25-50 years or whatever time horizon we are interested in. Among the issues which arise are how quickly will China slow down and can India maintain its growth rate. As an aside, it is worth mentioning that in principle, if EU becomes what we call a "virtual state", if it acts in external relationships as the single country then it would be a fourth pole but having said that, we will stick with the nation-states in this chapter.

Figure 1.6

Population Projections of the UN in 2004

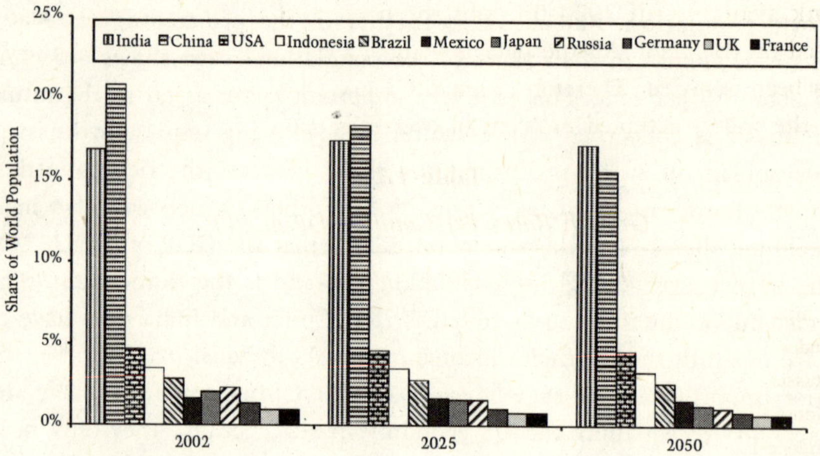

Table 1.2 presents our per capita GDP growth projections. We have done these projections from a macroeconomic perspective, based on the author's studies of the growth experience of India, China and Asia (see references). To some extent, we are also summarising the micro factors into these growth rates. As per the projections, China and India are the two fastest growing economies, followed by Russia. In this projection, Brazil is at the bottom. One interesting thing to observe here is that India's growth rate will go above China some time in the middle of the next decade (3rd column of the Table). These are based on a whole bunch of analysis of the Indian economy and a smaller but equally detailed analysis of the Chinese economy, on which of course, different experts may have different views. Russia will be the third fastest growing economy among the set of large countries. But its position does not change all that significantly; for the reasons already discussed above in relation to population. As far as Brazil is concerned, taking into account the views of the experts on Brazil, even if we modify the simulation and

double the growth rates for Brazil, it will not significantly change the global picture. The Brazilian economy does however become larger than 2-3 other countries by 2050.

Using these growth rates, it turns out that whether we look at the real growth rates in terms of local currency, PPP or in terms of GDP at current exchange rates, they are all the same. All the data that have been presented so far is from the World Development Indicators of the World Bank available till 2004-05, and the projections being made are also based on this data. All the data is standard data and data for no country has been adjusted. Therefore, even the China data has not been adjusted for the widely accepted problem of overestimation.

Table 1.2

Growth Rates Per Capita GDP at PPP

	1980-2002	*2003-2015*	*2016-2025*	*2026-2035*	*2036-2050*
China	8.2%	6.6%	5.6%	4.9%	4.0%
India	3.6%	5.2%	6.0%	5.7%	4.8%
Russia		4.9%	4.5%	4.1%	3.6%
Korea,S.	5.7%	4.3%	4.0%	3.7%	2.6%
Indonesia	3.7%	3.3%	3.7%	3.6%	3.5%
Taiwan, Ch.	5.4%	3.3%	3.1%	3.0%	2.3%
Spain	2.3%	3.0%	2.8%	2.6%	2.2%
Canada	1.6%	2.5%	2.3%	2.2%	2.2%
Australia	2.0%	2.5%	2.4%	2.1%	2.2%
UK	2.0%	2.2%	2.2%	2.2%	2.4%
USA	1.8%	2.0%	2.0%	2.0%	2.0%
Japan	2.0%	1.8%	2.0%	2.1%	2.0%
France	1.6%	1.8%	2.0%	2.1%	2.3%
Netherlands	1.8%	1.8%	2.0%	2.0%	2.0%
Mexico	0.8%	1.8%	2.1%	2.3%	2.3%
Italy	1.8%	1.6%	1.9%	2.0%	2.0%
Germany	1.6%	1.4%	2.0%	2.1%	2.2%
Brazil	0.7%	0.7%	1.5%	1.5%	2.2%

Figure 1.7 depicts what we would say, was the 100 per cent conventional wisdom amongst informed people, including analysts who had even done their own projections. This is the kind of picture which we believe that they had in 2004, and probably 95 per cent of the

analysts in the US and those who think about it in UK and Europe, still had till 2007 this kind of picture of the future. The GDP forecast depicted in Figure 1.7 has been obtained by applying the growth rate projections given in Table 1.2 to the GDP expressed in US dollars using the current exchange rate to convert from local currency units to US dollars. This has been done so that we can have a clear picture about what comes from this conventional wisdom (which in our view is fallacious).

Figure 1.7

Conventional Wisdom—A Unipolar Future

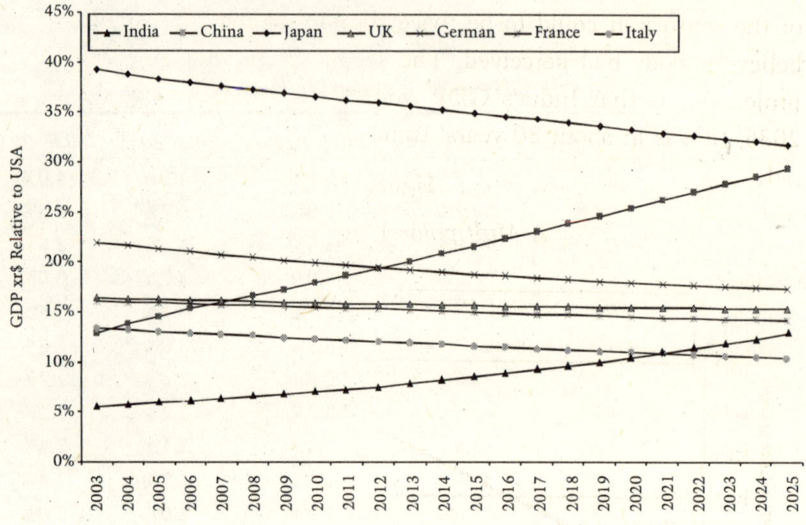

The main elements of this conventional view was that China (Figure 1.7) will continue rising but even 25 years from now it would only be 30 per cent of the size of the US economy. Therefore, though China was clearly recognised as the rising power, it was thought that it would be no threat to the US. Secondly, India at 5 per cent the size of the US economy was not really considered a significant player. There were perhaps a few isolated analysts who thought that maybe, at the end of 25 years, with about 15 per cent of the GDP of the US, it would/might become a *'swing state'*. Lastly, rich countries like UK, France, Germany etc., would more likely be competitively challenged by a rising China. These views were however, different from the author's conclusions, which are based on PPP projections. We believe that the correct measure for comparing size or economic power is to use the GDP at PPP. All the measures which we will be presenting are going to be relative to the US, because power is always relative, whether it is economic power or any other form of power. An absolute measure of power has little relevance or usefulness.

Figure 1.8 depicts our projection using the growth rates from Table 1.2, but now applied to GDP at purchasing power parity (PPP). They are also shown in relation to the US economy. There are just two things which stand out, one the size of the Chinese economy becoming larger than that of the USA within about 10 years i.e., 2015 and by the middle of the century, it could to be twice the size of the US economy. This we believe nobody had perceived. The second point that emerges, from this projection, is that India's GDP would be around the size of the US by 2035, that is in about 30 years' time.

Figure 1.8

A Multipolar World Economy

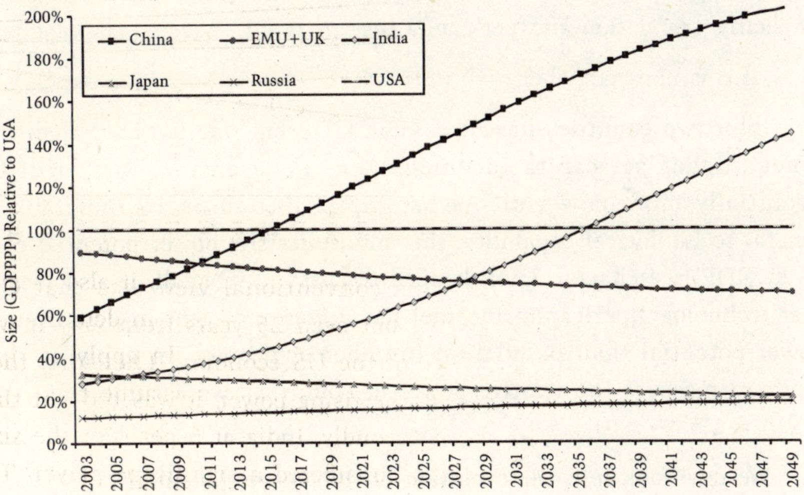

And finally, on Russia, according to this projection which was made before the recent oil price boom, they would just kind of catch up with Japan in about 50 years. Population plays an important part in these projections. Russia (as per these projections) has been placed as the third-fastest growing economy. It is not that we are saying they cannot grow faster. Oil price changes and natural resource price changes can change this a bit; with the crossover point occuring a decade earlier (5-10 years). But this does not fundamentally change the big picture.

And now we move on to the power of nation-states. The author has developed an index of power potential (VIP^2) which is the power potential of a country relative to the US (Virmani, 2004).

$VIP^2 = (Y/Y_{usa})^*(y/y_{usa})^\alpha$, where $0 \leq \alpha \leq 1$

Where,

Y = GDP at PPP,

y = Per capita GDP at PPP,

α = technology weight = 0.5

A number of conclusions follow this equation:

If $\alpha = 0$ ($\beta = 1$) then,

(a) The power potential of a country is measured by its GDP (at purchasing power parity) relative to that of the USA. A country with a higher GDP is potentially more powerful than one with lower GDP. Implicitly, population and per capita income (GDP) have equal weight.

If α is non-zero, then

(b) If two countries have the same GDP but one is richer than the other (higher per capita income/GDP)[2], the richer country will be potentially more powerful. As per capita income is an indicator of general technological capability, this multiplies the power potential of a given GDP (see chapter 3 for detailed discussion). Overall, it also means that technology (per capita income) has a greater weight in determining power potential than population (number of people). In applying this index to measure the relative power of countries, we assume that α = 0.5 (β = 1.5).

We now look into the evolution of the "power potential".

The picture that emerges is shown in Figures 1.9 and 1.10. Figure 1.9 is scaled to bring out clearly what is the position of India as per this

2. The other country therefore has a large population.

mean forecast. What it shows is that the power potential of India will equal that of Japan in about 16-17 years from now. The same growth projection used earlier (Table 1.2) is used in this power projection index. Figure 1.10 brings out the bigger picture. According to this forecast, China's power potential will equal that of the US by 2030, and this is a major contrast to the conventional view presented earlier. The implication of this scenario for the US is that China is going to be a major threat to their power in Asia in the not too distant future. The author's 2004 paper was the first time that anyone had made such a projection. The second point that emerges very clearly from both the figures is that India in this view would become a great power before the middle of the century.

Figure 1.9

Evolution of Power Potential—VIP²

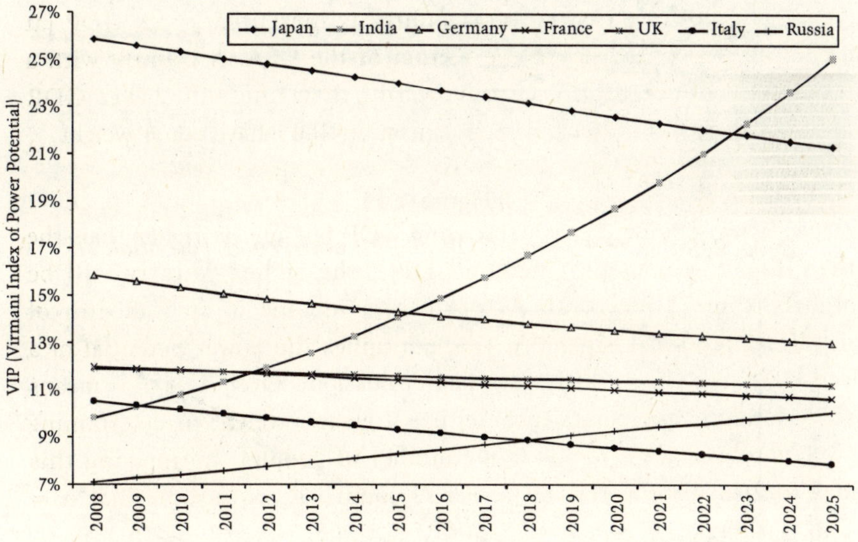

Finally, Figure 1.11 shows India in relation to China which follows straight from the growth projections. As we can see in the figure that India's size and power relative to China would keep declining till around the middle of the next decade, and then would start to catch up. But even 50 years from now, India would, according to these projections, be only 70 per cent of that of China. So it is a long haul for India to catch up with China.

Figure 1.10

Unipolar to Bipolar to Tripolar World

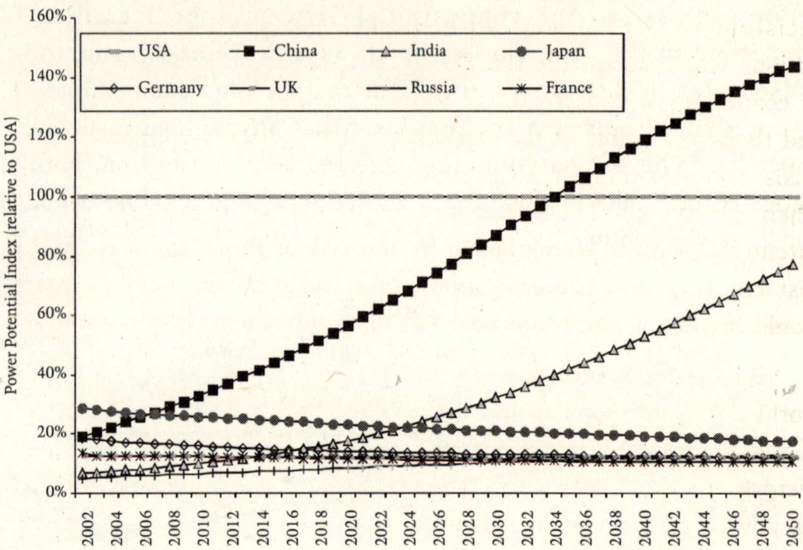

Figure 1.11

India Relative to China—GDP at PPP and Power Potential VIP[2]

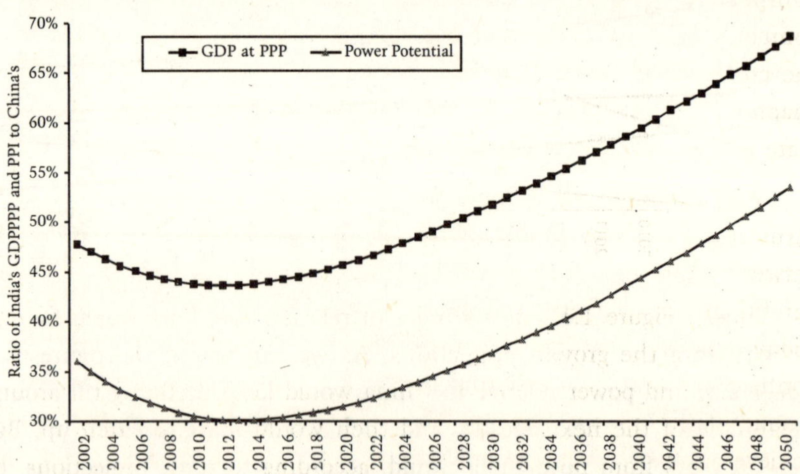

The conclusions from the mean scenario and the situation prevailing in 2005 were that, we have a multipolar world economy but only in economic terms and not in terms of the power. The EU does constitute an economic force; before the rejection of the treaty there was a belief among the supporters of EU that 70 per cent of the economic decisions of the EU were with the EU Secretariat and not with the nations which constitute the EU. If this was correct then at least as far as economics is concerned, we could consider the EU as a single power and therefore, a pole of the world economy. So before the global financial crisis, we went along with these experts because they get very offended when questioned. Thus, economic multipolarity already exists to some extent and will be strengthened by the rise of India. India is right now just entering into the economic game and over the next 25 years, it would become a significant pole in the world economy.

But as far as the power structure is concerned, in our view, the world is clearly unipolar and in fact, has been for far longer than most people imagine. Virmani (2005) applied the VIP index backwards in history, till the 18th century or 17th century and found that Russia lost its power, even before it collapsed in 1990 (see chapter 3 for details). Inherently, the world had become unipolar even before when people generally think. Therefore, the world as described here is unipolar with a multipolar fringe, by analogy with the concept of monopoly with a competitive fringe (in economics). We have the middle powers competing against each other but are no match for the US in terms of the concepts of power that have been used here (discussed further in chapter 2). These concepts do not incorporate aspects connected to non-state actors, which may be relevant.

And therefore, by around 2025, the world will, in terms of power structures, become bipolar with the rise of China and somewhere between 2035 and 2040 it will become tripolar. But we need to be very careful in remembering and distinguishing between the world position today and the one that is being forecast. It is very important not to confuse the two. It is essential that one's feet are firmly placed on the ground in the present, but one has to look up in the sky if one wants to achieve anything. It is extremely unproductive, perhaps even dangerous, if our whole body is lifted into the clouds along with our head. This can give us very misleading answers to what we should or should not be doing currently. We often read in the press, articles by various analysts repeatedly confusing between where we are today and where we might be 25 years from now. We have to be aware of both when planning current approaches and actions. Various aspects of this emerging world order will be presented and analysed in subsequent chapters.

Appendix: Virmani Index of Power

A nation's power potential (NPP) can therefore be defined as the multiple of the size of its economy measured by the GDP at purchasing power parity (Y) and its technological capability measured by its per capita GDP (y):

$NPP = Y^{*}y^{\alpha}, y = Y/L,$

L is the population and α is a parameter that can have a value between 0 and 1.

If we substitute $Y = y^{*}L$ in the above equation and put $\beta = 1+\alpha$, we obtain;

$NPP = L^{*}y^{\beta}$ where β is a parameter that can have a value between 1 and 2.

The Virmani Index of Power Potential (VIPP) or VIP^2 in short, is the power potential of a country (as defined above) relative to the USA:

(1) $VIP^2 = (Y/Y_{usa})^{*}(y/y_{usa})^{\alpha}$, where $0 \leq \alpha \leq 1$

Or equivalently as

(2) $VIP^2 = (L/L_{usa})^{*}(y/y_{usa})^{\beta}$, where $1 \leq \beta \leq 2$

A number of conclusions follow from these equations;

If $\alpha = 0$ ($\beta = 1$) then

(a) The power potential of a country is measured by its GDP (at purchasing power parity) relative to that of the USA. A country with a higher GDP is potentially more powerful than one with lower GDP. Implicitly population and per capita income (GDP) have equal weight.

If α is non-zero, then

(b) If two countries have the same GDP but one is richer than the other (higher per capita income/GDP)[3], the richer country will be potentially more powerful. As per capita income is an indicator of general technological capability, this multiplies the power potential of a given GDP. Overall it also means that technology (per capita income)

3. The other country therefore has a large population.

has a greater weight in determining power potential than population (number of people). In applying this index to measure the relative power of countries we assume that $\alpha = 0.5$ ($\beta = 1.5$).[4] The power potential of all countries with a GDP at purchasing power parity of more than $ 15 billion in 2002 (*WDI,* 2004) is estimated using this index.

'Actual power' depends on the amount and quality of strategic assets, including defence equipment, technology and skills, acquired by the country. Formally we can define the Virmani index of actual power (VIP) as a function (G) of power potential VIP^2 and the strategic assets K^s of the country (relative to the strategic assets of the benchmark USA K^s_{us}):

(3) $VIP = G(VIP^2\ ,\ K^s/K^s_{us})$

The function G allows for complementarities/synergy between economic and military/strategic elements (e.g., investment in strategic technology that has positive spin-off on the civilian economy and vice versa) or substitutability. For purpose of application a simple (Cobb Douglas) form of G with parameter σ, seems adequate. That is,

(4) $VIP = (VIP^2)^{1-\sigma}\ (K^s\ /\ K^s_{us})^{\sigma},\ 0 < \sigma < 1.$

If economic and strategic assets have equal weight in VIP, $\sigma = 0.5$. A lower (higher) σ means strategic assets have less (more) weight than economic. Note that if strategic assets ratio is the same as VIP^2 then VIP= VIP^2 for every value of σ. Unless otherwise stated, we assume in our empirical analysis that VIP and VIP^2 are have a high positive co-relation.

In the national accounts expenditure on public goods like defence and strategic technology, is treated as current expenditure valued at current cost. From the perspective of national power it is more like an investment in physical and human capital. Further as it is not a commercial tradable good or technology, its value (price) is not equal to the actual cost at which it is acquired (which will be inversely related to capability and efficiency $\in$). These expenditures have to be adjusted for

4. For this set of medium-large countries we estimated for 2002 the relationship between per capita GDP measured at current exchange rate x and per capita GDP at purchasing power parity y. On running a cross section regression for 2002 data, we find the following relationship: $x = A\ y^{0.5}$. This was one of the reasons for selecting $\alpha = 0.5$ after simulating the index for a range of α values from 0.25 to 0.75.

efficiency and price changes to make them comparable across countries and time. Formally this can be written as,

(5) $K^s_t = \in_t E_t/p_t - \delta K^s_{t-1}$, where t represents time.

K^s_t is the stock of strategic technology, E_t is the expenditure on this technology and p_t is the price deflator, $\in_t$ is an efficiency parameter and δ is the rate of depreciation of the stock. The stock of strategic assets is also subject to obsolescence. A technological breakthrough by one or more countries (e.g., the industrial revolution, atomic weapons) can make part or whole of the strategic assets of the rest of the countries obsolete, thus reducing their power (VIP) dramatically.

Strategic assets are a national 'public good'. Each government has to raise resources through taxation which can in general have a negative effect on growth of per capita GDP. The revenues raised have then to be allocated between different types of public goods such as strategic assets (E^s) and other public goods like roads (E^y) that have a positive effect on the growth of per capita GDP y. Thus, the direct positive effect of greater expenditure on strategic assets can be partly off-set by the indirect negative effect on economic growth. Such trade-offs and costs can be minimised (lower p, higher $\in$) by acquisition of strategic assets through an alliance with a more powerful country which already has such technology, skills and equipment. The latter will only provide strategic assets if the former is able to enhance its power or welfare in some way (e.g., provision of bases, supply of soldiers/guerilla fighters, oil contracts, help in anti-terrorist operations).

2 Multipolar Economy, Unipolar Power Structure

Economy is the foundation of power. Power, according to Mearsheimer, is always relative. Therefore, absolute size of the economy does not matter; it is the relative size that matters. Unlike perhaps in the 18th or 19th centuries where the economy and military strength were the only things that mattered, there are a number of other factors that we have to keep in mind in the 21st century. One is democratic accountability. Nations like India, the US, and the countries constituting the EU are constrained in what they can do by democratic accountability. One element of this is the effect of globalisation and human rights. Moral legitimacy of the use of power becomes important and soft power, in this case, plays an important role. The second factor is nuclear weapons, which have changed the dynamics of power in the 21st century. In that I believe, as Mr. K. Subrahmanyam has often said, war between global powers is not very likely. The third factor is the issue of non-State actors which complicates the situation. Most importantly, the fourth factor is the will to exercise power, which is an issue as far as India is concerned. Does India have the will to exercise power? The events of 2008 have heightened our apprehensions about it. We will return to these new elements at various points in this book including chapter 9. There are of course scholars who have asserted that India does not have a strategic culture and therefore, will have difficulty being a power and using power.

To compare the economic size of countries we have to select a measure. Historically many if not all analysts have used either GDP in terms of current exchange rates or component of this GDP like manufacturing. The author has insisted that the appropriate measure to compare the economic size of countries is gross domestic product (GDP) at purchasing power parity (PPP). The GDP PPP is a very simple idea. For example, if one can buy a certain basket of goods in the US at 1000 USD, how many Indian rupees are needed to buy the same basket of goods in India? This turns out to be around 12,000 rupees (pre UN

2005 revision). So the PPP exchange rate was 1:12 and not 1:40. Therefore, the PPP GDP, which is your ability to buy a certain basket of goods, is what measures the real economic size of a country. The welfare of the people depends on how much they can buy from their income. Hence, we have to measure GDP in terms of PPP. It is the only way to compare the relative size of economies and the relative welfare or per capita income. GDP mechanically can be thought of as population times per capita GDP. Similarly, when you think of national income, it is population times the average income per person.

In this chapter we start by looking at the historical role of Asian countries and Asia since start of the millennium. Figure 2.1 shows that at the start of the millennium, Asia had roughly 80 per cent of world GDP. It declined gradually till the Industrial Revolution to 60 per cent, and then there was a sharp decline to a low of 20 per cent. This was around the end of the Second World War. Similarly the corresponding rise in Europe is from 10 per cent to a maximum of roughly 40 per cent. In the case of the US, being a new country, it started at 0 per cent and then rose rapidly. At the end of the Second World War, the situation started to change. Asia began its rise again, Europe started declining and America was more or less stable.

Figure 2.1

Regional Shares of World GDP at PPP

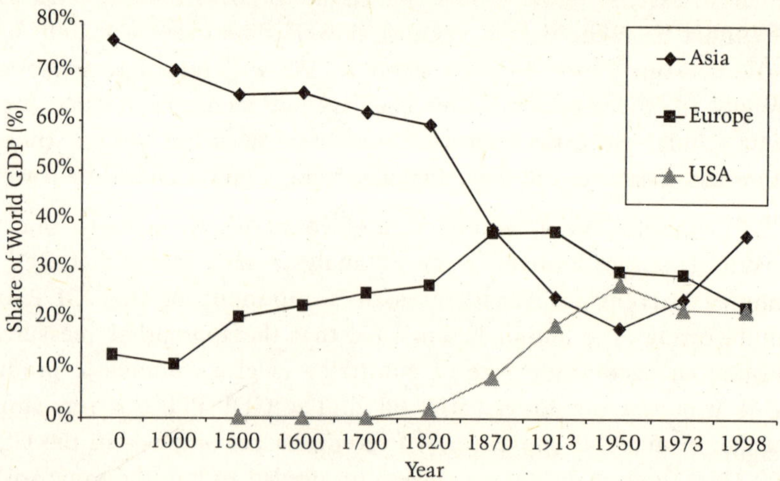

Source: Madison (2003).

Figure 2.2

Asian Countries' Share in World GDP

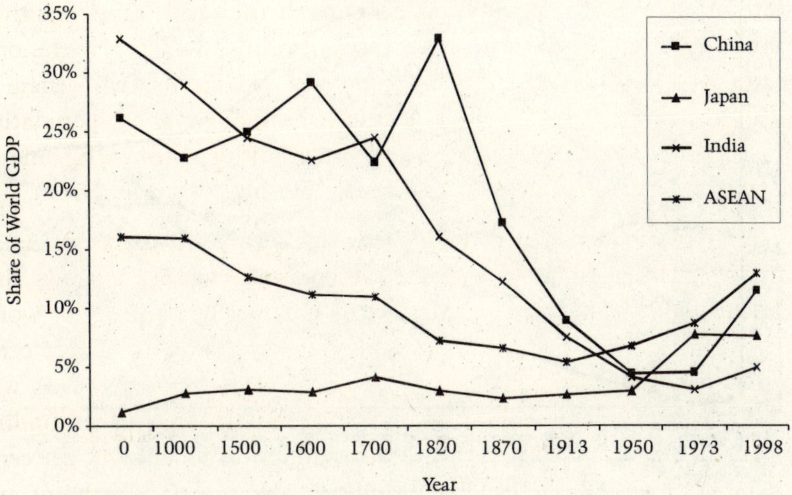

Source: Madison (2003).

Individual Asian countries also show the same pattern (Figure 2.2). India was larger than China only in two periods—at the start of the millennium and around 1700. Otherwise China's share of the world GDP has always been higher than India's. The second point to take note of is that Japan was the first country in Asia to start rising followed by ASEAN, China and India. Thus, the growth acceleration began between 1950 and 1970. Figure 2.3 shows the picture from 1975 onwards. There is a revival of Asia from 15 per cent of the world GDP to about 30 per cent, with Europe on the decline. The basic thesis today is that this is going to continue into the whole century.

What is the situation today? Figures 2.1 to 2.3 compares the economic size of continents and countries based on their share of world GDP. Figure 2.4 compares GDPs of countries relative to the US. The EU which is EMU+UK is taken as one unit because of the argument that as an economy, the EU acts as a single unit. Figure 2.4 allows for an argument that the world economy is multipolar. The US, the EU and China are more or less equal while Japan and India are less than half the size of the US, which shows the inequality in the size of the economies.

Figure 2.3

Changing Global Economy

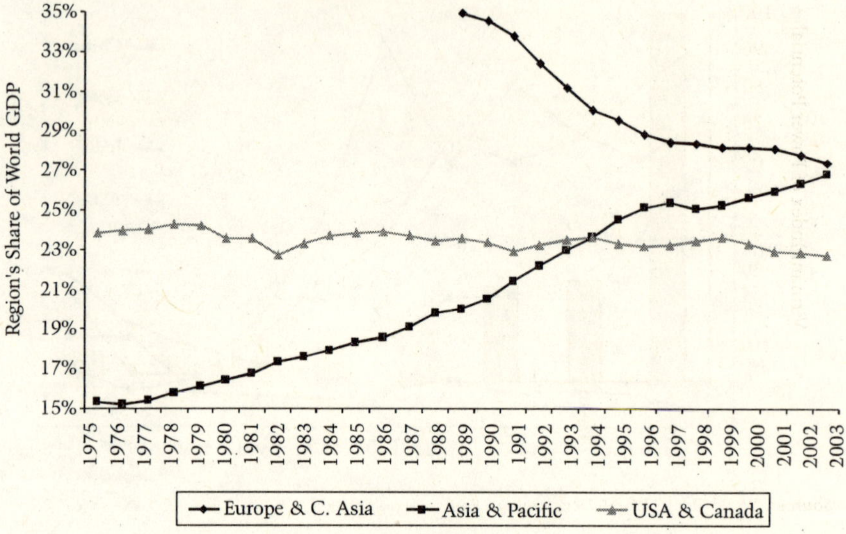

Figure 2.4

Multipolar World Economy

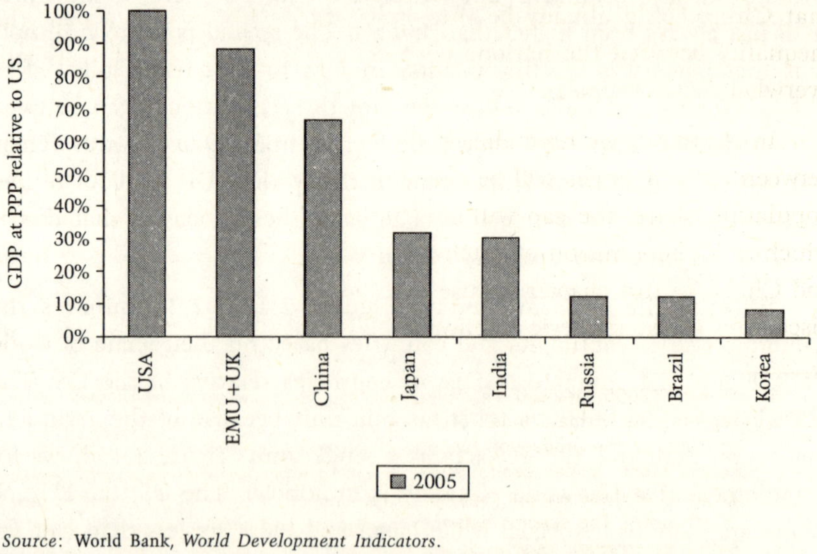

Source: World Bank, *World Development Indicators*.

Figure 2.5

Unipolar Global Power Structure

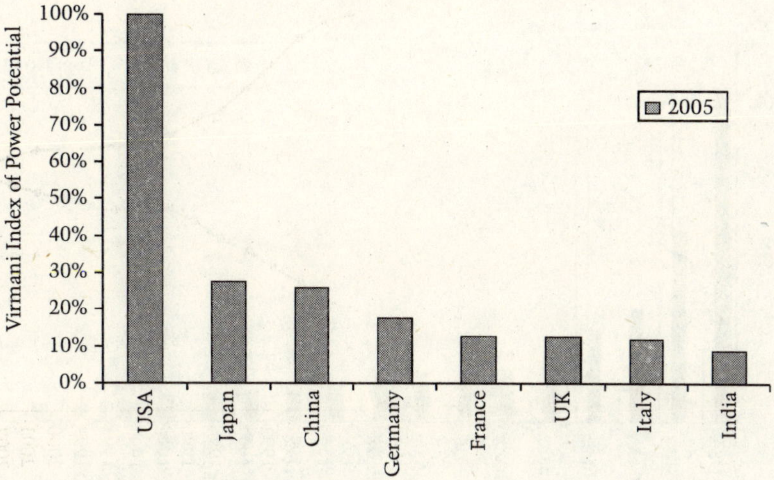

Source: World Bank, *World Development Indicators*.

This picture changes completely when economies are measured in terms of their power potential.[1] In Figure 2.5, the US lead over Japan and China, becomes huge. The US power potential is three times that of the next power which is Japan. Although this is changing so rapidly that China could already be interchanging positions with Japan, the inequality between the nations is evident. Therefore, the world is still overwhelmingly unipolar.

In chapter 1, we have already shown, how these inequalities or gaps between the economies will be closed. By comparing the GDP share and population share, the gap will close because of the per capita income, which is a phenomenon of catch-up growth currently occuring in India and China. In this chapter we use more recent data to set the stage for a discussion of the strategic implications.

1. Virmani (2005) devised a simple index of power potential based on economic factors, the Virmani Index of Power Potential (VIP^2). The VIP^2 is based on concepts of the production function of the economy which includes the physical capital stock, human capital stock, including educational skills and technology. When all of these are put together into a function, it gives us the economic power of a country. The specific defences, aerospace and nuclear equipment which we define as strategic assets, do not form part of the overall physical, human and technological capital. See, chapter 3 for details.

Figure 2.6

Global Imbalance: GDP and Population Shares

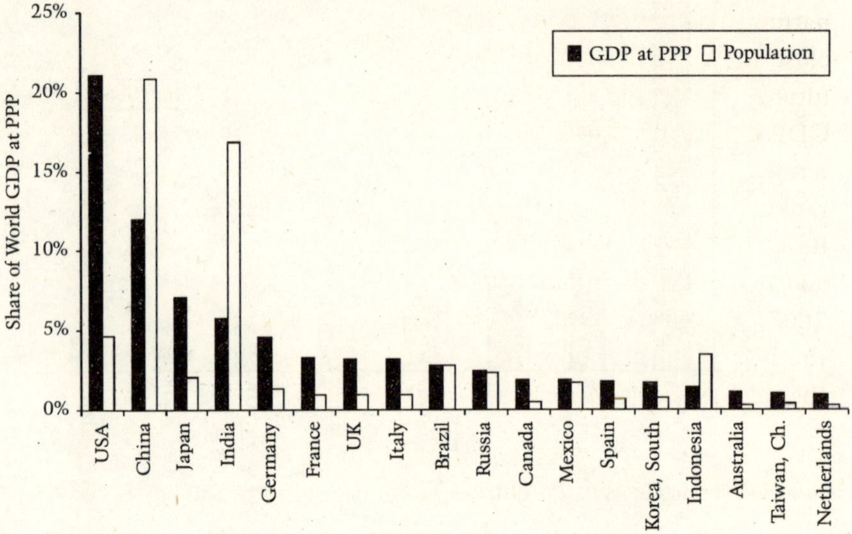

Source: World Bank, *World Development Indicators*.

The results are very similar to those in chapter 1 and can be summed up on follows. The US share of world economy is 21 per cent and China's share is around half of that of the US. Similarly, India's share is around one-fourth that of the US. In terms of population, China and India's share is much larger than that of the US followed by Indonesia, Brazil and Russia. In Figure 2.6, where both the GDP and population shares are shown together, the gaps become evident. The US has a huge positive gap i.e., its share of the world GDP is much larger than the share of its population. However in countries like China, India and Indonesia, it is the other way round. An important point to note is that there is a very small gap in the case of Brazil and Russia. Our assertion is that the negative gap in case of India and China and the positive gap in case of the US, Japan and other countries will close because of what is called 'catch-up growth'. Figure 2.7 shows the catch-up growth potential by taking the ratio of the per capita income of each country to that of the US. India's per capita income is 1/10th that of the US. The huge gap is seen as a positive factor in terms of catching up with the West and therefore, improving the relative position. India, China, Indonesia have this negative gap while most of the developed countries have a positive gap. Over this century, this gap is going to narrow and close. One may raise a question that while this gap did not close in the past what are the possibilities that it will happen in the future? The reason for this is the increasing per capita income and the GDP growth rates over the last 20-30 years. This can be explained in terms of the rate of growth of each country as well. Table 2.1 shows the ranking of countries by their rate of growth. China is on the top; both its GDP growth rate and per capita growth rate have been the highest and India is at the ninth position. For a period of 25 years from 1980 to 2007, the growth rates of both China and India have been high. With the higher growth rates, the per capita income gap is closing rapidly in the case of China and less rapidly in the case of India.

Figure 2.7

Catch-up Growth Potential—Globalisation and Growth Potential

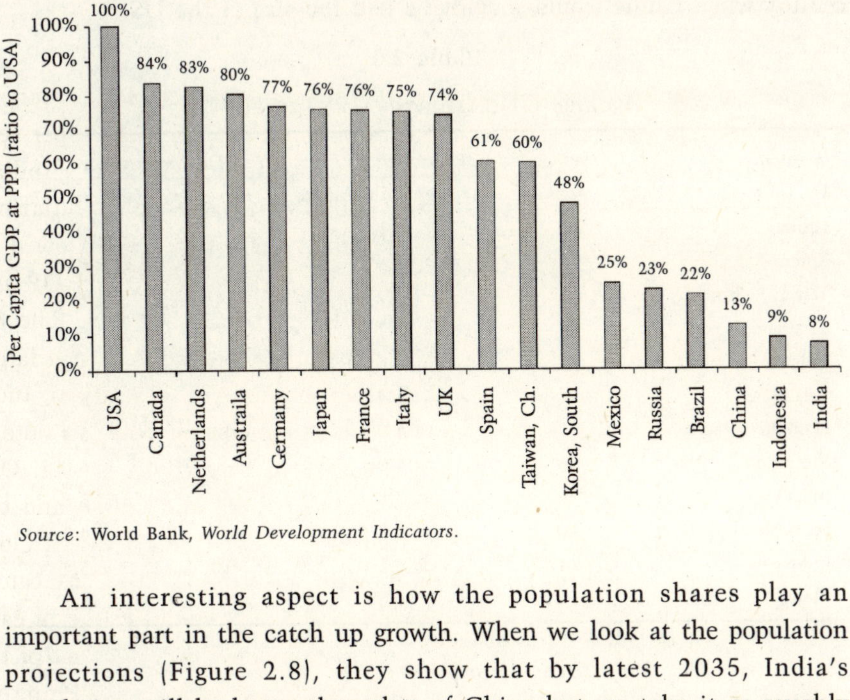

Source: World Bank, *World Development Indicators*.

An interesting aspect is how the population shares play an important part in the catch up growth. When we look at the population projections (Figure 2.8), they show that by latest 2035, India's population will be larger than that of China but we take it as roughly equal. The third largest in population is the US and the fourth is Indonesia. The population shares of Russia and Germany are going to decline sharply over this half century. The interesting point here is that just arithmetically India and China only need 1/4th per capita income to be equal in size with the US because they are four times the population, whereas any other country has to have a higher per capita income than the US to catch up. Our thesis, therefore, is that it is only India and China who over the next 50 years have the potential of challenging the US in terms of size and power potential. Hence, only tripolarity is possible. Alternatively, there are chances of quadripolarity if the EU becomes a virtual state. But this is not likely at least for the next 20-30 years and that is why the EU has been left out of this picture. The conventional wisdom (Figure 2.9) has been that even by 2025 China's economic size (GDP relative to the US) will still be smaller than Japan and India would be smaller than Germany, the UK and France. In terms of the US perceptions, China therefore will not be a major threat to the US and the world will still remain unipolar, even till the middle of the century when China would roughly be half the size of the US.

Table 2.1

Average GDP Growth—1980 to 2004

Economy	*Per Capita GDP Growth Rate*		*GDP Growth Rate (Avg.)*	
	Rank	*Average Growth Rate*	*Rank*	*Average Growth Rate*
China	1	8.2	1	9.6
Korea, Rep.	2	5.6	3	6.7
Taiwan, China	3	5.2	4	6.4
Thailand	4	4.7	7	6.0
Ireland	5	4.6	13	5.3
Singapore	6	4.4	2	6.9
Hong Kong, SAR	7	4.0	11	5.4
Vietnam#	8	4.0	8	6.0
India	9	3.8	9	5.8
Luxembourg	10	3.7	17	4.7
Indonesia	11	3.6	10	5.4
Malaysia	12	3.6	6	6.3

Note: # Growth for 1980 to 1984 is estimated.

Source: World Bank, *World Development Indicators*.

Figure 2.8

Population Projections—UN 2004

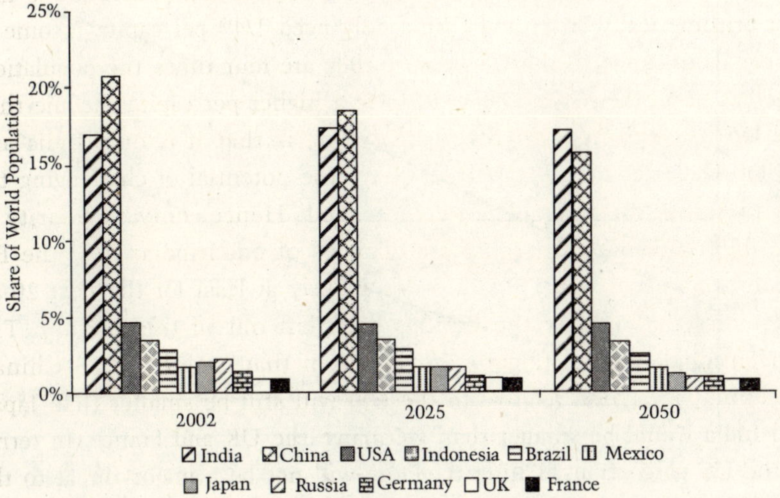

Source: World Bank, *World Development Indicators*.

Figure 2.9

Conventional Wisdom—Unipolar

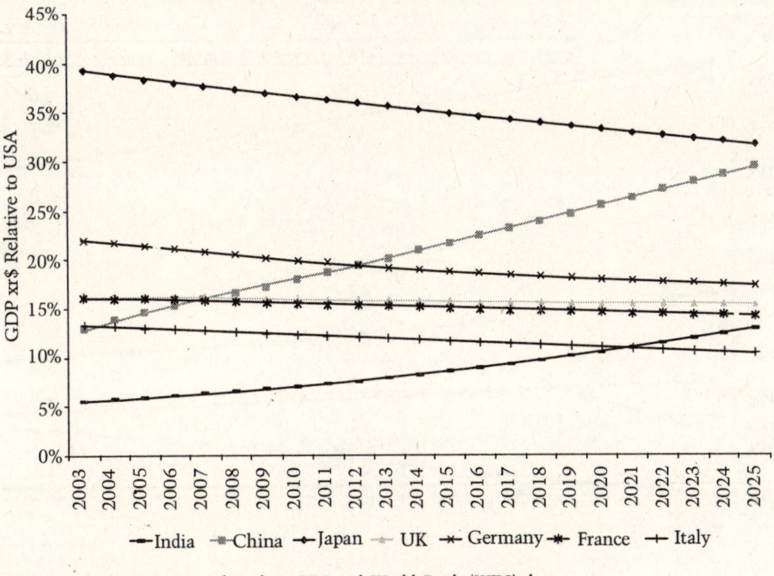

Source: Authors projections, based on UN and World Bank (WDI) data.

Figure 2.10

Multipolar World Economy

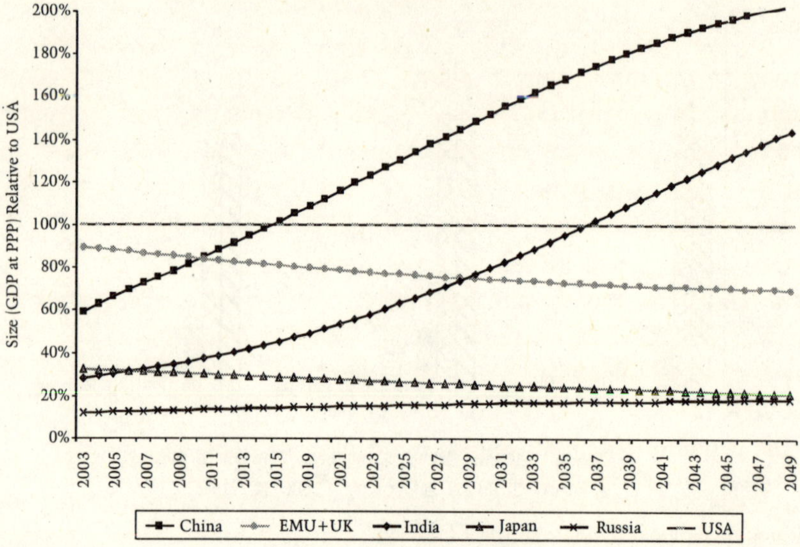

Source: Authors projections, based on UN and World Bank (WDI) data.

Figure 2.11

Evolution of Power Potential: VIP Squared

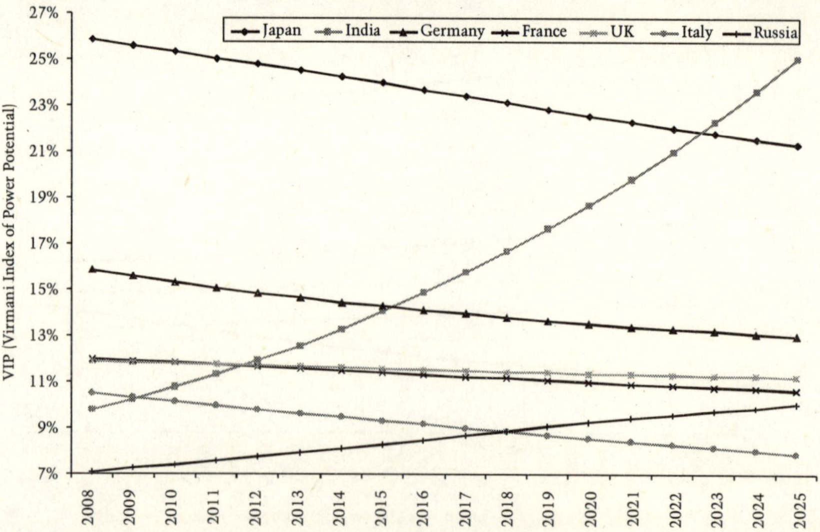

Source: Authors projections, based on UN and World Bank (WDI) data.

Figure 2.10 projects a completely different picture, extended up to 2050. China's economy is projected to become twice the size of the US by the middle of the century and around 2035 India's economy would equal the size of the US economy.

Let me come to power (power measured according to the power potential: VIP squared index). The projections in Figure 2.11 were more modest when the author first made them in 2004 and 2005, but in the last 3-4 years, China and India have been growing much faster than those projections had assumed. It is important to note here that the US strategic assets are huge and they will remain much larger than China's for a long time. But the projections in this chapter and this book are purely economic, since economic size is going to have a big effect on the way the world power structure will play out. The period between 2020 and 2035, where the world would basically be bipolar (in our view), will be the period of potential conflict and danger for many countries.

With regard to India, if it continues its current growth rate it will be a significant power. India is rising and will rapidly overtake many developed countries in terms of power potential—Italy first, then France, the UK, Germany and Japan. Japan will remain a significant power for the next 10 to 20 years. It is, therefore, very important for India to have good relations with Japan because it is an Asian power, a democracy and it still has general technological capabilities which are sustaining its power status in spite of the decline in its population. Russia's position is uncertain, as it will depend critically on the price of oil. The ones in chapter 1 to 7 are based on pre-boom prices.

What is the likely power structure in 2020? In Figure 2.12, China's power potential is shown at 60 per cent of that of the US. Since the power potential of the US still remains much higher, one may ask whether there is a change in the unipolar structure. Yes, there is. Virmani's (2005) backward projections showed that the USSR, at the peak of its power, had only 40 per cent of the power potential of the USA. China will have 60 per cent (see chapter 3). Therefore, in 15 years' time the world will be bipolar and it will be a very difficult period for Asia. India will have only 40 per cent of the power potential of the US by 2030 but that is the same figure that USSR had at its peak. It is in this period that India would become potentially significant and the tripolar structures will start to emerge.

Figure 2.12

Bipolar Global Power Structure

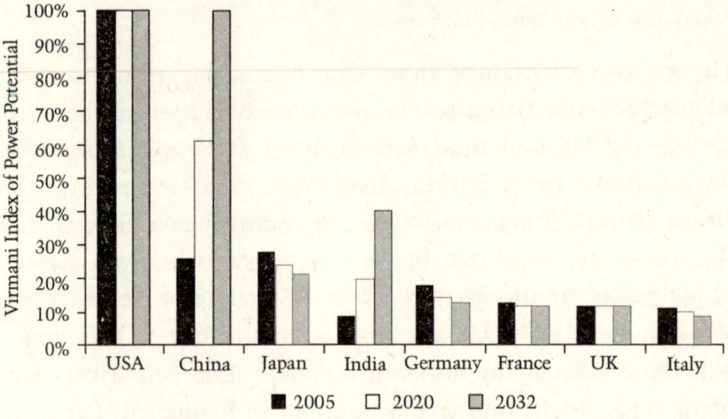

Source: Authors projections, based on UN and World Bank (WDI) data.

Actual power depends on strategic and defence technology, which in turn depends on public expenditure and development of such technology. This is affected by the will to exercise power. When discussing this, the examples of China and Japan come to mind. China clearly has the will and has shown it repeatedly. The Chinese have always had the idea of being a global power, as against which, Japan after losing in World War II, had a peace constitution. Japan has deliberately eschewed power even while it was still the second strongest power. There was no will to exercise, use or develop this power since the Second World War. Japan made this deliberate choice. The fact is that, a country that does not show the will cannot be powerful.

Strategic technology is a critical element in power. The cost and efficiency of strategic technology varies widely across the world. Alliances which give a country this technology and equipment, can both reduce the cost and improve the efficiency of the acquisition. Much of the Soviet and American technology after the Second World War was dependent on German technologists, who they stole from defeated Germany. When the Pentagon had hired consultants to study India, the author told them that in order to have good relations with India, it is important to remove the technological apartheid. Russia, France and the

UK have had an oligopoly in our market. Clearly, adding Israel and the US to the list of suppliers will improve our terms. It is a simple matter of economic logic. The more players there are on the seller's side, the better deal the buyer gets.

The lessons of history show that there is a significant risk of conflict between the rising power and the dominant power. The only exception is the US and the UK. One has to remember that China is ruled by a Leninist party. Private consumption in China was 37 per cent of GDP as against 70 per cent in the US and about 60 per cent in India in 2007. Therefore, in China, the rest of the economy—60 per cent—is directly controlled by the party. This gives it enormous control over the money it can spend. The US government would have to levy huge taxes to match the money at the disposal of the Chinese authorities. If China has a democracy in the future, this scenario will completely change. The fact that two middle income countries—China an upper middle income country and India a lower middle income country—will become a part of the global power structure is unprecedented in history. One can choose to be sceptical of the projections made above. The conventional Western wise men are still not willing to believe firstly, that this is going to happen and secondly, the serious implications this shall have for the world power structure.

With regard to maintaining a better balance of power in Asia, we advocate that we use the concept of democracy to develop better relations with Japan, Indonesia, Australia etc., because even put together, these will be smaller in power potential than China. There are new approaches and capabilities which India needs to focus on—one is power projection, the second is intelligence and the third is covert action, which is something India is very squeamish about. What has amazed us in observing the US is the way it controls the discourse, language and agenda of foreign policy. India should develop the same capability. Motivation, toughness and unity of purpose seem lacking right now. Institutions of governance are the greatest weakness and we have to improve, evolve and focus on these.

In the past, until the 1980s, India was very poor and weak with little prospects of major improvement. This is not true any more. Some of us who focus on the future forget about the present. Presently we are a low income country—in impolite terms, a poor country. The average income is still very low, but we have managed to become one among the powers in the current multipolar world. This is not contradictory but unusual. India is soon to become a lower middle income country. In the next 15 years, things are going to change drastically. People who are presently below the poverty line will rise above that level and people will be able to see this change physically. India will be a global power if we are able to maintain growth and inclusive development, which is important for our democratic system of governance.

References

Virmani, Arvind (2005). "Global Power From The 18th To 21st Century: Power Potential (VIP[2]), Strategic Assets and Actual Power (VIP)", *Working Paper* No. 175, ICRIER, November.

3 Power Potential, Strategic Assets and Global Power

A Simple Model

Introduction

The USA is often referred to as the most powerful nation on earth, particularly since the collapse of the USSR in 1990. It is well known that the US economy is the largest in the world. But does the size of an economy measure a nations power in a global context? During the cold war between the US and NATO on one side and the USSR and Soviet Bloc on the other, the world was treated as being bipolar, i.e., the two countries USA and USSR were recognised to be the two most powerful countries in the world of the time. The most visible part of their competition was in space, nuclear, defence and other technology. The possession of advanced military equipment such as ICBMs, submarines, aircraft carriers, bombers and fighters was also an element of the relative power of these two nations. Does this mean that military technology and equipment is the predominant factor determining a nation's power? Since then complex models have been built to define and measure a nation's global power. Economic and technological factors play a major role in these models [see e.g. Tellis *et al.* (2000)]. Other factors are natural resources, education and skills and investment in R&D and technology development.

Waltz (1979) defined State power as the "extent that (one) effects others more than they affect [one]". It is therefore a "combination of its capacity to resist the unwelcome influence of others and conversely to influence others to behave as it wants them to." International relations experts have been divided on the relative importance of economic strength and military might in the global power of a nation. We resolve this conflict by decomposing national power into two elements: (a) The 'power potential' of a country, which depends on economic strength and general technological capability, and (b) Military might or in modern terminology 'strategic capability'. This includes defence equipment, strategic technology and specific technologies needed for attaining military superiority. Together these define the actual power of a country. International ambition and determination, the 'will to power' play(s) a role in transforming the 'power potential' into 'actual power.' The chapter then goes on to discuss how to measure each of these elements in the simplest possible way and to define an index for measuring each. For the former, the chapter presents a simple index the Virmani index of power potential (VIP^2),[1] and for the latter, a measure of strategic/military assets/capability. The two are then combined to produce a single index of actual power (VIP).

Section 2 discusses the economic basis of national power. Section 3 formally defines the two indices, the VIP^2 and the VIP (Virmani index of power). The former index has been calculated for about 110 countries.[2] Section 4 delves into the past centuries by constructing the VIP^2 index for the major powers in the 18th, 19th and 20th centuries. The French, British and the US dominance during the three centuries respectively, emerges clearly. In post-war 20th century it finds that the USSR barely met the economic conditions for being classed as a 'great power' as its VIP^2 was less than that of the UK in 1913 when the latter had already been displaced by the USA. Section 5 presents and discusses the results for the global and regional powers. Section 6 looks into the future by constructing growth scenarios. It then explores the issue of whether the current 'unipolar world with a multipolar fringe' will become bipolar, tripolar or multipolar in the next 20 years. Section 7 concludes the chapter.

Economic Strength and National Power

An appreciation of the role of economic size and technological potential on the global balance of power has grown since the Second World War. Prof. Paul Kennedy, in his *Foreign Affairs* article and subsequent book,

1. This is an elaboration of the index of 'power potential' proposed in Virmani (2004).
2. Virmani (2005d).

The Rise and Fall of Great Powers gave economics considerable weight in the evolution of the global balance of power. He made the following points:

- Traditional field of international relations has not fully appreciated the role of economic strength, with the role of economic factors relatively neglected.
- Military power rests on and is sustained by economic power.
- The rise and fall of great powers can be traced to the change in their economic strength.
- Relative rather than absolute economic strength is the relevant variable.
- There may be leads and lags between the change in economic power, military power and national power.

Economic power is the foundation of national power. Economic strength is the only sustained and sustainable basis for national power and relative economic power is the basis for national power. Even though military power disproportionate to economic power can be used to enhance national power for a certain period of time, this may not be sustainable over long periods, particularly in the globalised world of the 21st century. This was illustrated to some extent by the break-up of the USSR, where the military and strategic competition could not be sustained by a declining economy. The role of economic factors in international affairs is, likely to be greater in the 21st century than it has been in previous centuries. With the growth of communication and the increased mobility of goods and services, labour, capital and technology, much technical knowledge is becoming the common heritage of mankind in reality. General technological capability is increasingly part and parcel of economic evolution, and economic factors, therefore, encompasses this technology. The process of modernisation and global economic integration has expanded the gains from economic cooperation between States, reduced the gains to the winner from war, and increased the potential losses to third parties from active war between States. The lags between the rise or decline of economic power and the rise or decline of great powers may shorten during the 21st century. This will not, however, eliminate the need for military capability.

Tellis *et al.* (2000) have developed a comprehensive and complex model for measuring power in terms of the ability of a State to achieve and sustain global hegemony. In their model, military capability is the outcome of an interaction between national resources and national performance. National resources consist of five building blocks of power, technology, enterprise, human resources, financial/capital resources and physical resources. National performance contains three factors, infrastructural capacity, ideational resources that augment or detract from the utilisation of these natural resources.

The factors mentioned in the Tellis model are all inputs into the productive capacity of an economy, though their economics nomenclature and definition may be different. Thus, a country's natural resource (e.g., oil), physical capital stock (including the stock of infrastructure), human capital (education and skills) and technology (including management, marketing and entrepreneurship) are all inputs into the production of national output and are formally included in the aggregate production function of the economy (see below). The gross domestic product of a country, which is the output produced by all these inputs, given the external (e.g., technology denial) and internal (e.g., quality of governance, social divisions/ conflicts) constraints facing economic agents, is therefore, a summary index of its 'national resources' and 'national capacity.' Even more broadly, the growth of a country's GDP and the level it has reached reflects both the strengths and weaknesses of its society (social capital, religion, culture, family) and institutions (political, market regulating, non-profit organisations, civil) in addition to its national policies.[3]

Commercial and Strategic Technology

There is a need to distinguish between two categories of technology; commercial and strategic.[4] Commercial technology is part and parcel of

3. The quality of institutions is an important determinant of growth. Social capital and related variables are also found to be significant.

4. "Dual use technologies" represent the overlap between the two types.

normal trade, financial flows and movement of managers and skilled personnel between open economies. FDI normally bundles two or more of these together. Any specific commercial technology (not available at a given time in the country) can therefore either be purchased from global markets or be attracted to the country through FDI (joint ventures etc.).

Strategic technologies are the technologies of power. They include military related technologies such as nuclear and aero-space, as well as technology for producing advanced weapon systems and defence equipment. By definition, strategic technologies are critical to national power and are not traded on commercial considerations. General technological capability forms the foundation of strategic technology, but its development requires special skills, directed R&D as well as focused attention. It has either to be developed through national effort or acquired through strategic/military alliances.[5]

General technological capability therefore has a dual role: It is the foundation of the productive capability of the economy and also the foundation for the development of specific strategic technologies. Thus, in the real world in which nations guard their strategic technological knowledge, those with higher technological capabilities have a greater ability to develop strategic technology and therefore greater power potential. Strategic technology also includes nascent technologies that may play a critical role in future defence systems. Because of the uncertainty inherent in forecasting the future, less developed technologies may at one stage be classed as 'strategic' and at another stage as 'commercial' and vice versa.

Productive Capability

The economic capacity of a country at any point in time is measured by its gross domestic product (GDP). This represents its output of goods and services during the year. The same economy can produce different goods and service in different amounts, with the actual pattern of output depending on the pattern of demand. In general two economies can differ not only in their productive capacity but also in the pattern of

5. Historically countries have also acquired it through conquest (USSR_East Germany) or theft (A.Q. Khan, Pakistan–URENCO, the Netherlands).

demand. So how do we know that one economy is larger than another i.e., has greater productive capacity? The only way to compare the size of different economies is by valuing all goods and services produced in each, by using a common set of relative prices. Such a measure of a country's economy is referred to as gross domestic product at purchasing power parity (Y).[6]

The technological capability of an economy depends on many factors. Virmani (2004) has used the principle of Occam's razor to define technological capability in the simplest possible way. This is done by using the familiar concept of an aggregate production function. When viewed from the perspective of productive capacity, an economy consists of different productive resources such as unskilled labour, stocks of physical capital, human capital in the form of education and skills, natural resources such as oil and minerals, disembodied technology (organisations) and technological capabilities embodied in capital goods and human beings. The aggregate production function shows how these resources can be combined to produce output i.e., it summarises the productive capacity of the economy. The aggregate production function and the related concept of aggregate factor productivity can be used to define the general technological capability of an economy.

The concept of total factor productivity growth (TFPG) is commonly used in economics to measure technological change in an economy. Conceptually the level or value of total factor productivity (TFP) could represent the technological capability of a country. Its operationalisation, however, requires the assumption that technology is disembodied and neutral. As we have indicated, technology is often embodied in capital and labour i.e., it is inseparable from the physical capital or the labourer/employee. In addition, historically we observe that capital intensity (capital per unit of labour input k), the education/ skill level of the labour force (human capital per person h) and technology (T) move broadly in tandem as an economy develops. In

6. If the economy is open and competitive, it also follows that it is producing things in which it has a comparative advantage and importing those which others produce relatively efficiently. If a policy distortion prevents this from happening, the economy's productive capacity will be reduced and this will be reflected in GDP at PPP.

other words, for new/better technology to be translated into higher output per person, an appropriate compliment of better skills and more capital per person is also needed. They form a package that together produces a higher level of productivity. Labour productivity or output per unit of labour is a summary measure of the level and quality of this package of technology, capital intensity and skill intensity. As it is also much easier to define and measure than TFP, it is operationally a more useful measure of an economy's technological capability than TFP. Per capita gross domestic product at purchasing power parity or GDP per person (y = Y/L, with L = labour force, proxied by population) can therefore, be used as a summary measure of the 'general technological capability' of an economy. This is illustrated more formally in the next section.

Index of Power

Aggregate Production Function

At the heart of the modern theory of economic growth and development is the aggregate production function of an economy. The aggregate production function summarises the supply capability of the economy, that is, its ability to produce a host of goods and services. The mix of goods and services actually produced depends on the pattern of domestic demand. The simplest algebraic representation of the aggregate production function is as follows:[7]

$$Y = T\,F\,(K, H, L)$$

Where Y is GDP, T is the level of technology or total factor productivity, F is a function of different factors of production such as K the stock of physical capital, H the stock of human capital (education and skills) and L the size of the labour force. Here, T represents the technological capability of the economy, assuming that technology is neutral and disembodied. Given this assumption, the aggregate production function can be estimated for any group of economies and

7. Each of the variables will change over time i.e., T(t), F(t), b(t), K(t), H(t), L(t) and Y(t). For visual simplicity we have dropped the time subscript from all the variables.

used to derive the level of technology for each country. This has indeed been done by many economists. This production function can be re-arranged to obtain per capita GDP:

$y = T f(k, h)$

Where $y = Y/L$ is the per capita GDP, $k = K/L$ is the amount of physical capital per person and $h = H/L$ is the average level of human capital.[8]

From the perspective of the current chapter, namely to define and measure economic power, this assumption of neutral technical change and disembodied technology is highly restrictive and unnecessary. We therefore propose to use a more general and complicated representation of the aggregate production function that paradoxically simplifies the measurement of economic power:[9]

$Y = T F(aK, bH, L)$ and on re-arrangement $y = T f(ak, bh)$

Where a, b represent capital and labour-based technical change respectively. In addition, technology is often embodied in capital, which makes the determination of K itself quite complicated. In this case, which is more realistic from our current perspective, it is not only very difficult to measure T, but T no longer fully captures the level of technology of a country. In general therefore, y captures all the relevant aspects of knowledge and technological capability, whether embodied in physical capital or existing in the brains of workers/professionals (i.e., education and learned skills). Thus, it is the simplest and best available index of general technological capability of an economy, in that per capita GDP across countries is highly (but not perfectly) co-related with the technological capability of countries.[10]

---

8. This requires an additional assumption of constant returns to scale that has been widely shown to be prevalent.

9. Another dimension of complication would be to include a term for natural resource stocks, i.e., $Y = T F (K, H, R)$, where R represents natural resources (e.g., oil, minerals). This can be an important element of economic power for major oil exporters like Saudi Arabia.

10. Our guess would be that differences in per capita GDP capture at least 90 per cent of the difference in technological capability.

Power Potential: VIP^2

A nation's power potential (NPP) can therefore be defined as the multiple of the size of its economy measured by the GDP at purchasing power parity (Y) and its technological capability measured by its per capita GDP (y):[11]

$$NPP = Y^* y^{\alpha}, \; y = Y/L,$$

L is the population and α is a parameter that can have a value between 0 and 1.

If we substitute $Y = y^* L$ in the above equation and put $\beta = 1+\alpha$, we obtain;

$NPP = L^* y^{\beta}$ where β is a parameter that can have a value between 1 and 2.

The Virmani Index of Power Potential (VIPP) or VIP^2 in short, is the power potential of a country (as defined above) relative to the USA:

(1) $VIP^2 = (Y/Y_{usa})^*(y/y_{usa})^{\alpha}$, where $0 \leq \alpha \leq 1$

Or equivalently as

(2) $VIP^2 = (L/L_{usa})^*(y/y_{usa})^{\beta}$, where $1 \leq \beta \leq 2$

A number of conclusions follow from these equations;

If $\alpha = 0$ ($\beta = 1$) then

(a) The power potential of a country is measured by its GDP (at purchasing power parity) relative to that of the USA. A country with a higher GDP is potentially more powerful than one with lower GDP. Implicitly population and per capita income (GDP) have equal weight.

If α is non-zero, then

(b) If two countries have the same GDP but one is richer than the other (higher per capita income/GDP),[12] the richer country will be potentially more powerful. As per capita income is an indicator of general technological capability, this multiplies the power potential of a given GDP. Overall it also means that technology (per capita income)

---

11. An alternative formulation could be $NPP = (Y^{1-\alpha})\, y^{\alpha}$.

12. The other country therefore has a large population.

has a greater weight in determining power potential than population (number of people). In applying this index to measure the relative power of countries we assume that $\alpha = 0.5$ ($\beta = 1.5$).[13]

The power potential of all countries with a GDP at purchasing power parity of more than $ 15 billion in 2002 (*WDI*, 2004) is estimated using this index (Virmani, 2005d).

Actual Power: VIP

'Actual power' depends on the amount and quality of strategic assets, including defence equipment, technology and skills acquired by the country. Formally we can define the Virmani index of actual power (VIP) as a function (G) of power potential VIP^2 and the strategic assets K^s of the country (relative to the strategic assets of the benchmark USA K^s_{usa}):

$$(3)\ VIP = G(VIP^2, K^s / K^s_{usa})$$

The function G allows for complementarities/synergy between economic and military/strategic elements (e.g., investment in strategic technology that has positive spin-off on the civilian economy and vice versa) or substitutability. For purpose of application, a simple (Cobb Douglas) form of G with parameter σ, seems adequate. That is,

$$(4)\ VIP = (VIP^2)^{1-\sigma} (K^s/K^s_{usa})^{\sigma},\ 0 < \sigma < 1.$$

If economic and strategic assets have equal weight in VIP, $\sigma = 0.5$. A lower (higher) σ means strategic assets have less (more) weight than economic. Note that if the strategic assets ratio is the same as VIP^2 then $VIP = VIP^2$ for every value of σ. Unless otherwise stated, we assume in our empirical analysis that VIP and VIP^2 have a high positive co-relation.

In the national accounts, expenditure on public goods like defence and strategic technology, is treated as current expenditure valued at current cost. From the perspective of national power it is more like an investment in physical and human capital. Further as it is not a

13. For this set of medium-large countries we estimated for 2002 the relationship between per capita GDP measured at current exchange rate x and per capita GDP at purchasing power parity y. On running a cross-section regression for 2002 data we find the following relationship: $x = A\ y^{0.5}$. This was one of the reasons for selecting $\alpha = 0.5$ after simulating the index for a range of α values from 0.25 to 0.75.

commercial tradable good or technology, its value (price) is not equal to the actual cost at which it is acquired (which will be inversely related to capability and efficiency $\in$). These expenditures have to be adjusted for efficiency and price changes to make them comparable across countries and time. Formally this can be written as,

(5) $K^s_t = \in_t E_t/p_t - \delta K^s_{t-1}$, where t represents time.

K^s_t is the stock of strategic technology, E_t is the expenditure on this technology and p_t is the price deflator, $\in_t$ is an efficiency parameter and δ is the rate of depreciation of the stock. The stock of strategic assets is also subject to obsolescence. A technological breakthrough by one or more countries (e.g., the industrial revolution, atomic weapons) can make part or whole of the strategic assets of the rest of the countries obsolete, thus reducing their power (VIP) dramatically.

Strategic assets are a national 'public good'. Each government has to raise resources through taxation which can in general have a negative effect on growth of per capita GDP. The revenues raised have then to be allocated between different types of public goods such as strategic assets (E^s) and other public goods like roads (E^y) that have a positive effect on the growth of per capita GDP y. Thus, the direct positive effect of greater expenditure on strategic assets can be partly offset by the indirect negative effect on economic growth. Such trade-offs and costs can be minimised (lower p, higher $\in$) by acquisition of strategic assets through an alliance with a more powerful country which already has such technology, skills and equipment. The latter will only provide strategic assets if the former is able to enhance its power or welfare in some way (e.g., provision of bases, supply of soldiers/guerilla fighters, oil contracts, help in anti-terrorist operations) or help offset the power of a rival (e.g., USA strengthening post-war Europe to counter the perceived threat from the USSR).

Though estimation of the strategic assets of countries is beyond the scope of the current chapter, it is useful to consider the relationship between power potential, strategic assets and actual power using equation (4). The following table illustrates the trade-offs:

Table 3.1

Power Potential (VIP²), Strategic Assets and National Power (VIP)

Table: VIP, Strategic Assets and VIP²

S.No.	VIP^2	K^s/K^s_{us}	σ	VIP
1	100%	1.25	0.5	112%
2	100%	0.75	0.5	87%
3	75%	1.00	0.5	87%
4	75%	0.75	0.5	75%
5	75%	0.50	0.5	61%
6	50%	1.00	0.5	71%
7	50%	0.75	0.5	61%
8	50%	0.50	0.5	50%
9	100%	1.25	0.3	107%
10	100%	0.75	0.3	92%
11	75%	1.00	0.3	82%
12	75%	0.75	0.3	75%
13	75%	0.50	0.3	66%
14	50%	1.00	0.3	62%
15	50%	0.75	0.3	56%
16	50%	0.50	0.3	50%

The 3rd column shows the actual power VIP that results from the VIP^2 and strategic assets shown in the 1st and 2nd columns respectively. Thus for instance a great power with a VIP^2 of 75 per cent and a strategic capability half of the dominant power, will have 60 per cent of its actual power. A great power with a VIP^2 of 50 per cent can attain only 87 per cent of the VIP of the dominant power even if its strategic capability is equal (assuming $\sigma = 0.5$). A lower σ changes these results by only a small amount.

The former USSR spent a lot of resources on strategic technologies and goods (E) and thus attained a level of VIP that was much greater than its VIP^2.[14] The accumulated strategic knowledge (K^s), though it has deteriorated over time, has not been lost. Consequently, the dissolution of the USSR has reduced the power potential of Russia much more than

14. Further its power potential was related not just to the economic size of the USSR but to economic size of the Warsaw pact which was like a Soviet virtual state. The Warsaw pact was in the context of power more integrated than the current EU (see below).

its actual power. Conversely, Japan after its defeat in World War II became a pacifist nation, which deliberately reduced expenditure on strategic technology, defence systems and forces. It also gave p any ambitions of being an independent power in Asia. Its 'actual power' is therefore lower than its 'power potential.' Post-war Germany also has some of these characteristics. In addition, some very small economies with low power potential have skilfully used formal or informal alliances to attain a level of actual power far in excess of their power potential.[15] In general, however, GDP is highly correlated with country expenditure on strategic assets and consequently, so is power potential with actual power.

Historical Evolution of Power

Though formal testing is not possible it is useful to see how well the Index tracks the evolution of power relations in the past three centuries. As official data on GDP at purchasing power parity from the World Bank and IMF is only available from 1975 onwards, we use the Kham-Geary purchasing power indices constructed by Angus Maddison (2003) for these purposes. These indices are however available only for selected years till 1950 after which annual data is available.[16] These are used to construct the power potential index.[17]

The industrial revolution made most of China's and India's strategic assets obsolescent *vis-à-vis* the strategic assets of the European countries. Thus, even though India's (China's) power potential (VIP^2) was 3.2 (3) times that of France (the strongest power) in 1700 and 1.7 (3.7) times that of the UK in 1820, India's (China's) actual power (VIP) became much smaller than that of many European nations. The failure of China and India to adopt the industrial revolution resulted in a sharp drop in the real value of their strategic capital, which dropped to a

15. 48th ranked Pakistan has been one of the most successful users of formal and informal alliances (in the last 50 years) to enhance its actual power way above its 'power potential' (lower than Algeria's 47).

16. The data for the year 1760 and 1800 (1880) has been constructed by using the growth rate from 1700 to 1820 (1870 to 1913) to interpolate.

17. These may not match for the WDI data. For instance, the average VIP^2 for UK for 1975-1990 calculated using Maddison data is 2 per cent (1/50th) less than that using WDI data.

fraction of that of these countries, thus opening a massive gap between their power potential (VIP^2) and their actual power (VIP). We therefore leave out these two countries from the analysis based on VIP^2.

More generally in the 18th and 19th centuries when the European powers were willing to conquer, colonise and subjugate non-white people and treat them as an intermediate species, the role of military might was much greater than it is today. Thus, the index of power potential VIP^2 may be less useful relative to the index of actual power VIP in the colonial era than it is today. In the globalised world of the 21st century, the importance of economic factors is greater than it was in earlier centuries and the VIP^2 rankings are likely to be highly co-related with the VIP rankings.

With conquest of Eastern Europe by the USSR at the end of the World War II, the Warsaw pact consisting of the USSR and Eastern Europe became what may be termed a 'Virtual State.' Though consisting of ostensibly separate nation states, it acted in its external dealings as well as among its members as a single State. The power potential of such a 'virtual state' can be approximated by treating it as a single State.

Multipolar Centuries: 18th and 19th

Figure 3.1 shows the power potential of the major European powers as measured by the index VIP^2. The UK is taken to be the benchmark nation so that the power potential is measured relative to it (i.e., it has an index value of 1 or 100 per cent). The broad picture that emerges is that France had the strongest global power potential in the 18th century and the UK in the 19th century. The second fact that emerges is that even at the height of British power around the middle of the 19th century, both the declining power France and the rising power, the USA had between 70 per cent and 75 per cent of the power potential of the UK. Similarly in the 18th century, the second ranked power had between 70 per cent and 80 per cent of its power potential (though the country in second position changed).

Third, the power potential index indicates that the world was inherently multipolar for much of these two centuries, with even the 5th ranked power having between 55 per cent (45 per cent) and 65 per cent of the power potential of the most powerful country in the 18th (19th) century. Balance of power strategies and diplomacy helped eliminate long debilitating wars within Europe (Kissinger, 1995) and thus increased their power *vis-à-vis* the rest of the world. Further, establishment of British predominance required exploitation of the economic resources (including labour and human capital) of the empire and particularly of India. Agreements regarding 'spheres of influence' outside Europe may also have contributed to the colonial conquest of Asia, Africa and Latin America, whose strategic assets had become obsolescent.

Bipolar or Unipolar 20th Century?

In 1913 at the start of the 20th century, the USA was clearly the dominant power (Figure 3.1). The UK however, still ranked second with Germany nipping at it heels at third rank after growing rapidly between 1880 and 1913. The USSR (3rd) and France (4th) had almost the same power potential, with Italy bringing up the rear (Figure 3.1). The US rise between 1880 and 1913 was meteoric with its power potential more than doubling, relative to the UK.

The USA has therefore clearly been the predominant power since the beginning of the 20th century. It is therefore interesting to note that the USA's share of the world GDP was only 8.9 per cent in 1870 and had risen to 19 per cent in 1913. It rose to a peak of 28 per cent in 1951 and declined thereafter to about 21 per cent in 1975. It has been fairly stable between 21 per cent and 22 per cent between 1975 and 1990.

Figure 3.2 shows the power potential measured by VIP^2 with the USA as the benchmark.[18] The United Kingdom was still the second most powerful nation in the world in 1913 with a power potential about 42 per cent of that of the USA. Combining the Indian economy (The Jewel of the Crown/British Empire) with that of the UK and treating the two as a 'virtual state' results in a power potential of 49 per cent (not shown). In other words, a subjugated India contributed about 7 per cent points or 1/6th to the power potential of the UK.[19] It has been noted by

18. These may not match for the WDI data. For instance, the average VIPP for UK for 1975-1990 calculated using Maddison data is 2 per cent (1/50th) less than that using WDI data.

strategic analysts that the UK was perhaps the first power in history to yield its dominant position without a war. In the light of the rapid fall in its power potential (as measured by the VIP²) till 1913 and its subsequent decline to 20 per cent by 1950, the UK seems to have acted very wisely. Germany's (West and East combined) power potential was down to about 75 per cent of the UK's by 1950.

Figure 3.1

Power Potential of European Powers in 18th and 19th Century

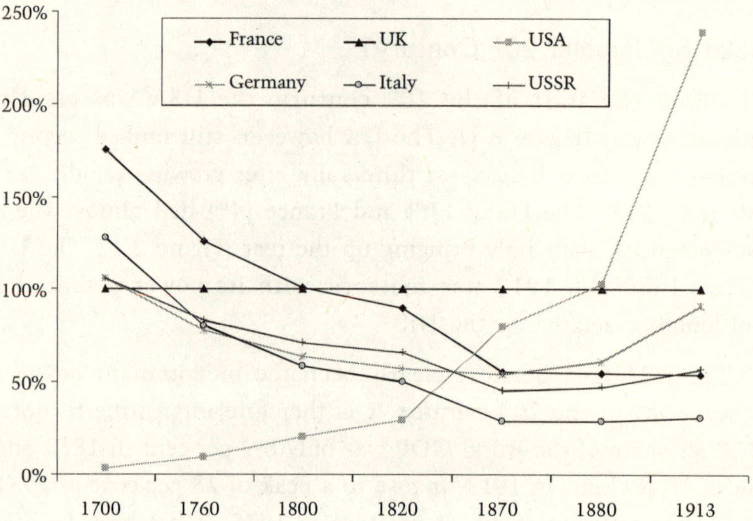

The power potential of the USSR in 1913, in contrast, was only 24 per cent, enough to classify it as a global power (≥ 20 per cent). As a result of the two world wars, its power potential had fallen to 17 per cent by 1950 (Figure 3.2). This would have lowered its status to a regional power (≥ 5 per cent), if it had not in the meantime acquired an 'empire' by incorporating Eastern Europe under the guise of the Warsaw Pact. Measured in terms of VIP² the power potential of the Soviet Virtual State (SVS) consisting of the USSR and Eastern Europe was 25 per cent in 1950 allowing it to retain its status as a great power, second only to the USA. The power of the Soviet Virtual State (USSR) was on a rising trend till 1975 when it peaked at 37 per cent (27 per cent) in 1975. At

19. This is not shown in the figure.

this point Eastern Europe contributed 10 per cent points or over 1/4th of the power potential. Historical evidence suggests that the rising power of the USSR from 1950 to 1975 led to greater assertiveness. As the USSR's own power potential and that of Eastern Europe started declining after 1975, the former's hold over the latter also weakened gradually. As disaffection grew among the people of Eastern Europe their contribution to the strength of the empire would in any case have declined from 10 per cent towards zero (even if USSR had remained at 27 per cent).

Figure 3.2

Power Potential of the USSR and the Soviet Virtual State

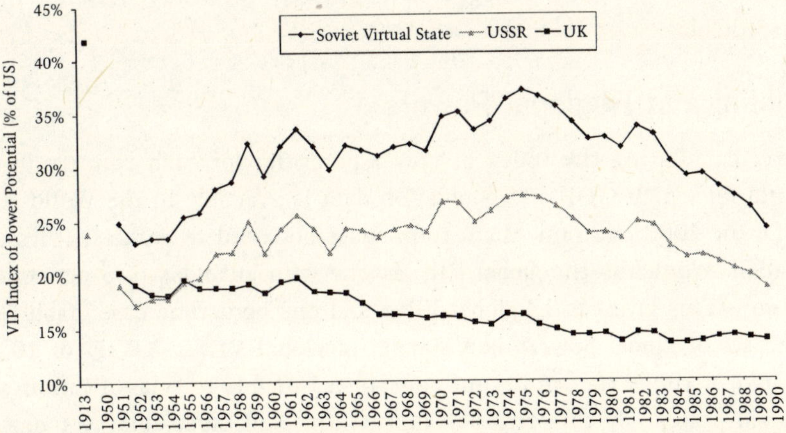

Figure 3.2 also shows that the power potential of the USSR (SVS) declined continuously since the mid-70s to reach less than 20 per cent (25 per cent). Thus, in terms of power potential (only), the USSR had ceased to be a 'global power' at the time of its break-up in 1990. Post-1990 economic research has shown that the Soviet economy was declining (relatively and perhaps absolutely in later stages) because of dysfunctional "socialist" policies of autarchy and centralised party/bureaucratic control. The USSR accelerated this decline by trying to maintain the illusion of bipolarity and strategic (near) parity with the USA, through excessive public investment in strategic technology. This

helped maintain its actual power above its 'power potential' but accelerated the decline in power potential.[20]

From this we reach several tentative conclusions about national power: (a) That an aspirant for 'great power' status must have a power potential of at least 35 per cent of the predominant power. (b) A nation state must have a power potential of (at least) 40 per cent to be a credible 'great power' and to maintain that status. (c) A rising power can be more assertive and credible than is perhaps warranted by the level of its power potential. (d) Acquisition of strategic assets is critical for a 'great power' with less than 50 per cent power potential to challenge the dominant pole and to convert the world into a bipolar one. (e) The minimum cut-off level of 'power potential' for bipolarity may be higher in an open globally integrated economy, but may also be more sustainable.

Global and Regional Powers

After calculating the index of power potential for each country in the world for which GDP and population data is available in the World Bank WDI for 2003, we rank them from most powerful to weakest (Virmani, 2005d). We define the global VIP² as one with an index of 5 per cent or more.[21] This gives us 13 global VIP²s and one borderline case (Table 3.2). The set of global powers is a sub-set of global VIP²s. A VIP² of 20 per cent or 4 times the minimum appears reasonable for classification as a 'global power.' By this criterion only China and Japan qualify today (in addition to the USA). Germany which was a potential global power till a decade ago is no longer one. The global VIP²s that are not global powers can be defined as 'regional powers.' By this criterion there are six regional powers in Europe, two in Asia and one each in North America and Latin America (Table 3.2).[22]

20. Ferguson (2001) has argued that the existence (non-existence) of a financial market helped the UK (hindered France) in its quest for Empire. India's developed capital market is an advantage, but this is offset by China's heritage of socialist ownership of assets and dictatorial control over financial intermediaries (banks). In terms of our analysis in Section 3, a capital market allows a State to borrow against future taxes and thus focus resources on a particular period of war or conflict.

21. The alternative would be to take the top 10 or 15.

22. Leaving aside the three global powers, the USA, China and Japan.

According to our index, China is now the third strongest power in the world and will displace Japan in second place in the next few years. The larger rich countries of Europe, Germany, France, the UK and Italy are long time members of the global VIP^2 club and will remain more powerful than India for some time even though the latter's economy is the fourth largest in the world.[23] India has just moved into 8th rank in the global VIP^2 club displacing G7 member Canada. Its GDP will become larger than Japan's in the next three years. Its power potential is greater than that of Russia, which is in 10th place behind Canada. The other members of the global power club are Spain, Brazil and South Korea. South Korea's power potential is rising relative to that of Spain and Brazil and is likely to exceed it in the next five years.

Table 3.2

Global VIP^{2}s in 2005

Economy	*VIP^2 Rank*		*GDP Rank*		*VIP^2*	
	2003	*2005*	*2003*	*2005*	*2003*	*2005*
Global Powers						
United States	1	1	1	1	100%	100%
Japan	2	2	3	3	28%	27%
China	3	3	2	2	22%	25%
Regional Powers						
Germany	4	4	5	5	18%	17%
France	5	5	6	6	13%	12%
United Kingdom	6	6	7	7	13%	12%
Italy	7	7	8	8	12%	11%
India	9	8	4	4	7.8%	8.5%
Canada	8	9	11	11	8.0%	7.8%
Russia	11	10	10	9	6.0%	6.5%
Spain	10	11	13	13	6.5%	6.4%
Brazil	12	12	9	10	5.7%	5.8%
Korea, Rep.	13	13	14	14	5.5%	5.5%
Australia	14	14	16	17	4.8%	4.7%

23. In GDP at PPP, the only way to compare the size of two economies. Their GDP converted at the current exchange rate is much larger than India's.

The 21st Century

Emerging Global Power: India

To outline the shape of the emerging future, recall that India and China are still relatively poor countries and their high rank in the global power club is due to their large population (relative to the USA and other countries) and despite their relatively low per capita income. The other side of this coin is that they have the greatest potential for increasing power, by raising their per capita income. For instance, if Russia's and Brazil's per capita income was raised to the level of the USA, their 'power potential' would still be 50 per cent and 60 per cent that of the USA respectively. In contrast China's and India's power potential would equal that of the USA if their per capita income was about 40 per cent of that of the USA in 2005.[24]

The potential for closing the power gap is illustrated in Figure 3.3, which shows all countries with the greatest gap between their share of the world GDP at purchasing power parity and their share of the world population. India, China and Indonesia have the largest negative gap, while the USA, Japan and Germany have the largest positive gap followed by France, the UK and Italy. The other countries in the global power club such as Russia and Brazil have negligible gaps and are consequently not shown here. Indonesia is still not a member of the global power club, and will only become a serious contender once it reaches there in the next two decades or so. Among the members of the global power club, India and China have the greatest gap (Figure 3.3) and therefore the greatest opportunity for closing it.

Population changes slowly over time and the UN population projections till 2050 do not show major changes in relative population, with the exception of Russia and Japan whose population will decline by 25 per cent and India whose population will increase to equal that of China. Thus, the major increases in power potential will come only through increases in per capita income relative to USA's. China and India have been among the ten fastest growing countries in the world for the past 25 years. Virmani (1999a, b) had forecast that they are likely

24. India 42 per cent and China 37 per cent.

to be among the 3-5 fastest growing economies in the next two decades. Thus, the current unipolar world can become bipolar or tripolar over the next 25 to 50 years if either or both of these countries continue to grow at a much faster rate than the USA. The demographic situation of other nation states makes it highly unlikely that any of them can compete with the USA for great power status in the next 50 years.

Figure 3.3

Global Imbalance; GDP Share—Population Share

The only other possibility is for the European Monetary Union (EMU) or European Union (EU) to coalesce into a Virtual State. This does not appear very likely in the next decade or two, because the larger countries of the EU (the UK, France, Germany, Italy and the Netherlands) would have to emasculate themselves in the process of transferring power to the EU Virtual State. On the contrary, the people of these countries are currently moving in the opposite direction by rejecting moves for further integration and trying to get back some of the powers ceded to the EU secretariat. Euro-optimists however expect that the movement towards integration will resume within 5 years and that the previous peak level of integration would be re-established in 10 years. Thereafter they project that the EU Virtual State could be created within 15 years from now. Even the optimists concede, however, that the process of EU integration could be delayed because of the problems of EU expansion and the issue of admitting Turkey into the EU. Thus, even an over optimistic time line for the EU would be to target becoming a Virtual State in about 20 years.

Figures 7.4 and 7.5 give the projected evolution of the power potential of some of the larger members of the global VIP^2 club. The growth rate assumptions are primarily those used in Virmani (2005a). A few minor corrections are made for the period 2006 to 2008 because new data is available from WDI and IMF WEO. Demographic and other factors are taken into account in a qualitative way in making the growth forecasts.[25] Shocks such as a major oil/energy crisis, political transformation/collapse would have to be taken account of by building alternative growth scenarios.[26]

Figure 3.4

India, An Emerging Global Power

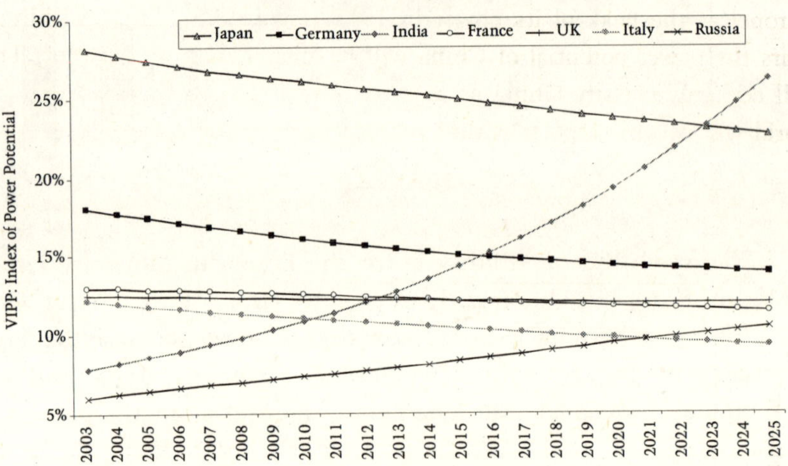

One noteworthy change is the projected rise in India's power ranking over the next 25 years (Figure 3.4). India will become more powerful than Italy in about five years, and France and the UK in about seven years. In about 10 years (2016), it is projected to become more powerful than Germany. By 2022 India's power potential will exceed 20

25. Other factors such as the slowing of growth as the country approaches the global technology frontier/production possibility frontier, are sought to be taken into account when making these projections.

26. An oil shock would slow down the growth rate of oil importing countries such as China, India and Japan relative to the USA.

per cent, making it a global power along with China and Japan (in addition to the USA). As shown in Virmani (2005b) and reflected in our projections, no other country has the potential to join the ranks of global powers over the next 25 years. Within 20 years India's power potential will exceed that of Japan (Figure 3.4).

New Great Power: China

More dramatically, China will become the second strongest global power within this decade. In 15 years it will become a great power, reaching about 75 per cent of the USA's power potential by 2025 (Figure 3.5). The speed with which China is rising almost mirrors the speed with which the USA rose at the turn of the 20th century. In 1983, China's power potential (VIP[2]) was the same as that of India. In 2006 its power potential will equal that of Japan. In another five years its power potential will equal that of the Soviet Virtual State (USSR + Eastern Europe) at the peak of its power in 1975 (Figure 3.5). Thus, within 10 years the power potential of China will be greater than 40 per cent. This will certainly classify China as a 'great power.' Does this mean that the world will become bipolar within a decade?

Figure 3.5

The End of a Unipolar World

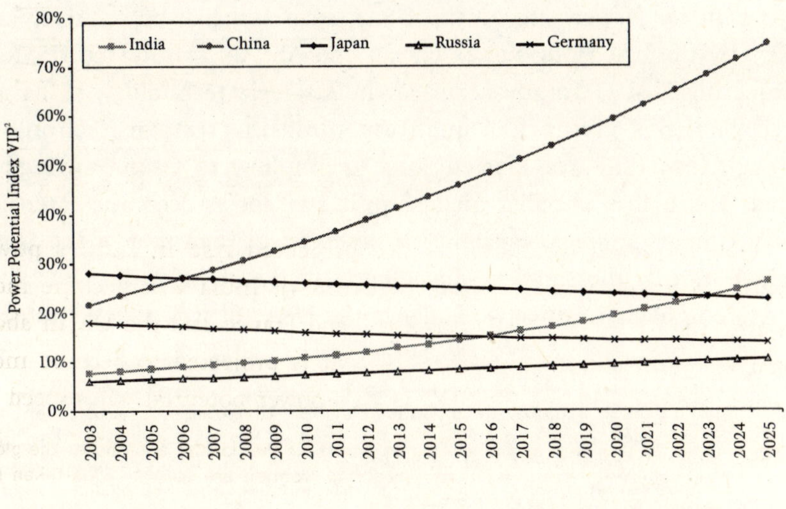

Let us first address the question of what is the minimum power potential (VIP^2) or actual power VIP needed for this purpose. A complete answer must await the detailed calculation of the strategic assets of great powers of the past and consequently their VIP. We can however shed some light by comparing the position of communist USSR in the second half of the 20th century and of communist China at the start of the 21st century.

China is ruled by a Leninist communist party just as the USSR was after World War II. There are, however, several differences between the 21st century and the 20th century and between the two countries that suggest that China will have to have a higher power potential before the world becomes bipolar. The nature and extent of globalisation is much greater in this century than it was in the previous one. The degree of economic interaction and interdependence among the major economies is far greater than before. In addition, globalisation now extends to every other sphere of human activity such as society and politics. Second, the model of economic development followed by the two countries is completely different.[27] The USSR followed an autarchic development model which minimised interaction with the rich, developed countries. China has since the mid-1980s followed a development model that fully uses the potential of globalisation and global economic integration. The FDI-Export model adopted by it goes further and makes it heavily dependent for fast growth on the USA, Japan and EU, both directly and indirectly through Hong Kong, Taiwan and ASEAN. Third, the USSR by conquering East Germany acquired the strategic technology, skills and R&D facilities giving it a quantum jump in strategic technology. Though the USSR transferred some technology to China during the decade and half of socialist friendship, it was not as deep and extensive. Thus, China's strategic capability is much lower than that of the Soviet Virtual State at the same power potential (VIP^2). Unlike the USSR it is therefore unlikely to directly challenge the USA till it is much stronger.

27. Though China is ruled by a Leninist communist party, as was post-war USSR, Mao put in place a highly decentralised system of economic management and development compared to the highly centralised system followed by the USSR. Thus, the movement to set up backyard electric furnaces in villages during his regime represented a degree of government decentralisation unmatched by democratic regimes.

In our judgment, China will be in a position to challenge the US power in Asia when its power potential reaches 60 per cent i.e., by around 2020. Even then, the challenge is unlikely to be of a direct military nature, such as an invasion of Taiwan. However, the use of pressure to achieve the same objective is likely to rise progressively.

Figure 3.6

Emergence of Tripolarity or Multipolarity?

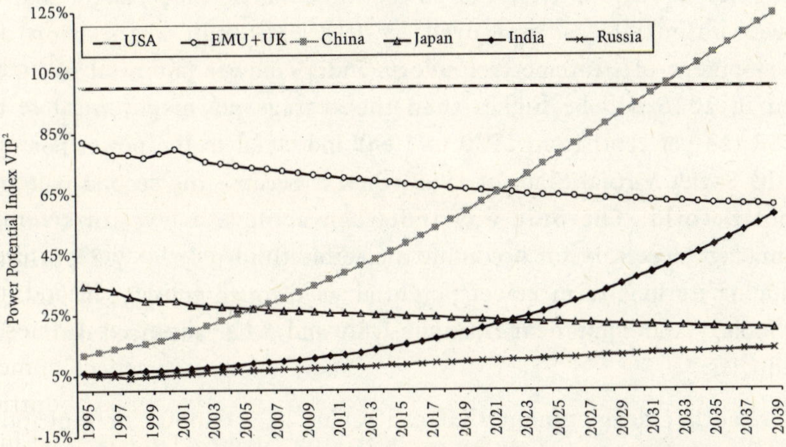

With China's power potential reaching 74 per cent by 2025 and the third ranked power, India having a power potential of only 26 per cent (1 per cent less than that of the USSR at its peak), the world is likely to become bipolar (Virmani, 2004). What this means is that China would likely challenge the USA in the economic and geopolitical context and could conceivably initiate a creeping annexation of the South China Sea. China's ruling party, about a year ago, talked about the 'peaceful rise of China.' This statement has however, been hedged since then, apparently because it is not intended to apply to Taiwan. One of the key tests of the ruling Chinese communist party's intentions will be whether it applies the same principles and approaches to a rising India, that it expects the USA, Japan and the EU to apply to a rising China. If it takes a positive approach to India's rise (e.g., on permanent membership of UNSC, founding of EAEC, NSG clearance of India-USA nuclear agreement), then it can rightly expect the same positive approach from others.[28]

Tripolar or Multipolar World?

There are two hypothetical developments that can result in a tripolar or multipolar world instead of a bipolar one in 25 years. From the history of the USSR and current day Russia, it is apparent that it is possible for a country to achieve a level of power (VIP) that is much larger than its power potential (as measured by VIP^2) through acquisition and development of strategic technology. India's power potential of 26 per cent in 2025 will be higher than the average power potential of the USSR (23 per cent) from 1950 to 1990 and equal to the power potential of the Soviet Virtual State in 1955 when it became the second pole in a bipolar world. The only way India can achieve a level of strategic technology necessary for becoming a credible third pole by 2025, without reducing its long-term power potential, is through transfer of strategic technology and equipment from the USA and other advanced democratic countries.

Another development that can result in a tripolar or multipolar world around 2025 is if the emergence of China and India on the global scene forces the residents of the large countries of the EU to reconsider their stand on EU integration. Twenty years from now, they may decide to constitute an EU government, based on direct elections by EU citizens, with complete powers to act on all matters connected with international relations (defence, foreign affairs). Such an EU would be a global power. The power potential of the European Monetary Union countries plus UK is in 2005 a little less than 75 per cent and is projected by us to decline somewhat to about 60 per cent (Figure 3.6). However, the power potential of an EU Virtual State would be about equal to that of China in 2025.

---

28. In seminars on China-India comparison, Chinese scholars frankly talk about 'competition and cooperation' between the two countries, while Indian scholars mention only 'cooperation'. No Chinese will however admit that "competition" includes proliferation of nuclear technology (e.g., atomic weapons design, medium-long range missiles and technology) to Pakistan.

If neither of these developments take place, the world will still become tripolar in about 30 years, with India as the weakest pole (Figure 3.6). Though the power potential VIP^2 of China is projected to be greater than that of USA in 30 years, its actual power VIP is likely to remain less for several decades because of the accumulated strategic assets of the USA.

Conclusion

In this chapter we presented a simple index of power potential, the VIP^2© that can be easily applied to any one of the 200 or so countries for which GDP and population data is available. The index measures potential power relative to the USA, which therefore, has an index value of 100 per cent. We specify benchmark values of the index for a country to be considered a great power (40 per cent), a global power (20 per cent) or a regional power (5 per cent). We find that there are currently two potential global powers, China and Japan in addition to the undisputed and unique USA. Germany, which was a potential global power till a decade ago, is no longer one.

As expected the largest number of regional powers are found among the rich countries of Europe, namely Germany, France, the UK, Italy and Spain (somewhat more surprisingly). Canada, another rich country meets the grade, while Australia just misses it today but is likely to meet it in a few years. Asia is clearly a rival to Europe in that it now has two global powers and three regional powers, India, South Korea and Australia. Brazil is the sole regional power in Latin America, while no country in Africa or Middle East meets the criterion.

The chapter also shows that in terms of power potential the world ceased to be bipolar sometime between 1975 and 1985. Thus, the world can in our view currently be best described as "unipolar with a multipolar fringe" constituted by the middle powers such as the UK, France, Germany, Russia, Japan, China and India (by analogy to the market structure, 'monopoly with a competitive fringe'). This situation is likely to last for another 10 to 15 years, when China becomes a 'great power'. Therefore this constrained unipolarity will have prevailed for 40 years before a bipolar world emerges.

The number of global powers will increase from three to four in less than 20 years, with the addition of India. At that point China's power potential would be about 75 per cent of the USA's while the sum of Japan and India's power potential would be 2/3rd of China's. Virmani (2005a) forecasts that the world would become bipolar by 2025 and tripolar by 2050. This chapter suggests that such a projection could induce behaviour that results in a tripolar or multipolar world by 2025. This is supported by recent developments in the US-India relations. The bold decision of President Bush to remove restrictions on the flow of commercial nuclear power technology to India and to facilitate the flow of dual use and strategic technology could transform power relations in Asia and the world.[29] If followed to its logical conclusion this could raise India's actual power (VIP) above its power potential (VIP^2), leading to a tripolar world by 2025. More realistically, it could accelerate the arrival of a tripolar world. In other words, the period of bipolarity will be shortened, an outcome that is in the mutual interest of both the USA and India.

The following policy implications emerge from the analysis of the chapter:

(1) Maximisation of economic growth will maximise power potential.[30] Since Deng's market revolution, China's Leninist ruling party has absorbed this lesson fully and has been acting on it. India's democratic ruling elite has for too long ignored this lesson. Further, acceleration of economic growth in India will not only increase its power but also (unlike in China) eliminate poverty faster (Virmani, 2005c).

---

29. Just as President Nixon's opening to China did. This will in my view, be one of the decisions that mark President Bush's (and his Indian counterpart Dr. Manmohan Singh's) place in history. India should not however let this go to its head. Size gives India an advantage, but the large number of poor people reduces the influence and respect that it enjoys. Though projections indicate that poverty (as currently defined) will be eliminated in 15 to 20 years, analysts should be realistic, remembering both the strength and weakness.

30. To find an answer to the question of how to do these in India, please see Virmani (2005c).

(2) Investment in strategic technology must be commensurate with the power potential of the economy so as to convert the 'potential' into actual power.[31] Too little investment will result in the potential remaining unrealised and aggressive powers will be tempted to exploit this weakness. Excessive investment in strategic assets can raise actual power in the short-run but can undermine long-term power potential by diverting funds from other essential public goods and services.

(3) Alliances (formal or informal) with a country having a large, high quality stock of strategic capital can be highly beneficial to a relatively poor country with a lower level of general technological capability and strategic assets but large stock of under utilised brains. Such a partnership can lower the financial and time cost for the latter of building strategic assets and improving their quality. The growth of strategic capital can therefore be accelerated resulting in faster rise of VIP.

(4) The previous point has two implications for India:

a. A strategic partnership with the US, the dominant power (uni-pole), can be beneficial to India if it gives India access to the US strategic technology. The US spokesman's statement on March 25, 2005 in Washington that the USA would "..help India become a World Power," has a value for India if it means that the USA is willing to "supply India the Strategic technology to ensure that India's actual power (VIP) matches or exceeds its growing power potential (VIP^2)."[32] This is not, however, a commercial transaction where financial price equals marginal revenue. The US president had authorised such a statement because he perceived a strategic benefit to the USA from having a natural and stable balance of power in

31. The global balance emerging from such a policy by all countries would result in a "natural balance of power" (Virmani, 2004). Such an equilibrium among the major powers is therefore likely to be more stable.

32. President Bush's commitment to supply the requisite technology to India is confirmed by informed strategic analysts in Washington as is the resistance of the bureaucracy.

Asia. The USA can also benefit in the medium-long term from India's large stock of young but underutilised brains.[33]

b. A strategic partnership between India and each member of the 'democratic, multipolar fringe' (Japan, the UK, Germany, France, and Russia) can also be mutually beneficial, particularly if it involves joint R&D and production. This is because these countries' strategic assets, though inferior to that of the USA, are superior to India's. They also have some technologies that match those of the USA in quality and/or cost and are therefore competitive. Increasing the number of competitors levels the playing field for the buyer. In the medium-term they too can benefit from India's high stock of young underutilised brains.[34]

(5) Acquisition of technology or skills from others is not a substitute for, but a complement to indigenous development for a potential global power or aspiring great power. Acquisition of strategic assets (materials, equipment, technology, skills) from others must be used to: (a) Fill gaps and cover weakness in domestic capability, (b) Speed up indigenous development of strategic assets and improve the effectiveness and quality of strategic R&D, (c) Widen the ambit of strategic R&D into frontier areas not accessible previously.

(6) The dominant power will try to reduce the flow of strategic technology from it to the potential challenger. As shown above, China will be strong enough to challenge the US power by 2025. The US government has therefore taken steps over the last few

---

33. See Rummel (1994) and Ray (1998) for the hypothesis that liberal democracies do not wage war against each other. In our view the probability of war between liberal democracies is indeed likely to decline in the 21st century for the theoretical reasons given in this thesis. Thus, it is in the interest of democracies to collaborate both to strengthen each other and to jointly promote democracy throughout the world.

34. See Rummel (1994) and Ray (1998) for the hypothesis that liberal democracies do not wage war against each other. In our view the probability of war between liberal democracies is indeed likely to decline in the 21st century for the theoretical reasons given in this thesis. Thus, it is in the interest of democracies to collaborate both to strengthen each other and to jointly promote democracy throughout the world.

years to stop such flows from the US, the EU and Japan. In response China has been emphasising that it is a middle-income country whose per capita income will not equal the USA's for 50 years or more. This chapter shows that as far as global power relations are concerned, the relevant comparator is either the power potential VIP^2 or the actual power VIP, not the relative per capita income.

(7) As long as the EU does not become a "Virtual State", it is not a global power and its incentive for stopping the flow of strategic technology to China will be much lower than that of the USA. On the other hand, if the EU becomes a 'Virtual State' it will be a rival of China and its incentive to restrict the flow of strategic technology to China will rise sharply.

References

Ferguson, Niall (2001). *The Cash Nexus: Money and Power in The Modern World*. Basic Books.

Kennedy, Paul (1988). *The Rise and Fall of the Great Powers: Economic Change and Military Conflict from 1500 to 2000*. USA: Random House.

Kissinger, Henry (1995). *Diplomacy, Simon and Schuster*. Reprint edition. April.

Maddison, Angus (2003). *The World Economy: A Millenial Perspective*. OECD Development Centre Seminars. Overseas Edition. Overseas Press (India) Pvt. Ltd.

Ray, James Lee (1998). "Does Democracy Cause Peace?", *Annual Review of Political Science* 1:27-46. *http://www.mtholyoke.edu/acad/intrel/ray.htm*

Rummel, R.J. *(1994). Death by Government.* Transaction Publishers. *http://www.hawaii.edu/powerkills/note1.htm*

Tellis, Ashley J., Janice Bially, Christopher Layne, Melissa Mcpherson (2000). *Measuring National Power in the Post-Industrial Age: Analysis Handbook*. Santa Monica: Rand.

Virmani, Arvind (1999a). "Potential Growth Stars of the 21st Century: India, China and The Asian Century", *Occasional Paper*, Chintan, October. *www.icrier.org/avpapers.html*

———. (1999b). "Star Performers of the 20th (21st) Century: Asian Tigers, Dragons or Elephants", *Occasional Paper*, Chintan, September. *www.icrier.org/avpapers.html*

———. (2004). "Economic Performance, Power Potential and Global Governance: Towards a New International Order," *Working Paper* No. 150, ICRIER, December. *www.icrier.org/publications.html*

———. (2005a). "A Tripolar Century: USA, China and India," *Working Paper* No. 160, ICRIER, March. *www.icrier.org/wp160.pdf*

———. (2005b). "A Tripolar World: India, China and USA," *ICRIER Public Lecture*, May. *www.icrier.org/public/TripolarWrld_IHC4c.pdf*

———. (2005c). "Policy Regimes, Growth and Poverty In India: Lessons of Government Failure And Entrepreneurial Success", *ICRIER Working Paper* No. 170, October. *www.icrier.org/WP170GrPov9.pdf*

———. (2005d). "Global Power From the 18th To 21st Century: Power Potential (VIP^2), Strategic Assets and actual Power (VIP)", *ICRIER Working Paper* No. 175, November. *www.icrier.org/wp175.pdf*

Waltz, Kenneth (1979). *Theory of International Politics*. Reading: Addison-Wesley.

4 World Economy, Geopolitics and Indo-US Relations

Introduction

The USA has been the predominant or sole global superpower since the collapse of the USSR at the end of the 1980s and arguably since the beginning of the 1980s (Virmani, 2005e and chapter 3). At the same time the European Union has emerged as an economic rival in certain global contexts such as WTO negotiations and in certain sectors such as civil aircraft. Many member States of the European Union, however, feel less constrained to support all the US actions across the world, since the collapse of the USSR. The US action in Afghanistan and Iraq has also demonstrated both the military predominance of the USA and its limitations in the globalised, relatively democratic world of the 21st century. The terrorist attack on the World Trade Center in New York (9/11) has thrown a challenge to US security that will take it many decades to address. Co-incidentally what are new threats and challenges for the USA have been so for India for decades (Jehadi terrorism, nuclear proliferation, see chapter 8). These problems are likely to continue to confront and challenge the USA for decades.

As long as China is ruled by a party based on the Leninist concept of monopoly of political power, a rapidly growing China with increasing military expenditures could emerge as another threat to the USA in the coming decades. Elements of the US strategic community have therefore started looking for new allies and friends. There is increasing recognition in the USA that India could be one such friend because of the shared values (democracy, respect for rule of law and human rights), the highly educated/skilled and prosperous Indian diaspora in the USA and overlapping (not identical) interests.[1] Much of the US establishment (political and academic), steeped in non-proliferation theology, was not however willing to end the nuclear apartheid structure that it had built to contain India's strategic advancement after the 1974 atomic test.[2]

Indian analysts and national security strategists were equally clear about India's world view and approach to India-US relations:[3]

(1) India has no extra-territorial ambitions and had never in its history tried to rule other countries. The Indian empires in South East Asia had no political connection with India, but were independent cultural entities. Thus, the probability of India taking an offensive territorial posture after it became a global power was negligible.

(2) Because of centuries of rule by a foreign power and the humiliation of being ruled by the British East India Company, the Indian elite was extremely sensitive about its independence and freedom of action. India would therefore never be a client State or a formal (inherently junior) ally of the USA.

(3) A closer long-term relationship between India and the USA could only be built on the principles of equality. Just as equality under law in a democracy does not eliminate differences arising form IQ and wealth, India with 8 per cent of the per capita income and power potential of the USA would be financially and technologically weaker than the USA for many decades.

(4) A genuine, enduring, partnership based on the principle of equality could not be built on a foundation that patently

1. Many observers have pointed out that the US government's approach to India started to change in the last years of the Clinton administration, after the Indian nuclear tests of 1998. To what extent the hearts and minds of those connected with that administration have changed is unclear!

2. Nuclear Suppliers Group (NSG), Missile Technology Control Regime (MTCR), The Wassenaar Agreement to control dual use technologies, initially directed against India.

3. Some of this was in response to US queries and dialogue with US interlocutors over the last two years. For instance, the Pentagon had hired independent consultants such as Booze Allen Hamilton, USA, who visited India and met many strategic analysts and thinkers during 2004. In addition, numerous US government officials and congressman visited India and interacted with Indian think tanks during 2004 and 2005.

discriminated against India, with $1/6^{th}$ of the world population, independent technological capability and power potential.

(5) A natural balance of power, based on economic size and strength, was not possible if one of the potential stabilisers (India) had its strategic hands tied behind its back while other, more aggressive countries had no such restrictions.

(6) Consequently a removal of restrictions on 'Dual use' and civilian nuclear technology and materials was a pre-requisite for a long-term, mutually beneficial relationship between India and the USA (Virmani, 2004).

This message was apparently heard and accepted by the second Bush administration, because of its prior positive view of India[4] and new/revised assessment of both the emerging challenges in Asia and of India's potential capability to meet these challenges.[5]

The new approach of the Bush administration provided India with an opportunity to advance its own national interest. One must, however, be realistic enough to remember that India's short-term approach to some issues, such as Pakistan's nurturing of Jehadis, may differ. This should not deter the two countries in cooperating in areas where their respective national interests coincide. The first step in this process is to have a realistic view of the world and India's role in it. The second step is to define what India needs to do to enhance its chosen role in the world. The third step is to determine what strategic technology and assets we need and can get from the USA, Russia and France etc., that will accelerate the process of attaining these objectives. The role of diplomacy then is to get the best deals available from any source to further India's national interest. The fourth step is to ensure the indigenous us development of those technologies and assets that are necessary for attaining India's strategic objectives and that none of them is either able or willing to give to India.

---

4. *A la* the Vulcans including Robert Blackwell and Condoleezza Rice and the latter's *Foreign Affairs* magazine article in 2000 and its references to the emerging importance of India in global matters.

5. This re-assessment was apparently made some time in 2004 and culminated in a new CIA National Security paper in December 2004 that explicitly mentioned a new global role for India.

There are no free lunches in the world of diplomacy and national power. The USSR veto on Kashmir in the UNSC and the Indo-Soviet friendship treaty's insurance against a second front during Bangladesh liberation, came at the cost of explicit or tacit support to the USSR's suppression of Eastern Europe (Hungary, Czechoslovakia) and its invasion of Afghanistan. China's freedom for unlimited export to the USA and other OECD countries requires it to cooperate with the USA in the UNSC. All cooperation entails mutual adjustment and mutual gain. Though India's government has not been stranger to the truth propagated by Kautilya, pure hearts sometimes confuse personal sentiment and individual morality with national interest. Global powers like France in the 18th century, the UK in the 19th century, the USA in the 20th century and China in the 21st do not make such mistakes. They pursue their national interest without sentimentality and without being bound by personal morality, whatever the (above the surface) rhetoric.

The next section documents the relative economic and geopolitical position of the major countries. Section 3 outlines the new challenges facing the USA, and to a varying and perhaps lesser degree the other major countries, including India. Section 4 gives a projection of the world economy and polity over the first half of the 21st century. This helps clarify the challenges and opportunities for the USA and India and the imperatives for mutually beneficial cooperation. Section 5 concludes the chapter.

Unipolar World with Multipolar Fringe

We start by looking at the world today, five years after the start of the 21st century, first in terms of the world economy and then in terms of geopolitical power.

Multipolar World Economy

The economic importance of a country in the world can be measured either by its share in the world GDP or by its ratio to the US GDP, the largest economy in the world. Any such comparison of economic size is valid only in real term, that is, using the same set of prices to weigh different baskets of goods. The closest approximation to this is the GDP measured in purchasing power parity terms.[6]

One contentious issue is whether to treat the constituent countries of the European Union (EU) as individual nations or to consider one single entity called the EU. Strong supporters of the EU in the European academic community assert that 70 per cent of the economic decision-making of these States is in the hands of the European Union based in Brussels rather than in the individual nations constituting the EU.[7] We observe that the EU does operate as 'virtual state' with a common EU view in the context of the WTO negotiations. However, in other contexts such as the World Bank and the IMF, individual nation states continue to play a role, though there may be a large degree of coordination so as to present a common viewpoint. Giving the benefit of doubt to the EU optimists, we can treat the EU as one economic entity. We approximate this entity by the EMU, which is indeed much more closely integrated with respect to monetary policy, plus the UK. The global financial crises has however revealed gaping holes in integrated financial governance.

US GDP was about 21 per cent of the world GDP at PPP in 2005 (down about 1 per cent point from 1975). Figure 4.1 shows the distribution of economic size among the largest economic powers relative to the USA. This figure suggests that the world economy may indeed be considered multipolar today. The size of the EU economy is almost the same as that of the USA, while China's economy is 66 per cent of that of the USA.[8] The USA, the EU and China therefore have approximately the same size. Japan and India, though half the size of China, have enough bulk relative to the USA to count in the world economy especially if they can build coalitions and/or represents the aspirations of other countries. India, a low income country having a large fraction of the poor in the world can clearly play a credible role as the spokesperson/representative of

6. Most analysts have used the GDP of a country converted to US$ using the current exchange rate, both for a comparison with the USA and for deriving world aggregates. This in our view gives a misleading view of a country's relative economic and global power.

7. Academics from France and Netherlands seem to be the most optimistic.

8. A 16.5 per cent increase in size (as proposed by China's statistics bureau) would raise this to 77 per cent.

the low income and lower-middle income countries of the world as it had done at the WTO ministerial in Hong Kong. Thus, an argument can be made that the global economic scene is multipolar rather than unipolar, bipolar or tripolar.

Figure 4.1

Distribution of World GDP: Large Countries Relative to USA

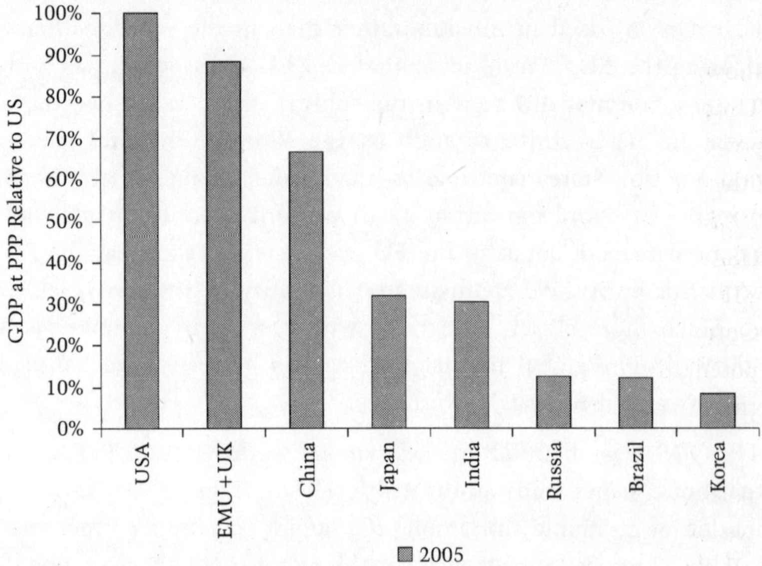

Source: World Bank, *World Development Indicators.*

Unipolar Power Structure

State (geo-political) power is the "extent that (one) effects others more than they affect [one]" (Waltz, 1979). It is therefore a "combination of its capacity to resist the unwelcome influence of others and conversely to influence others to behave as it wants them to." Geo-political power depends on economic strength, technological capability and military power. Virmani (2004, 2005a) index of power potential (VIP²) combines economic strength and commercial technological capability. This is an approximation of the actual power of nation states that depends on additional factors such as strategic technological capability and assets.[9] In

9. Strategic assets include military, nuclear, aero-space assets and the technological capability to develop these. They are difficult to quantify/measure for a large number of countries (Virmani, 2005e).

this context it is difficult to treat the European Union as a 'virtual state' because in the context of global security and foreign relations each member state is individually represented in every country as well as in the World Bank, the IMF and the UN organisations and acts in its own interests. Even passionate academic supporters of the European Union do not claim that it is currently a 'virtual state' but are very hopeful that it would become one in 20-25 years. We therefore consider only nation states in this context of global power politics.

The distribution of power potential as measured by the VIP^2 is shown in Figure 4.2. The figure suggests that the world is currently 'Unipolar with a multipolar fringe'. The USA is clearly the predominant power in the world today; some would call it the 'sole superpower', others a 'constrained hegemon'. The second and third ranked powers in 2005, Japan and China have a little over 1/4th the power potential of the USA. According to Virmani (2005c) a cut-off value of 20 per cent for the VIP^2 can be used to define a potential "global power" (see chapter 3). Germany, the fourth ranked power has only 17 per cent of the power potential of the USA and is thus no longer a global power (according to this definition).

According to Virmani (2005e) actual power depends on both "power potential (VIP^2)" and "strategic assets (military, aero-space, nuclear)."[10] If we accounted for 'strategic assets', the actual power of the USA *vis-à-vis* all the countries shown in Figure 4.2 would be even stronger, while that of Japan and Germany would be much weaker. One indicator is that the US defence expenditures are currently more than the sum of the defence expenditures of the next 25 powers. The relative position of Russia (not shown as it is less than India) would however be stronger relative to the other countries, including India and Italy, because of its much larger stock of strategic assets. Thus, currently it is quite clear that the world is unipolar, though there are a number of middle powers that constitute a polycentric fringe that are competing with each other for a distant second position.[11]

---

10. He defines an index of power (VIP) that incorporates both VIP^2 and "strategic assets/technology" and shows how the latter differs from the "commercial technology" included in the former. See also Virmani (2005c).

11. By analogy with the economic structure called 'monopoly with a competitive fringe.'

Figure 4.2

Distribution of Power Potential (VIP²)

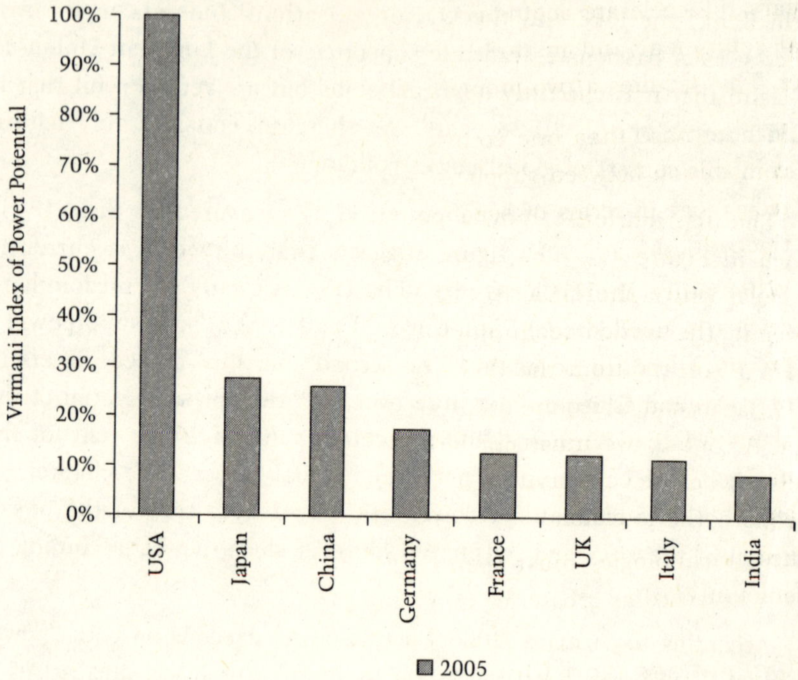

The strategic technological capability and assets of the USA are far in excess of those of the other powers.[12] One way in which this manifests itself is the use by European and Japanese military/strategic equipment of critical parts or sub-assembly originating in the USA over whose transfer/sale to other countries the USA exercises absolute control. Its defence spending is equal to the sum of the next 25 powers. It can plausibly be argued that the US strategic capability is currently equal to or greater than that of all the other powers put together. France, Russia and other countries have strategic technological capabilities in certain areas that match those of the USA. But there are also many areas in which the strategic capabilities of the USA are more than a decade ahead of each. India is on the other end of the scale. Despite

12. For instance the USA is a leader in RMA, the revolution in military affairs, ABM technology, space weapons, remote intelligence gathering and ECM (electronic counter-measure) technology.

India's capabilities in the nuclear and space field, its overall strategic assets are currently a fraction of those of France and Russia. Thus, it is necessary to accelerate acquisition of strategic technology, skills and critical equipment and materials to move India closer to the global frontier. This requires a two-pronged acquisition strategy:

(a) Where more than one country possess the strategic capability, competition between suppliers should be used to procure the best technology in terms of benefit-cost ratio (appropriate quality-price trade-off).

(b) When only the USA has the technology, we must identify critically needed technologies, equipment and materials and procure these from the USA through strategic cooperation. This may sometimes require a degree of determination and persistence about which we must not be squeamish (in the interest of the nation). No country, even a strategic partner will hand us anything on a platter.[13]

These technologies must then be internalised, adapted to Indian conditions and used as a base for further development (R&D).

New Challenges and Opportunities

The last five years have thrown up new challenges for the USA, the 'sole superpower'/'constrained hegemon' since 1990, and new opportunities for India, which has been facing some of these challenges for decades. Their impact on Europe, Japan and Russia were mixed, throwing up new challenges and opportunities.

Proliferation and Failed States

Weapons of mass destruction acquire a specially menacing aspect when they are in the hands of either failing States, failed States or 'rogue' States that have no stake in the modern world and its interlocking system of trade and investment. Taliban Afghanistan with access to

13. Rosy views about the days of strategic partnership with the USSR are just that. There was no dearth of problems and difficulties even with this much-vaunted friend. But we must be realistic enough to accept this as part of the geo-political game.

proliferating scientists in Pakistan and North Korea, who in turn had access to Chinese technology and materials, fell into this category.[14] Pakistan, the primary destination as well as source and major conduit for nuclear proliferation during the 1990s, seemed to be slipping into the failed State category around the time of the US intervention in Afghanistan. It has now reversed the process and recovered considerably though the fundamentalist Frankenstein created by it continues to thrive. There is therefore a possibility of leakage of WMDs to fundamentalist and a fundamentalist challenge to army power and authority, particularly if the US leaves Afghanistan before a moderate regime is firmly in control of the entire country.[15] Though India has faced the challenge of Pakistani WMDs (nuclear weapons and missiles) for more than a decade, the new found concern of the USA about WMDs is welcome and should be used for joint planning and action wherever this is in mutual interest.

India is a close geographical neighbour of many of the heavily populated States that are potential candidates for failure. India with its manpower, military and strategic capability, is one of the few countries that can build up the capability to intervene in an explosive situation with the help and cooperation of the USA. It is also quite possible that India's judgment about which States are failing or rogue States may differ from that of the USA. Clearly joint action should occur either when the two country's interests coincide or when additional strategic benefits make the benefit-cost ratio to India sufficiently positive.

Jehadi Terrorism

India has been coping with cross-border terrorism since 1980. In the 1990s this cross-border terrorism increasingly took on a fundamentalist Jehadi character as it targeted J&K. In the 2000s this cross-border terrorism was spread to the whole of India and has diversified its bases from the West to the North and East, though this may be partly a tactical move by the controllers/handlers/planners across the border.

14. Virmani (2006) forthcoming.

15. It is not outside the realm of possibility that a similar situation develops in Iran.

The USA and the West were rudely shaken from their supreme indifference to this phenomenon by 9/11. Their great concern is the global nature and reach of this terrorism in contrast to the national or sub-national terrorism seen in earlier decades. This terrorism though merely a limited (fundamentalist and violent) offshoot of Wahabi/Salafi Islam assumes a global character because it seems to rest on the foundation of belief about a Muslim Ummah that is above the nation states. It is therefore a threat to many democratic countries with substantial Muslim populations, as well as to the USA, which arouses particularly strong emotions among Arabs for its support to Israel's policy towards the Palestinians. Post 9/11, over-reaction by some US authorities has reinforced negative emotions among Muslims.[16]

The Indian experience of externally financed and orchestrated terrorism since 1980, the experience of political integration of Indian Muslims into the democratic mainstream is a valuable example for other countries. Further, India is at the geographical centre of the Islamic world with Bangladesh, Indonesia and Malaysia to the west of India and Pakistan, Iran and the Middle-East to the west and Central Asia to the north-west. Historically its was also one of the intellectual centres of Islamic thought (Deoband). There are therefore areas in which India's and the US's interests coincide just as there are obvious areas in which they differ (Pakistan).

There are however new threats that may limit the extent of cooperation. External financing and propagation of Wahabi education, 'Babri Masjid' and 'Gujarat riots' have planted the seed of discontent that the ISI and other agencies are all too happy to exploit. Thus India has to be extremely careful and cautious in actively supporting military action initiated unilaterally by the USA in or against Muslim countries, while being open to jointly determined and managed military interventions against terrorists.

16. In truly democratic countries such negative departures are usually corrected through the political process and the same is likely to happen over the next three years in the USA.

Rise of China

As China is ruled by a Leninist party, its phenomenal growth rate has occasionally raised concern among political leaders in Western democracies; given the limited respect such parties have historically had for human rights and the Rule of Law. A few analysts and leaders have also started worrying about the future imbalance of power in Asia. China's proliferation of nuclear weapons designs and critical technology/equipment/materials to Asian friends (Pakistan and North Korea) and indirectly through them to other countries (Libya, Iran, Syria/Saudi Arabia) has heightened these concerns[17] (chapter 8). The most recent example is the supply of cruise missiles and cruise missile technology to Pakistan in 2004-05.

To what extent can a country that has: (a) for decades tried to undermine its Southern neighbour's security and indirectly stymie its rise as a regional power, and (b) exploited its modernised and democratic Eastern neighbours guilt about World War II to keep it from converting its global power potential into actual power, be believed when it talks about its own "peaceful rise"? Its actions over the next decade on three key issues will show its real intentions (the proof of the pudding is in the eating). China's support for India's case for access to peaceful nuclear technology at NSG,[18] its support for its case for a permanent veto bearing seat on the UN Security Council and acceptance of the concept of an inclusive Asian Economic Community, then its statements would acquire greater credibility. The evidence so far, on all three issues is mixed.

The US along with Japan has sufficient power to ensure a balance of power in Asia, in the next couple of decades. In the long-term (around mid-century), India is the only country that has the potential to sustain the balance of power in Asia (Virmani, 2005b). The medium-term situation is marked by a great deal of uncertainty and there is a danger that the independence and freedom of action of the smaller States of Asia would be seriously compromised or constrained if the balance of power in Asia was disrupted. This uncertainty can be reduced

17. See Milhollin and White (1991, 1995), Gelb (1984), Gertz (1996), Shuey and Kan (1995) and Albright *et al.* (1997). See also Weismann and Krosney (1981). See also Virmani (2006) for a historical review.

18. Without trying to muddy the waters by supplying additional, new nuclear power plants to Pakistan.

by accelerating the growth of India's economy and enhancing its strategic capability, thus ensuring a better balance of power in the interregnum.

China's demand for oil and mineral imports is rising rapidly. Its share of the world imports of natural resources including oil is likely to rise over the next two decades. As oil, uranium and certain other minerals are owned by the US, Canadian and other Western countries or their multinational companies, the Chinese are concerned about this increased vulnerability. This perceived vulnerability is sought to be minimised through purchase of natural assets in other countries. The initial steps in this direction have already raised serious concerns in the USA and lesser concerns in Canada and a few other Western countries.

High rates of saving and reinvestment by its Socialist enterprises gives China the ability to purchase global assets through such enterprises. Suppression of private consumption by channelling private savings into banks and from there into loss making socialist units assists this process (chapter 6). China's share of the world's natural resources (oil, minerals) owned and operated/managed by Chinese socialist enterprises is therefore likely to rise over the next 20 years. This will increase China's power/influence over natural and agricultural resource rich countries such as Australia, Iran, Saudi Arabia, Indonesia, Malaysia, Thailand and the natural resource rich countries of Africa and Latin America. High socialist saving rates could also lead to purchase of high tech companies and brand icons in the developed world arousing concerns and counter action in the USA and perhaps in the other countries.

In contrast, Indian corporate purchase of western companies is viewed as being much more benign, as it is not driven by any national/ government geopolitical design. Positive relations with the USA will also allow greater freedom to the Indian public sector oil companies to purchase oil assets abroad.

US Economic Risks and Hedging

Education

A developed country like the USA can maintain its growth rate only by keeping up the pace of innovation and technological change ("commercial technology"). This depends on: (a) the institutional/market structures for innovation, (b) the level and quality of higher education including associated research and (c) the average level of education of the population/labour force. The first and second, which also form the foundation on which US leadership in 'strategic technology' is built, are unmatched by any other country and are likely to remain far superior for many decades. The greatest weakness is in the average level and quality of education, particularly in maths and sciences, which (uncorrected) may decline further as the share of Hispanics in the population rises, given the latter's lower average educational attainment.[19] The average education level and quality of maths/science education of many Asian countries is already superior to that of the US. Though the US government and elites will make an effort to raise the level, there is a significant probability that other countries will catch up and eventually exceed the US. China with its flexible, open (to FDI), pragmatic and result-oriented policy is likely to catch up in a few decades. Given its population/labour force size, this represents a competitive economic threat to the USA, in a way that the higher educational attainment of smaller countries do not.

Though India could follow with a lag, its rigid education policy structure and deteriorating State dominated and bureaucratically controlled education system makes it unlikely to do so unless fundamental reforms are carried out.[20] A new education policy framework and regulatory system that allows and encourages private and foreign educational institutions (non-profit and commercial) to provide quality education at all levels, could rapidly increase the supply of education to meet anticipated demand increase (Virmani, 2005e). India's past attainment in higher education, respect for intellectual property and rule of law and its legal system also make it a more reliable and trustworthy partner for collaborative efforts in many areas of medium-

19. Their share of the US population would nearly double, from 12.6 per cent in 2000 to 24.4 per cent in 2050 as per the US census projections: *www.census.gov/Press-Release/www/releases/archives/population/001720.html*

20. This makes it almost impossible for sincere and honest educational entrepreneurs and non-profit institutions to enter and survive while permitting quasi-legal, low quality, educational institutions, including many set up and run by politicians, to flourish.

high skill labour-intensive R&D. Such partnership can help the US maintain its technological edge *vis-à-vis* EU, Japan and China while simultaneously helping India acquire technological skills and capabilities at a much faster pace.[21] Thus, if India can reform its education polices and regulations expeditiously there is enormous scope for export of educated personnel and for mutually beneficial cooperation with the USA and other advanced countries in developing 'commercial technology'.

Strategic Technology

Because of the new threats from non-State actors, failing States and their secret supporters, the US dissemination of 'strategic technology' is in the process of becoming even more restrictive than before. Even a close US ally like the UK has complained that the US is denying it access to 'strategic technology' developed under a joint fighter development programme. This is because the US is unsure whether even an ally such as the UK, which is part of the EU, will never pass on technology embodied in physical capital to potential adversaries.[22] Under the new National Security Strategy, frontier (F) strategic technology is likely to be denied even to allies.[23] Allies and partners of the USA may get access to one generation old (F-1) 'strategic technology,' while others will have access only to two generation old (F-2) technology. India's developing strategic relationship with the USA will put it in the second category, with access to F-1 technology. We should however attempt to access, pre-frontier or F-1/2 technology, particularly in areas that will help us meet the non-conventional threats that are motivating the new

21. The competitive economic threat to the USA from these three is greater than that from India and this relative situation is unlikely to change for many decades.

22. Major non-NATO ally Pakistan gave China uranium enrichment technology that A.Q. Khan had stolen from Urenco in the Netherlands, in return for Chinese weapons designs, HEU and Tritium for weapons. More recently it is reported to have given unexploded Tomahawk cruise missiles that landed in Pakistan in 2004-05 to China for reverse engineering, in return for Chinese cruise missiles and related technology.

23. The JSF or F-35 is currently under development. The F22A Raptor entered service in 2004 and can be considered at the frontier today. The Stealth Bomber B2 which became operational in 1993 is F-1 technology. The F18 (F117A) that entered service in 1983 (1982) has F-2 technology base with upgrades having varying degrees of F-1 technology.

USA strategy. This requires that we position ourselves to contribute technologically to the US development of frontier (F) technology. This may be possible in areas such as software and information systems and nuclear technology.

Globalisation and Interdependence

Globalisation has increased economic interdependence and thus increased the costs of war and open conflict between major powers. Unlike during the cold war no country stands outside the global economic system or desires to create a separate parallel system independent of the developed countries—the USA, Europe and Japan. The degree of interdependence of China (the putative rising power), as well as of other big countries such as India, Russia and Brazil, with advanced/rich countries has increased progressively and is likely to continue. Global trade and capital flows have risen over the past few decades. China's trade surplus with the US and its accumulation of US government debt creates mutual dependencies. China's dependence on the US market is matched/countered by US consumer's dependence on cheap (sometimes subsidised) exports. Even FDI and equity flows from one nation to another, instead of creating dependence of the recipient on the source, create mutual interdependence. Thus US, EU and Japanese FDI investors in China are among the strongest geopolitical defenders of China in these countries as the profitability of their investment would be affected by any conflict and would be at risk of expropriation in the event of war. Conversely China's integration into the global economy (high trade share) and its dependence on FDI, particularly export-oriented FDI, makes it less likely to initiate war or open conflict with countries that receive a major part of its exports or are the source of its FDI.[24] History however, cautions that a rising Germany was not constrained from aggressive action against countries with which it had intense bilateral economic relations.

24. We can similarly increase the US dependence on us by sharply raising the level of FDI flows from and related trade with the USA. There are great opportunities for trade in services such as health care where US costs are rising rapidly, resulting in declining health insurance coverage and rising pension costs. Joint ventures between the US and Indian companies to provide health care to the old and poor US citizens in India can also help moderate pension costs and increase the competitiveness of the US industry.

Similarly China's large holding of US government debt ($265 billion or 12 per cent of total) creates interdependence.[25] Historically, large public debt and inability to borrow to finance wars has been the reason for the sudden demise of a great power. The USA has demonstrated during the Clinton administration that it can solve its government debt problem with relative ease when it politically decides to do so. There are, however, a few analysts who believe that political consensus on the means to do so will be much more difficult in future.[26] The fiscal problem has since taken a quantum jump due to the policy measures taken to keep the US financial crises from turning into another great depression.

One upshot of this rising dependence of the USA on China (even though mutual) is that a prudent US government would like to reduce the risk of such dependence through diversification. India provides an ideal hedge to overdependence on China, in terms of opportunities for FDI, equity and debt flows, trade and transfer/sale of technology. To become a true safe haven for the US *vis-à-vis* China, however, India needs a major reform of its policy, rules and procedures to make them 'non-corrupt' investor-friendly.[27]

Energy and Environment

Energy supply (prices) and environmental degradation are two global threats that affect all countries though to different degrees and with different consequences. Environment quality (e.g., air) is a superior good that is inherently of greater value to richer people (and countries). Rising energy (oil and natural gas) prices will in contrast have greater negative impact on poor people (and countries). The projected rise in energy demand from China and US by accelerating the rise in prices is therefore likely to slow the rise in average income of all energy deficit countries like India. Greater use of nuclear power can moderate the rise in energy prices. As the rise in India's energy demand will start impacting the

---

25. The second highest holding after Japan with $673.1 billion at end-February 2006. India's were $12.1 billion (1 per cent of total). *Source: www.ustreas.gov/tic/mfh.txt*

26. The new political divisiveness between the christian right and the liberal left and independents as well as between Democrats and Republicans who support cuts on income from capital are also a source of concern by themselves, as is the rising level of income inequality driven by the rising share of the top 1 per cent.

27. The alternative, a pro-foreign investor or FDI-biased model is less acceptable in democratic India.

world demand significantly only in a couple of decades, the immediate freeing of India's access to uranium and to global nuclear technology, can ensure (given the gestation lags) that the impact of India's rising demand for energy will be minimal. There would also be an additional bonus to the US and other rich countries in terms of reduced output of greenhouse gases and pollutants (e.g. from coal).

Democratic Limits to Military Power

In the 19th and 20th century great powers could undertake military campaigns against foreign countries and occupy other nations relatively unfettered by public opinion. The spread of democracy and human rights in the 20th century and the globalisation of information impose limits on the unilateral use of military power by democracies. Democratic countries are severely constrained in their use of fatal force against peoples even those who are citizens of a hostile/enemy nation. Use of murder and torture by a democratic State against its own citizens is banned and is normally unacceptable even in times of conflict or war. Globalisation of democratic values has made such action by a State against the citizens of other democratic countries largely unacceptable. These internal and external democratic pressures limit the power of even militarily strong States to use indiscriminate force, over a prolonged period of time, against opponents when passive civilians (particularly women and children) are likely to be killed or maimed. This limits the ability of a militarily strong nation to occupy another country (whose population does not accept such occupation as legitimate). This has been amply demonstrated in Iraq, where the US military victory over the Saddam Hussein's armed forces has been thwarted by individual insurgents that operate among the general public. Even a traumatic event like 9/11 cannot indefinitely sustain democratic support for "Guantanamo" and "Abhu Gharib" type of dirty war in the 21st century. Thus even the USA at the height of its power, perhaps the strongest military superpower in history, is limited by its own democratic system and the democratisation of the world.[28] In this context, the US has aptly been referred to as a 'Constrained Hegemon.'

---

28. A dictatorship is less constrained about human rights internally and abroad and its effective military power, to suppress and subjugate domestic and foreign populations, is therefore greater.

The USA therefore needs to garner democratic support from across the world, particularly from other democratic countries, to sustain its own and global public opinion in 21st century conflicts. The support of democratic India constituting 1/6th of the world population (projected to be the most populous country in 25 years), can therefore be vital in shaping global public opinion on military actions against common threats like Jehadi terrorists, failed States, WMD proliferation and aggressive non-democratic/dictatorial States. At a practical level, the USA and India will have a different hierarchy of specific threats to each and the general unity of purpose must be translated into a clear understanding of individual threats to each country. This will ensure that any Indian support for the US actions against threats that are of greater importance to it are balanced by the US help and support for Indian action against those threats of greatest importance to it. Without such understanding and mutual support, a supportive public opinion cannot be maintained indefinitely for another countries' use of fatal force.

Emerging Scenario

Conventional Wisdom Circa 2004

The CIA by itself or through various think tanks in the USA is known to analyse the development of the world economy and its impact both on the US economy and on its global power. De-classified reports have also periodically appeared on the official websites and in the press based on these studies. The conventional wisdom as of early 2004 (CW 2004) was very similar to that represented in the following figure. Figure 4.3 shows the GDP in local currency and prices of the large countries converted to US$ value using the exchange rate prevailing in 2003 as a proportion of USA's GDP. The GDP of each country is projected over the first quarter of the 21st century using the author's projections of the real growth rate of these economies.[29] Real growth rates can be derived either from GDP at constant prices in local currency units or from GDP at PPP at constant prices, and analysed and projected forward based on

29. With no adjustment for real exchange rate appreciation.

historical comparative data.[30] The application of these real rates to GDP at current exchange rates and their projection and application to the same gives incorrect results for the future. It is nevertheless presented here for comparability.[31]

Figure 4.3 brings out elements of the conventional wisdom (CW), namely the rise of China's economy and the slower rise of India's economy as well as the relative decline of Japan.[32] The implications drawn by the rest of the world (CW) was that for the foreseeable future (i.e., next 20 years) China is not a competitive challenge to the USA, though it may be for Japan and the advanced European countries (Germany, France, UK). It was also believed/hoped that the contradictions between a relatively free market economy and a very closed political system would manifest themselves in a gradual political liberalisation and movement towards democracy.[33] Thus most of the US and many European analysts believed till early 2004 (and many still believe), that the US geo-political predominance in the world would remain unchallenged during the first half of the 21st century. The same analysts also thought of India's development and rise as a global power a very distant prospect. It was therefore (as per CW 2004) not to be taken very seriously as an Asian power, much less a global power. The only exception were the neo-conservatives in the USA, particularly those that were part of the group of 'Vulcans' who advised Republican candidate George Bush, some of who envisaged India having 15 per cent of the US GDP by around 2025 and thus becoming a 'swing state' in the asian/ global context. The CW, with minor variations, appears still to be the

30. Based on this analysis, the growth rates of China, India and Russia are projected to decline as the gap between their per capita income and that of the USA is reduced.

31. A few prominent recent studies have estimated the cross-sectional convergence of GDP at current exchange rates to GDP at purchasing power parity as per capita income rises and applied these to inter-temporal data. Inter-temporal data for fast growing (mainly Asian) economies since 1960, however, shows little evidence of systematic convergence. The application of cross-sectional ratios to inter-temporal data is flawed. An unpredictable degree of convergence will however take place, so that the GDP of India and China at current exchange rate will eventually be higher than that projected here, even if the real growth rate is exactly as assumed.

32. The US share of the world GDP (xr $) will decline from over 28 per cent to between 22 per cent and 23 per cent by 2050.

33. As had happened earlier in Japan and South Korea.

predominant view in the USA as revealed through comments on the signing of historic nuclear agreements between the two countries in July 2005 and March 2006.

Virmani (2004) showed that such projections using GDP at current exchange rate as the basis for comparison gave an incomplete and misleading picture about the rise of China and India (see below). A new CIA report in December 2004 also contradicted the existing CW by naming India as a potential stabilising force in the balance of power in Asia.

Figure 4.3

Conventional Wisdom about China and India

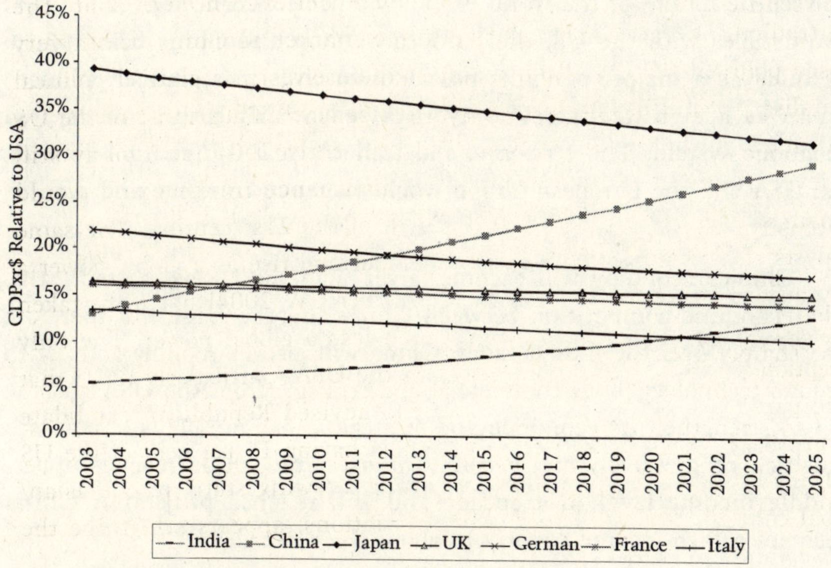

Source: Author's projections, based on UN and World Bank (WDI) data.

A New View 2005

Virmani (2005a, 2005e) has projected the economic size and power of the large countries into the future (Figures 4.4 and 4.5 and Tables 4.1 and 4.2). These should be viewed as the author's estimate of the mean or most probable scenario (with a probability of about 0.75). Other scenarios presented by different scholars, such as: (a) a dramatic slowdown in China's growth rate, either due to pressures for democratisation or to internal disturbances due to rising inequality, (b) a higher growth trajectory for China than observed historically in the fast growing countries of East Asia, are not ruled out but are judged by us to have low probability. Similarly for India, a deceleration in growth due to weakness/deterioration in governance or faster growth due to accelerated reform are also possible but are judged to be of low probability.[34]

Future of the World Economy

The US share of the world GDP (at purchasing power parity) will decline from about 21 per cent to between 16 per cent and 17 per cent by 2050. Figure 4.4 and Table 4.1 shows that the multipolar or polycentric nature of the world economy will be enhanced over the next two decades with the US, the European Union and China being joined by India as a major economic pole. Russia will join relatively reduced Japan as a significant economy in a reasonably non-concentrated economic system. The economic and technological competition between the USA and the European Union would therefore continue and perhaps intensify.

China's economy will become larger than the USA's around 2015. The economic competition between China and the USA will therefore rise sharply over the next decades. China will also be looking actively to acquire technology, both commercial and strategic from the USA and the EU to strengthen its economic and strategic capability. This search will heighten progressively and become intense after China reaches upper-middle income level in a decade and will reach a peak after China becomes a high-income country in about three decades.

The Indian economy will become larger than the US in about 30 years (Figure 4.4 and Table 4.1). India will transit from being a 'low income' to a 'lower-middle income' country within the current decade, but will take a couple decades after that to reach 'upper-middle income' level. It therefore poses the lowest competitive threat to the USA and the European Union from among the current and potential economic powers. Given the evolution of global demographics with declining and ageing labour force in the European Union and a shortage of young

34. Please see Virmani (2005f) and chapter 6 for the strengths and weaknesses of China and India and its likely impact on future growth. An even more detailed evaluation of the Indian economy is in Virmani (2005d).

educated/skilled labour in the USA and a corresponding acceleration in labour force growth in India and the availability of young knowledge workers, the latter could also be the best partner for the former.

Table 4.1

Relative Size of Large Countries, Current and Future

	GDP at PPP Relative to USA				
	2005	*2015*	*2025*	*2037*	*2050*
USA	100%	100%	100%	100%	100%
China	66%	98%	134%	175%	203%
Japan	32%	29%	26%	24%	21%
India	31%	44%	66%	102%	144%
EMU+UK	88%	82%	77%	73%	70%
Germany	20%	18%	17%	15%	15%
France	15%	14%	13%	13%	12%
UK	15%	14%	14%	14%	14%
Italy	14%	12%	11%	10%	9%
Spain	9%	9%	9%	9%	8%
Russia	13%	14%	16%	18%	19%
Brazil	12%	12%	12%	11%	11%
S. Korea	8%	10%	12%	13%	13%

Note: Under alternative scenario, Brazil's ratio could rise to 14 per cent.
Source: Author's projections, based on UN and World Bank (WDI) data.

As the USA will no longer be the largest economy in the next decade, it is useful to recalibrate the picture by measuring the smaller economies relative to China. In this case the global economy would be better described as Quadripolar in 2025, as Japan's economy would be 1/5th the size of China's. In this projection (based on data available in 2004), the Russian economy is about the size of Japan's by 2050. A sharp rise in oil prices over the last year and a half has raised the size of its economy relative to Japan. It is also possible that rising prices of oil over the next several decades and the increased demand for raw materials will give a further boost to the Russian economy relative to Japan's. It is therefore within the realm of possibility that Russian economy will become larger than Japan earlier than indicated in Figure 4.4.

Figure 4.4

Quadripolar or Multipolar World Economy

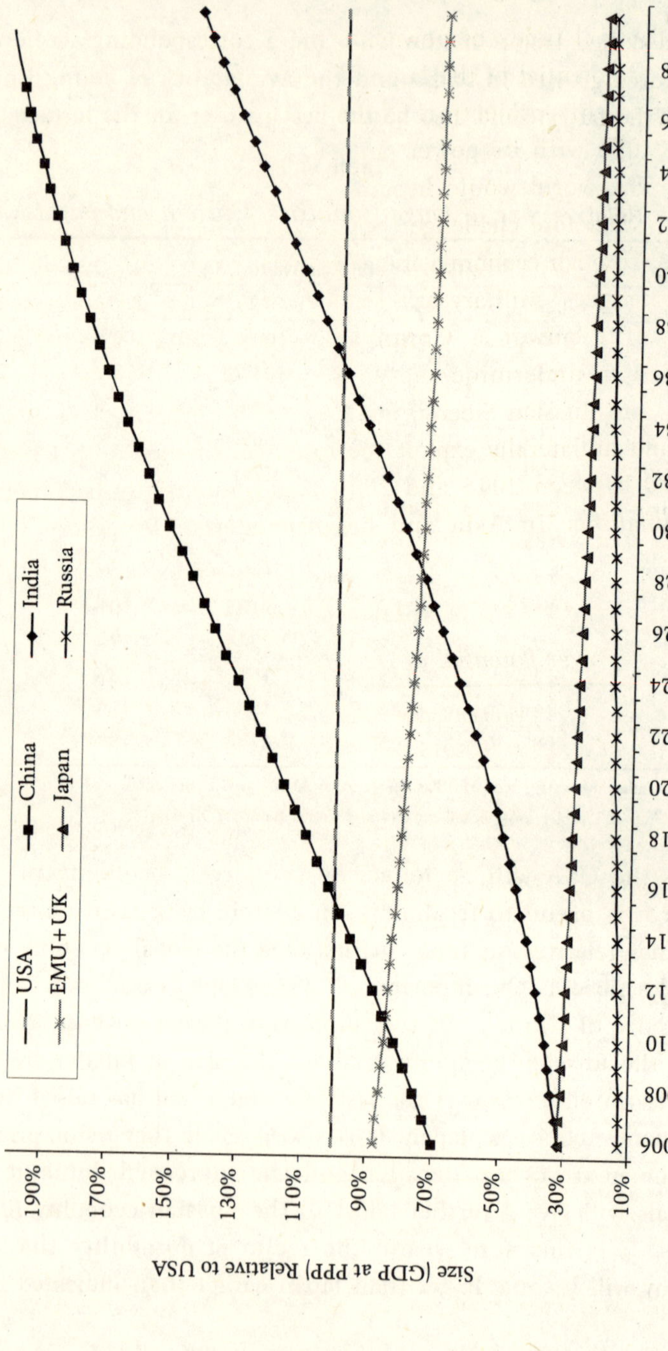

Source: Author's projections, based on UN and World Bank (WDI) data.

Geopolitics: Emerging Tripolarity

Virmani (2005c) index of power potential VIP² is used to derive the future power potential of the large countries (Figure 4.5 and Table 4.2).[35] According to this projection China would become a potential great power by 2020 with its power potential equalling that of the USA by 2030 and the world would become bipolar between 2020 and 2030. China may therefore challenge the US power in Taiwan and the South China Sea, through economic inducement and pressures, as well a build up of naval forces, military and strategic assets. In the absence of any countervailing power a Communist party ruled China may be emboldened to undermine the power of India and Japan, encourage migration into Russian Siberia, put pressure on Taiwan to surrender its freedom and unilaterally exploit the resources of the South China Sea. The period between 2025 and 2040 could potentially be a period of power imbalance in Asia and heightened risk for all of China's neighbours.

Table 4.2

Power Potential of Nations (Relative to USA)

	Virmani Index of Power Potential: VIP²				
	2005	*2015*	*2025*	*2040*	*2050*
USA	100%	100%	100%	100%	100%
Japan	27%	25%	23%	20%	19%
China	26%	47%	77%	128%	154%
Germany	17%	15%	14%	13%	13%
France	13%	12%	11%	11%	11%
UK	12%	12%	12%	12%	13%
Italy	12%	10%	9%	8%	7%
India	9%	15%	27%	59%	86%
Spain	7%	7%	8%	8%	8%
Russia	6%	8%	11%	13%	15%
Korea S.	6%	8%	10%	13%	13%
Brazil	6%	5%	5%	4%	5%

Note: Under an alternative scenario, Brazil's VIP² could rise to 7 per cent.

Source: Author's calculations based on projection given in Table 4.1.

35. $VIP^2 = (Y/Y_{usa})*(y/y_{usa})^{0.5}$. Y and y are the GDP at PPP and the per capita GDP at PPP of the country. Y_{usa} and y_{usa} are the GDP and the per capita GDP of the USA (respectively).

Figure 4.5

Emerging Tripolar Power Structure

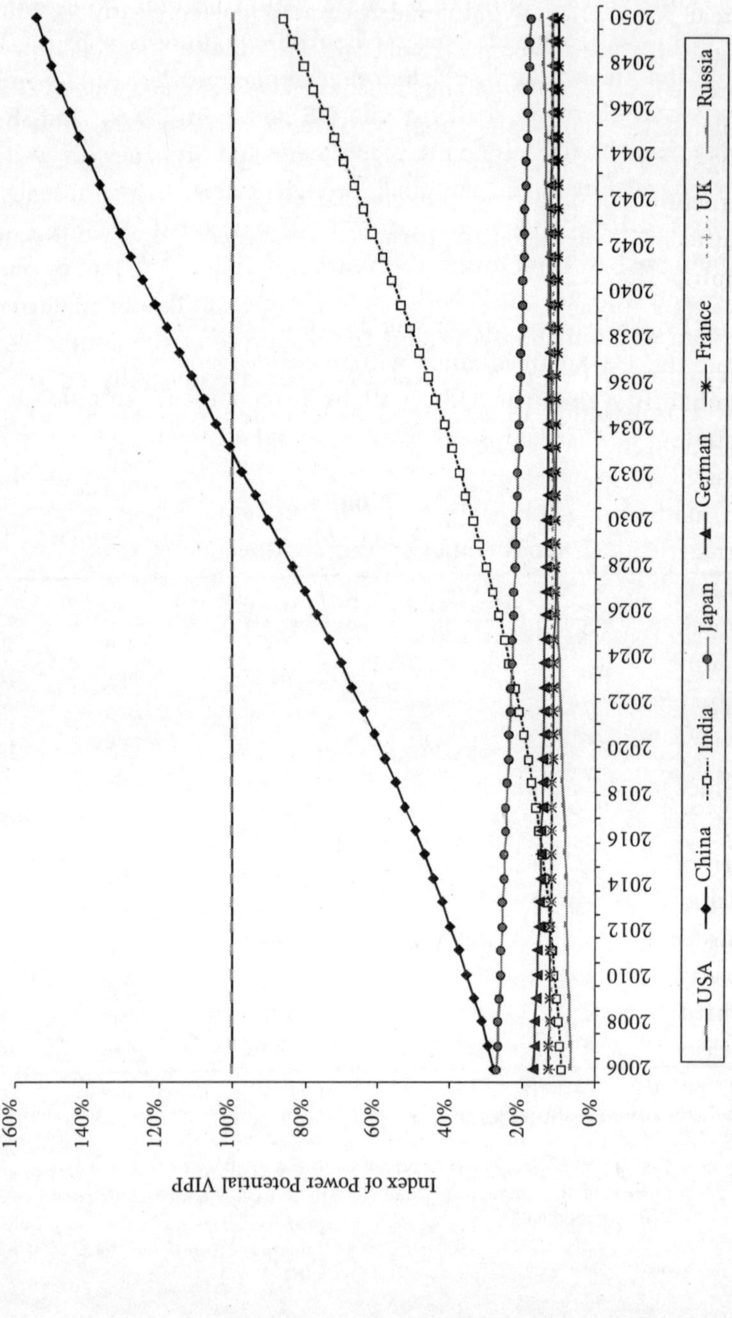

Source: Author's projections, based on UN and World Bank (WDI) data.

As per these projections, India will become a 'global power' by 2020, and a potential 'great power' between 2030 and 2040.[36] With three 'great powers' the world could become tripolar as early as 2035 and is highly likely to become tripolar by the middle of the century. Of the three poles USA, China and India, the last is expected to be the weakest pole. If the European Union becomes a 'virtual state' sometime after 2025 it would be a fourth 'great power' making it a quadripolar power structure in 2035. It is unlikely that either Japan or Russia would have sufficient power relative to the USA/China for the world to be called multipolar.[37]

Even with the optimistic assumption (from the US perspective) that the US-Japan alliance will remain strong, there is a significant probability that the USA will be forced to accommodate China's interests in East and South East Asia and surrender its primacy. This is less likely to happen if the democratic nations of Asia, partner the USA in maintaining the balance of power in Asia. US-India cooperation in strengthening India's strategic capability and overall power is thus in the interests of both countries. This would also help to preserve the independence and freedom of action of India as well as the other countries in Asia. Ideally, the USA and India should work towards a situation in which the period of bipolarity is shortened or eliminated.

Though some analysts have asserted that a bipolar geopolitical structure is more stable than a tripolar one, this is valid only if all three are completely different from each other. It is not necessarily true of a tripolar structure in which two poles share the same human and democratic values while the third pole has little respect for these values. Two independent democratic poles are more likely to ensure the rule of law and respect for human rights, while deterring the non-democratic third pole from aggressive or adventurous foreign policy. By this reasoning the existence of a fourth pole (the EU) that shares the same

36. The USSR was a 'great power' with a VIP^2 of 40 per cent while China is likely to need a VIP^2 of 60 per cent (Virmani, 2005e). India would need an intermediate power potential of about 50 per cent (say).

37. Even if the per capita income of either one or both is 50 per cent more than we have projected. See Virmani (2005b) for an exposition of why only two nation states, have the possibility of matching the power of the USA during the 21st century. Indonesia is a third possibility but only towards the end of the century.

human, democratic values of two of the other three poles, would add to global stability and increase the probability of a peaceful world, rather than increasing instability. This does not, however, rule out economic and technological competition among the democratic poles, nor does it ensure that they would always cooperate in propagating the rule of law, democracy and human rights. Depending on national interest, they may do so in some countries but not in others. They are however very unlikely to engage in open conflict with each other.

Globalisation of National Security

The changing role of India in the global environment requires a change in the institutional arrangements and approaches that it has for interacting with the current and potential global powers as well as with other countries and regional organisations. Over the next decade or so, India has to change its approach from one in which it reacts to the actions of other more active and hyper active countries to one in which it tries to influence the policies of others. It needs to bring about a greater conceptual clarity to its foreign policy and revamp its international intelligence capabilities. India also needs to ensure that the rise in its 'actual power' is commensurate with the rise in its 'power potential,' by developing a comprehensive approach to strategic technology. Among the changes needed are the following.

Foundation: Internal Security

The most fundamental role of the State or the government that claims to govern it is to provide security of life, limb and property to all its citizens. The State is defined by its monopoly over violence. In return it must provide physical security to all. Only the latter can legitimise the former. The rule of law is a basic foundation of a modern market economy. It is a pre-requisite for development and equitable economic growth. A country that cannot ensure the rule of law and public security within its borders cannot become a global power. The writ of the government must be established over the Naxalite dominated interiors of the country and lawlessness (kidnapping and murder industry) eliminated from states/regions of the country where it had become prevalent, because of the abdication of responsibility by the political rulers of these states and the gross failure of governance. Given the limited capabilities of the governments in these states/regions they must focus on universal provision of the basic public goods and quasi-public goods such as police, courts, roads, (water) aquifer development and management, public health, primary education, civic/urban planning and public utilities, connectivity, access to information/knowledge. Citizen's organisations (NGOs, NPOs), the media and the higher judiciary should focus their public efforts on increasing the accountability of the rulers/administrators with respect to these basic and essential functions of government.

Foreign Policy Constructs

If India is to play the 'Balance of Power' game to its advantage the perspective planning functions, intellectual effort/output, information/knowledge base and training systems for operational personnel must be reoriented and strengthened. Similarly, the conceptual basis of India's foreign policy approach to its region (South Asia, East and South East Asia and West and Central Asia) must be widened and developed with greater sophistication.

To illustrate, if we define South Asia as the land mass from Afghanistan to Myanmar plus the Arabian Sea, Bay of Bengal and the Northern Indian Ocean, India's foreign policy objectives regarding South Asia could be defined as follows:

(a) To create a South Asian economy that is regionally integrated, globalised and fast growing. This requires good quality multi-modal transport infrastructure and communications within the region and with the rest of Asia and the Indian Ocean littoral.

(b) To have a South Asia in which all citizens are educated to the best of their ability, progressive, fully empowered with respect to human rights and modernised yet grounded in their great cultural/religious heritage.

(c) To make South Asia a terrorist free and terrorism free zone.

(d) To ensure that there is no proliferation of WMDs from this region to others (and from one country to another within the region).

(e) To ensure that countries from outside this region do not proliferate WMDs to this region (i.e., clandestinely violate their freely/voluntarily entered international treaty commitments).

Once the goals are enunciated, they should be discussed with powers who share India's democratic principles and goals and who can influence the other countries of this region. India's diplomacy must persuade them that such a South Asia is in their own long-term interests even though short-term interests may differ in some respects. A short, medium and long-term plan of action must be drawn up and jointly implemented to achieve these objectives.

Global Intelligence

The Subrahmanyam Committee long ago recommended the revamping of institutional structures for intelligence collection, integration, analysis and assessment and others have reiterated these recommendations since then. This becomes even more imperative in the changing context. Modern technology must be introduced to upgrade and widen the intelligence network (satellite, internet, radio waves) while strengthening traditional methods of human intelligence (e.g., foreign language training). We must develop an extensive capability for covert action to address asymmetric threats from non-state actors, fundamentalist terrorists, their handlers/controllers/motivators/ financiers.

Strategic Technology and Assets

Strategic technology and assets [major defence platforms (submarines, fighter aircraft), nuclear and aero space technology, robotics, communication (interception/eavesdropping), internet (pattern recognition), radar (stealth, ECM)] are critical to India's becoming a global power in the next 15 years or so. This requires better planning of procurement and development of strategic technology and an integrated view across different organisations and departments currently engaged in them. Issues like the nature and amount of offset purchases and the trade-offs between acquisition and development would have to be addressed. Attention has to be given to specialised education and training of scientists and technicians (perhaps in-house) in nuclear, space, oceanic and other technologies. The National Security Council should have a special wing that carries out the planning and monitoring of the development of strategic technology and skills.

Defence: Flexible Response

The nature of the challenge that India has been facing has evolved over the years. The nature of constraints under which defence and foreign policy operates will also change—some will loosen, others will tighten. As open violent wars between major powers becoming increasingly unlikely, those who wish us ill have developed indirect means of undermining India's security. We need to increase the range of options available to us to attack the source or fountain head as well as to pay back in the coin that they choose to use or which are more cost effective from India's perspective and reduce the potential adversary's benefit-cost ratio. This requires a sharp increase in capability for unconventional warfare and unconventional means of defence. A wider range of options must also be developed and/or enhanced for dealing with asymmetric threats from non-state actors, fundamentalist terrorists, their handlers/controllers/motivators/financiers.

Economic Interdependence

In this age of globalisation the size of the market you offer for other countries' exports is a measure of the (actual or potential) influence you have over them. It is easier to switch most imports from one country to another than to switch exports from an established buyer/country to others.[38] Thus paradoxically the size of a country's imports is a better measure of its economic power over others that the size of its exports. In some cases the latter can even be a source of dependence and weakness in terms of power relations.

In 2005, the USA imported 16.1 per cent of the world's merchandise imports, ranking it as the biggest importer of goods. It is therefore the largest market for global exporters and exporting countries

38. Perhaps the only exception is oil imports, where there is a monopoly/oligopoly (OPEC cartel) with a small competitive fringe. It is highly misleading to treat the highly volatile spot and futures markets where most of these small competitive suppliers operate as market for oil.

and this is a factor in the economic influence and power that it has over others. The share of the second largest importer, Germany at 7.2 per cent was about 45 per cent of that of the USA and that of China at 6.1 per cent the third largest importer was less than 40 per cent of that of the USA. The next three largest importers, Japan (4.8 per cent), the UK (4.7 per cent) and France (4.6 per cent), import 30 per cent or less of that of the USA. They are followed by another group of importers with a group of countries with around 20 per cent of the imports of the USA (Italy (3.5 per cent), the Netherlands, Belgium, Canada (3 per cent)). Thus for the World, these countries would be ranked high as destination for their exports. In contrast India's and Russia's imports constituted only 1.2 per cent of world imports placing it at 17th-19th position. If we want to increase the economic influence of India over other countries we must aim to increase India's share of world imports above 3 per cent so as get into the top ten.[39] What is true globally also applies bilaterally. A progressive and corresponding increase in Indian imports from the USA will also increase the dependence of US exporters and US economy on the Indian market. Though world imports of commercial services are 21 per cent of merchandise imports, India with 2.9 per cent of world imports is ranked 10th.

The picture changes somewhat if we treat the EU as a single economic entity. The WTO has carried out the exercise of eliminating intra EU trade (i.e., among the 25 members) to obtain its trade with the rest of the world. The USA is the largest importer with 21.4 per cent of world imports, a share that is higher than its share of the world GDP at PPP. As noted earlier, this is an important component/channel for the USA's economic influence on the rest of the world. The EU (25) is the second largest importer from the rest of the world with an 18 per cent share of world imports. Though the import ranking of these two entities is the same as their GDP (at PPP) ranking, the USA's share of world imports was higher than its share of world GDP (20.7 per cent), while that of the EU (25) was lower (20.4 per cent). Next in the ranking are China and Japan with world import shares of 8.2 per cent and 6.4 per cent, respectively. India with an import share of 1.6 per cent and Russia

39. The share has increased by less than 1 per cent in 10 years. At this rate it will take at least two decades.

with 1.5 per cent are ranked 11th and 13th, respectively. We must reach the top five by 2020, by exceeding the 4 per cent share of 5th ranked Canada.

Germany (9.3 per cent), USA (8.7 per cent) and China (7.3 per cent) are also the three largest exporters in the world.[40] The USA is however least dependent on exports while Germany and China are much more dependent on exports for their growth than the USA is. Fourth ranked Japan (5.7 per cent) falls in the former category, while fifth ranked France (4.4 per cent) falls in the latter category. Similarly, 13th ranked Russia (2.4 per cent) and 29th ranked India (0.9 per cent) fall in the former and latter category respectively. Though world exports of commercial services are 23 per cent of merchandise exports, India with 2.8 per cent of world exports is ranked 10th in both. If the EU is treated as a single entity, the export shares are EU (17.2 per cent), USA (11.7 per cent), China (9.9 per cent) and Japan (7.7 per cent). Russia (3.2 per cent) and India (1.2 per cent) are ranked 8th and 20th respectively. The EU, the USA and India are less dependent on exports while China, Japan and Russia are more dependent on exports for their growth.

FDI inflows into an economy also measure the relative attractiveness of an economy.[41] Though the stock of FDI, equity and debt owned by foreigners in an economy denote a mutual dependence of the host and the source country, once invested and to the extent they are difficult to disinvest, the balance of advantage shifts to the host country. Thus the share of a country in the world FDI is an indicator of its economic power over the rest of the world. China with 9.3 per cent of the world FDI flows was the second largest recipient in 2003, followed by France in third place with 8.3 per cent and the USA in fourth place with 7 per cent. Germany (2 per cent), Russia (1.4 per cent), Japan (1.1 per cent) and India (0.7 per cent) were ranked at 14th, 17th, 22nd and 23rd. India's share of FDI has risen significantly over the last two years, and is expected to rise further with the removal of sector FDI share limits in telecom, insurance, real estate, banking and retail trade. In particular, a sharp increase in FDI from the USA would increase the

---

40. Numbers in brackets are shares of world exports.

41. Luxembourg has shown a surge of investment as many European MNCs have shifted their headquarters to it in recent years.

interdependence of the two economies and thus help in reducing the asymmetry in economic power.

Conclusion

In the 21st century all major countries recognise that international trade and financial flows are in the interests of both the source and destination countries. All countries therefore promote economic relations between themselves for mutual gain. The intensity of these relations may differ because of history and the relative economic gains from competition and cooperation. Any economic or political risks from excessive economic dependence on any one country (whether in terms of oil imports, trade or FDI), are best addressed through diversification across countries and the development of hedging strategies. This is an application to countries of the well known and accepted principles of portfolio diversification and hedging of risk.

Strategic cooperation and competition is in contrast a different matter depending on strategic perceptions. These perceptions are based not just on current threats and power relations but also on potential threats and relative power. Though the future is inherently uncertain, each country must formulate a view of the future and base its actions on it. In this chapter we have argued that China and India will play a critical role in the future balance of power. It has been shown that China is likely to become the second pole in the global power system within 20 years and India a third pole in about 35 years. Thus, a great power like the USA must pay great attention to the potential threat and the potential gain from closer relations with each of these countries.

The Bush administration had made such an evaluation and had come to the conclusion that closer strategic collaboration with India is in the long-term interest of the US. Thus the US government seem prepared to make a strategic investment in India, whose returns will accrue to the USA after a decade or two in terms of a more stable balance of power in Asia and consequently a more peaceful Asia. This approach, if continued by subsequent US administrations, will also reduce the risk that in a couple of decades an aggressive power may overtly or covertly undermine its technological and geopolitical leadership. Many strategic analysts in the USA did not yet share the

Bush administration's assessment that India will become a global power, which can help reduce the future risk to the US global leadership. These US analysts therefore believe that the Indo-US nuclear agreement is a bad bargain for the USA.[42] In contrast, Indian analysts who appreciate the potential of strategic cooperation predicted a setback to Indo-US cooperation if the US Congress had failed to make the necessary legislative changes to allow India to access uranium ore and civilian nuclear technology. This is because a complete and comprehensive elimination of technology denial to India was and remains a litmus test, which will determine the degree of trust in and support for the USA in democratic India.

Given the enormous gap between the US and Indian strategic capability and assets, India has (potentially) more to gain in the next two decades from genuine strategic cooperation with the USA than the latter can gain from India (including profits from sales of defence equipment). It was in India's interest to use the opportunity provided by the Bush administration, to enhance India's strategic capability and global power. This does not mean abandoning traditional sources of strategic technology like Russia, but widening and deepening the sources of supply so that we can get a better bargain for ourselves. The chapter shows that Russia and Japan are unlikely to be global powers 20 years from now though their regional influence will remain significant. Nevertheless, these countries along with Germany, France and the UK currently have strategic capabilities that would be more readily supplied to India at reasonable price because of competition from the USA. India must obtain the most appropriate strategic technology from the most cost-effective source and build upon it. This will allow an acceleration of acquisition and development of strategic technology within the allocated resources.

Better relations with the USA will also open the door to better relations with many US friends and former allies in Asia and Africa, such as Saudi Arabia and Indonesia. It may also encourage China to take a more positive view of genuine (transparent) friendship with India and

42. They believe that India would have been satisfied with a permanent seat on the UNSC. Analysts like Strobe Talbot perhaps base such an assessment on their interaction with the Indian government during the Clinton administration.

perhaps abandon what some analysts have called the 'containment of India' through creation of Trojan Proxies in South Asia. The benefits that accrue to India will depend on the skill with which it plays the balance of power game. Despite the heritage of Bhisma and Kautilya, there is a lot that the Indian administration and political system have to learn to maximise the global advantage to India.

Though there are strong interest groups in both countries arguing for a slow, ultra-cautious pace of development of Indo-US relations, the benefit-cost ratio is currently favourable. Though India's share of the world economy and its relative power will likely increase over time (and USA's bargaining power correspondingly decline), India can accelerate its rise to power if the arrangements and understandings reached earlier can be carried forward in an atmosphere of trust.

References

Albright, David, Frans Berkhout, and William Walker (1997). *Plutonium and Highly Enriched Uranium 1996: World Inventories, Capabilities and Policies*. New York: Oxford University Press for Stockholm International Peace Research Institute. p.276.

Asia-Pacific Defence Reporter (1991). "Incidental Intelligence: China Emerging as Third World Weapons Supplier," *Asia-Pacific Defence Reporter*, September, p.19.

Gelb, Leslie (1984). "Pakistan Link Perils U.S.-China Nuclear Pact," *New York Times*, June 22 and "Peking Said to Balk at Nuclear Pledges," *New York Times*, June 23.

Gertz, Bill (1996). "China Aids Pakistani Plutonium Plant," *Washington Times*, April 3.

International Monetary Fund (2006). *World Economic Outlook*. April.

Milhollin, Gary and Gerard White (1991a). "Bombs from Beijing: A Report on China's Nuclear and Missile Exports," Washington D.C; Wisconsin Project on Nuclear Arms Control, May, p.17.

———. (1991b). "A New China Syndrome: Beijing's Atomic Bazaar," *The Washington Post*, 12 May, p.C1, C4.

———. (1995). *The Risk Report*. Washington D.C: Wisconsin Project on Nuclear Arms Control. May p.8.

Rice, Condoleezza (2000). "Promoting The National Interest," *Foreign Affairs*, January/ February.

Shahid-ur-Rehman (1999). "Z.A. Bhutto, A Man in Hurry for the Bomb," *Long Road To Chagai*. Islamabad: Print Wise Publication.

Shuey, Robert and Shirley A. Kan (1995). "Chinese Missile and Nuclear Proliferation: Issues for Congress," *CRS Issue Brief*, 29 September, p.9.

Spector, Leonard S. (1988). *The Undeclared Bomb*. Cambridge, MA: Ballinger Publishing Company. p.72.

Virmani, Arvind (2004). "Economic Performance, Power Potential and Global Governance: Towards a New International Order," *Working Paper* No. 150, ICRIER, December. *www.icrier.org/wp150.pdf*

———. (2005a). "A Tri polar Century: USA, China and India," *Working Paper* No. 160, ICRIER, March. *www.icrier.org/wp160.pdf*

———. (2005b). "Tri polar World, India, China & US," May 18, *Lecture Paper*, ICRIER. *http://www.icrier.org/public/TripolarWrld_IHC5.pdf*

———. (2005c). VIP^2: A Simple Measure of Nations (Natural) Global Power," *Occasional Paper*, July. *http://www.icrier.org/VIPP4.pdf*

———. (2005d). "Policy Regimes, Growth and Poverty in India: Lessons of Government Failure and Entrepreneurial Success!" *Working Paper* No. 170, ICRIER, October. *http://www.icrier.org/WP170GrPov9.pdf*

———. (2005e). "Global Power from the 18th to 21st Century: Power Potential (VIP^2), Strategic Assets & Actual Power (VIP)", ICRIER *Working Paper* No. 175, November.

———. (2005f). "China's Socialist Market Economy: Lessons of Success," ICRIER *Working Paper* No. 178, November.

———. (2006a). *Propelling India from Socialist Stagnation to Global Power: Growth Process and Policy Reforms*. New Delhi: Academic Foundation. Volumes I & II.

———. (2006b). "Trilateral Proliferation: Pakistan's Euro-Chinese Bomb," forthcoming.

Waltz, Kenneth (1979). *Theory of International Politics.* Addison-Wesley, Reading.

Weissman, Steve and Herbert Krosney (1981). "The Kindly Dr. Khan," *The Islamic Bomb: The Nuclear Threat to Israel and the Middle East.* New York: Times Books.

World Trade Organization (n.d.) *International Trade Statistics, 2006*. Press Release (Tables and charts) *www.wto.org/english/news_e/pres06_e/pr437_e.htm*

World Bank (2006). *World Development Indicators*. CD Rom 2005 and e-data base, April.

5 Global and Regional Powers and the Asian Balance of Power

Introduction

The focus this chapter is on the role of Asia in the world economy. To see where we are going, we first look backwards, a little into history and speak discuss things which are not normally talked about and then move forward into a projection of the future. With the help of tables and figures, this chapter deliniates Asia's role in the world economy in the past century and in recent decades. It then digresses briefly to cover some definitions. Though one would like to avoid any economic jargon, these are necessary for distinguishing between a lot of contradictory numbers that are put out by different writers and the media. Then very briefly it will describe indicators and indices of power. Finally, the chapter will I touch upon the likely projections for the future of Asia and the world. The basic approach underlying this chapter is to link economics with security issues.

Regional Shares of World GDP (PPP)

Figure 5.1 shows regional shares of world GDP over the long period of history from the beginning at year 0 to 1998. Figure 5.2 depicts regional shares of world population and Figure 5.3 shows per capita GDP ratio to the world average. All this data exists all the way back to the beginning of the millennium. The degree of accuracy that far back will obviously not be as much as in recent data. The Second World War provides, very roughly an appropriate divide from the perspective of directional trends. During the pre-war period Asia's economy has been more or less in continuous decline with its share of the world GDP on a downtrend. Conversely Europe's share of the world GDP has been rising. In the millennial perspective, America was a late comer till its settlement by Europeans, and then in 1820 it took off. So basically before WW II there was a decline of Asia in the world economy. The figures reflect relative importance of regions in the world. Up to 1820 Asia had 60 per cent of the world economy with Europe around 25 to 30 per cent.

Figure 5.1

Regional Shares of World GDP at PPP

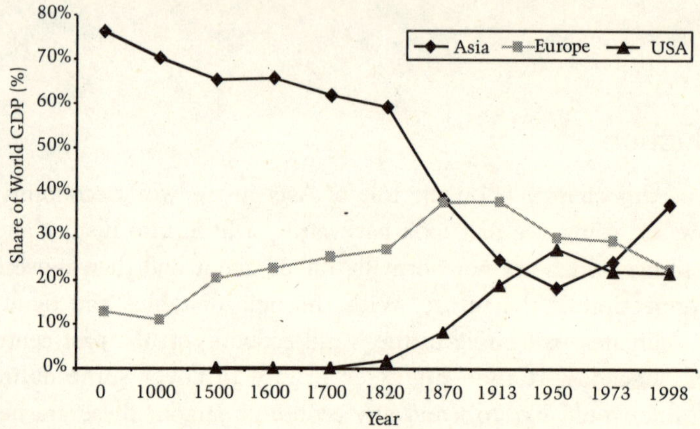

Source: Madison (2003).

Figure 5.2

Regional Shares of World Population

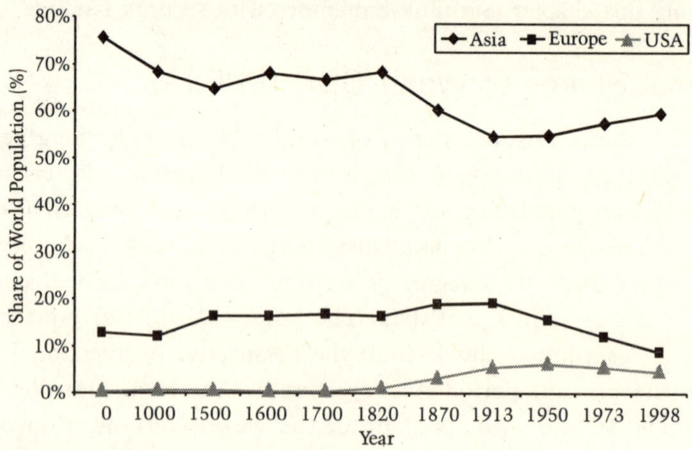

Source: Madison (2003).

Figure 5.3

Per Capita GDP-Ratio to World Average

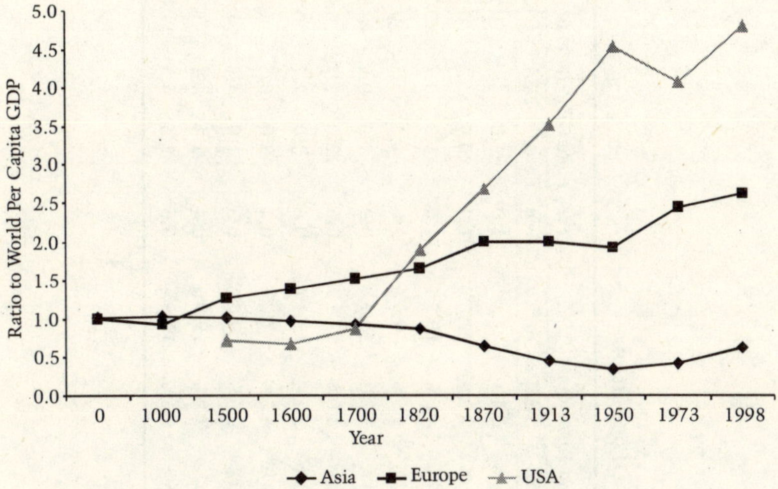

Source: Madison (2003).

A small part of the relative decline of Asia and the rise of Europe and the USA was due to differences in population growth, which resulted in a decline in the population share of Asia and a rise in that of Europe and USA (Figure 5.2). Most of the change in relative economic position was however due to the dramatic rise in per capita GDP (or income) of Europe and the USA as a consequence of the industrial revolution and the diffusion of technologies spawned by it (Figure 5.3).

In the post-war period, we see a reversal of the pre-war trends for Asia and the USA with the share of the former beginning to rise and that of the latter starting to fall (Figure 5.1). This was actually preceded by a turn around of Europe with its share of GDP starting to rise at the beginning of the First World War. This reversal was driven initially by a reversal in the population shares of each of these continents. As shown below it is now increasingly driven by the closing of the per capita income (or GDP) gap that had opened up and widened over the previous centuries.

Though the overall story is going to hinge on three continents, Asia, Europe and the USA, it is useful to look briefly at Latin America and Africa as well. Table 5.1 contains data pertaining to 'Share of World GDP

Table 5.1

Regional Shares of GDP and Population

	Share of World GDP at PPP					Share of World Population					Per Capita GDP: Ratio to World				
Year	*Asia*	*Europe*	*USA*	*LAC*	*Africa*	*Asia*	*Europe*	*USA*	*LAC*	*Africa*	*Asia*	*Europe*	*USA*	*LAC*	*Africa*
0	76%	12.7%		2.2%	6.8%	75%	12.8%	0.3%	2.4%	7.1%	1.0	1.0		0.9	1.0
1000	70%	10.9%		3.9%	11.8%	68%	11.9%	0.5%	4.2%	12.3%	1.0	0.9		0.9	1.0
1500	65%	20.5%	0.3%	2.9%	7.4%	65%	16.2%	0.5%	4.0%	10.5%	1.0	1.3	0.7	0.7	0.7
1600	66%	22.7%	0.2%	1.1%	6.7%	68%	16.3%	0.3%	1.5%	9.9%	1.0	1.4	0.7	0.7	0.7
1700	62%	25.3%	0.1%	1.7%	6.6%	67%	16.6%	0.2%	2.0	10.1%	0.9	1.5	0.9	0.9	0.6
1820	59%	26.9%	1.8%	2.0%	4.5%	68%	16.3%	1.0%	2.0%	7.1%	0.6	2.0	2.7	0.8	0.5
1870	38%	37.7%	8.5%	2.5%	3.6%	60%	18.9%	3.2%	3.1%	7.1%	0.6	2.0	2.7	0.8	0.5
1913	25%	38.0%	19.1%	4.5%	2.7%	55%	19.0%	5.4%	4.5%	7.0%	0.4	2.0	3.5	1.0	0.4
1950	18%	29.7%	27.3%	7.9%	3.6%	55%	15.5%	6.0%	6.6%	9.0%	0.3	1.9	4.5	1.2	0.4
1973	24%	29.2%	22.0%	8.7%	3.3%	57%	12.0%	5.4%	7.9%	9.9%	0.4	2.4	4.1	1.1	0.3
1998	37%	22.6%	21.9%	8.7%	3.1%	60%	8.6%	4.6%	8.6%	12.9%	0.6	2.6	4.8	1.0	0.2

Source: Madison (2003).

at PPP', the 'Share of World Population' and 'Per Capita GDP Ratio'. Note that the share of Latin America in the world GDP is 8.7 per cent and in the world population is 8.6 per cent. There is very little imbalance between these two. Consequently, their per capita GDP is also about equal to the world average. We do not expect big changes in future in Latin America because there is no imbalance. On the other hand, Africa's per capita GDP is very low relative to the world average. We do not however, expect large changes in Africa over the next 50 years and therefore will not be saying much more about Latin America or Africa.

Comparing Economic Size

It is important to understand why we see in public discourse, different estimates of relative income or GDP of various countries. What has been used in this chapter and book, because it is the right and proper way to measure relative size of economy of different countries or regions, is GDP measured at purchasing power parity (PPP). As already mentioned, GDP can be divided into population and per capita income or the average income of persons living in the country. The latter is correctly measured only if PPP is used.

In simple terms, purchasing power parity can be explained by assuming that somebody having $100 in the US buys a certain basket of goods and services. To have parity, there is a need to ascertain as to what is the amount of rupees that will buy the same basket of goods and services. Let us say that its equivalent is rupees 1200. Then that is the purchasing power parity, 100 dollars to 1200 rupees. It means the exchange rate in terms of purchasing power is 12 rupees per dollar and not 45 rupees as we see in the market. The purchasing power parity is really a measure of the size of what people (in India in this case) can buy which is what the GDP is supposed to be.

In contrast the GDP measured in dollars is merely the Indian GDP in rupees converted to dollars by multiplying with the current exchange rate (Rs. 45/US$ in our example). In certain cases this grossly underestimates the true purchasing power of the economy or its residents. This can be seen from Figure 5.4.

Figure 5.4

GDPxr Underestimates GDP at PPP

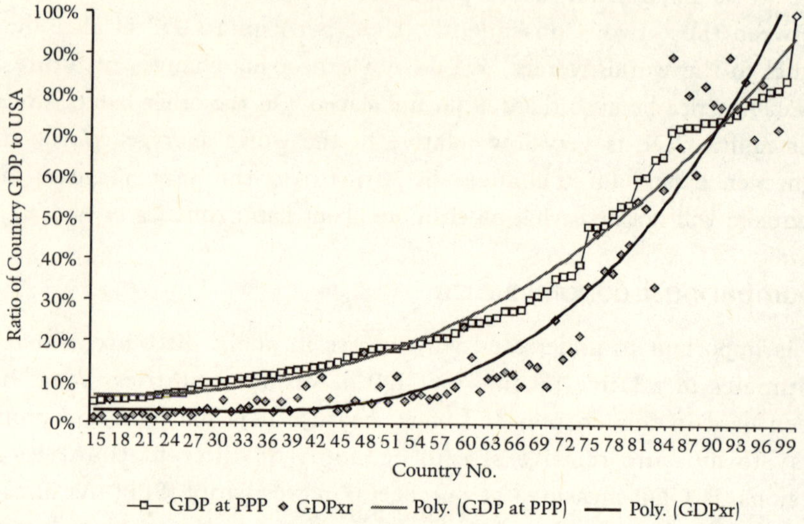

Source: World Bank, *World Development Indicators*.

Very briefly, what has been done here is to arrange all the countries of the world in the year 2005 along the X-axis. Then their GDP at PPP and at the 2005 exchange rate is plotted. -▫- denote the GDP at purchasing power parity and the ◆ denote the GDP measured in terms of the current exchange rate. A trend line has then been put through each set of dots for the GDP at PPP and a — for GDP at the market exchange rate. The important thing here is that when you go from almost zero income to about middle income or 24 per cent of the US income, the gap between these two widens. That means the current exchange rate measurement is getting further and further away from the real measure of the economy, the GDP at PPP. Once a country has 25 per cent of the US GDP, the gap starts to narrow.

Now most people have heard about the first BRIC'S (Brazil, Russia, India and China) report. This report assumed that we are on the side of the curve where the gap is going to narrow. It is just not true of India and China. Russia, however, is now at the turning point and hereafter the gap is going to start narrowing as Russia grows. Brazil is somewhere in the middle between China and Russia. So there is the fundamental error in the way many reports have projected GDP at market exchange rates and then used conversion factors to obtain the GDP at PPP.

Country Trends: Asia and Europe

Figure 5.5 depicts the large Asian countries' share of the world GDP at PPP. This shows that the GDP shares of India, China, Japan and rest of Asia all declined in line with the overall downtrend shown in Figure 5.1 from year 0 to 1998. There are three additional points emerging here. One is that during the period 0 to 1500, India's GDP was larger than China's. Since then it has generally been smaller. The second is that Japan had a relatively small GDP share till the end of the War, but thereafter it rose rapidly and overtook both India and China. Finally, the up tick in the overall share of Asia was led by Japan, followed by the rest of Asia, then China and finally India. In other words, all countries of Asia are participating in the come-back of Asia.

Figure 5.5

Asian Countries' Share in World GDP

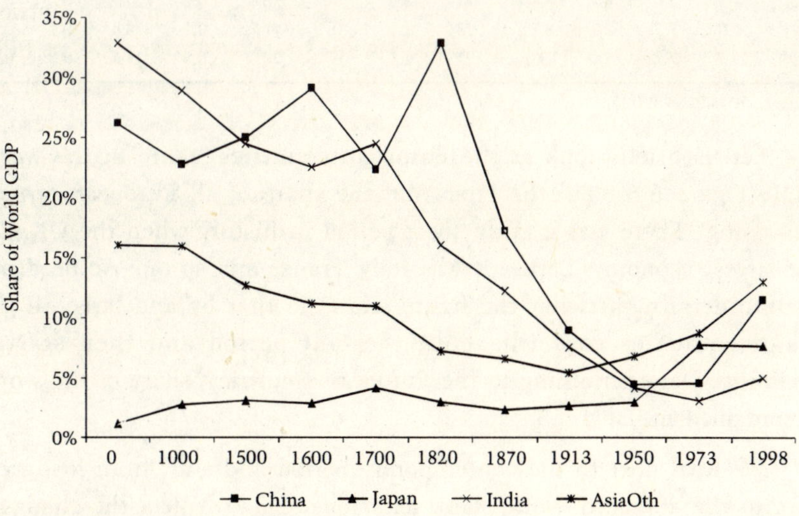

Source: Madison (2003).

Details of Asian countries' share of world is shown in Table 5.2. This suggests that the decline and rise of the population share of rest of Asia has played a role in the decline and recovery of its GDP share.

Japan's modest rise and fall in the pre-war period was also related to population shares, but the post-war rise has been driven by increase in per capita income (catch-up growth). During the pre-war period, India's population share was on a declining trend while China's was highly erratic. In both cases, however, the predominant driver of the decline in GDP share was the rising gap between their per capita income (or GDP) and that of USA, Europe and some Latin American countries (Table 5.2).

Table 5.2

Asian Countries' Share of World

	Share of World GDP at PPP				*Share of World Pop*				*Per Capita*			
Year	*China*	*Japan*	*India*	*Asia*	*China*	*Japan*	*India*	*Asia*	*China*	*Japan*	*India*	*Asia*
0	26.2	1.2	32.9	16.1%	26	1.3	32	16%	1.0	0.9	1.0	1.0
1000	22.7	2.7	28.9	16.0%	22	2.8	28	15%	1.0	1.0	1.0	1.0
1500	25.0	3.1	24.5	12.7%	24	3.5	25	13%	1.1	0.9	1.0	1.0
1600	29.1	2.9	22.5	11.1%	29	3.3	24	12%	1.0	0.9	0.9	1.0
1700	22.3	4.1	24.4	10.9%	23	4.5	27	12%	1.0	0.9	0.9	0.9
1820	32.9	3.0	16.0	7.3%	37	3.0	20	9%	0.9	1.0	0.8	0.8
1870	17.2	2.3	12.2	6.6%	28	2.7	20	9%	0.6	0.9	0.6	0.7
1913	8.9	2.6	7.6	5.4%	24	2.9	17	10%	0.4	0.9	0.4	0.5
1950	4.5	3.0	4.2	6.8%	22	3.3	14	16%	0.2	0.9	0.3	0.4
1973	4.6	7.7	3.1	8.7%	23	2.8	15	17%	0.2	2.8	0.2	0.5
1998	11.5	7.7	5.0	13.0%	21	2.1	17	20%	0.5	3.6	0.3	0.7

Source: Madison (2003).

Let us briefly look at the European countries' share in the world GDP (Figure 5.6). Till the First War, the share of all European powers was rising. There was a fairly short period in history when the UK was the largest economy. Earlier it was Italy, France and so on. We need not go into details but what the figure shows is that by and large all the major countries rose till about the War period and then started declining. Data pertaining to the European countries' share of the world is contained in Table 5.3.

We turn next to the contemporary period and shift from historical data to the standard World Bank data. Figure 5.7 depicts the changing pattern of global economy in terms of share of country's share of world GDP at PPP. North America (the US and Canada), as a region has a share of world GDP which has been more or less constant except for a small decline from the 1970s onwards. The share of Asia-Pacific has

Table 5.3

European Countries' Share of World

	Share of World GDP at PPP					Share of World Population					Per Capita GDP: Ratio to World				
Year	UK	France	Italy	Germany	USSR	UK	France	Italy	Germany	USSR	UK	France	Italy	Germany	USSR
1500	1.1%	4.4%	4.7%	3.3%	3.4%	0.9%	3.4%	2.4%	2.7%	3.9%	1.3	1.3	1.9	1.2	0.9
1600	1.8%	4.7%	4.4%	3.8%	3.5%	1.1%	3.3%	2.4%	2.9%	3.7%	1.6	1.4	1.9	1.3	0.9
1700	2.9%	5.7%	3.9%	3.6%	4.4%	1.4%	3.6%	2.2%	2.5%	4.4%	2.0	1.6	1.8	1.5	1.0
1820	5.2%	5.5%	3.2%	3.8%	5.4%	2.0%	3.0%	1.9%	2.4%	5.3%	2.6	1.8	1.7	1.6	1.0
1870	9.1%	6.5%	3.8%	6.5%	7.6%	2.5%	3.0%	2.2%	3.1%	7.0%	3.7	2.2	1.7	2.1	1.1
1913	8.3%	5.3%	3.5%	8.8%	8.6%	2.5%	2.3%	2.1%	3.6%	8.7%	3.3	2.3	1.7	2.4	1.0
1950	6.5%	4.1%	3.1%	5.0%	9.6%	2.0%	1.7%	1.9%	2.7%	7.1%	3.3	2.5	1.7	1.8	1.3
1973	4.2%	4.3%	3.6%	5.9%	9.4%	1.4%	1.3%	1.4%	2.0%	6.4%	2.9	3.2	2.6	2.9	1.5
1998	3.3%	3.4%	3.0%	4.3%	3.4%	1.0%	1.0%	1.0%	1.4%	4.9%	3.3	3.4	3.1	3.1	0.7

Source: Madison (2003).

been rising rapidly for the last 25 years or so. Europe and Central Asia as a region have been declining. So the figure here currently depicts the US share at par and the relative rise of Asia and relative decline of Europe.

Figure 5.6

European Countries' Share in World GDP

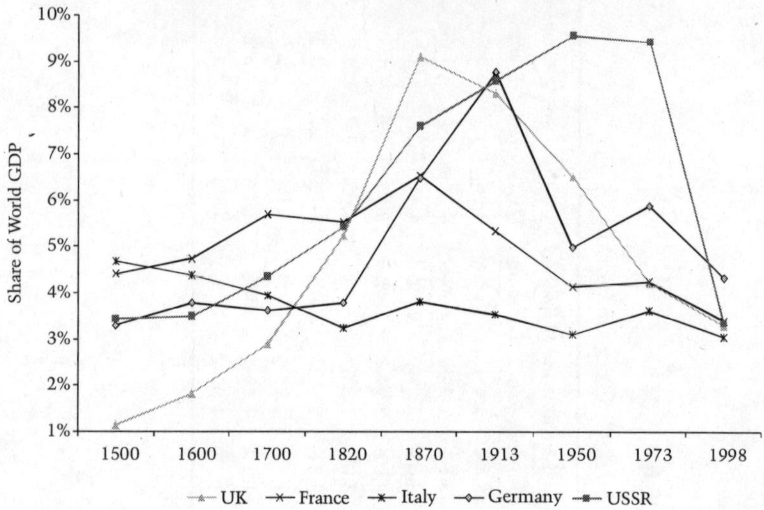

Source: Madison (2003).

Figure 5.7

Changing Global Economy

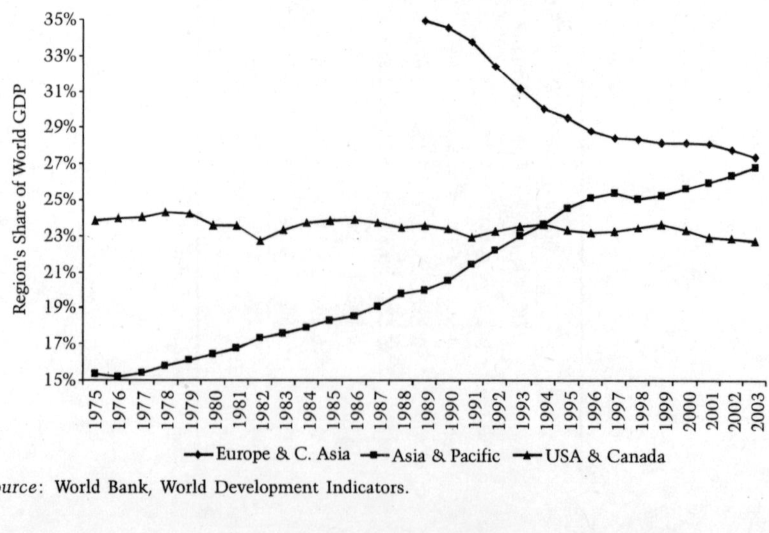

Source: World Bank, World Development Indicators.

Table 5.4, compares the position in 2003 with that in 1979 for GDP shares, population shares and relative per capita income. The relative per capita GDP of Asia has risen over this period because of the rise in China and India; India's per capita GDP relative to the world has doubled from 0.2 per cent of the world average to 0.4 per cent. China's per capita income was much smaller in 1979, about half that of India. It has jumped six times to 0.6 of the world average and is now 50 per cent more than India's.

Table 5.4

Region/Asian Country Share Growth

	GDP PPP		*Population*		*PCGDP*	
	1979	*2003*	*1979*	*2003*	*1979*	*2003*
Europe and C. Asia		27.6%	18.9%	13.8%		2.0
Asia and Pacific	15.6%	27.0%	35.1%	32.9%	0.4	0.8
USA, Canada	24.0%	23.0%	5.9%	5.1%	4.1	4.5
Latin America	9.4%	7.6%	8.0%	8.5%	1.2	0.9
N. Africa, Mid-East	4.2%	3.9%	4.0%	5.2%	1.0	0.8
Sub-Saharan Africa	3.0%	2.5%	8.5%	11.2%	0.4	0.2
China	3.0%	12.4%	22.3%	20.5%	0.1	0.6
Japan	8.2%	6.9%	2.7%	2.0%	3.1	3.4
India	3.3%	5.9%	15.4%	17.0%	0.2	0.4
ASEAN	2.5%	4.1%	8.0%	8.6%		0.5
Russia		2.6%	3.3%	2.3%		1.1
European Union	25.5%	21.5%	9.8%	7.2%		3.0

Source: World Bank, *World Development Indicators*.

World Today: Economy and Power

There has been a lot of discussion that the world is unipolar, multipolar or polycentric. To get a fix on this issue let us start with a look at the world economy. On the basis of the shares of different countries and unified economic groupings, we conclude that the world economy is multipolar. Figure 5.8 depicts the economic power of major countries relative to the US. Considering that the US is the largest economy in the world we measure each country's GDP relative to the USA. We take the European Monetary Union (EMU), along with the UK (which is not in the EMU, but is an important member of the European Union) as a measure of an almost unified Economic Union. At this time the size of the EU economy is almost 102 per cent of the USA. The size of China's economy is 70 per cent of the US economy. Next in size we have the Japanese and the Indian economies which are roughly 30 per cent of the USA (Figure 5.8). So there are multiple sources of economic influence even though they are not equal to the US. We believe, that it is not necessary for all economies to be of equal size to have a significant impact on the world economy and to have a role in the world. Historically the Italians, the French, the UK etc., have been powerful nations despite wide variations in different parameters. Roughly 30 per cent is a good measure. With this criteria we have five large economies and consequently, can conclude that the world economy is multipolar.

Figure 5.8

Multipolar World Economy

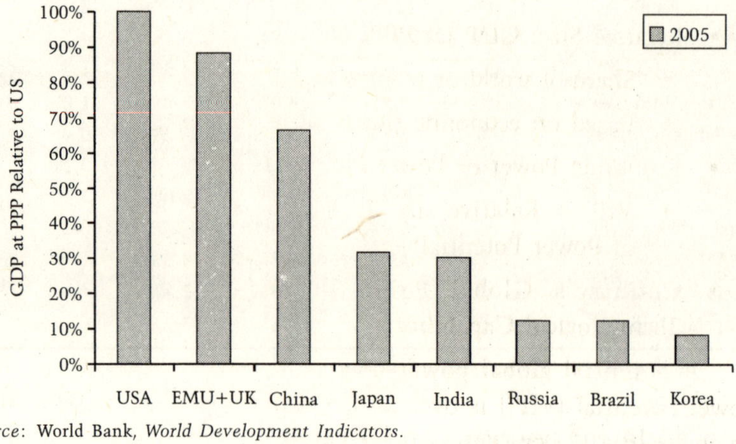

Source: World Bank, *World Development Indicators*.

As defined by Waltz, State power is the "extent that (one) effects others more than they affect [one]", it is therefore a "combination of its capacity to resist the unwelcome influence of others and conversely to influence others to behave as it wants them to." Power of a State or country has therefore to be measured relative to another country, and in the contemporary context it is most appropriate to measure it relative to the USA. In our analysis we consider only the power relations between States (countries). That is, we do not address the issue of non-State actors.

Economic power depends not just on the size of the economy but also on its technical capabilities. In chapter 3, we have applied economic concepts to measure technological capability and economic power. In very simple terms, this involves the definition of a technology-skill factor based on the economic theory of production. This is combined with measures of relative economic size, used above, to define an index of economic power or the over 'power potential' derived in relation to the US.

Part of the attraction of this index is that it can be used to calculate the power potential of over 200 countries in the world and can be extended backwards into past centuries to calculate the relative power potential of all important countries of those eras. These calculations have been done and are available in the references. Here we use this index along with the relative size to identify the global and regional powers. The index of power potential (VIP^2) is calculated as follows:[1]

Index of Power Potential: VIP^2

- Relative Size: GDP (at PPP)
    - Share of world or relative to USA technology-skill factor
    - Based on economic theory of production
- Economic Power or Power Potential
    - VIP^2 = Relative size*Tech-skill-capital factor (Virmani Index of Power Potential)
- Country's Global Power depends on VIP^2 and Strategic Technological Capability

A potential global power may be defined as one whose index of power potential (VIP^2) is over 25 per cent. The USA, by definition, has an index of 100 per cent as other countries' power is measured relative to it. Only two countries meet the criterion for defining a potential global power—China and Japan.

We define a regional power as one that has an index value of 5 per cent or more.[2] There are five European countries, which have a fairly high value of the index and easily meet this criterion. There are only

1. Though the abbreviation VIP was choosen for its obvious implication, particularly in India, it can also stand for Virmani Index of Power.

2. There is view that there is no such thing as a regional power as such, a country can only act in this capacity either if it can carve out a global space for itself or is explicitly or tacitly permitted by the global power(s) to do so.

two Asian countries, India and South Korea, which can be classed as regional powers. Other countries that can be called regional powers are Russia, Canada and Brazil. Details pertaining to global and regional powers are given in Table 5.5.

Table 5.5

Global and Regional Powers: 2005

	Relative GDP	*Size Rank*	*Tech-Skill*	*Power VIP*[2]	*Potential Rank*	*PCadp (24vr)*	*ar rt Rank*
Global Powers							
USA	100%	1	100%	100%	1	1.8%	32
China	69%	2	40%	27.4%	2	8.2%	1
Japan	32%	3	86%	27.3%	3	2.0%	26
Regional Powers							
Germany	19.5%	5	84%	16.3%	4	1.7%	39
UK	15.5%	6	88%	13.6%	5	1.9%	30
France	14.7%	7	85%	12.6%	6	1.6%	43
Italy	13.4%	8	83%	11.2%	7	1.8%	33
Spain	9.1%	11	80%	7.3%	10	2.3%	21
India	30.7%	4	29%	8.9%	8	3.7%	9
Korea S.	8.5%	13	72%	6.1%	12	5.5%	2
Russia	12.6%	10	51%	6.4%	11		82
Canada	8.6%	12	89%	7.6%	9	1.6%	40
Brazil	13.1%	9	46%	6.1%	13	0.6%	56

Source: World Bank, *World Development Indicators*.

The Indian value of the index is 8.9 per cent. It is still less than the value of the index for most of the European regional powers. Russia's power index at 6.4 per cent is less than that for India. Yet it appears to be more powerful. Its power does not arise from its economy, but its strategic capital or assets, something that we will touch upon below.

As there are so few countries in the list of regional powers and countries such as South Africa, which are commonly mentioned in this context are not in this list, we weaken the criterion. We define a category of global VIPs that have an index value of 2.5 per cent or more and regional VIPs that have an index value of more than 1.5 per cent. These countries may play a significant role either globally or regionally

(Table 5.6). South Africa is the only African country that makes it to this list while other Asian countries in the list are Turkey, Iran, Saudi Arabia, Taiwan, China, Indonesia, Thailand and Hong Kong.[3]

Table 5.6

Global and Regional VIPs

	Relative Size		*Tech-*	*Power Potential*	
	GDP	*Rank*	*Skill*	*VIP²*	*Rank*
Australia	5.2%	16	87%	4.5%	14
Taiwan, Ch	5.1%	17	82%	4.1%	16
Mexico	8.5%	14	49%	4.2%	15
Argentina	4.5%	19	60%	2.7%	18
Netherlands	4.3%	23	89%	3.8%	17
Poland	4.3%	24	58%	2.5%	19
S. Africa	4.5%	20	53%	2.4%	20
Relgium	2.7%	29	88%	2.4%	21
Austria	2.2%	34	90%	2.0%	25
Sweden	2.3%	33	86%	1.9%	26
Switzerland	2.1%	37	90%	1.9%	28
Greece	2.1%	36	75%	1.6%	30
Norway	1.5%	45	98%	1.5%	32
Turkey	4.9%	18	45%	2.2%	22
Iran	4.4%	22	44%	1.9%	27
Saudi Arabia	2.9%	27	60%	1.8%	29
Indonesia	6.8%	15	30%	2.1%	23
Thailand	4.4%	21	46%	2.0%	24
Hong Kong	1.7%	41%	86%	1.5%	31

Source: Authors calculations, based on World Bank (WDI) data.

There is a slight problem with the VIP² index because it treats natural resource riches at the same level (or on par with) real technological power. This creates some anomaly.

Global Imbalances

Before looking at the future of Asia and the world, it is useful to look at the figure summarising the current global imbalance, that we believe

3. Pakistan however, does not meet the cut-off criterion.

will be substantially corrected over the next half century. This shows for each country the difference between the share of a country in the world GDP and its share of the world population. Then the countries with the greatest discrepancy or imbalance (positive or negative) are depicted in Figure 5.9. The three largest negative discrepancies are three large Asian countries. Those with positive imbalance are European countries along with Japan and the US.

Figure 5.9

Global Imbalance: GDP Share—Population Share

Source: World Bank, *World Development Indicators*.

As these imbalances get reduced over the next 50 years or so, Asia will rise. As Japan has a positive imbalance, as this is corrected it will slow the growth of Asia, but overall the effect will still be a rising Asia. A legitimate question can be asked, that for many centuries these imbalances have not been corrected, even though there have seen glimmering of change even earlier.

However, if we come to the more recent period, Table 5.7 shows the average GDP growth over the last 25 years. When we look at the performance in terms of per capita GDP growth we find that with the exception of two European countries the fastest growing economies are all Asian. In terms of GDP growth, the two European countries are replaced by countries from other continents. The rapid growth of many Asian countries has resulted in a closing of the per capita income gap with the rest of the world. Note that India is ranked 9th in both cases. So what is happening is that with globalisation and policy reform the countries of Asia, which were earlier left behind, are beginning to catch up. We expect a number of Asian countries to continue to be among the fast growing economies in the world.

Table 5.7

Average GDP Growth (1980 to 2004)

Economy	*Per Capita Growth Rate*		*GDP Growth Rate (avg.)*	
	Rank	*Average gr rt*	*Rank*	*Average gr rt*
China	1	8.2	1	9.6
Korea, Rep.	2	5.6	3	6.7
Taiwan, China	3	5.2	4	6.4
Thailand	4	4.7	7	6.0
Ireland	5	4.6	13	5.3
Singapore	6	4.4	2	6.9
Hong Kong, SAR	7	4.0	11	5.4
Vietnam#	8	4.0	8	6.0
India	9	3.8	9	5.8
Luxembourg	10	3.7	17	4.7
Indonesia	11	3.6	10	5.4
Malaysia	12	3.6	6	6.3

Note: # Growth for 1980 to 1984 is estimated.

Source: World Bank, *World Development Indicators*.

Population and Growth Projections

The basis of our projections of economic size and the power potential index projections, are the population projections of the UN and our own projections of per capita GDP (or income). The UN population projections are shown in Figure 5.10. There are two big spikes one pertaining to China and other to India. The figure shows that China's population will grow more slowly than India's over the next 50 years or so. Therefore, the population of the two will become almost equal around 2030-2035 and India's will be marginally larger by 2050. Secondly, relative population of Japan, Russia and parts of Europe such as Germany is likely to decline. So population is going to play a role in the relative decline of Russia, Europe and Japan.

Figure 5.10

Population Projections: UN 2004

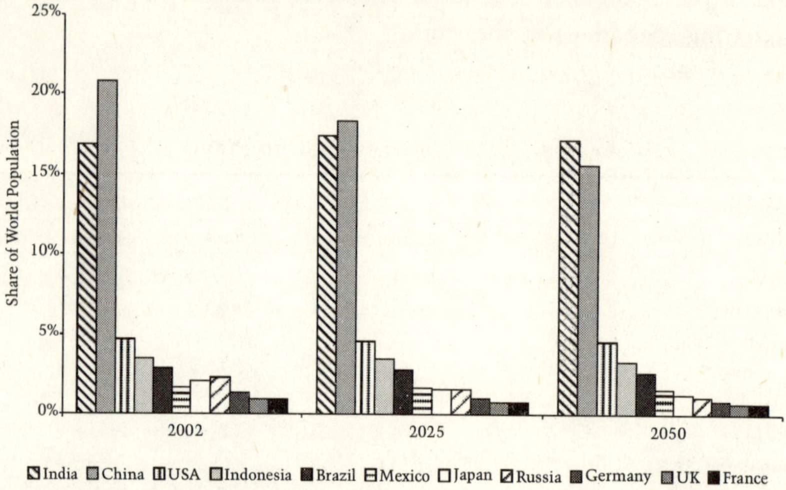

Source: UN World Population Prospects, 2004 revision

We have to digress somewhat to discuss why the EU can be treated as an almost unified economy but not a single power. In economic matters it acts as a unified whole in several dimensions such as at the WTO negotiations. However, at the World Bank, G8, G20 etc., each country has a separate presence even when the EU may coordinate certain aspects. In matters pertaining to national security such as the question of raising a small force in Europe, the issue is being debated endlessly. Thus, the EU is not even a 'virtual state,' like other virtual states in history like the British empire and the USSR. The British empire, even though it contained a separate entity like India, was a virtual State in the sense that the empire acted as a unified whole in projecting power. The USSR consisted of Russia and countries of Eastern Europe and was a virtual State because it acted as a unified State. The EU is far from it and the prospects of it becoming one over the next 10 to 15 years are very low. Of course, if it becomes a 'virtual state' then it would be a power, but the prospects have become bleak after the rejection of the new constitution and the rise of nationalist sentiment in several countries.

So given this uncertainty about the EU, our conclusion is that the world can only become tripolar. For China and India to equal the US, they have to have a per capita income only one fourth of the US because their population is about four times. Though nothing is inevitable the likelihood of this happening over the next 20 years for China and the next 40 years for India is quite high. For any other country, such as Russia, Brazil, Germany or Japan to equal the USA in terms of economic size or power, they have to have a much higher per capita income than the USA and there is little prospect of that during the next 20 years or more.

Per capita GDP growth projections are shown in Table 5.8. The only important thing to note here is the forecast that India will start growing faster than China sometimes in the next decade (2010-2019). To appreciate this, we need to briefly outline how the Chinese economy functions. First, China's objective is growth maximisation. The basic objective of the Communist Party of China is to retain power and they have come to the conclusion since 1980 or perhaps a little earlier that the best way to do that is to maximise the rate of growth of the economy. Some analysts have in the past confused this with the very different USSR system which collapsed. The Chinese system is a highly decentralised system, unlike the USSR. It was decentralised in Mao's time long before China started moving to a market-oriented system. The growth objective is very easy to translate to even public sector companies. Basically, at a firm level it becomes a corporate growth maximisation strategy. So the strategy prevails not only at the national level, but at the provincial, city and down to the public sector company levels (see chapter 6 for further discussion).

Secondly, there are two ways in which they have sought to achieve fast growth. The first is public investment. A lot of people forget, that in 1980 China was a Communist country and 100 per cent of the assets of the country were owned by the Government/Communist Party. All the profits and returns to capital generated in the economy could be used by the party/State without the need for tax distortions. The system they have maintained is that all returns from public assets (which constitute a very large fraction) are re-invested. So there is a very high rate of investment. That is one prong of the strategy but this strategy alone would not have worked just as it did not work in the USSR. The second prong is the market. This is coupled with two engines of growth, FDI and exports. Exports by State linked entities enjoy virtually free run on the banks, while export-oriented FDI and most other FDI enjoyed a host of freedoms (including from labour rules) that is not available to domestic private parties. FDI has been critical to China's growth over the last 25 years because their entrepreneurship was decimated by the Communist party. Historians report that two million entrepreneurs were killed during the Communist Revolution. Therefore, reforming China did not have any entrepreneurship base of the kind we have in India. Therefore, to have a productive growth they instituted and evolved the market-led, FDI-export led growth model. That is the basic reason for their success.

Table 5.8

Per Capita GDP Growth Projections

	1980-2004	*2000-2009*	*2010-2019*	*2020-2030*
India	3.8	4.6	5.6	6.0
China	8.2	7.4	6.0	5.4
Japan	2.1	1.6	2.0	2.1
Russia	-0.9	5.9	4.7	4.3
USA	1.9	1.7	2.0	2.0
EMU+UK	1.8	1.7	2.0	2.1
UK	2.1	2.2	2.2	2.2
Germany	1.6	1.2	1.8	2.1
France	1.6	1.8	1.9	2.0
Italy	1.7	1.5	1.8	1.9
Spain	2.3	2.8	3.0	2.8
Brazil	0.6	0.6	1.3	1.5
S. Korea	5.6	4.7	4.2	3.9

Source: Authors projections, based on UN and World Bank (WDI) data.

To project their growth into the future we need to know what are the weaknesses and risks pertaining to China. People who want to see China fail emphasise the weaknesses but one has to be realistic. We are of the opinion that strengths and weaknesses are the two sides of the same coin. First, look at government ownership which enables high rate of investment in China. One of the failings is that it leads to the creation of excess capacity which further results in falling returns and rising non-performing assets (NPAs). China analysts keep writing about the weakness of the banking sector. In reality it is a deliberate subsidy provided through the government-owned banking system. It is therefore a disguised form of fiscal deficit. So they pump money into unprofitable and/or failing public sector units whenever there is a demand shortfall or cost competitiveness problem. This is a systemic weakness, the other side of the coin of strong re-investment by profitable public sector companies. They will have to resolve this contradiction if they want to keep growing.

The second thing is that rising exports are critical to growth when the public sector has such high investment rates irrespective of expected returns on investment. The Chinese were already the second largest exporters in the world in 2008 and there is a limit to the export share they can garner for themselves. If it keeps growing, eventually it would become 100 per cent which is impossible. So at some point the high growth of exports that has sustained overall growth has to slow down. This overdependence on exports will soon turn into a weakness as export-led growth cannot continue indefinitely. The third weakness is that the FDI-export model has a knife edge character. We learnt this during the 1997 'Asian crisis,' when the high growth economies of ASEAN and East Asia suddenly slowed down considerably. Before the crises it looked as if high growth would go on for ever, then a sudden unexpected shock derailed them resulting in drastic reduct in the growth rate. The global economic crises that resulted in a collapse of global export demand is a test. A growth collapse has been started off by using the fiscal-financial system to inject massive subsidies into the system and increase infrastructure investment. In our view this can be maintained for several years but eventually the FDI-export model would have to be transformed.

The fourth weakness is the worsening income distribution, much unlike other Asian countries. The Chinese Communist Party drastically curtailed spending on social welfare and diverted all the money including profits into investment. Consequently, hardly any money went into social sectors. So the income distribution has worsened drastically. Anyway, given all these strengths and weaknesses they will have to chart an appropriate course, but the economy will gradually slow down.

Regarding India, the author's book, *Propelling India from Social Stagnation to Global Power*, shows that the pre-1980 period was characterised by socialist policies and stagnation. The economy grew at 3.5 per cent and poverty actually worsened. That is the greatest contradiction of this period of "Indian socialism." Contrary to what numerous economists and development experts said there was no trade-off between growth and poverty reduction, slow growth went hand in hand with rising poverty rates. A policy shift toward freer markets occurred in the 1980s, starting slowly from the second term of Smt. Indira Gandhi in 1980. It was fully underway by 1985 after Shri Rajiv Gandhi became PM in 1984. This raised the growth rate of economy by about 2 percentage points to 5.5 per cent. The 1990 reforms raised the growth rate further by 1.3 per cent to about 6.8 per cent. More importantly, the effect of the 1990 reforms have spread slowly throughout the economy so that the underlying growth rate of the economy has been rising gradually. Figure 5.11 depicts the rising growth of the Indian economy. At the end, in 2006 it is roughly between 7 and 7.5 per cent. The issue is whether this will keep growing. Our view is that an average growth rate of 8.5 per cent to 9 per cent is feasible over the next five years (See Figure 5.12). Sustaining such rates of growth over a longer period of 15 years or so will only be possible if government systems are seriously reformed. There are some people who think it will continue rising even further to 10 per cent or more, but this is over-optimistic (see Virmani 2009 for an update).

Figure 5.11

Rising Growth Trend: Market Reform

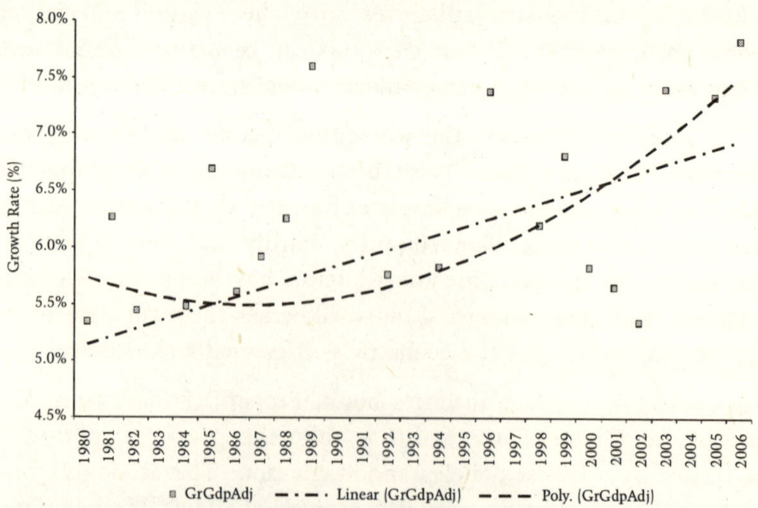

Source: National Accounts Statistics, CSO, Dept. of Statistics, Govt. of India.

Figure 5.12

Growth Trend—New Data Series

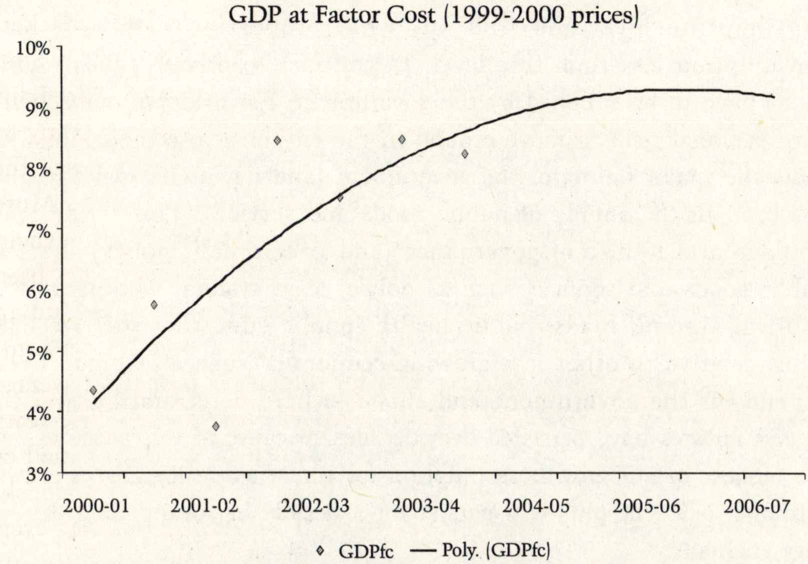

Source: National Accounts Statistics, CSO, Dept. of Statistics, Govt. of India.

Poverty rate in India in 2004 was about 22.5 per cent (MRP). This is not unusual for a country of our per capita income. Given our 1.1 billion population, the number of poor is about 250 million. There are only two countries in the world (China and USA) whose total population is more than the number of poor in India even if the poverty rate is normal. The size is huge because the population is huge, this must be kept in mind.

We have, however, not done badly in terms of relative per capita income. As far as income distribution is concerned if you rank all the countries for which data is available, we come out at 31 out of 127. That is, we are in the top 1/3rd bracket whereas China is in the bottom 1/3rd. This is one thing in which we are much better off than China.

The reason for giving so much importance to economic growth is because an improvement in the welfare of the people is directly related to the increase in average income of the country (for any given income distribution). It is important to keep in mind that there are two types of goods—private goods and public goods. Private goods are those which people can buy with their income and can consume themselves. This consumption is the basis for calculating poverty rates. We define some consumption level and find out what proportion of people have consumption less than this level. In contrast to private goods, public goods have to be supplied by the government. For example, nobody can have personal road to move around in the city or across the country. In India the major failing of the government (and its intellectual advisors) has been in the supply of public goods and services. This is the most fundamental failure of governance (and government policy). It is in public goods and services such as police, legal system, administration, political system, roads, public health, public education that we have failed relative to other fast growing economies such as China. These depend on the government and this is where deterioration and the biggest failures have persisted over decades. Because of this weakness we are modest in our growth assumption for India, assuming that a growth rate of 7 per cent plus will persist for a decade or so and then decline very gradually.

Evolution of Major Economies

Figure 5.13 reflects conventional wisdom (2004) GDP growth trend for major countries relative to the USA over the period up to 2049. This was based on an erroneous use of GDP at current exchange rates. It suggested that Japan's economy would decline gradually and that of China would rise at a faster pace to replace it as the second largest one with its GDP about 30 per cent of the US. India's economy would rise from very low to moderate level approximately equal to that of Japan at that time. The US would therefore continue to be the predominant economy and power for most of this century. China, though a significant player would not be in a position to challenge the USA, while India would at most be a swing State. In the case of Europe, even the conventional wisdom, expected that it would decline relatively and that China and India would rise relative to Germany, France, UK, Italy, etc.

The author's academic work during the second half of 2004 (December 2004 working paper) sharply contradicted this projection. There were also reports that a CIA study had given more importance to

India than that given by the prevailing conventional wisdom (CW). The author's 2005 paper showed that the CW is totally wrong because over the next 50 years the size of the Chinese economy would be two times that of the USA and the Indian economy could be as much as 140 per cent of the US economy. This was a completely different view of the world from the prevailing conventional wisdom.[4]

Figure 5.13

Conventional Wisdom (2004): Unipolar

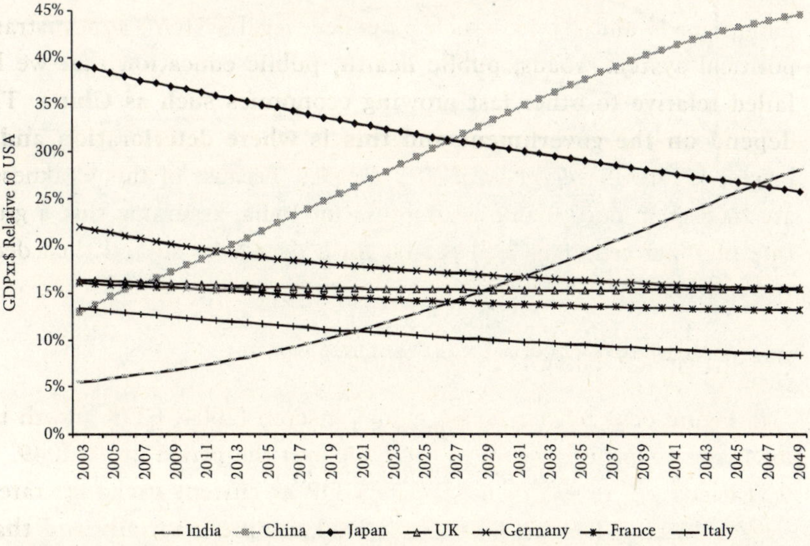

Source: Authors projections, based on UN and World Bank (WDI) data.

Figures 5.14 and 5.15 show the GDP at PPP of countries relative to the US GDP at PPP. The former depicts the multipolar world economy, with the EU (EMU+UK) included, while the latter shows the large countries of Europe separately. We see that China's economy will equal the US in about 10 years. India is likely to take 30 years to reach parity. It is therefore a lesser economic competitor of the USA. Russia's economy will rise to equal a declining Japan by around 2050 (Figure 5.14).

4. This attested to by the fact that in 2005, the top 5 to 10 international relations journals refused even to consider a paper based on these projections for publication.

Figure 5.14

Multipolar World Economy

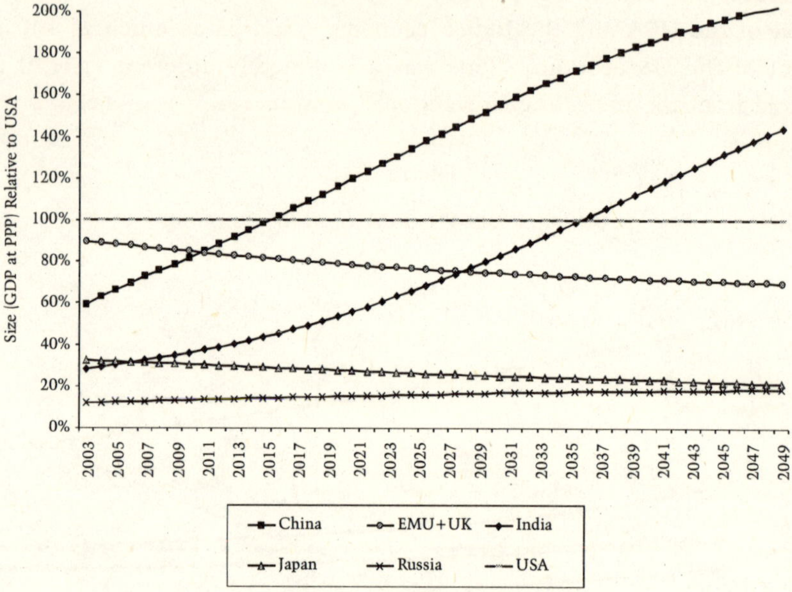

Source: Authors projections, based on UN and World Bank (WDI) data.

Figure 5.15

GDP at PPP (Relative to USA)

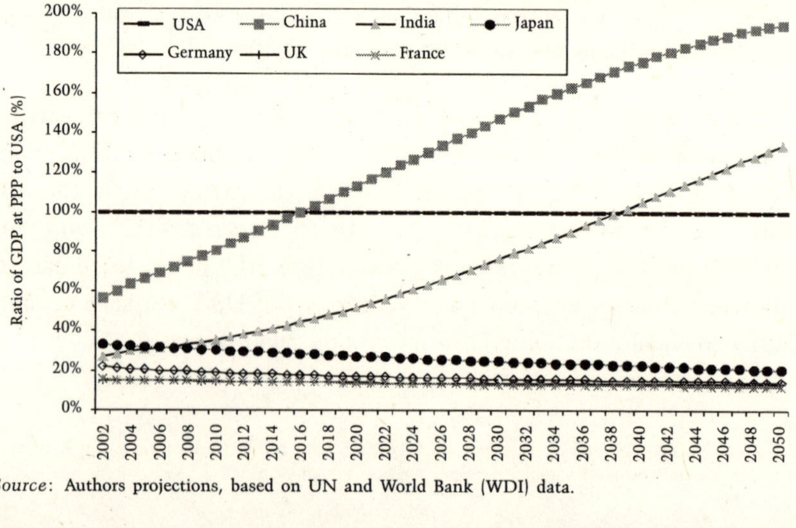

Source: Authors projections, based on UN and World Bank (WDI) data.

Figure 5.16 depicts GDP (PPP) relative to the USA for ASEAN and other Asian countries like South Korea and Australia. Korea in global terms has increasing relevance and will become significant over the next 20 years as Europe, Russia and Japan decline relatively. The problem with ASEAN is that it is not even a cohesive economic bloc like the EU was even in its earlier avatar of an economic community. ASEAN can therefore not even be called an economic power. The potential exists. The size of ASEAN will by 2050, be about 42 per cent of the USA, compared to about 60 per cent for the EU.

Figure 5.16

ASEAN and other Asian Countries

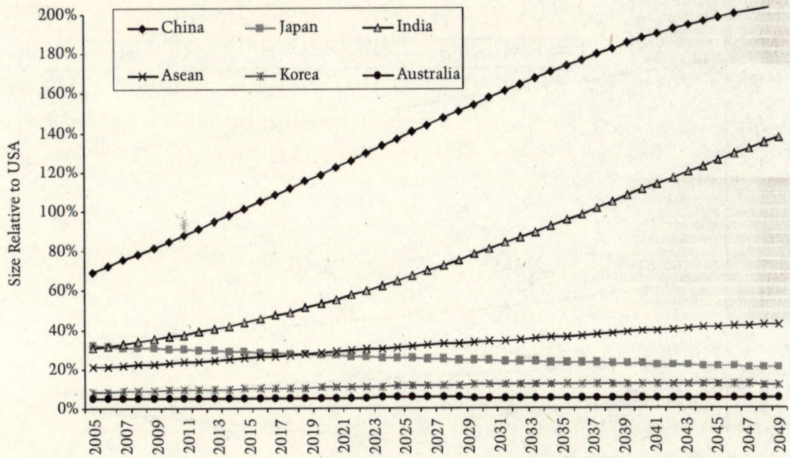

Source: Authors projections, based on UN and World Bank (WDI) data.

What ASEAN does quite successfully is to use its high growth rates and favourable location to get a lot of attention. ASEAN is located strategically in relation to China, India and the Middle East, and thus has leverage. But in terms of becoming a power to reckon with, they must first get much more integrated and strengthen ASEAN institutions. Only then can they hope to become a 'virtual state'.

Figures 5.17 and 5.18 depict the evolution of the power potential of different powers in terms of the index of power VIP² discussed earlier. The former gives the picture of India *vis-a-vis* the current regional powers that it is likely to overtake. The latter shows the bigger picture with respect to the USA and China. In about 20 years or less, India would become a global power (Figure 5.17). Its power potential would reach 25 per cent. By that time Japan would have declined to below 25 per cent and soon cease to have a power potential to classify it as a global power. However, for the next 20 years or so, Japan will remain a global power and can still play a significant role in the world. Indo-Japan will therefore remain of great importance for us. It will also be in India's interest to collaborate with the EU and/or the developed countries of EU to accelerate our development in the next 20 to 25 years.

Figure 5.17

Evolution of Power Potential: VIP[2]

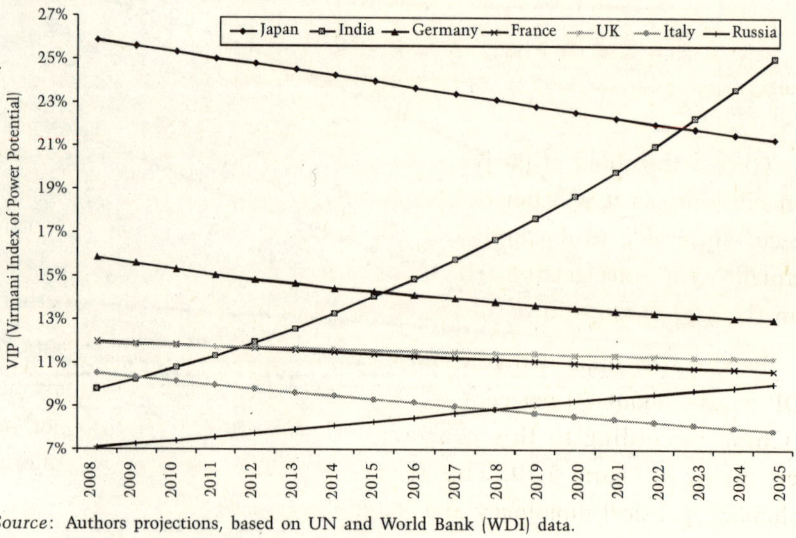

Source: Authors projections, based on UN and World Bank (WDI) data.

Figure 5.18 depicts the transformation of global power equations from unipolar to bipolar and subsequently to tripolar world order. Currently, it is a unipolar world given that China's power potential is far below the US. The huge current disparity will narrow substantially in about 25 years to become about 60 per cent of USA, and the world will start becoming bipolar again. It is not essential for the power of the challenger to equal that of the dominant power for this to happen.

Figure 5.18

Global Power: Uni to Bi to Tripolar

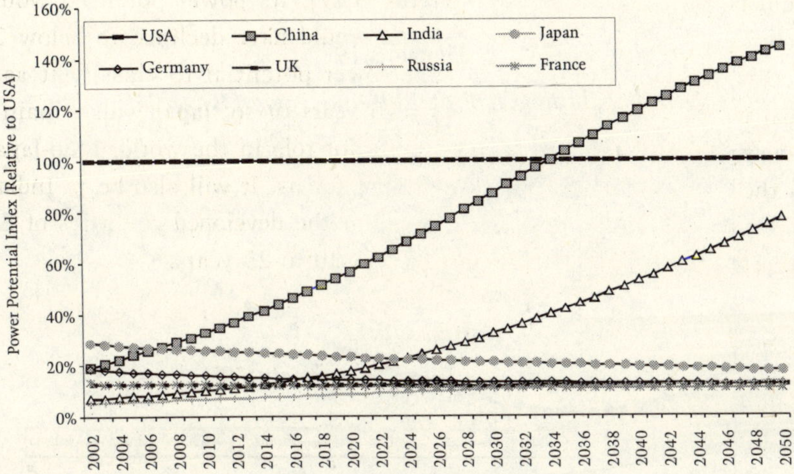

Source: Authors projections, based on UN and World Bank (WDI) data.

Once a threshold of 60 per cent or so is crossed, the US policy will start changing as it will not be able to do the things in Asia which they are currently able to do. Similarly, the effect of China on all the other countries will start getting felt. China's power potential will be larger than the arithmetic sum of all the other countries of Asia put together.

Beyond this India will continue to catch-up slowly and by 2050 our GDP will be about 70 per cent of China and power will be roughly half of China (according to this conservative projection). This aspect has been shown in Figure 5.19. This is very important for India's economic diplomacy, political diplomacy and national security.

When the author first presented this graphical depiction in 2004-05 there were many people who felt that China's growth will decline rapidly. Consequently, he projected different scenario's including one of faster catch–up (Figure 5.20). There are three trend lines for each of the two countries indicating high, mean and low. The scenario termed "China low and high India scenario" is most optimistic from India's point of view. In this scenario if China grows according to the low scenario and India according to the high scenario, then India's will catch up in terms of GDP growth in about 20 years. Remember the other scenario which we consider more realistic, even by the year 2050 India would only be 70 per cent of China (See Figure 5.19).

Figure 5.19

India/China: GDP at PPP and Power Potential

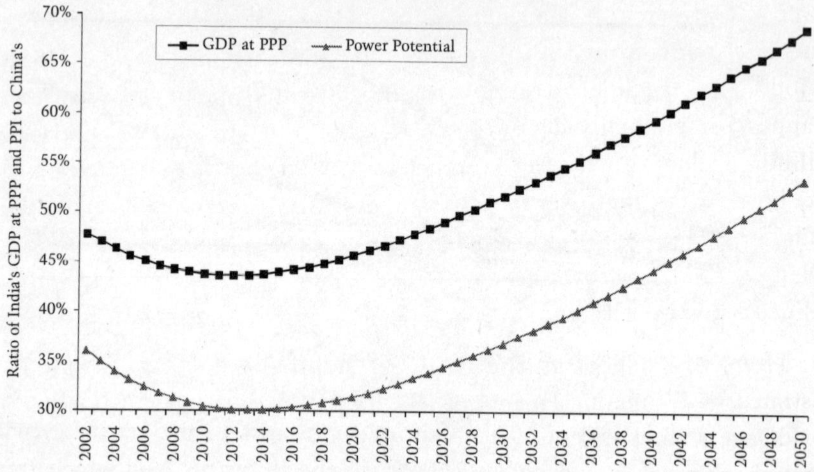

Figure 5.20

India-China: Alternative Scenarios

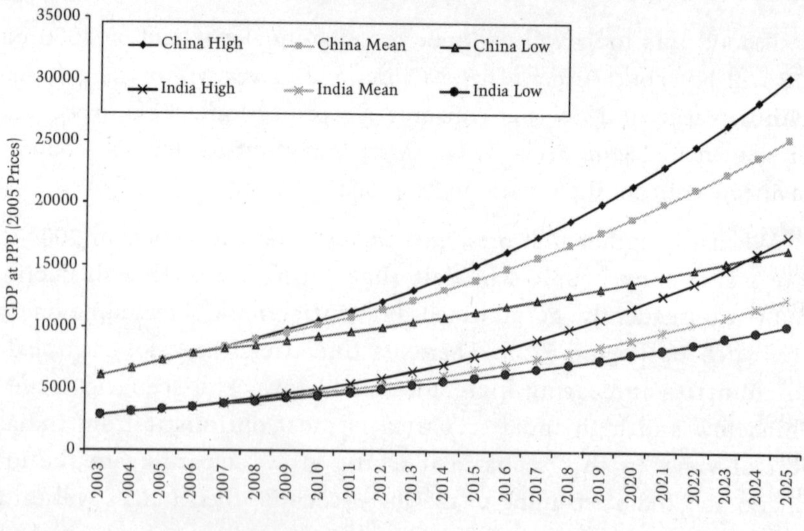

There is generally a lot of difference between the power potential and actual power of a country. Actual power depends on the power potential (index), strategic assets and technology and the 'will to power.' Strategic technology encompasses defence technology, nuclear technology, space platforms and so on. It is driven by public expenditure on development of strategic technology which also depends on economic power and strategic assets. For example, Russia is really cashing in on and benefitting from the huge investments made during the USSR period. The stock of strategic technology they built up does not disappear, it gradually declines but it is still there and they are very skillfully exploiting whatever is left, to maintain their power. There is a risk, however, in that over-investment in strategic assets can reduce the funds available for investment in the economy, consequently kill the golden goose. Russia over-invested in strategic technology and therefore, declined economically.

The third aspect is the 'will' to acquire power. This can be illustrated by comparing Japan and China. For 50 years since the Second World War, Japan had no desire to become a powerful country and therefore, they have not become and they have not looked at it in those terms. They were not interested in strategic technology. Only recently has this begun to change. This window of 25 years in which Japan can still be classed as a global power is going to be very important for Japan and I believe for India also. Both must utilise it to develop wider and deeper interaction for mutual benefit.

An alliance with technologically advanced countries can play a major role in acquisition of strategic and defence technologies. We seem to have had a brahminical attitude that we must develop everything ourselves. That is not what major countries have done historically. Russia, after World War II grabbed the German scientists, the German equipment and German blueprints and took them to Russia. They did not develop everything from scratch. If you really have the will to acquire power you just have to go after it wherever you can get it from. Another example is Pakistan. In economic terms it is not even a regional VIP, yet it has a strong will to counter India. It therefore, went out and got the strategic technology from wherever it could lay its hands on it (see chapter 8).

Conclusion

To conclude, there is a likelihood of change in global world order from a unipolar to bipolar world by 2025, and to tripolar by 2050. If the European Union becomes a virtual state by then, the world would be quadripolar. The balance of power in Asia is going to be critical. China will equal the collective power of Asian democracies—India, Japan, Indonesia, Russia, South Korea as well as Australia. I believe Russia is likely to use its Asian connections to enhance its power in Europe. China's economy will be only a little smaller than the US plus India and we know from history that there is heightened risk of conflict when a power rises so quickly. The only exception has been the rise of USA relative to the UK. These two had very similar values and systems, which is not true for the USA and China. As long as China has the single party rule (Leninist party), its system is not likely to change enough to become similar to the USA. We cannot however, completely rule out the possibility that 30-40 years later China may become a democracy. If this happens, then of course there will be a different situation.

Given the most likely scenario, it becomes essential to reduce the risk of conflict in Asia. Closing the economic and technological gap between India and China would produce a better balance of power and less temptation for China to use its rising power and result in greater stability. It would also permit a greater freedom of action for smaller Asian countries to rise. As far as ASEAN is concerned, it is not even a proper economic entity. Media reports suggest that Brussels in Europe has a huge bureaucracy of the EU. ASEAN does not even have a proper secretariat. So unless it changes, ASEAN does not have a major role in the next few decades. If 25 to 30 years later, they realise that they need to do something, then things may change.

Regarding technological cooperation, India has traditional connection with Russia and with Japan cooperation is being strengthened. The EU appears to be quite receptive. With the USA, how the nuclear agreement is carried forward is quite critical to facilitate better mutual trust. As an economist one believe in more competition. If a country is exclusively tied with one country, the latter has a monopoly and the former is at its mercy. If there are more countries trying to sell equipment and technologies, the buyer is in a stronger position. India can gain substantially if there is competition and that should be our objective. We should also utilise our democratic credential to have access to better technologies.

Relations between India and China are going to be critical for a stable balance of power. Normalisation of bilateral relations between India and China are very important and we must exploit our huge market potential. They are heavily dependent on exports for economic growth. There has to be some limit beyond which China cannot raise export share of the US market. Somebody will wake up and say you should not go further. So China is looking for new markets and one of them is India. There are a lot of barriers. We can start by removing barriers. We should trade with China like other countries—Japan, Russia or anybody else. We can then move to free trade in goods and services through a bilateral agreement that encompass both goods and services (chapter 7).

With regard to Sino-Indian relations, there are three key issues, which are important from the Indian perspective. One is a fair and equitable border settlement where one can have a simple rule that the terms should be 'no worse than' offered by Chinese Prime Minister Chou en Lie in 1960. Secondly, China must stop nuclear proliferation to countries hostile to India. The author's research on nuclear proliferation to Pakistan revealed that every single piece of equipment they needed for the bomb, was purchased in Europe. Yet they were not ready. The record shows that they got plutonium for the bomb and everything they needed for the final explosion from China, despite having got all the equipment from Europe (chapter 8). That is something we should be concerned about. It cannot be that China wants good relations with India but then goes on doing this. That should be part of our diplomatic engagement with them. Obviously, we don't need to fight and swear at each other but it must be part of our diplomatic effort. Finally, it is important that China should recognise India's due role in Asia and in the world. Five years ago they thought India was a nobody and China could behave in any way. That appeared to change during these five years and it is a good thing. But still we find that China is trying to build economic structures which exclude India. If we want to have genuine peace and security in Asia, we must build inclusive structures where both India and China have equal roles. One of these ideas is, as the Prime Minister of India said, the Asian Economic Community. There are also some ideas floated about the Asian Energy Community. Other areas must also be explored which include all major countries of Asia including India and China.

References

Madison, Angus (2003). *The World Economy: A Millennial Perspective*. OECD.

Untied Nations (n.d.). *World Population Prospects: The 2004 Revision.* Population Division of the Department of Economic and Social Affairs of the United Nations Secretariat, *http://esa.un.org/unpp*

6 China's Socialist Market Economy

Introduction

Through the 1990s China was widely and often held up as a paragon of economic policy reform driven growth and an example for others to follow. We in India were not immune to the temptation to do the same. There is no doubt that China has lessons that India and many other countries can learn, lessons that will help improve their growth rate. Some of these lessons have been correctly learned, for instance those related to the export-led growth model adopted by many South East Asian and East Asian countries. There is however a great danger of learning wrong lessons. This danger arises from the fact that information can and is controlled much more easily in a communist party ruled State than it is in a democracy, even a flawed one. China has also gone out of the way to make economic interaction with it (e.g. FDI, outsourcing of manufacturing) profitable for foreigners (non-Chinese), so their interests are best served by publicising information that ensures that profitable interaction with the Chinese Communist Party (CCP) and the State continue.

The present chapter is an attempt to derive a more balanced picture of China's past success so that better and more fruitful lessons can be drawn for the use of other non-communist countries. In this context the economic history of India, characterised as it is by 30 years of Indian socialism can be quite beneficial as it comes closest to the market-based "Socialism with Chinese Characteristics". In contrast, comparisons of China with Soviet socialism (USSR) can be very misleading and those with Cuba or North Korea are deliberate red herrings. With the exception of the degree of external openness (FDI & foreign trade), China's economy in 2005 is still much more 'socialist' than India's was in the heyday of the Indian version of socialism.

Overview

In the late 1930s, Oskar Lange put forward the idea of "Market Socialism," an economy in which assets (means of production) were owned socially (by the communist party or State), but which mimicked the supply-demand price adjustment of the competitive market economy. Aba Lerner, Lange and others then debated this issue during the 1930s. The key element that is common to 'market socialism' *a la* Lange and Lerner and 'socialism' (*a la* Lenin and Stalin) is socialist (i.e. party) ownership and (managerial) control of assets. The key difference is market-based allocation of goods and services *versus* centrally planned allocation of goods and services.

In China, the 'market' element has expanded gradually since the start of the agricultural reforms in 1979[1] and the introduction of urban reforms in 1984. In 1992 China publicly stated that its goal is a "socialist market economy with Chinese characteristics". Though China has successfully expanded the scope of the market, "socialist" (communist) control of factors remains very important. An understanding of these elements is essential for an understanding of the economic performance of China.[2] The chapter starts by giving a stylised version of China's economy in terms of the mix of socialist and market elements. This leads to an explanation of the growth performance of the Chinese economy and appropriate lessons for other countries, particularly non-socialist ones.

The primary "market" economy is in products (goods and non-infrastructure services) where even CCP controlled enterprises compete to maximise growth, as in a private corporate economy. The other market elements are external capital (100 per cent foreign invested enterprises and joint ventures) and external trade. Exports and FDI have played such an important role in China's economy that its growth has been characterised as 'export-led growth,' and could since 1990 be characterised as 'FDI-export led growth'. The extent to which import

1. After the third plenum in December 1978.

2. The reforms that China is currently undertaking or plans in future, have no relevance to past performance. The focus of the chapter is on industry, so early agriculture reforms are not discussed.

trade is now free is not entirely clear, though on balance this could be put into the market category. There is also a competitive fringe of individual capitalists/private capital that operates in export production.

The socialist planning system still operates, however, in factor markets (land, labour, capital) and infrastructure, the pricing of these inputs is used to provide (indirect) subsidies to foreign investors and domestic exporters. Cities/provinces can and do price land to any buyer at any price. The labour responsibility system determined where a person can work legally and where he cannot. The banking system has evolved little from a government department where loans are decided on the basis of provincial/national objectives and the ability to repay is irrelevant (variable cost of capital).[3] Infrastructure pricing and supply (particularly to foreign invested enterprises) is similarly decided on the basis of national/provincial/city objectives and can vary with enterprise. This is also true to some extent for the output of the State owned enterprises (SOEs) which remain subject to central department (their bosses) orders and directions.

In moving from the "socialist" to the "socialist market" economy, China has borrowed aspects from the "nationalist market economies" of developing Japan, South Korea and Singapore. The primary objective of the latter government's was to catch-up with the advanced countries through fast growth of average income. They therefore developed a national consensus to maximise GDP growth. The whole nation was mobilised to achieve this goal. The simplicity of this objective (growth, investment, production) made it much easier to decentralise it and ensure accountability at every level including that of the private corporate sector (Zaibatsu, Chaebol). Democratic accountability was however stronger in these countries, so that much greater attention had to be paid to democratisation of the gains from growth and the welfare of all citizens.[4]

---

3. For SOEs it varies downward from the formal rate to zero. The implicit interest rate could be negative if partial repayment is expected. For non-SOEs it varies upward from the formal rate for SOEs plus 20 per cent.

4. Even though in theory we can always devise a set of assumptions that shows welfare maximisation and growth maximisation as equivalent, we are talking about the effect of adopting and trying to implement the two approaches in the real world (outcome).

Both types of economies contrast with 'democratic market' economies like India that are driven primarily by democratic concerns in which the multidimensional nature of welfare maps into multiple, often contradictory, objectives. The means adopted to achieve one objective often contradict those required to achieve another resulting in cross-cutting actions. Multiple objectives lead to diffusion of accountability and provide liberal scope for pursuing ones personal goals (agency problems) as failure to achieve any one objective can always be blamed on the need to ensure another.

Socialist Elements

Leninist Party

The standard Marxist-Leninist description of the Communist ruled State is the "Dictatorship of the Proletariat". In China, as in other communist/socialist states, this means the dictatorship of the Chinese Communist Party (CCP).[5] To paraphrase Perkins (1994), "All political power in China is monopolised by the Chinese Communist party, a party that is organised along Leninist lines. Power is centralised at the top and not easily challenged from below." The party is a hierarchy stretching from the party general secretary at the top to the party honcho in the smallest settlement/village. The objectives, broad approach to achievement of these objectives and the parameters within which lower levels can take initiatives, are decided at the top. Within this framework there is a multilevel decision-making process from the national to provincial, metro cities and town and village level.

Decentralisation of Socialist Production[6]

This decentralisation is not a post-1978 development but has evolved since the 1960s, with the decentralisation of planning authority first to

5. The only reasonable political benchmark is the former USSR/Soviet Union. North Korea is a personal dictatorship, not a party (proletariot) dictatorship. Similarly Cuba is better described as a kind of feudal or virtual dictatorship. Even though Castro is the unchallenged dictator of Cuba, his stature in the party, rather than use of terror, ensures that nobody challenges him (i.e., he is a virtual dictator). Therefore to say that China is far removed from North Korea and cannot therefore be called a 'dictatorship' is a red herring.

6. The discussion also draws on Shirk (1985), Jin and Qian (1998), Che and Qian (1998), Smyth (1998), Oi (1995), Putterman (1995) and Mood (2005).

the provinces and then to the county. To paraphrase Perkins (1988), "By the 1970's a large proportion of Chinese enterprises were under the authority of the provinces rather than Beijing. In most cases, particularly with large enterprises and strategic sectors, Beijing retained effective control even if planning formally was at the provincial level."[7] "The Collectively owned and the Township and Village Enterprises (which were then called the Commune and Brigade Enterprises) accounted for 22 per cent of industrial production in 1978, where the ownership rights over such enterprises resided not with the community but with the local government" (Walder, 1995).

Evidence is provided in Wong (1985) that local governments (provincial levels and below) in addition to having gained greater autonomy over allocation of materials from the Centre during the Cultural Revolution, were also to a large extent able to bypass the material allocations of the central plans by setting up local enterprises with local funds. The level of Central government control fluctuated from then onwards, but decreased during the Cultural Revolution. Some materials which had been under direct allocation by the State Planning Commission or by the Central ministries were now allowed to be locally allocated. In 1966, "almost all output from local small scale industries" came to be under local allocation. These small scale industries included iron and steel, cement, chemical fertilisers, coal and farm machinery and therefore, this decentralisation was not trivial to increasing local government's ability in making and implementing investment decisions. Each level of local government invested in its own enterprises decentralised to their control even if the profits from these enterprises was not formally available to them.

The immediate effect of Chinese Communist Party campaigns such as the "Great Leap Forward" and the "Cultural Revolution" were clearly highly destructive in many ways. These campaigns were however a training ground for a unique communist party structure that was highly centralised in that the party at all levels had to implement the policy orders emanating from the leadership of the party (and anybody who dared oppose the Mao set objectives of these campaigns came to a

7. In fact decentralisation of industry was carried to an unsustainable extreme under Mao, with the setting up of thousands of steel furnaces in the villages of China.

horrible end). It was also highly decentralised in its implementation and operation in that party cadres had to use their own initiative in finding (reallocating) financial resources, obtaining the capital goods for setting up furnaces and finding the raw materials for producing steel. Even the red guards had a lot of freedom in defining the 'Capitalist Roaders' and inventing re-education campaigns and punishments for them. The Maoist period of socialist experimentation, though harsh and destructive, established an experimental approach to party and State action. In our view this experimentation and experience has been an important foundation for converting party cadres and State employees (often indistinguishable) into public entrepreneurs.

The Party Core

The party has undoubtedly changed and evolved over the last 25 years and is different from what it was under Chairman Mao. But it is also very different from any ruling party in a genuine democracy or 'quasi-democratic' State. For instance, one of the most important departments of the party is the personal department. This department (at different levels) vets and selects all official appointees to positions with decision-making authority[8] and every CEO of every government owned/controlled company/firm/organisation. These appointees are therefore not just state officials or company/cooperative CEOs, but part of the network of the Chinese Communist Party. Even if the CEO is not a party member there will be a party member (or group of members) ostensibly juniors in the organisation who can over rule him on 'ideological' grounds.[9]

Other vital departments of the Chinese Communist Party are the ideology and propaganda departments. The management of information is one of the important responsibilities of the party and its senior leadership. Democratic country citizens' too readily forget that the communist state has to ensure that its citizens believe, decade after decade, that every thing the party does is for their good. Good chits from foreign business partners are also helpful in this endeavour, so it is

---

8. Equivalent to our Joint secretary and above.

9. The Chairman of one of the policy banks in China, complained in an interview in the *Financial Times* that all his decisions were reviewed every month by a committee whose members included party officials with little or no expertise in financial matters.

important to ensure that foreigners believe the party line. In any case, positive expectations among foreigners is essential for maximising FDI, exports and investment, all of which are critical to the attainment of Party (CCP) objectives.

China is not immune to the deterioration in governance that is seen in many non-OECD countries, particularly those that try to control economic activity. The systems of government and party are therefore fraying as in these countries, leading to increased corruption. The lack of control arising from the general deterioration in governance can easily be confused with a deliberate decision to reduce, dismantle or eliminate the control network, given the level of transparency regarding internal working of Chinese Communist Party.

Post-1980 Financial Incentives

The degree of operational freedom and flexibility within the designed and designated sphere of operation of the lower levels has however, increased since 1980. The most important impact of the post-Mao period reforms was to increase the financial incentives of the local governments to promote investment in their regions—as not only the means to hedge against shortages under planned quotas—but as a means to increase local revenue (and hence the bonuses and perks they could award themselves), local employment and incomes (including those of their family and friends, through control over local enterprises). The three reforms that are considered in the literature to have been the most important in this change of incentives were:

(a) Enterprises were now to be taxed at fixed rates, leaving all residual profits with them.

(b) Each level of government now had to pay a fixed amount out of taxes collected from enterprises under its jurisdiction to the next higher level.

(c) The introduction of household responsibility system gave the households the right to income from sale of above-quota produce, making it necessary for the township and village governments to look for other sources of income.

Within the overall structure of decentralisation, the degree of autonomy and nature of accountability for managers of organisations and enterprises can vary from province to province, from township (village) to township (village) within the same province. Thus, appointment of the CEO by the party/government can go along with a relatively high degree of operational autonomy for the CEO in a production firm.[10] For instance, the town or village CCP boss who appoints the T&V enterprise CEO could leave him free to maximise the growth of the firm subject to specified obligations to the village/town administration (e.g. local purchase or hiring) and/or the local party boss. Similarly the CEO of a joint venture may be free to pursue a growth/sales maximisation strategy subject to either promoting exports (with any losses covered by State loans i.e., disguised as NPAs) or below cost supply of intermediates to an FDI investor to attract it to that area. On the other hand, the professional CEO of an investment company or bank, may have limited market autonomy, with most of his decisions vetted or reviewed by a committee of party members (formally junior to him in his and other organisations).[11]

China's governance system is therefore a mix of centralised and decentralised elements, bearing little resemblance to Stalinist USSR.

Factor Markets

The socialist control over factor markets is pervasive, compared to any 'democratic market economy,' though it may appear liberal relative to the former USSR or Mao's China. This includes the land, labour and capital markets.

Land

All land is owned and controlled by the State. Because of the historical legacy of cooperative ownership of farmland, the system is slightly different in the rural areas. In many provinces, farming households ostensibly have an ownership share in village and farm land, but lose

10. But not in the financial sector where the party/government still controls capital flows.

11. Indian public sector managers have always enjoyed this type of freedom. This does not mean that we can arbitrarily classify the Indian public sector or the TVEs as private.

this right if they move to the urban areas to work. Brandt *et al.* (2002) examine the realities of land rights and tenure security, over a decade after China introduced reforms and de-collectivised agriculture. They find that although the allocations were supposed to be for 15 years, which was increased to 30 years in late 1990s, only 28 per cent of the villages in the survey had seen no reallocation of land since 1983 and in the rest of the cases the reallocation decision was never made by the households concerned. Most of the reallocation decisions were made at the village level, and a small percentage at the township level, and in almost half of the villages, the date of reallocation hadn't been announced in advance. Not only are the household not entitled to own land they cultivate or to have a say in the change of their holdings, they also do not get any compensation for investments in land improvement that they might have made on the land transferred away. Although 71.6 per cent of the villages reported that their households were free to transfer land use rights to other households, which is a short term contract in the nature of land rental, called Zhuanbao, only 3 per cent of the land was actually rented out in 1995.

Many urban municipalities in market economies own urban land that is normally acquired rural land on the outskirts of a city for conversion into urban land. They have, however, to operate within a system of zoning laws, rules and procedures. In a socialist economy, land use can be changed overnight at the stroke of a pen. To whom, at what price and for what purpose the land is given, can vary with category of the person/firm. For instance, the acquisition of new land for industry involved complex negotiations with suburban communities or townships in which it gives up part of its land in exchange for guaranteed jobs for some of its members (Perkins, 1988). Buying and selling of long term leases was allowed in urban areas in the 1990s, but the process of acquisition of rural land for factory purposes remained unchanged. It is however very important to remember the positive discrimination in favour of foreign invested enterprises. The fact that such enterprises have been legally allowed to trade leased land does not mean that domestic private enterprises or individuals (as against 'socialist owned/controlled enterprises) have the same rights. Further, even if formal legal rights have been given the situation, in practice it may be quite different (worse) for the (genuine) domestic private sector than it is for the FD investors.

Citizens can be evicted from the land if the CCP/government decides to rebuild an urban area or build a new township on rural land.[12] Till mid-2005 there was no formal system of government registration of the ownership rights of households over apartments. Thus, the second owner of an apartment does not have the legal right to mortgage it to a commercial bank and get a loan, despite the fact that the original/first owner of the apartment may have had mortgaged the apartment to get a loan. The latter is the result of a cosy deal between the urban authorities, the developer and the bank, that cannot be repeated for the resale because the urban authorities are no longer involved and have nothing to gain from winking at the 'law' (the so-called owner has no legal right to sell i.e., has only usurfruct rights).

The urban authorities can also price the land to suit their purpose. It can therefore be reduced to a fraction or nil for a 100 per cent foreign invested firm that brings in skills, technology or products that are thought desirable or one that commits to export part or whole of its output. It can similarly be reduced for a real-estate developer who shares part of the profit with the urban authorities.

The rapid development of coastal cities and their absorption of such villages has left an interesting anomaly in places such as Shenzen. There is a rich 'village' in the middle of Shenzen that is owned collectively by the households that lived there and farmed the land more than three decades ago when it was a real village collective. Currently it looks more like an 'urban jungle' than a 'village,' but is still called a village.[13]

Labour[14]

In every Communist country the party controlled the labour unions and therefore the terms and conditions of work. This is also true in China

12. 30 million people have had their land taken over by property developers since 1994. According to Gao Zhi Sheng, a public interest lawyer, a majority of Chinese judges are members of the CCP and therefore ensure that its objectives are fulfilled.
13. Presumably because that is the only way in which urban land can be owned by these citizens. It is therefore a show case of the "private ownership" and development of land in urban areas.
14. The discussion also draws on World Bank (2005), Au and Henderson (2002), Whalley and Zhang (2004) and Hertel and Zhai (2004).

and therefore the overall policy approach to terms and conditions of employment, work hours and wages is decided by the CCP (at an appropriate geographical level or level of government). If the CCP decides to apply different work and pay rules in a particular province, sector, industry or type of enterprise (e.g. foreign invested) from those applied to general domestic enterprises, neither the (so-called) labour unions nor the employees can do anything about it. They can either like it or lump it.

In addition, in China the labour market is also controlled through the Hukou system that determines where a person is entitled to live and work and receive State-provided social benefits. If people move without formal CCP permission they are in effect illegal migrants with no rights. Chinese government's restrictions on rural-urban mobility primarily operate through the Hukou system—a system of household registration—which establishes a person's place of legal residence (where a child's residence is established initially at the mother's place of legal residence). Legal residence in an area entitles one to access public schooling and health care, housing and job opportunities and/or land for farming. Legal change of residence is possible if either a person succeeds in getting a place at a senior middle school and then at a city college by clearing competitive exams for the same, or if the state allows it, say allowing firms in a city to hire permanent workers from nearby rural areas. A worker may live legally in an urban area, without acquiring an urban *hukou* as a permanent resident on a long term permit or as a contract worker. Permits for legal residence are neither easy nor cheap to come by, and illegal migration has been increasing throughout the reform period.

Surplus labour in rural areas (due to underemployment) was estimated to be about 100 million of which the 'floating population' of illegal migrants from rural to urban areas constituted 'tens of millions' (Perkins, 1994). Total rural to urban migrants in China were estimated to be about 76 million in 2000 and total number of migrants around 131 million. In 1999, 16.87 million migrants were legally allowed to migrate to counties other than their home counties. Though the figures aren't directly comparable, being for different years and the 16.87 million includes both rural urban and other migration, but they give a rough idea about the extent of illegal migration. A variety of factors ensure that illegal migrants find it extremely difficult to get employment in better paying industries, among them local governments' pressure on enterprises to give employment to local residents. And there is always the risk of deportation.

When the special economic zones were first opened, all labour contracts were with a Chinese labour bureau (CCP controlled) that effectively controlled terms and conditions of employment. Later when the demand for unskilled labour exceeded the local labour pool, people were brought in from neighbouring areas and by this act given (temporary) legal right to live and work in that Special Economic Zone. If every unskilled labourer was expected to work 100 hours a week 52 weeks a year in the SEZ, the new migrants would "voluntarily" even "happily" do so. There was no other option to earn that kind of annual wage in their own place of legal residence and the legal right to work/live in the SEZ could and was easily revoked if (s)he was not willing to accept the rules decreed by the CCP. If FDI investors were willing to produce and export labour intensive goods, if a docile pool of unskilled labour willing to work day and night was available, this was ensured by the local party bosses. The extreme restrictions on labour have undoubtedly eased over time, but likely remain stricter than in any market economy (or one that claims to be a "market" economy).

Formally labour is allowed to work for 76 hours a week of which 40 is normal and 36 overtime. Reports suggest that 100 hours a week (at normal wages or piece rates) is not uncommon in labour intensive units producing for export.[15] This ironically results in a reduction in per hour productivity below what it would be if working hours were the same as in state owned enterprises.

Some steps towards reform of the *Hukou* system have been taken in recent years. In 2001, the Ministry of Public Security reduced the minimum requirements to be eligible for *hukou* in small towns and cities to the applicant having a permanent source of income and legal

15. As an increasing number of western companies have made commitments to stake holders to enforce labour standards in their overseas production units and suppliers, records are falsified and labor coached to provide the 'right' answers to visiting social auditors.

housing in the locality. And in some medium and large cities, such requirements have been reduced to having a work contract of specified duration, say more than 2 years. It is now illegal to charge migrants' children extra school fees and in early 2004, fees for temporary resident permits in urban areas were eliminated. Nevertheless, legal migration remains difficult, Central directives are subject to local implementation or the lack thereof.

In a survey by the World Bank and the Development Research Center (DRC) of the State Council, in 2003 of 3156 enterprises in all 31 provinces, 60 to 70 per cent of enterprises considered labour market distortions arising out of *hukou* status—whether due to direct pressure on enterprises to employ local residents and not to employ migrants for certain jobs and positions (Beijing specified 100 such occupations in 2000) or due to inability of local governments to provide pension, medical, unemployment benefits to migrants and education to their children—as serious or very serious protectionist practices affecting their region or industry.[16]

Capital

Socialist Enterprises

In 1980, 100 per cent of capital assets were owned and controlled by the State/CCP. The management of these assets was (is) distributed to different levels of government, which in turn was (is) controlled by different levels of the party. Some were (are) controlled at the national level through the departments of the Central government and their CCP bosses. Others are managed/controlled at the provincial, city and village level (village cooperatives, T&V enterprises). All industrial enterprises (now SOEs) were what in Indian parlance would be called departmental public enterprise. Some of these industrial enterprises have been converted into (what in India we call) Public Sector Units (PSUs), i.e., companies that may or may not be listed on the stock exchange. In China the listing could also be (solely) on the Hong Kong stock exchange or even a foreign exchange. This does not convert them into

16. Apparently illegal migrants are henceforth to be allowed to use certain urban social services like schools for enrolling their children.

private enterprises as management control remains with the same CCP boss or his nominee/appointee.[17]

Similarly, Town and Village Enterprises (TVEs), though (in theory) collectively owned by the workers, are subject to local government direction (Perkins, 1988, 1994).[18] This would in practice mean that the CEO is appointed by the local party boss/government and works under his supervision/direction within the operational autonomy given by the latter. It would be an extremely foolhardy T&V manager who could ignore the objectives and guidelines set down by the local party boss/ government. However, party appointed managers have a sphere of autonomy assigned by the CCP/government within which they run the firm and compete in a market environment. Thus, managers of county firms may maximise value added, so that they can increase the benefits (wages, perks, employment of children) to enterprise employees. This would result in competitive behaviour in input/output markets.[19] As long term value added maximisation is the same as growth maximisation, the conflict between local and national goals is minimised. Fierce competition in product markets (both input and output side) is also consistent with party appointed management, given the growth objective.

China's State owned enterprises (SOEs) can be formally owned/ managed by the national, provincial or municipal governments. Listed companies are largely national or provincial SOEs as even collective enterprises were not allowed to raise capital on these exchanges till 1997.[20] TVEs are classified as non-state sector, but often this is mistaken as private sector.[21] TVEs are SOEs controlled by the lowest

17. In India, the Tata's exercised absolute control over TELCO & TISCO with 6-8 per cent of the share holding till the mid-nineties.

18. The township was basically the old commune which carried out both production and government functions. Even in (so called) 'individual private' enterprises started by workers or managers, the local government would invariably play a role and have a share in their earnings.

19. Competition can however be thwarted by local/provincial protective barriers to trade.

20. Regional stock exchange on which the latter raised capital were abolished in 1995. Listing quotas were abolished in 2000.

21. The correct picture as painted for instance by Gelb and Byrd (1990) and Perkins (1988, 1994) seems to have been lost along the way.

level of government with a greater degree of autonomy in terms of market operation.[22] However, township governments own and operate township enterprises and village enterprises have substantial and numerous ties to village government. Village committees perform government functions but village officials are not civil servants.

Urban collective enterprises can be wholly owned subsidiaries of SOEs or township promoted or hived off units.[23] Thus, they have organic links to the government. By way of comparison, cooperatives in India, operate under explicit rules and regulations and can be termed as private, even in those cases in which their dependence on government funds, makes them vulnerable to government interference.[24]

We call these corporate enterprises together as socialist enterprises. Kuijs (2005) has shown that these enterprises are not required to pay any dividends to the government and consequently have 100 per cent reinvestment of profits. Kuijs (2005) also shows that the exceptionally high saving rate of China is due solely to the high saving and investment by the enterprise sector, while the household and government saving rate and the latter's investment rate is in line with other Asian economies.

Institutional Reform

Limited reforms in ownership and operational flexibility led to remarkable improvements in output and productivity of SOEs. Xu (1997) estimates that that the labour productivity of these enterprises grew at the rate of 2.6 per cent per annum during the period 1980-1989. Among the reforms were:

22. According to Huang (2003), the revenue objectives of the local officials are much more closely aligned with the profit maximisation objectives of the enterprise as both depend on income maximisation, in contrast to higher levels where many macro objectives come into play and dilute autonomy and accountability (pp. 140, 127, 106).

23. With the township contributing old machinery from existing township production unit but legally owning the entire enterprise even it is subsequently nurtured/built-up by the managers with their own funds.

24. They have a choice not to get funds from the government If they choose to become dependent on government funds then they have to abide by the conditions imposed on provision of these funds.

(a) Increasing marginal profit retention rates, on average from 11 per cent in 1980 to 27 per cent in 1989 (though these retained profits were subject to many constraints over use).

(b) Granting firms greater autonomy over six main productions decisions—value and quantity of output, type of product, technology and scheduling of production and exports.

(c) Contract responsibility system, which granted managers the legal right and some discretion to operate the firm for the contracted period. 88 per cent of the firms in the sample had a CRS contract in 1989, while almost none did in the beginning of the sample period.

(d) Granting managers some discretion over exact wages paid to the employees.

(e) Increasing management turnover, though any arbitrary increase in management turnover cannot *per se* be considered a reform, but insofar as it might have made managers more accountable, this may influence firm performance.

Li (1997) finds a marked improvement in the marginal products of labour and capital in the 1980s, with the former increasing by 54 per cent between the pre- and post 1985 periods. There were also efficiency gains due to reallocation of labour—though how this might have come about is uncertain, as labour allocations continued to be controlled by local governments and layoffs were virtually prohibited. One possible explanation is that the ownership rights that the local governments won over SOEs in the 1980s could have induced them to allocate labour more efficiently. Another lies in the rights given to enterprises to set up collectives to place their redundant workers.

Banks

The household savings rate has fluctuated between 16 per cent and 22 per cent of GDP during the nineties. Because the share of household income in GDP is very low in China, household saving rates out of disposable income were quite high in the mid-nineties. They had declined to around 24 per cent of disposable income or 15.5 per cent of GDP by 2000 (Kuijs, 2005). Investment by households, largely residential, is estimated by Kuijs at 5-6 per cent in 2003. The remaining household savings ranging from 9 per cent to 12 per cent of GDP are transferred to the banking system.

The policy banks and commercial banks are 100 per cent owned by the national government while the regional banks are owned by local governments, State owned enterprises or business federations (government controlled).[25] Till 1998 there was a formal lending quota system operated by the central bank for SOEs. The only financial intermediary that could be called private, the Urban Credit Cooperatives (UCC) was compelled to hand over a majority of shares to the municipal governments in 1995.[26] Up to 1998 only the urban and rural credit cooperatives, whose deposit base was limited to the non-State firms were allowed to lend to private firms.

In the Communist State, capital has no price or cost. Even in Socialist China, banks are not intermediaries but instruments of the State (departments) for channelling capital into desirable activities. According to Perkins (1994), "Though formally commercial banks were separated from the Central bank early in the reform period, in reality they follow the direction of the central bank and of the government policy makers in general." Below market interest rates are standard (Perkins, 1988, 1994). More important, capital costs can vary by borrower (in the same category), among borrowers of different categories in the same industry, place and time. Interest rates on loans to non-State firms (i.e. non-SOEs) have to be equal to or greater than the rate of interest to SOEs plus 20 per cent.

According to official figures non-performing assets (NPA) for the four commercial banks were 25 per cent in 1998 of which 20 per cent were loss assets. NPAs constituted 30 per cent of GDP.[27] NPA has no meaning for loans to SOEs, because credit is given if it is needed to maintain an activity or organisation that has an assigned role in the economy. In other words, if partial or no repayment is expected when

---

25. Minsheng Bank is owned by the All-China Federation of Industry and Commerce, a government organisation overseeing private firms.

26. Huang, 2003: 118.

27. See Lardy (1998) for a detailed discussion of NPAs.

the loan is made, it is a misnomer to call it an NPA later when the expected happens (in this situation full repayment is a low probability event and therefore unexpected). The repeated capitalisation of China's "banks" shows that this description is not far from the truth, for a large share of loans.[28] Such bailouts since the Asian crises aggregate to between 50 per cent and 100 per cent of GDP.

This stylised picture for the entire period till 2004 should not be taken to mean that there are/is no liberalisation/market reform over time or that truly market-oriented lending based on technical criterion is nil in 2004. The extent of such lending is however, very hard to know accurately and is likely be a much smaller fraction of the total than is assumed by CW (Conventional Wisdom). Further sale of some shares to foreign banks or the public will not dilute CCP (management) control of these commercial banks in any way.[29] It will merely result in transfer of technology and skills to the bank for them to use within the circumscribed autonomy authorised by the CCP, perhaps with a gradually expanded scope for market lending over the next few decades.

Technology and IPR

Realising the extent of its industrial backwardness in 1979, China did not hesitate to send thousands of students to the US and the West to close the gap in education and skills. Most of these early students were the children and kin of party officials who could be trusted to collect as much information and knowledge and bring it back for socialist dissemination. Even later a large fraction of students was connected to CCP.

Technology as a factor is largely part of the socialist system (collective ownership). There is no genuine market for technology in socialist China in the sense that individual buyers and sellers of technology can transact among themselves. In the socialist system, if any government firm acquires technology from abroad either through

28. A Mckinsey journal volume on China (2004) gives just of hint of this.

29. A recent (2005) report in the *Financial Times* quoted the Chairman of one of the commercial banks complaining about how all his decisions were subject to review (and were reviewed monthly) by a committee consisting of party cadres holding mid-level positions in the financial system.

purchase or through a joint venture with a foreign firm, that technology could be disseminated to every government firm that needs it.[30] Reverse engineering where feasible would also be viewed as part of the natural right. Even in the case of ostensibly private firms, such acquired technology may be transferred to others.

China has partly avoided the pitfalls of stagnating commercial technology that was one of the factors in the falling behind/collapse of the USSR, by allowing relatively free import of capital goods (embodied technology) and welcoming FDI. FDI helps avoid stagnant or negative technical change in the civil economy (i.e. all non-strategic areas) that characterised the last decade of the USSR. China has also tried to undertake research in new scientific areas with some success. The output of Chinese scientists as measured by the citation index increased rapidly to respectable levels.

Increased pressure on China not to allow the widespread use of Western registered brand names and openly violate copyright and patent rights is likely to increase over time. In our view, this will have the effect of reducing the violation of IPRs on consumer goods where the violation is blatant and visible. It will have little effect (for decades) on the way IPRs on capital goods and intermediate products are regarded/treated within the socialist-owned enterprises.

Infrastructure

As in many developing countries a large part of China's basic physical infrastructure is owned by the State. Other countries also control prices and implicitly cross-subsidise certain categories of users such as low and lower middle-income consumers. Some do the opposite by setting lower rates for industry. China, however, has the ability to tailor supply, including the supply price, to the individual user to meet other objectives such as exports or FDI. Thus for instance, a distribution line could be laid or a road constructed to a new FDI investor's location if this is necessary to attract it. Utility prices could be similarly changed

30. A research-oriented company in each industry may be selected to import, adapt, modify and develop technology for that industry and then disseminate it to all SOEs in that industry. This perhaps includes reverse engineering of imported capital goods.

to suit any requirement if that helps meet an objective. There is no incentive for the receiver of this munificence to disclose or publicise such hidden subsidies, because they could just as easily be withdrawn.

Market Elements

Product Market

The most important market innovation that China introduced into its socialist economy was the product market. In 1979 it started with agriculture output markets. Initially agriculture markets were partially liberalised in a manner similar to that used in India for sugar and other markets in the sixties. This was a 'dual pricing and distribution' system in which part of the produce continued to be handed over to the government at a controlled price, while the rest could be sold freely at the market price.

Many of the rules circumscribing small-scale service activities were also abolished or ignored, resulting in a boom in collectively and individually owned restaurants and shops. Labour contracting services also developed in the interior provinces to supply construction workers to urban areas.

Dual pricing in industrial goods was introduced by China in 1985-1986, with prices on the market channel allowed to fluctuate according to market conditions.[31] At this point, more than half of all industrial goods were still distributed at administered prices. Product liberalisation was gradually extended to the entire manufacturing sector. It has also been selectively extended to the real estate sector and retail trade.

Domestic markets are however far from perfect, particularly for goods and services that were produced and traded at the county level and at the province level (to a smaller extent). As the county/province owns the local/provincial firms, there is a tendency to modify regulations to favour local production and create protective barriers against import of competitive goods from other counties/provinces. This tendency will be least in cities and provinces whose CCP bosses are part of the central

31. "Low level government officials did extract informal payments of various kinds" Perkins (1994).

party leadership and therefore more interested in national growth. Further, the collective enterprises that constitute the most competitive firms are limited in their physical reach by capital, transport and other constraints. Inter-provincial market integration has increased from very low to moderate levels.

International Markets

Foreign Trade

In the early years external trade was carried out largely by State trading companies and provincial trading companies and by 1993 there were 4000 such government controlled foreign trade companies. External trade can now be taken as largely market-based even though the system retains a strong bias against imports. Though policy biases against imports by domestic firms have been gradually removed government and managers have an asymmetric attitude to exports and imports. In 1979, reforms were introduced to facilitate exports of manufactures and (for the first time) to allow for foreign investment (Lardy, 1992). Special economic zones (export processing zones) were set up to free foreign investors and other exporters from red tape. Input tax offsets and export subsidies were introduced. The currency was devalued from 1.7 yuan per US dollar in 1981 to 2.9 yuan per USD in 1985. Though exports grew rapidly from 1977 onwards, imports remained tightly controlled till the mid-1980s (Perkins, 1988).

Exchange Rate

In early 1980s foreign exchange was tightly controlled by the Bank of China even for foreign investors who needed to repatriate profit or import inputs for export. To attract export-oriented FDI from Hong Kong and other overseas Chinese, government created 'foreign exchange adjustment centers' or swap markets on which those with surplus foreign exchange (e.g. joint venture hotels) could sell their surplus FE to foreign firms at market determined rates. The establishment of these centres effectively freed imports for FDI producers. The currency was devalued further to 4.8 yuan per USD in 1990, the dual exchange rate integrated in 1994 and current account convertibility formally introduced in 1995. External trade was therefore effectively freed for foreign producers between mid-1980s and mid-1990s.

FDI

The third important market element is foreign capital in the form of foreign direct investment (FDI). Compared to the control exercised over domestic capital, FDI is attracted through the application of market principles. Namely FDI will only come if the expectation of profit is high. Conditions have therefore been created using every socialist control (indirect subsidy) at its command to attract FDI to China and to ensure that it finds it profitable to keep expanding exports. Policy has been liberalised whenever it was necessary to keep inflows of FDI and outflows of exports from faltering. This has included fairly early opening of both the real estate sector and of retail trade.

The first FDI investors to take advantage of the freeing of trade were producers from Hong Kong and Macao who shifted their export production to Guangdong SEZs in China starting in the mid-1980s.[32] In 1990, 55 per cent of all (realised) foreign investment came from Hong Kong and Macao and by 1992 Hong Kong's share in total Chinese exports had risen to 44 per cent. Producer-exporters from Taiwan (to Fujian) and other overseas Chinese followed with the shift from their home countries to China accelerating in the early 1990s.

Private Fringe

There is also a small proportion of the domestic (i.e. non-FDI) manufacturing sector that could be classified as a genuinely private sector. This consists mostly of individual (atomistic) producers who supply labour-intensive goods to exporters and FDI producers. Though there is no direct management control by the CCP, the latter always has the residual power to destroy anyone who steps too much outside the limits acceptable to higher party authorities.

---

32. In 1979, 22.6 per cent of China's total exports were to Hong Kong, of which only 21 per cent were exported. By 1987 the shares had increased to 31.1 per cent and 62 per cent. Hong Kong's share in China's manufactured exports was even higher ranging from 46 per cent in textiles to 62 per cent in clothing to 87 per cent in machinery. (Sung, 1991).

Genuinely private enterprises consist of two types: Individual (e.g. push carts) and those with one or more employees. In 1998 the former constituted 99.8 per cent of the 6 million such enterprises. Further out of the total, 56 per cent were in the service sector (mainly food and retail). Thus there were probably as little as 6000 (1/2 of 0.2 per cent of 6 million) private manufacturing enterprises in 1998. Some progressive provinces/cities such as Guangdong (Shunde) and Wenzhou (Zhejang) did try to promote private entrepreneurship and privatisation (Huang, 2003: 110, 129). Given existing laws this required innovative steps like joint government-private structure and labelling of firms as collective enterprises.

According to Huang (2003), there is a systematic bias against domestic private entrepreneurship, arising from the need to minimise any potential threat to the CCP's monopoly of political power. FDI investors cannot pose a political threat to the CCPs rule so the party has been quite willing to provide a playing field that is heavily tilted in their favour. In contrast, a strong independent group of private domestic entrepreneurs could at some time in the future become an alternative source of political power. Thus, the capital and other markets under government control are heavily biased against genuine private domestic entrepreneurs, if not completely closed to them.

Growth Model

China is a nationalist State with a clear vision of national power through economic growth and technological catch-up. The Chinese Communist Party translates this vision into explicit objectives suitable for different levels (nation, province, city, firm) that are broadly coherent but far from perfect (not devoid of contradictions). Among the sub-goals that this translates into are increased sales/production, value added investment and technology transfer from the advanced countries. The growth strategy for achieving these objectives has evolved over time. Starting from the mid-1970s it first became an export-led growth strategy and then from the mid-1980s an FDI-export led growth strategy. Underlying these has been the development of domestic product markets and the evolution of the management structures of government enterprises to meet the challenges of competition in domestic and global markets.

Objectives

In general terms the objective of the CCP is to increase China's global power subject to itself retaining power internally and indefinitely. In the process of achieving the primary objective, the people should be reasonably content and no significant sub-group should become so unhappy as to revolt against CCP rule. More formally, the objective is the maximisation of economic growth subject to the maintenance of existing welfare of all groups. The objective differs from that adopted by "nationalist market economies," or "corporate States," such as Japan and South Korea prior to their becoming high-income countries, where growth maximisation was subject to the constraint that welfare of all groups of citizens must be rising. Both approaches however contrast with the social welfare maximisation objective of the governments of most "democratic market economies".[33]

The growth maximisation objective percolates down the CCP network and becomes the major, if not primary objective of every level of government (province, city, town, village) as well as of the managers of firms appointed by them. There is enough flexibility in the system to adapt the objectives to the particular circumstances and constraints of each level and the area in which it operates. At the level of the firm, the growth maximisation objective could be translated either into a market share objective similar to corporate capitalism or a value added maximisation objective that combines the interests of labour/managers and capital. Thus, even CCP appointed managers compete in product markets. Unlike managers in corporate capitalism, however, they are subject to the guidelines and constraints arising from national/provincial/city objectives set (and conveyed) by the CCP (boss). They therefore often have to balance (trade-off) firm against national or provincial objectives (e.g. employment).

Means

The primary means of achieving high growth is a high investment rate. This has two prongs. One socialist/public sector investment and the

33. Though a model can always be constructed in which the two objectives result in identical policies, we are talking about the real world of layers of government servants working on dozens of sectors and hundreds of sub-sectors.

second is foreign direct investment (FDI). This is combined with an unprecedented degree of export orientation. Thus public investment, FDI and exports are the three pillars of China's successful growth maximisation strategy.[34] The policy framework and the CCP network has been moulded to maximise these three critical elements of the growth strategy. Everything else has a secondary or marginal role in explaining non-agricultural growth to date, though it may become more relevant in future. FDI-export led growth has earlier been an important part of the growth strategy of Singapore, Thailand, Malaysia and Indonesia, but China has taken this to a new level and scale. China has (so far) successfully combined this with levels of public investment not seen since the collapse of the USSR.

Foundation: Public Investment

The public ownership of assets has been an important contributor to the fast growth of China's economy as it allows a motivated government to use these profits either for public investment or to provide subsidies to FDI or exporters and thus indirectly boost investment. Unlike a democratic market economy like India, China did not need to generate funds for public investment (or subsidies) through taxes that distort markets and reduce efficiency and productivity. Government appointed/ controlled managers cannot however match the innovativeness of private entrepreneurs or the efficiency of growth maximising private firms (e.g. Zaibatsu, Chaebols). Though public ownership of assets has driven growth so far it can become the greatest source of weakness as public profits decline and disappear reducing public investment and stalling the entire economy. Past strength and future weakness are two sides of the same coin.

A very large fraction of assets are still owned and controlled by the State/CCP network, which appoints the top management in listed companies, cooperatives, T&V enterprises and State owned enterprises ("socialist enterprises"). Kuijs has shown that enterprise investment has ranged between 27 per cent and 35 per cent since 1990. Though government/State saving is between 4.8 per cent and 8.1 per cent of GDP (low government consumption on social services), it is in line with

34. Econometric evidence is presented in the section 4.5.

those of other countries. The government has been investing about 2.2 per cent to 4.3 per cent of GDP and transferring the rest to socialist enterprises for investment. The public sector (state + socialist enterprises) therefore has a high share of national profits and consequently China can have both low tax rates and very high investment rates.

As an illustration, consider the situation when the State owned 100 per cent of the capital assets. A capital-output ratio of 4 along with an 8 per cent rate of return on assets would have resulted in non-tax revenues of 32 per cent of GDP.[35] Thus reinvestment of public returns to capital along with FDI inflows of 8 per cent of GDP (7.4 per cent in 1993, 5 per cent in 2002) would result in a 40 per cent investment rate without recourse to any taxes. Gross fixed investment was less than 31 per cent of GDP till 1992 and reached 40 per cent in 2002. Any tax revenues could therefore be used to subsidise certain types of exports/FDI.

As the Table 6.1 shows, Chinese government's direct investment (including in infrastructure) was the same in China as in India during 1993 to 2000. It rose sharply in China during 2001 and 2002 but has returned to earlier levels in 2003.

Table 6.1

Gross Investment of Government as a Per cent of GDP

	Average		*1993-94*	*1994-95*	*1995-96*	*1996-97*	*1997-98*	*1998-99*	*1999-2000*	*2000-01*
	93-2000	*93-2002*								
India										
Admin. Dep+DPE	3.1%	3.0%	3.6%	3.7%	3.5%	3.2%	3.0%	3.0%	3.2%	1.8%
Admin. Depts	1.7%	1.7%	1.7%	1.9%	1.8%	1.7%	1.4%	1.6%	1.7%	1.7%
China										
Govt Invest	3.1%	3.3%	2.8%	2.9%	2.7%	2.7%	3.1%	3.5%	3.4%	3.5%

Source: China's data from Kuijs (2005); India's data from NAS.

High rates of investment in infrastructure since the mid-1990s may have reflected a change in the allocation of public expenditure, initially

35. According to Prof. Xianon Xue of the China Europe International Business School, Shanghai, the earning before interest and tax (EBIT) has fallen from 12 per cent of assets in 1992 to 4 per cent in 2003. He also indicated that FDI was 7 per cent of total investment and that the bulk of investment was still made by government firms.

driven by the unemployment created by SOE closure and weaker export demand during the Asian crises.[36] This investment was not however, carried out directly by the government. The government however, "financed investment via capital transfers to state-owned enterprises in the power, electricity, water, transport and other infrastructure sectors (Kuijs, 2005).' The transfers were 6.2 per cent of GDP in 2001 (*op cit*) and the excess of government saving over investment was only 3.7 per cent of GDP. This implies that 2.5 per cent of GDP must have gone as subsidy from government to SOEs. In any case a substantial part of China's infrastructure investment seems to be through enterprises (socialist and foreign JVs).[37]

Table 6.2

Enterprise Investment and Saving

	1990	*1991*	*1992*	*1993*	*1994*	*1995*	*1996*	*1997*	*1998*	*1999*	*2000*	*2001*
Enterprises												
Investment	24.7%	25.3%	28.5%	35.5%	33.2%	32.9%	30.6%	29.1%	28.6%	28.4%	27.3%	29.0%
Saving	11.5%	13.0%	13.4%	16.2%	16.0%	16.4%	13.4%	14.2%	14.1%	14.1%	15.5%	15.0%
Invest-Saving	13.2%	12.3%	15.1%	19.3%	17.2%	16.5%	17.2%	14.9%	14.5%	14.3%	11.8%	14.0%

Source: Kuijs (2005).

Table 6.2 shows the very high rates of investment by enterprises ranging from 24.7 per cent of GDP to 35.5 per cent of GDP during the 1990s. It is consistent with the hypothesis of this chapter that investment by 'socialist owned' enterprises ('public sector') has played an important role in China's growth.

The USSR's early growth was also founded on high levels of government investment. Growth however stalled after the economy reached middle-income, because the USSR was largely cut-off from the global economy and the global technology pool. This lack of concern for

36. Around 1994-95 many SOEs were shut resulting in large pockets of unemployment. The Asian crises added to this by weakening of global demand for China's exports, thus increasing the losses from exports by government owned firms. Infrastructure spending was therefore increased in the second half of the nineties so as to increase job creation (Keynesian aspect). The positive effect on China's image were soon recognised and publicised effectively to attract more FDI, including export-oriented FDI.

37. See Virmani (2004d) for an analysis of the policy approach needed for development of infrastructure in India.

social benefit-cost means that the marginal product of public capital may fall to zero or even become negative because of excess capacity. We know from the USSR experience that this can lead to unsaleable inventory stock, falling capacity utilisation and collapse. Though inventory investment in China reached a peak of 10.4 per cent of GDP in 1989 it had declined 0.2 per cent of GDP by 2002.[38] China therefore appears to have successfully dealt with this problem so far by liberalising output/product markets and orienting its system to push exports. The former helps avoid obvious mismatches between consumer/user demand and public sector output. Despite this, exports are an important channel for utilising excess capacity in tradable goods, a version of the old 'vent for surplus,' with marginal cost pricing and indirect subsidies aiding this effort. Such exports can (also) help in exploiting scale economies by building plants with capacity larger than domestic demand. The unabashed promotion of export-oriented FDI has proved to be a vital means for achieving efficient and sustainable export growth. Because global export shares have to be raised at such a frenetic pace a fall in unit values is inevitable in some goods and markets.[39]

Rising implicit subsidies and declining returns to public capital will eventually make it difficult to maintain such high rates of public investment. Listing of government owned companies and banks on foreign and domestic stock exchanges is a clever way to get foreign equity capital to finance public investment. This suggests return on capital may already be so low as to create a shortage of funds for investment and implicit subsidy. Lardy (1999) estimates that the rate of return on capital in State owned enterprises has fallen from 25 per cent at the start of reform to 6 per cent in 1997.[40] Lardy also estimates that the consequent decline in public saving from 30 per cent of GDP to 20 per cent has been more than offset by a rise in household saving from 0 per cent to 20 per cent of GDP (overwhelmingly in banks or currency).[41]

38. The previous peak was 8.4 per cent of GDP in 1978.

39. This is happening for instance in textile exports to the USA.

40. If ROC has fallen over a decade by 8 per cent points in (showpiece) publicly listed companies (Prof Xue, foot note 10), then the ROC in other government firms is likely to average between 0-4 per cent.

41. Profitability of SOEs has however jumped up sharply in the last two years of phenomenally high growth.

It would not surprise if international capital markets readily provide these funds on the illusion that this means privatisation of government companies or banks.[42] If these funds are not forthcoming or when they run out, China will have to alter its development strategy more fundamentally.

The exceptionally high aggregate growth rates of the past few years have made even normally loss making units temporarily profitable. This is however unlikely to be maintained when growth rates return to normal levels (historical averages).

Engine: FDI and Exports

Foreign direct investment is the second pillar of China's growth. China has learnt from and built upon the experience of Singapore, Thailand and Malaysia, the pioneers of FDI-export led growth. It has aggressively pursued FDI by identifying potential FDI investors across the globe, including in other successful low and middle-income countries. It has then laid out a red carpet for every FD investor that can help raise China's technological levels, skills and expertise or can directly or indirectly raise the level of exports on a sustainable basis. The welcome mat included all inducements needed to ensure that they set up base in China (including capital subsidies). Since 1997, FDI has been between 3.2 per cent and 4.9 per cent of GDP. According to Kuijs (2005) net external financing of enterprise investment—from the banking sector and via net foreign direct investment (FDI)—is high compared to other countries and contributes 1/3rd of investment finance.

FDI and exports have been the engine of efficient economic growth since 1985 though their relative importance has varied over time. Adoption of an FDI-export led growth strategy converted China from an autarchy into an essential link in the global production chain developed between 1965 and 1985 by the newly industrialising economies and the ASEAN-4. China created conditions (suspension of labour rights, capital subsidies to counter every negative) for a wholesale shift of labour-intensive (LI) production by Chinese entrepreneurs from Hong Kong,

42. As Abraham Lincoln said, "You can fool all the people some of the time," perhaps in China a lot more time than he imagined.

Taiwan and other countries in South-East Asia to the special export zones and regions. 59.3 per cent of FDI between 1978 and 1999 came from Hong Kong, Taiwan and Macao.[43] The share was much higher in the initial years and has declined over time. It was 68.2 per cent in 1994 and 40.2 per cent in 2003 (Prasad and Wei, 2005). Detailed data for 1995 shows that the share of foreign invested enterprises (foreign equity share $\geq$ 25 per cent) in manufactured exports was 51.2 per cent. FIE's share in exports of electronics and telecommunications was 94.5 per cent, in instruments 71.8 per cent, in plastic products 77.2 per cent, in printing and record pressing 79.4 per cent, in furniture 79.4 per cent, in leather products 73.2 per cent, in metal products 61.1 per cent and in garments and footwear 60.5 per cent (Huang, 2003, Table 1.4). Another 17 per cent of manufactured exports take place through export processing where the buyer supplies the inputs, detailed designs and specifications and quality inspection and control personel and gets back the output for export.[44] Thus these labour-intensive (LI) export goods are now highly competitive. Along with the support system provided by the socialist-corporate state, this gives China a comparative advantage in organised labour-intensive mass manufacturing.

The conventional wisdom is that China's phenomenal success in LI exports is due to the superior productivity of Chinese workers. In reality the per-hour worker productivity is not much different from that in any other country at a similar level of income (perhaps lower). The output per man-month is however much higher because hours worked per week/month are up to 100 per cent higher than in equivalent democratic market economies, being unconstrained by (implementation of) bourgeois labour laws. Now that China has developed a comparative advantage in mass manufacturing and construction, it is likely to persist even if hours worked gradually decline from 'socialist' to 'democratic' levels.

Non-labour intensive exports (even those produced by FDI) are not necessarily competitive. The banking system provides loans to State enterprises (e.g. SOEs) and provincial/city governments producing

43. Almost 50 per cent was from Hong Kong during 1979 to 1999 (Huang, 2003: 6, 48).

44. Huang, 2003: 15. The share of HK & Taiwan in FDI was 61.8 per cent in 1995, and another 4.9 per cent was from Singapore.

intermediate goods and infrastructure services respectively at zero or negative effective capital cost. These implicit subsidies are then transformed through below cost prices, into explicit subsidies to the FDI-export complex and to hi-tech industry.[45] This is a significant factor in attracting hi-tech/skill-intensive FDI and capital-intensive exports. Through this process some competitive items are undoubtedly discovered or created and these, along with less than competitive items, are part of the set of capital-intensive (KI) and skill-intensive (SI) exports.

The banking losses arising from these implicit subsidies have been repeatedly capitalised by the government budget during the last five years. If this is a real rather than a paper transaction, the enterprise profits available for re-investment will be reduced. In this case either taxes on the FDI-export sector have to increase or the supply of free public services has to be reduced.[46] The former either undermines the usefulness and sustainability of the high public investment that is the foundation of China's growth maximisation strategy or offsets the subsidies given to the FDI export sector (increasing inefficiency).

In the post Asian crises decade, the first class infrastructure in and around the FDI-export hubs is advertised as an important factor in the high share/growth of KI and SI exports from China. The building of showpiece infrastructure well ahead of demand certainly helps in attracting attention and approbation from investors and adds to the attractiveness of China as an FDI location. Further, even if infrastructure is highly underutilised it is a permanent asset that will become useful at some time. However, if its marginal social return is zero or negative, the sustainability of the public reinvestment strategy becomes doubtful as returns dwindle making it necessary to raise distorting taxes. It should also not be forgotten that poor infrastructure in Jakarta, Indonesia and Bangkok, Thailand did not prevent these two countries from growing fast for decades.

Tseng and Zebregs (2002) estimate that FDI contributed 2.5 per cent per annum to TFP growth and about 3 per cent per annum to

45. The prices of intermediate goods in China are reportedly less than their price on the high seas outside India—i.e before taxes, delays or red tape.

46. The latter is related to the income distribution point discussed below.

overall GDP growth. This suggests that the difference between China's and India's growth rate since 1980 can largely be explained by the difference in FDI inflows (including export-oriented FDI).

Empirical Analysis

The following OLS growth regressions for China for the period 1982 to 2002 based on data available in World Development Indicators 2002, support the analysis presented above. All variables are in growth rates (represented by the preface Gr). The independent variable is growth rate of per capita GDP. Dependent variables are the rates of growth (Gr) of Gross Fixed Capital Formation (GFCF), World GDP (Gwrld) and FDI gross in US $ (FDIg$):

GrPcGdp=0.54+0.24*GrGfcf+0.12*GrGfcf(-1)+1.03 GrGwrld+0.017*GrFDIg$

(1.0) (3.6)*** (3.9)*** (4.6)*** (2.5)***

R^2 = 0.96, R^2 (adjusted) = 0.95, DW = 2.1. Numbers in bracket are t values. *** is significant at 1 per cent level.

Similar results are obtained using TSLS.[47] The export dependency of the Chinese economy is suggested by the fact that a 1 per cent increase (decrease) in the rate of growth of the world economy raises (lowers) China's growth rate by 1 per cent.

If we replace gross FDI by net FDI (FDIn$ is in US $) the equation becomes;

GrPcGdp=132-0.07*Year+0.26*GrGfcf+0.1*GrGfcf (-1)+0.78*GrGwrld-0.54*GrFDIn$

(1.8)* (-1.8)* (7.6)*** (4.0)*** (3.6)*** (-2.1)*

R^2 = 0.94, R^2 (adjusted) = 0.92, DW = 2.1. Numbers in bracket are t values. * is significant at 10 per cent level, *** is significant at 1 per cent level.[48]

---

47. Instruments include growth rates of world imports, China's population & labour force and exports (lagged).

48. If the same equation is run with TSLS, year and FDIn$ become non-significant. If year is dropped from the equation, FDIn$ is significant at the 10 per cent level.

Thus, a 1 per cent increase (decrease) in net FDI inflow increases the per capita GDP growth rate by 0.5 per cent.

These regressions show the strong investment led nature of China's growth and the role of world demand GDP on China's growth. The latter represents the opportunity for exports at unsubsidised rates or without lowering unit values. FDI plays an important role in China's growth. These results are consistent with an FDI-export led growth.

The importance of FDI is also brought out by the following sources of growth equation (estimated for 1966 onwards) in which the prefix Gr represents the growth rate, Gdp_L represents GDP per unit of labour and Kf_L is fixed capital per unit of labour:[49]

GrGdp_L = 1.47+0.832*GrKf_L+0.283*AR(1)

(1.9) (2.9)*** (1.9)*

R^2 = 0.29, R^2 (adjusted) = 0.24, DW = 1.79.[50]

Using the parameters of this equation we can calculate TFPG as,

TFPGa = GrGdp_L – 0.832*GrKf_L or TFPG= TFPGa-1.47.

Then by OLS,

TFPG = 478 – 0.24*year + 0.04*FDIg$z

(4.4)*** (-4.4)*** (5.9)***

R^2 = 0.83, R^2 (adjusted) = 0.81, DW = 1.88.

This equation shows that,

(a) FDI is a driver of productivity growth.

(b) There is a secular down trend in productivity growth. We hypothesise that this is the result of excessive investment by socialist enterprises and the consequent decline in marginal productivity of capital in these enterprises. The high investment is the counterpart of the party encouraged/sanctioned objective of growth (value added) maximisation, low or zero dividend payment

49. The capital stock series is built using perpetual inventory method using GFCF and assuming a 5 per cent depreciation rate.

50. Capital's share is much lower (0.54) and DW very low if we estimate from 1977 onwards.

requirement, transfer of saving from the government budget and subsidies provided through the controlled banking system (so called NPAs).

During the period of fast world GDP and world trade growth starting around 2003-04, the importance of exports in driving growth increased relative to that of investment. The global economic crises of 2008 has returned the growth drivers to the earlier position. In fact, the relative role of investment is likely to remain very high for 3 to 5 years.

Outcome

Income Growth

If we go by the official statistics, China's economy grew at an average rate of 9.5 per cent per annum during 1980 to 2003, the fastest in the world. During this period the world share of China in merchandise trade saw the largest expansion and China became the largest recipient of FDI. Collins and Bosworth (1996), corroborated later by the World Bank and IMF, have shown that China's growth from 1980 to end-nineties was overestimated by 1 per cent to 2 per cent. Young (2000) shows that non-agricultural growth is overestimated by 2.5 per cent. If we make an adjustment of 2 per cent, China has demonstrated its ability to sustain growth at about 7.5 per cent per annum over 25 years. This is still the fastest in the world, but only 30 per cent higher than India's, the 9th fastest growing economy.[51] The IMF (2004) has, however, shown that China's growth (as measured by official statistics) was on a trajectory similar to that of Japan and the NIEs in a similar period of their development, though it was faster than that of the ASEAN-4.

In the last few decades, China's growth has benefited from the demographic dividend. As the demographic transition is coming to an end this dividend will soon be reduced to zero.[52] The 1990s were a period of above average international trade growth and the current decade could see a slower growth in goods trade. As China's share of the

51. About 60 per cent higher in terms of per capita growth.

52. After a decade or two it will become negative because of the rapid ageing of its population.

world's goods exports rises to US levels its export growth will slow. China has also benefited from the large gap between its per capita income and its manufacturing wage relative to India and other labour intensive exporters. The gap is likely to be eliminated as its per capita income rises to upper-middle income levels and then to high-income levels. The closing and inversion of the wage gap will contribute to the slowdown in export growth and FDI inflows. Most observers have been forecasting a slowdown in China's growth rate and a few have even predicted a dramatic slowdown.[53] On balance, China's growth rate is likely to decline gradually to more normal levels from the stratospheric double digit rates achieved recently.

Income Distribution

The distribution of income has worsened dramatically since 1979. Part of this deterioration is the reversal of unsustainable levels of equality reached during the Maoist years. The rest of the deterioration was a conscious decision to accelerate growth by focussing subsidies and infrastructure development into the FDI-export areas in the coastal regions during 1985 to 2000. Given the restrictions on internal movement of workers (the labour responsibility system) this translated into growing income inequality. Out of total of 127 countries China ranks 91 in terms of the Gini co-efficient of inequality, and 94th in terms of the consumption share of the poorest 20 per cent of the population. Further, the retreat of the State from provision of social goods has also translated into greater inequality in the receipt of public and quasi-public goods. Rising inequality and declining public social services have a potential for socio-political upheaval and counter repression that could disrupt growth.

Risks

The FDI-export drive is critically dependent on building and sustaining optimistic expectations about the economy and the Asian crises demonstrated the vulnerability of this model. The obverse of high social ownership of domestic assets and consequent high investment rates is a

53. See IMF, World Bank and ADB reports on China and Chang (2001). See also Virmani (1999).

low share of private consumption in GDP. The rate of capacity build up is much faster than the growth of private consumption, leaving exports as the only means for balancing supply and demand. China's membership of WTO and rising job fears in OECD countries will result in increased scrutiny of and resistance to subsidised exports. Its socially regressive labour rules for export oriented manufacturing, may also be questioned more seriously, if not by governments then by Western labour unions and NGOs. China has however taken premtive action by changing the formal labour laws.

Given the resumption of generation of non-performing assets, China is somewhat more vulnerable on these issues than the Asian crises countries.[54] Its income distribution is also worse than in other successful Asian economies. On the other hand, China's large economy has domestic strengths and bargaining power that were absent in the smaller Asian countries. These will result (in our judgement) in a slowing of growth and not a sudden collapse if the CCP/government continues to adapt its policy to the changing circumstances and imperatives as it has repeatedly done since 1980.

One of the ironic effects of China's export-led growth is the recreation of centre-periphery relationship that a Latin American economist talked about 50 years ago. Instead of the USA of the fifties, China of the 21st century is the manufacturing workshop of the world, diverting FDI in manufacturing (including export-oriented FDI) out of other developing countries, while sucking in mineral and agricultural imports from them. Thus the resource rich countries of Asia, Africa and Latin America are the (new) periphery supplying primary commodities to China, the new manufacturing centre of the world. Just as in the case of 20th century America, a reaction may build up against 21st century China.

Politics

There are political arguments for a sharp slowdown in economic growth arising from rising inequalities and social tensions. Some have gone further to argue that there is an inherent contradiction between the

54. Which have resulted in a (World Bank estimated) national debt of 50 per cent to 100 per cent of GDP. See Jia Kang & Quan-hou (2001).

market economy whose success requires competition and plurality and the centralised political system that suppresses independent democratic thinking and impulses.[55] If the contradiction cannot be managed, it has within it the seeds of a socio-political explosion that will bring growth to a halt for a substantial period of time (after which it could resume at a much slower rate). This contradiction is much more than it was in South Korea (say) and the latter eventually succumbed to the democratic impulse. The counter-argument is that dictators can and have maintained highly repressive regime for decades after upheaval. Whether growth rate can be maintained along with repression depends on the response of the rest of the world.

Comparative Performance: India

Reform Impact: J Curve

According to India's national accounts data, GDP and per capita GDP have grown at an average of 5.8 per cent per annum and 3.8 per cent per annum respectively during 25 years from 1980-81 to 2004-05.[56] The comprehensive reforms instituted in the 1990s have increased competitive pressures on the Indian economy while at the same time enhancing its ability to compete globally. The growth rate had however increased by only about 0.6 per cent point.[57] The opening of the economy to international trade seems to produce a J-curve effect. The direct negative effects of competition appear immediately as capacity utilisation falls in uncompetitive product lines. With capital immobile, reduction in capital stock is limited by the rate of depreciation. The positive effects of competition on productivity appear gradually. New technology is first adopted by the pioneers and effected through new investment. It diffuses gradually to other firms in the industry.[58]

55. K. Subrahmanyam.

56. The WDI data underestimates the GDP growth rate substantially though the per capita GDP growth rate is almost the same.

57. From 5.5 per cent per annum during 1980-81 to 1991-92 to 6.1 per cent during 1992-1993 to 2003-04. Per capita GDP growth accelerated by 1 per cent point from 3.3 per cent to 4.3 per cent per annum.

58. There are numerous cases of firms that have transformed their systems and shown large increases in productivity. The effects of these are not however available in the sector data.

Improvements in productivity will therefore appear at the aggregate level only after a lag. The underlying medium term trend rate of growth in India was around 6.5 per cent in 2004 and was anticipated to move up to 6.8 per cent.

Figure 6.1

Medium Term Trend in India's Growth—J Curve of Liberalisation

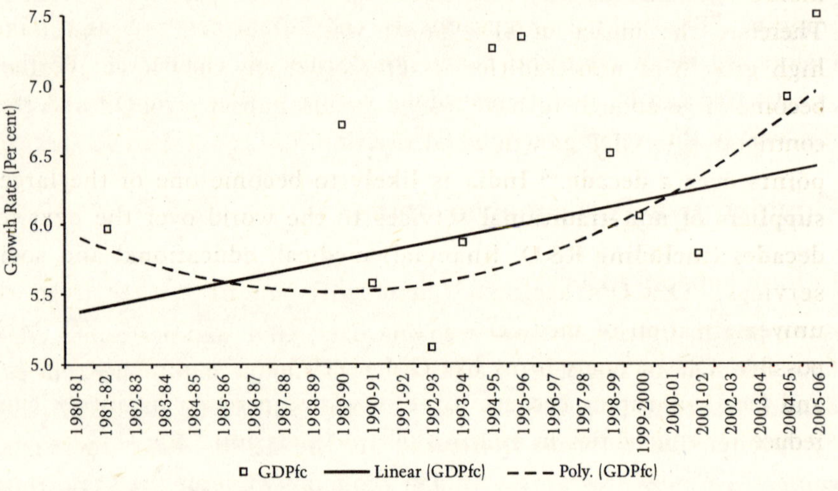

Source: Authors calculations based on World Bank, WDI and Poverty data.

It was argued in 2005, that the growth rate could be raised further to 7 per cent to 7.5 per cent thereafter if policy and institutional reforms resume. The policy reforms include removal of controls on a host of sectors and sub-sectors that are the basis of the jungle of red tape and lead to bureaucratic delays, labour reform and lifting of entry restrictions in education (see Virmani, 2004a for details).[59] Three specific (modern services, FDI, demographic transition) and three general factors were cited in justification of the feasibility and sustainability of a higher growth rate.

59. This book summarises the reforms proposed in a series of internal papers done in the Ministry of Finance (Department of Economic Affairs), Government of India, from 1995 onwards. The underlying theme of these suggestions is to increase competition in every market and sector by removing the distortions introduced by the Indian version of socialism and to focus government effort on the supply of public and quasi-public goods and services.

Services: Exports to GDP

First, the one area in which the improved competitiveness of the Indian economy is clearly visible is in the double-digit (20 per cent to 30 per cent per year) growth of information technology (IT) and IT-enabled services (ITES) export. Though such non-traditional (i.e., excluding transport and tourism) service exports are already a significant share of India's total exports, they constituted a very small part of the economy. Therefore, the impact on GDP growth was limited. With the continuing high growth of non-traditional service export, they have gradually become large enough to have a measurable impact on GDP and their contribution to GDP growth could rise from 0.5 per cent to 1.5 per cent points over a decade.[60] India is likely to become one of the largest suppliers of non–traditional services to the world over the next few decades (including R&D, financial, medical, educational and social services). OECD's ageing citizens will benefit greatly from the universalisation of medical services that their lower cost will make possible. Old economy firms like GM which have become uncompetitive and face bankruptcy because of accumulated pension liabilities, could reduce these liabilities in exchange for provision of health services.

FDI: Unexploited Potential

The second factor is the unexploited potential of foreign direct investment (FDI). The proportion of FDI in total investment and GDP was very low in India compared to other high growth Asian countries such as Singapore, Malaysia, Thailand, China, Indonesia and Vietnam. In contrast to China's FDI-export led growth model, India's growth has been led by domestic investment and entrepreneurship.[61] The positive role of FDI in growth (marketing, technology, management systems) is gradually being exploited with a rise of FDI flows to $8bi to $10bi per annum and then to over $ 30billion (inflow). This will give a substantial boost to productivity and growth.[62] India is already an attractive location for skill-intensive manufacturing because of the high quality and availability of

60. Starting at the lower end and going up to the higher end of the range.

61. See Khanna and Huang (2003) for a comparison with China.

62. Several ICRIER working papers by Rashmi Banga have shown the positive effects of FDI in India.

middle management/technical skills and knowledge workers. Several areas of competitiveness related to such skills are already visible, namely biotechnology, auto engineering (parts) and specialised chemicals.[63]

With China's per capita income more than twice that of India's and its per capita consumption 50 per cent more than India's, its hourly wage will eventually attain the same ratio. Membership of the WTO and scrutiny by global NGOs will make it increasingly difficult for foreign invested firms in China to make people work 100 hours a week. India will therefore become a more attractive location for small & medium scale labour-intensive manufactured exports *vis-à-vis* China. The special economic zone (SEZ) law can reduce red tape/bureaucracy. However, it has not introduced much needed flexibility in labour laws, rules and procedures and has still to accelerate development of high quality infrastructure.[64] FDI can continue to play a role in integrating India into the global supply chain for a host of products. If domestic hurdles to global operation are removed, FDI could add at least a point to growth.

Demographic Dividend

The third important factor is the demographic transition that is taking place across the world. The high growth of East and South East Asian countries was to a substantial degree due to the demographic transition (Bloom *et al.*, 2001). This is the ∩ (inverted U) shape followed by the ratio of labour force to population.[65] With the supply of labour rising faster than population per capita GDP growth accelerates. Further the changes in the age profile (a decline in the average age of the labour force) results in a rise in the aggregate saving rate ensuring sufficient funds for investment. China is nearing the end of its demographic transition with the labour force beginning to age and its faster growth period coming to an end. India in contrast has entered the most positive phase of this demographic transition. This could add between 0.5 per cent to 0.8 per cent points to the growth of the Indian economy.

---

63. With the introduction of a product patent regime from this year, the protection of the legal system will now be available to drug developers.

64. Sadly the provision for labour flexibility was dropped from the law at the insistence of the CPM & CPI.

65. The dependency ratio follows a U shape first falling then rising.

In addition the population of Europe and Japan is ageing rapidly and there will be a great demand from these economies for 'youth-intensive' goods and services, including R&D services.[66] Over the next half century India will have the youngest labour force in the world. India is therefore likely to become the largest exporter of such 'youth-intensive services'.[67]

Intangibles

There are also several general factors that will sustain growth. One is the existence of a large underutilised pool of free thinking, autonomous working, high IQ people. The normal distribution of IQ in a population means that 2 per cent of population has very high IQ and 10 per cent has high IQ. Applying this to India we get 20 mi and 100 mi people respectively. Bad economic policies till 1980 contributed to gross underutilisation of this resource. The utilisation rate of underutilised brain power will increasingly rise along with the literacy rate, universalisation of primary education and better information about opportunities.

The second is the high quality and diversity of India's institutions and the social capital built over centuries.[68] The democratic system, including the relatively new non-governmental institutions and free and vibrant media, is a great source of long-term strength. Rodrik and Subramanian (2004) estimate that India's (China's) income level is 15 per cent lower (higher) than that predicted by the quality of its institutions. India's income will therefore rise to the predicted level with the correction of wrong policies, while China will not be able to sustain the same growth at higher income levels where these institutions are critical.

The third is the experience of working with citizens of very diverse backgrounds (religious, ethnic, language, sub-culture) and the facility

66. For instance a study has shown that Nobel Price winners in Physics did their most productive work below or around the age of 25.

67. As China's population will age much earlier than that of India, it is not in a position to exploit this opportunity.

68. China had similarly high levels of social capital but much of this was destroyed during the communist revolution and the cultural revolution.

with English. This pluralism and language facility is a unique advantage in the globalised 21st century. India is also ideally placed to partner OECD countries in the emerging global knowledge economy of the 21st century. These specific and general factors were viewed in 2005 sufficient to overcome any negative growth factors, to raise growth to a sustainable 7 per cent to 7.5 per cent.[69]

The analysis of Virmani (2009) shows that the trend rate of growth of the Indian Economy has risen to 8.5 to 9 per cent by 2008-09. This has happened despite the weakness and risks noted in this chapter. However, Virmani (2009) points out that maintaining high growth of this order requires continuing reforms.

Poverty

There are some questions raised by India-sceptics about poverty and inequality in India, which have to be viewed in the light of the following facts. India is a low-income country, so the proportion of poor is still high (about 22 per cent according to conventional methods).[70] The absolute number of poor is thus larger than the total population of all but two countries (USA and China). It is democratic so the poor are free to live and work anywhere and are therefore visible everywhere. India's income distribution is, however, among the top quarter of the 127 countries for which the Gini co-efficient is available.[71] It does very well for the poorest 10 per cent whose consumption share is the 6th highest among these 127 countries.[72] India is one of a handful of high growth countries whose income distribution has not worsened significantly during the high growth period.[73] By 2010, when India becomes a lower-middle income country, the conventionally measured poverty rate will be

69. A more optimistic scenario is also possible in which growth reaches the 7.5-8 per cent range and remains there for a decade or so. The probability of this is 10-15 per cent in our view. Surjit Bhalla has been asserting for the last three years that India's growth rate will soon exceed 8 per cent.

70. The poverty rate or head count ratio is 29th out of 87 countries for which data is reported.

71. 32nd to be precise.

72. 14th for consumption share of bottom 20 per cent and 25th for bottom 40 per cent of the population.

73. Cornea and Court (2001).

reduced to about 15 per cent.[74] Poverty is likely to be completely eliminated by the time it becomes an upper-middle income country around 2025.[75]

According to Bhalla (2003) the poverty rate is about 12 per cent. This is the correct rate for comparison with that of China as shown by the following simple exercise. China's poverty level based on an income survey was estimated by the World Bank to be 16.5 per cent using a $1 a day poverty line and 46.7 per cent using a $2 a day poverty line. As India's poverty rate is based on a consumption survey, we have to either assume that the consumption share of China are the same as its income shares (estimate 1) or that its consumption shares in the two lowest (10 per cent each) brackets are higher than its income shares in these brackets (estimate 2). In the latter case we assume further that in China the consumption share of the bottom 10 per cent is 50 per cent higher than the income share and of the next lowest 10 per cent is 25 per cent is higher.[76] From the data we also see that China's per capita GDP at PPP in current international dollars was 1.6 times India's (average ratio for 1999 to 2001). As the share of private consumption in GDP in China was 71 per cent of that in India,[77] China's per capita private consumption was only 1.1 times India's (average for 1999 to 2001). Using the consumption distribution along with the per capita private consumption we can calculate the per capita consumption of the bottom 10, 20 and 40 per cent of the population in each country (Table 6.2).

The results in Table 6.3 show that the per capita consumption of China's poorest 10 per cent to 20 per cent is between 52 per cent and 80 per cent of India's poorest 10 per cent to 20 per cent in real terms. Thus

---

74. Based on official rate in 1999-2000 (26 per cent) adjusted for survey changes (i.e., 28-29 per cent). We assume a decline of 1 per cent point per year based on the average decline since 1980.

75. Before that the national poverty line will probably be raised.

76. As the rich are widely accepted to save a larger share of their income than the poor, the consumption distribution is expected to be better than the income distribution.

77. China's private consumption (Total consumption-Government final consumption) is 46.8 per cent and India's 65.5 per cent of GDP (LCU). All data is from WDI, World Bank.

the 1$ a day poverty rate in India must be lower than in China (16.5 per cent). Similarly the $2 a day poverty rate in China (46.7 per cent) is unlikely to be lower than India's because the per capita consumption of the bottom 40 per cent in China is 80 per cent to 100 per cent of that of the lowest 40 per cent in India.

Table 6.3

Per Capita Consumption of the Poor in China Relative to India

	Estimate 1		*Estimate 2*
Lowest 10%	0.52		0.78
Lowest 20%	0.59		0.79
Lowest 40%	0.82		0.97
China Share		*Adj Factor*	
Lowest 10%	1.8	1.5	2.7
Lowest 20%	4.7	1.35	6.3
Lowest 40%	9.0	1.18	10.6
India Share			
Lowest 10%	3.9	1	3.9
Lowest 20%	8.9	1	8.9
Lowest 40%	12.3	1	12.3

Note: Estimate 1 assumes China's consumption distribution. Estimate 2 obtains China's consumption share by increasing its income share of lowest 10 per cent by 50 per cent and increasing that of next 10 per cent by 25 per cent.

Source: Authors calculations based on World Bank, WDI and Poverty data.

Governance Issues

The greatest long-term weakness in India is on the political side. Infirmities in its political system have led over the last four decades, to a deterioration in the quality and quantity of public goods (roads, policing, legal system.) and quasi-public goods supplied. The high fiscal deficit is a symptom of this deterioration in governance. Differences in quality of governance across States are also an important cause of rising interstate differences in growth rates and poverty (head-count ratio). The governments' lack of success in suppressing Maoist and other insurgencies in the interiors of the country is another reflection of government failure. The issue is not, however, one of corruption but the supply of public and quasi-public goods and services (e.g. public safety and security, urban planning, water supply, sewage and sanitation, roads, airports, highways) and government monopolised utilities (electricity). China's government(s) at different levels are not less corrupt than India's but the former produce the public goods and services necessary for growth while the latter do not.[78]

Political/governmental reforms are necessary over the next decade to ensure that the system remains on even keel.[79] This downtrend in governance must be reversed and one is optimistic that it will be reversed, given the strength of non-governmental institutions such as the media and non-profit organisations and the more active role of the higher judiciary and independent bodies such as the Election Commission. Though Indian democracy responds slowly to such intangible threats, it has always been able to deal with them in a democratic and non-disruptive manner.

Future: Mean Forecast

Based on the above analysis we project the size of China and India relative to the USA and relative to each other (Figures 6.2 and 6.3) based on the assumptions in Table 6.3.[80]

Table 6.4

Rate of Growth of GDP at PPP (per cent)

Period	*India*	*China*
2006 to 2010	6.4	7.3
2011 to 2020	7.0	6.5
2021 to 2030	6.9	5.5
2031 to 2040	6.0	4.4
2041 to 2050	5.0	3.5

Source: Authors calculations based on World Bank, WDI and Poverty data.

78. Sadly the public has for too long let governments get away with non-performance on public goods under the obfuscation that it is working for (spending resources on) the welfare of the poor. This appears to be changing along with greater competition in the media.

79. See Virmani (2004a) for the new development paradigm needed for high growth in India.

80. See Virmani (2005a) for the assumptions and more detailed discussion.

Figure 6.2 shows that the Indian economy is likely to become larger than Japan's (GDP at Purchasing Power Parity) in the next few years. It also shows that both the Chinese economy and the Indian economy will

Figure 6.2

Size of China and India Relative to the USA

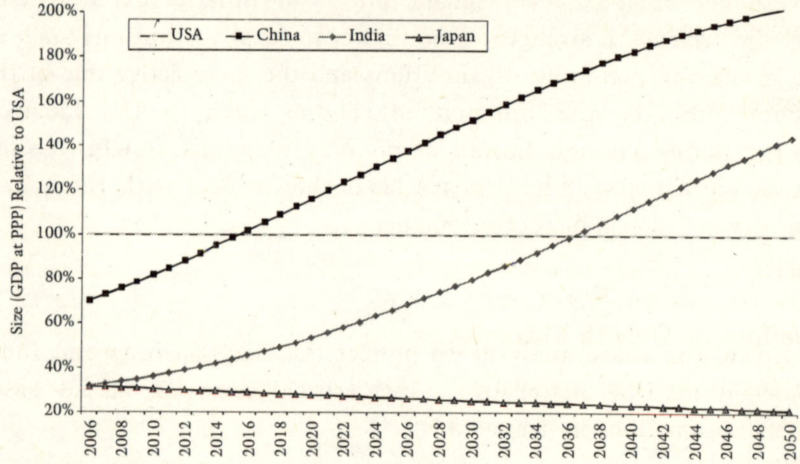

Source: Authors calculations based on World Bank, WDI and Poverty data.

Figure 6.3

Indian Economy Relative to China

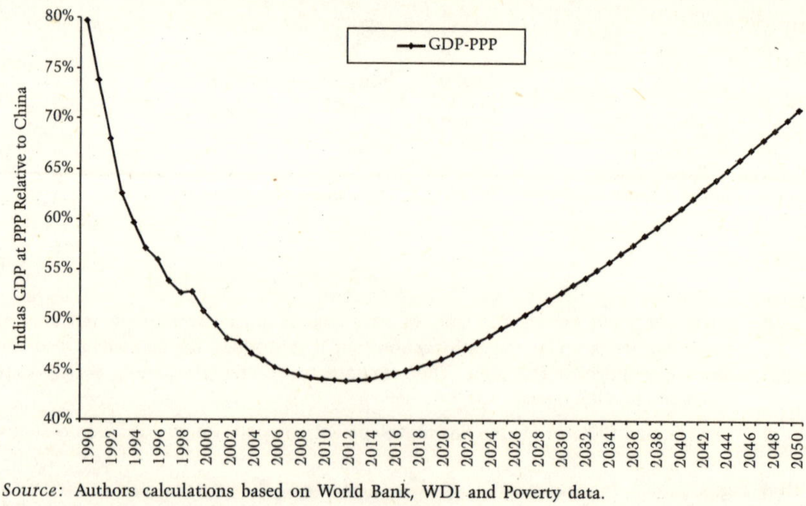

Source: Authors calculations based on World Bank, WDI and Poverty data.

become larger than that of the USA in about 10 years and 30 years respectively. Figure 6.3 shows the size of India's economy relative to China's. India's economy which was equal in size to that of China in 1983 was already down to 80 per cent by 1990. It is currently about 45 per cent of China's and will decline further before starting to recover sometime in the next decade. According to our mean projections, however, the catch-up process will take decades. By 2050, India's economy will be only 70 per cent the size of China's.

Lessons

In this section we summarise some of the lessons arising from the above analysis of the Chinese economy, viewed from the perspective of the Indian economy and India's growth experience. These lessons therefore implicitly incorporate an India-China comparative perspective.

Welfare or Growth Maximisation

In theory, we can always construct a set of assumptions in which growth maximisation is identical to social welfare maximisation. The issue here is about the outcome of one or the other strategy in practice.

A growth maximisation strategy is clear, focused, easy to understand and implement. Growth maximisation is related to maximisation of value added, sales/production, and long term employment at the firm and local government level. It can therefore be relatively easily decentralised down to the lowest levels of government and implemented more efficiently even with low quality of governance. The public sector can also be integrated into this objective without creating dissonance.

A welfare maximisation strategy leads to multiple, often contradictory, objectives. Though rational trade-offs are possible in theory, they are not made in practice and confusion and cross cutting actions are common. This in turn leads to: (a) Detailed rules regulations and procedures for making choices—red tape and bureaucratic functioning. (b) Lack of accountability. It is easy to use one or more objectives (those that are hardest to measure) as an excuse for non-achievement of all others. It also becomes easier to substitute ones personal objectives for the official ones by disguising the former as the latter. (c) Given serious agency problems in governance, particularly in democratic systems, this provides an incentive for inefficiency and corruption.

A growth maximisation strategy subject to reasonable social welfare constraints is superior to a welfare maximisation strategy implemented through subsidiary growth objectives. The former is much more likely to take the largest number of citizens from low-income to high-income category in the shortest possible time. The latter provides greater opportunity to those charged with implementation to increase their own welfare in the name of the poor, consequently resulting in faster deterioration of governance *ipso facto* (other things equal).

Institutions: Micro-Structures

The importance of institutions, defined as laws, rules and social conventions in long run growth is now widely accepted. There are also studies showing the importance of social capital. Institutional micro-foundations or micro-structures, the organisations that implement these laws, rules and conventions have a critical role in economic growth (Virmani, 2004a). One of the lessons that we draw from our study of China and India's growth is, "Do not destroy institutions, modify and adapt them to your development objectives". It is very easy to destroy institutions very difficult and time consuming to build them.

The communist party government that came to power in China in the middle of the last century systematically destroyed what it considered 'capitalist' institutions and organisations. But they also built communist party run organisations during the next 50 years. The post-Mao reformers have adapted the latter to fill the gap left by the former. China has shown that: (a) Even a communist/socialist institution like the CCP can be used to nurture and support capitalist growth. (b) That communist controlled and managed cooperatives, which in the Maoist period undertook a combination of governing and production functions at the local level can be converted into competitive production organisations (town and village enterprises).[81]

81. Even ostensibly negative social institutions such as caste organisations could have been used by India for productive purpose e.g., for promoting literacy or group credit.

The destruction of centuries-old social and market institutions (e.g. private entrepreneurs) under Chairman Mao will, however, prove costly in the long run. Such institutions are particularly important at high income levels, when investors from countries at the same (high income) level are unlikely to find it as advantageous as it is today to set up either export-oriented or high-tech operations in a "socialist market economy" like China relative to a "democratic market economy" like India.

FDI and Trade Liberalisation

FDI bundles capital, 'technology' and entrepreneurship, where 'technology' is defined broadly to include information, knowledge and skills relating to management, marketing and production. The technology part of the bundle is much more important than capital for countries like India and China. For China, the entrepreneurial role of FDI has also been very important.

FDI can be an extremely effective instrument for growth if it helps a country enter the global supply chain. A successful diaspora in a more advanced country is even more effective if it still has a connection to and an interest in the development of the country of origin. The effectiveness of trade liberalisation in promoting growth is enhanced if it can be coupled with attraction of export-oriented FDI. FDI-export led growth has clearly worked in Asia, even if there are both positive and negative examples from other parts of the world. Democratic market economies are unlikely however, to be able to replicate the breakneck expansion of exports and FDI seen in China's socialist market economy (and perhaps even in some "nationalist market economies").

Technological change (embodied in capital goods or intermediates or disembodied) is greatly facilitated by free imports and therefore import restrictions on these have added costs. When bureaucrats decide what and from where capital goods and intermediate goods should be imported by entrepreneurs (QRs), innovation inevitably suffers.

Labour Laws and Rules

The special labour laws and rules for foreign invested enterprises and export producers in China has undoubtedly played a role in attracting export-oriented FDI and increasing labour-intensive exports. India is at the other extreme with very socially advanced labour laws and rules since 1950s (similar at that time to those in the richest countries). These were implemented in a manner that introduced extreme rigidity and restriction in the organised labour market. Rigid rules and bureaucratic procedures have limited the inflow of export-oriented FDI, discouraged the mass production of labour-intensive exports (e.g. garments, toys and consumer electronics) and resulted in slower employment growth in the modern manufacturing sector. India's workers could obtain the full benefits of an open economy if these laws and rules provided for greater flexibility. There is no need for India (or any other country) to go to the other extreme typified by China. In fact, China has finally started the journey away from the extreme by formally notifying some changes in labour laws.

Competition and Public Monopoly

Artificial monopolies, created by reserving industries for the government/public sector i.e., exclusion of private investment, have the most negative effect on efficiency and growth (as they have no redeeming merit). Setting up of government production companies *per se* is not obviously bad, creation of government monopolies and oligopolies clearly is. A competitive market structure is much more important than private ownership for efficient economic growth. Growth maximising and profit maximising monopolies, whether private or public can theoretically be equally (in)efficient initially, but eventually succumb to X-inefficiency. Highly motivated political and administrative leadership (as in post-Independence India or post-Mao CCP rule) can even be more effective initially, but this level of motivation and honesty is seldom sustained over long periods.

The public sector is, however, more likely to be characterised by multiple and incompatible objectives and agency problems. This is primarily responsible for the negative effect of public ownership. Soft budget constraints, poor selection of managers and lack of incentives arise in a context in which everyone and no one owns the firm. Public monopoly multiplies these problems. A monopoly/oligopoly structure coupled with social objectives (even secondary ones) and agency problems distort incentives for managers and can be disastrous for efficient growth. This applies in banking as much as in manufacturing.

The threat of imports (even where imports are low) is the greatest competitive force. In general, free access to imports (i.e., no bans or QRs) is the simplest way to ensure competition, a method that is available to economies of all sizes. Only large economies have the luxury of limiting themselves to domestic competition, but even in their case there will always be some products for which market size and minimum economic scale do not permit much competition.

High-Risk, High-Return Policies

India invested well ahead of demand in higher education in the 1960s just as China is doing in infrastructure since mid-1990. In India's case there was a clear imbalance between investment in basic education relative to higher education. In China's case there is an imbalance between private and public consumption relative to public investment. In hindsight, India's higher education strategy appears to have been highly successful (vide IT and other service exports).

The supply of infrastructure in ASEAN high growth economies generally lagged demand for it, in complete contrast to China, which is building well ahead of demand (eight-lane highways where four-lanes would be sufficient). China's infrastructure investment strategy appeared, till 2007, to be equally successful. India's investment could have been totally wasted if globalisation did not provide a channel of migration and utilisation of skills for which there was no demand in India. China's investment in rich country-style infrastructure could still be wasted if growth slows dramatically. Both are therefore high-risk high-return policies. Large countries like India and China can have diversified portfolio of policies, including a few high risk, high return ones. Small, poor countries should be extremely cautious in adopting any such strategy.

Democracy *versus* Dictatorship

Oligarchies such as Communist party ruled China or dictatorial democracies such as Singapore, post-war Japan and South Korea appear to have been more successful in organising a country to develop from low-income to high-income category. They also have an advantage in mass production and large-scale organised activity including construction. The disadvantages of dictatorship include the stamping out of diversity (language, culture, religion) and dissent.

"Democratic market economies" like India appear to be more successful at generating entrepreneurship, independent thinking and individual responsibility, that is an advantage in the service sector. Even the humblest service provider has greater scope for individual initiative than an assembly line worker and these characteristics are more important in services than in modern manufacturing. These skills are also advantageous in moving from the bottom to the top of the high-income category. India, with its great diversity, coupled with English language facility has an additional advantage in the globalised 21st century. Most managers and professionals have worked with others of different ethnicity, religion, native language etc., and can therefore work easily with people of any nationality or background.

There is however a simultaneity problem in comparing dictatorship with democracy. The former group seem to have adopted a growth maximising strategy and the latter group a welfare maximising one. Would a swapping of objectives make the latter more successful even in the low and middle income range?

Governance

The problem of governance is not the same as the problem of financial corruption. Even though the latter is associated with the former it is a very small sub-set of the governance problem. Mental corruption (intentions, objectives and motivation) is much more important than financial corruption (bribery). The governance problem is at its a core a problem of performance. Does the government (its leaders, bureaucrats) perform the functions that are its reasons for existence or are these secondary/tertiary to the objective of self aggrandisement? For instance, in urban areas does the government carry out effective urban planning, provide clean drinking water, sewage and sanitation, roads, street lights and parks so that it grows in an efficient and organic manner? Does the government build the national and intra-state highways necessary for commerce to flourish?

One of the lessons from China is that this is the most critical issue, not whether the government is spotlessly clean. The different levels of government in China are not less corrupt than in India, but China's government(s) supplies public goods and quasi-public goods and services, while the Indian governments has/have failed to do so to the level and quality that can reasonably be expected in a low income country. The second related lesson is that the Chinese governments have their eyes firmly focused on the goal, the production and supply of these public goods (appropriate to each level of government). The means are of secondary importance. Pragmatism is essential for achieving fast supply growth; all necessary means (privatisation, private-public partnership), are adopted to fulfil the goals and objectives. In India the goals can be forgotten for years in debates of the best means for achieving them as it is often more important to win elections/get power than to fulfil the goals and objectives of the entity over which you have power.

Conclusion: FDI-Export Led Growth

Many eminent scholars who studied China's phenomenal growth rate had earlier come to the conclusion that it has basically adopted the 'East Asian model of growth'. An essential element of this model was "export-led growth". Though the approach to growth among these countries has common elements there is also a great deal of variation. Singapore for instance, lacked domestic capitalists and initially depended heavily on FDI as a source of capital, technology and entrepreneurship. Though the role of the State in investment gradually expanded, the importance of FDI is still very high, perhaps the highest among Asian countries. Singapore therefore followed an FDI-export led growth model rather than an export-led one. China, for its own political reasons and socio-economic dynamics, shares with Singapore this significantly greater emphasis and dependence on FDI as a source of entrepreneurship, technology and competitive growth. During the eighties and early nineties it moved gradually from an export-led growth strategy to an FDI-export led growth then back to an export-led one in the 2000s. This strategy and the associated policies (whatever their short term costs and long term risks), have been a very important engine of growth in China during the last 25 years.

The greatest difference between China and the other countries of East Asia that followed the East Asian model was that at the start of reforms China was a Marxist 'socialist' State ruled by a Leninist Communist Party. Most of the East Asian States in their early years of reform/growth could perhaps be classified as authoritarian (one man or one party) democracies. There is a fundamental difference between the two. The socialist State (communist party) owns all the means of production, controls all factors and manages all production and sale of goods and services. China's reforms have moved the economy from socialist economy to a "socialist market" economy with a mix of old 'socialist' and new 'market' elements. The 'socialist' control of China's domestic assets (i.e., excluding FDI) was perhaps still around 95 per cent, at the beginning of the century.

As is well known, the market has two key elements: individuals and organisations that supply and demand a good and a mechanism for determining prices by matching total supply and demand that good. The efficiency and productivity depends on the behaviour of the supplier (objectives, incentives and skills) and the structure of the market (competition). The external elements of the market are well understood technically and relatively easy to institute. For instance 'dual' pricing and distribution systems were used as intermediates step in moving agricultural goods from a rationed/controlled rationed controlled system to a market based one in India during the mid-sixties. In the 1970s such transitional arrangements were applied in India to control manufactured goods well before the reforms in China. It is much more difficult to design, introduce and operationalise systems of management in which government owns and controls virtually all the capital/assets.

At the start of reforms in late 1970s, China had an administrative system that combined a high level of centralisation of policy-making with a relatively decentralised system of governance and production. The lowest level of government, the township and villages had a level of autonomy that was greater than in democratic India with a free and competitive agriculture sector. Similarly the level of production decentralisation was much greater than in the USSR or Eastern Europe, partly due the disastorous Maoist experiments in decentralising manufacturing of steel and other capital intensive goods to the local level. These experiments facilitated the creation of (party controlled) organisations and managers with experience of producing goods and services at the local level. With the creation of output markets these organisations formed the nucleus of the town and village enterprises (TVEs), which played a vital role in the success of market reforms during the 1980s. Governance decentralisation also facilitated the closer matching of the objectives and incentives of local governments and TVEs than was possible at the provincial and national levels.

China's economic growth has been driven by a highly motivated communist party (CCP) leadership that had fast growth and income catch-up with richer/advanced countries as its primary objective. This objective was successfully diffused and decentralised to the lowest level of government, the towns and villages, to a degree that was perhaps unmatched even by Japan and South Korea that had similar objectives in the corresponding point in their development.[82] This objective did not necessarily exist from the beginning of the reforms in 1977 or 1978, when the focus was on correcting the abysmal policies of the past decade that had put the economy well below its 'normal' trajectory. In 1975 China's GDP at PPP was about 81 per cent of India's and its per capita GDP at PPP 54 per cent of India's. Market reforms in agriculture led to a growth spurt in this sector. Renewed interest in exports to generate foreign exchange for imports helped support this growth and helped spread growth to the other sectors. The growth spurt between the mid-1970s and early 1980s represented normalisation of agriculture and foreign trade (export thrust) policy from a self-destructive Maoist extreme. As a consequence, the GDP gap with India had been closed by 1982-83.[83]

Product market and managerial reforms then shifted to manufacturing sector and the policy focus shifted to an export-led growth strategy. This evolved into an FDI-export led strategy. The policy could be described as a combination of attracting FDI at any cost and promoting exports at any cost. The public ownership of capital assets

---

82. Singapore also had similar objectives, but decentralisation is not an issue in a city state.

83. It took another decade to close the income gap.

and land has provided the profits that were used to push up public investment and provide the subsidies needed to maintain incredibly high rates of export and FDI growth. The output of this investment was absorbed by further investment, consumer demand expressed through output markets and exports.

Though economic policy has constantly evolved to expand the scope of the market and to develop market institutions a large area of socialist inefficiency remains. The strengths and weakness of socialist ownership are two sides of the same coin. Government ownership of most domestic assets eliminates the need for high taxes that create distortions and disincentives for private entrepreneurs. In combination with absolute control of individual saving, it allows high rates of public investment and high levels of subsidies to attract FDI and push capital intensive exports. The other side of the coin is that rates of return to public capital have progressively declined and will continue to decline as long as centralised social ownership and control (of national and large provincial SOEs) is maintained. At some point therefore both the amount of subsidy and the rate of public investment must fall, leading to a lower growth rate. Though in principle policy reform that expands the scope of the (genuine and more efficient) private sector can help maintain growth, this appears unlikely to happen at a speed that will keep the rate of growth from declining albeit gradually.

References

Au Chun-Chung and Vernon Henderson (2002). "How Migration Restrictions Limit Agglomeration and Productivity in China", *NBER Workling Paper* No. 8707, January.

Bhalla, Surjit S. (2003). "Recounting the Poor: Poverty in India, 1983-99", *Economic and Political Weekly* XXXVIII(4): 25-31, January.

Bloom, David E., David Canning and Jaypee Sevilla (2001). "Economic Growth and the Demographic Transition", *NBER Working Paper* No. 8685, December.

Brandt, Loren, J. Huang, Guo Li and Scott Rozelle (2002). "Land Rights in Rural China: Facts, Fictions and Issues", *China Journal* 47: 67-97, January.

Chang, Gordon G. (2001). *The Coming Collapse of China*. New York: Random House.

Che, Jiahua and Yingyi Qian (1998). "Insecure Property Rights and Government Ownership of Firms", *Quarterly Journal of Economics* 113(2): 467-496.

Collins, Susan and Bosworth, Barry (1996). "Total Factor Productivity", *Brookings Papers on Economic Activity*, p.2.

Cornea, Giovanni A. and Julius Court (2001). "Inequality, Frowth and Poverty in an Era of Liberalisation and Globalisation", *Policy Brief No.* 4, UN University, WIDER.

Dooley, Michael, David Folkerts-Landau, Shunming Zhang (2004). "Inequality Change in China and (Hokou) Labour Mobility Restrictions", *NBER Working Paper* No. W10649, July.

Eichengreen, Barry, Yeongseop Rhee and Hui Tong (2004). "The Impact of China on the Exports of Other Asian Countries", *NBER Working Paper* No. W10727, September.

Gelb, Alan and William Byrd (1990). "Township, Village, and Private Industry in China's Economic Reform", *Policy Research Working Paper*, World Bank, April.

Hertel, Thomas and Fan Zhai (2004). "Labour Market Distortions, Rural-Urban Inequality and the Opening of China's Economy", *World Bank Policy Research Working Paper* 3455, November.

Huang, Yasheng (2003). *Selling China: Foreign Direct Investment during the Reform Era.* Cambridge University Press.

International Monetary Fund (2004). "Advancing Structural Reform", *World Economic Outlook*, April.

Jia Kang and Zhao Quan-Hou (2001). "The Size of China's National Debt", *World Economy and China. http://www.iwep.org.en/wec/english/article/2001_01/jiakang.htm*

Jin, Hehui and Yingyi Qian (1998). "Public versus Private Ownership of Firms: Evidence from Rural China", *Quarterly Journal of Economics* 113(3): 773-808. August.

Khanna, T. and Y. Huang (2003). "Can India Overtake China", *Foreign Policy*, July/August.

Kuijs, Louis (2005). "Investment and Saving in China", *World Bank Policy Research Paper* 3633, June.

Lange, Oscar (1971). "On the Economic Theory of Socialism", in M.I. Goldman (ed.), *Comparative Economic Systems*. New York.

Lardy, Nicholas R. (1992). *Foreign Trade and Economic Reform in China, 1978-1990.* Cambridge: Cambridge University Press.

———. (1998). *China's Unfinished Economic Revolution*. Washington DC: Brookings.

———. (1999). "The Macro-economic Context: The Challenge of Bank Restructuring in China", *Strengthening the Banking System in China: Issues and Experience*. BIS Policy Papers No. 7, October.

Lerner, Abba, P. (1934). "Economic Theory and Socialist Economy", *Review of Economic Studies*. (Rejoinder in RES 1935).

Li, Wei (1997). "The Impact of Economic Reforms on the Performance of Chinese State-Owned Enterprises", *Journal of Political Economy* 105(5): 1080-1106 (October).

Mood, Michelle S. (2005). "Opportunists, Predators and Rogues: The Role of Local State Relations in Shaping Chinese Rural Development", *Journal of Agarian Change* 5(2): 217-250, April.

Oi, Jean C. (1995). "The Role of the Local State in China's Transitional Economy", *The China Quarterly* 144: 1132-1149, Special Issue, December.

Perkins, Dwight (1988). "Reforming China's Economic System", *Journal of Economic Literature* 26(2): 601-645, June.

———. (1994). "Completing China's Move to Market", *Journal of Economic Perspectives* 8(2): 23-46, Spring.

Prasad, Eswar and Shang-Jin Wei (2005). "The Chinese Approach to Capital Inflows: Patterns and Possible Explanations", *NBER Working Paper* No. 11306, April.

Putterman, Louis (1995). "Role of Ownership and Property Rights in China's Economic Transition", *China Quarterly* 144: 1047-1064, Special Issue (December).

Rodrik, Dani and Arvind Subramanian (2004). "Why India Can Grow at 7 Percent a Year or More: Projections and Reflections", *IMF Working Paper* No. 04/118, July.

Sheng-Jin Wei (2005). "Pitfalls of a State Dominated Financial System: The Case of China", *NBER Workin Paper* No. W11181, March.

Shirk, Susan L. (1985). "The Politics of Economic Reform in China", in Elizabeth Perry and Christine Wong (eds.), *Economic Reform in Post-Mao China*. Harvard University Press.

Smyth, Russel (1998). "Recent Developments in Rural Enterprise Reform in China: Achievements, Problems and Prospects", *Asian Survey* 38(8): 748-800, August.

Sung, Yun-Wang (1991). *The China-Hong Kong Connection: The Key to China's Open Door Policy*. Cambridge: Cambridge University Press.

Tseng, Wanda and Harm Zebregs (2002). "Foreign Direct Investment in China: Some Lessons for Other Countries", *IMF Policy Discussion Paper*, February.

Virmani, Arvind (1999a). "Star Performers of the 20th (21st) Century: Asian Tigers, Dragons or Elephants", *Occasional Paper*, Chintan, September, *www.icrier.org/avpapers.html*

———. (1999b). "Potential Growth Stars of the 21st Century: India, China and The Asian Century", *Occasional Paper*, Chintan, October. *www.icrier.org/avpapers.html*

———. (2004a). *Accelerating Growth and Poverty Reduction—A Policy Framework for India's Development*. New Delhi: Academic Foundation. January.

———. (2004b). "India's Economic Growth: From Socialist Rate of Growth to Bharatiya Rate of Growth", *Working Paper* No. 122, ICRIER, February. *www.icrier.org/wp122.pdf*

———. (2004c). "Sources of India's Economic Growth: Trends in Total Factor Productivity", *Working Paper* No. 131, ICRIER, May. *www.icrier.org/wp131.pdf*

———. (2004d). "Forex for Infrastructure", *Economic and Political Weekly* XXXIX(52): 5559-5562, December 25-31.

———. (2005a). "A Tripolar Century: USA, China and India", *Working Paper* No. 160, ICRIER, March. *www.icrier.org/wp160.pdf*

———. (2005b). "Institutions, Governance and Policy Reform: A Framework for Analysis", *Economic and Political Weekly* XL(22 & 23): 2341-2350, May 28-June 03/June 04-June 10.

———. (2005c). "Policy Regimes, Growth and Poverty in India: Lessons of Government Failure and Entrepreneurial Success!", *Working Paper* No. 170, ICRIER, October. *http://www.icrier.org/WP170GrPov9.pdf*

———. (2009). *The Sudoku of India's Growth*. New Delhi: BS Books. *www.business-standard.com/books*

Walder, Andrew G. (1995). "China's Transitional Economy: Interpreting its Significance", *The China Quarterly*. 144: 963-979. Special Issue, December.

———. (1995). "Local Governments as Industrial Firms: An Organizational Analysis of China's Transitional Economy", *American Journal of Sociology* 101(2): 263-301, September.

Whalley, John and Shunming Zhang (2004). *Inequality Change in China and (Hukou) Labour Mobility Restrictions.*

Wong, Christine (1985). "Material Allocation and Decentralization: Impact of the local sector on Industrial Reform" in E.J. Perry and C. Wong (eds.), "The Political Economy of Reform in Post-Mao China", *Harvard Contemporary Economic* Series: 2. The Council on East Asian Studies. Cambridge, MA & London: Harvard University.

World Bank (2005). "China: Integration of National Product and Factor Markets", *Economic Benefits and Policy Recommendations*. June 13.

Xu, Lixin Colin (1997). "The Productivity Effects of Decentralized Reforms: An Analysis of the Chinese Industrial Reforms", *World Bank Policy Research Working Paper* 1723, Febuary.

Young, Alwyn (2000). "Gold into Base Metals: Productivity Growth in the People's Republic of China during the Reform Period", *NBER Working Paper* 7856, August.

7 India-China Economic Cooperation

The legacy of relations between India and China began to change in the 1980s, with the opening of both economies. As long as their relationship was seen through a geopolitical prism, it was easy for both countries to view it as a zero-sum game. With the shift in both countries from an import substitution to an export promotion strategy during the 1980s, the focus shifted gradually to economics. With the acceleration of globalisation during the 1990s, the imperatives of global interdependence and an appreciation of the possibilities of mutual gain have also increased. This is particularly so in China, whose share of world trade is now about eight times that of India; they have similar shares of foreign direct investment (FDI) and capital flows. Starting in 2000 these developments led to the establishment of an India-China Joint Study Group (JSG) on accelerating bilateral economic cooperation, of which the author was a member as Director and Chief Executive of the Indian Council for Research on International Economic Relations (ICRIER). ICRIER also did a number of background studies for JSG, covering goods and services. After the presentation of this report to the two governments, the two countries formed an agreement for economic cooperation when Premier Wen Jiabao visited India in April 2005. However, the following discussion has nothing to do with that group or the government; these are the personal views of the author.

We will first review the trade between the two countries and then briefly mention issues connected with comprehensive economic cooperation and a multilateral context.

India-China Trade

In 2004, India was among China's top 20 trading partners, 15th in imports and 18th in exports. China was a much more important trade partner for India in 2004, ranking in the top five, second in imports and third in exports. The details of India's trade with China, from India's perspective, are shown in Table 7.1.

Trends in the export, import and trade shares are depicted in Figure 7.1. China's shares in India's overall imports and exports have been rising rapidly over the decade (2000s). It is interesting to note that the gap that opened up between the import share and the export share in the middle of the period has now closed.

Figure 7.2 gives the rate of growth of bilateral trade as well as the growth of China's share in India's international trade from 1997-98 to 2004-05. The main point is that the trend rate of growth of trade is somewhat faster than the rise in the share of China in India's trade. That is because India's trade has been growing quickly over this period. But still the trade share has been rising and accelerating over this period at 3.4 per cent per annum (the bottom line in the figure).

Figure 7.3 depicts the volatility of exports and imports along with the rate of growth of total trade. The figure shows that there is much less variability in India's imports from China than in India's exports to China. There is much more fluctuation in the rate of growth of the export trade.The precise degree of volatility is shown in the second column of Table 7.1, which shows that the coefficient of variation of the export growth rate is double that of the import growth rate. More precisely, the coefficient of variation of exports is 1.2 and that for imports is 0.6. This can bring up a number of hypotheses. One is that India's imports are driven by normal market considerations. In contrast, there is much more implicit or explicit government intervention in China's imports from India; there is an element of government signaling to the socialist/public sector part of the economy. These signals have apparently turned positive around 2002-03. This is probably also the reason for the closing of the gap between the import and export shares that had opened up in the middle of the period (Figure 7.1). So perhaps the positive signals from the Chinese government were partly responsible for this growth in trade. However, these signals appeal to have been diluted in subrequest years.

Table 7.1

India's Trade with China

Year	*Mean*	*CV*	*1996-97*	*1997-98*	*1998-99*	*1999-2000*	*2000-01*	*2001-02*	*2002-03*	*2003-04*	*2004–05*
Trade (US$ billion)											
Exports to China			0.6	0.7	0.4	0.5	0.8	1.0	2.0	3.0	5.3
Imports from China			0.8	1.1	1.1	1.3	1.5	2.0	2.8	4.1	6.8
Trade with China			1.4	1.8	1.5	1.8	2.3	3.0	4.8	7.0	12.1
Trade Balance	–0.8	–0.5	–0.1	–0.4	–0.7	–0.7	–0.7	–1.1	–0.8	–1.1	–1.4
(Per cent of Trade)	–25%	–0.5	–10%	–22%	–44%	–41%	–29%	–36%	–17%	–16%	–12%
Growth Rate											
Export	39%	1.2	17%	–41%	26%	54%	15%	108%	50%	81%	
Import	33%	0.6	47%	–1%	17%	17%	36%	37%	45%	67%	
Trade	34%	0.8	33%	–17%	20%	28%	28%	60%	47%	73%	
Trade Share	18%	0.9	27%	–16%	4%	17%	28%	33%	18%	29%	
Share in All/Total											
Export	2.9%	0.6	1.8%	2.1%	1.3%	1.5%	1.9%	2.2%	3.7%	4.6%	6.6%
Import	3.6%	0.4	1.9%	2.7%	2.6%	2.6%	3.0%	4.0%	4.5%	5.2%	6.2%
Trade	3.3%	0.5	1.9%	2.4%	2.0%	2.1%	2.5%	3.1%	4.2%	4.9%	6.4%

Source: *www.dgft.delhi.nic.in*, Department of Commerce.

Figure 7.1

China's Share in India's Total Trade (in per cent)

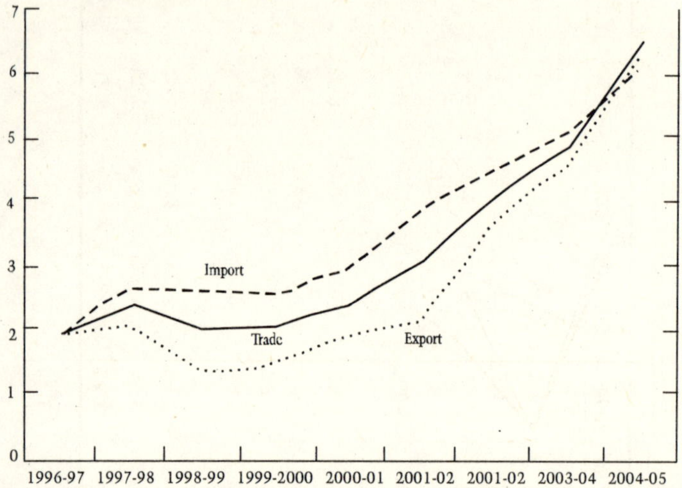

Source: *www.dgft.delhi.nic.in*, Department of Commerce.

The commodity composition of trade in Table 7.2 lists India's top 10 exports to China and top 10 imports from China. Similarly, Figure 7.4 depicts the concentration ratio for exports and imports at the two-digit level by ordering them from those with the highest to the lowest share and then cumulating the share. So, on the horizontal scale, if we look at the number five and track it to the graph, we get the five-product concentra-tion ratio at the two-digit level.

The bottom line in Figure 7.4 shows the concentration with respect to imports. The concentration is very high: the top five commodities account for almost 70 per cent of India's imports from China. The concentration in India's exports to China is even higher. The top five exports account for more than 80 per cent of the exports from India to China. Now we return to Table 7.2 to see the list of commodities. The top export from India to China is the two-digit category "ores, slag, and ash" (26) with 52 per cent of total export value. The category of salt, sulfur, lime and cement (25) has another 2.6 per cent of export value. So there is a very high concentration of basic raw material exports.

Figure 7.2

Growth Rate of India's Trade in China (in per cent)

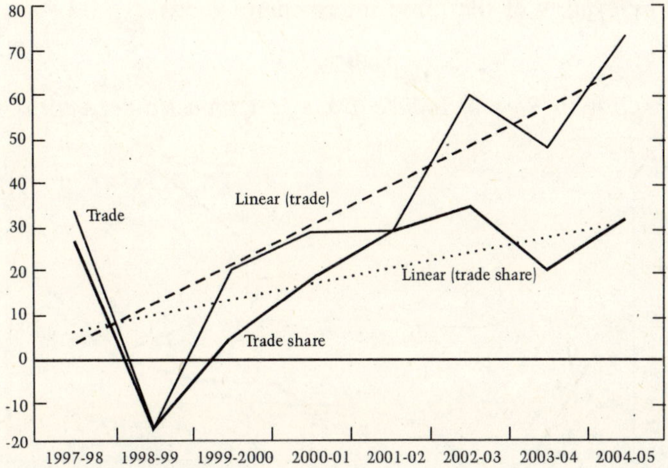

Source: *www.dgft.nic.in*, Department of Commerce.

It seems that this has a more general implication beyond India. China is now drawing many raw materials from all over the world—from Latin America, Africa and Asia. Thailand, for example, is a raw materials exporter to China. Indonesia, another raw materials exporter, has seen a surge in exports to China. This is going to be a factor around the world. A theory that was very prominent in Latin American economist literature envisioned countries in the "centre" as an exporter of industrial goods and the periphery as an exporter of raw materials. Some element of that arrangement is emerging with respect to China and other developing countries, particularly in Africa and Latin America.

The second noteworthy point is with respect to intermediate goods. The next-largest exports from India to China are iron and steel, followed by plastics. There are a number of undifferentiated products, and this, again, has certain implications for India and for other countries. That is, intermediate goods industries are subject to much cyclical fluctuation. Till 2006, the fluctuation has been driven by very high aggregate investment rates in these products in China. High aggregate investment creates a demand for these commodities, which results in a jump in investment in these industries, so the supply rises eventually. Thus, temporary imbalances lead to higher imports by China, but these are eliminated by higher supply and could even be followed by exports of the same intermediate goods.

Figure 7.3

Growth Rate of India's Trade in China (in per cent)

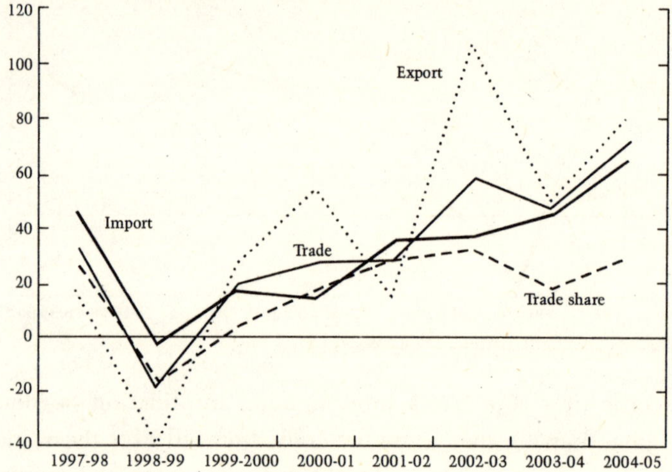

Source: *www.dgft.delhi.nic.in*, Department of Commerce.

Table 7.2

Composition of India-China Trade

India's Top 10 Exports to China			*India's Top 10 Imports from China*		
HS	*Commodity*	*Share*	*HS*	*Commodity*	*Share*
26	Ores, slag, ash	52.1%	85	Electrical machinery and parts	25.6%
72	Iron and steel	11.5%	84	Nuclear reactors, boilers, machinery	14.8%
39	Plastic and articles	7.4%	27	Mineral fuels, oils, and waxes	12.0%
29	Organic chemicals	6.5%	29	Organic chemicals	11.7%
28	Inorganic chemicals, compounds	3.9%	50	Silk	4.3%
25	Salt, sulphur, lime, cement, etc.	2.6%	71	Pearls, stones, jewellery	2.2%
3	Fish and aquatic invertebrates	1.9%	28	Inorganic chemicals, compounds	2.1%
84	Nuclear reactors, boilers, machinery	1.8%	72	Iron and steel	1.8%
52	Cotton	1.5%	59	Textile fabrics, industrial textiles	1.5%
74	Copper and articles	1.2%	54	Man-made filaments	1.5%

Source: *www.dgft.delhi.nic.in*, Department of Commerce.

Figure 7.4

India's Import and Export Concentration of Trade with China (cumulative share, in per cent)

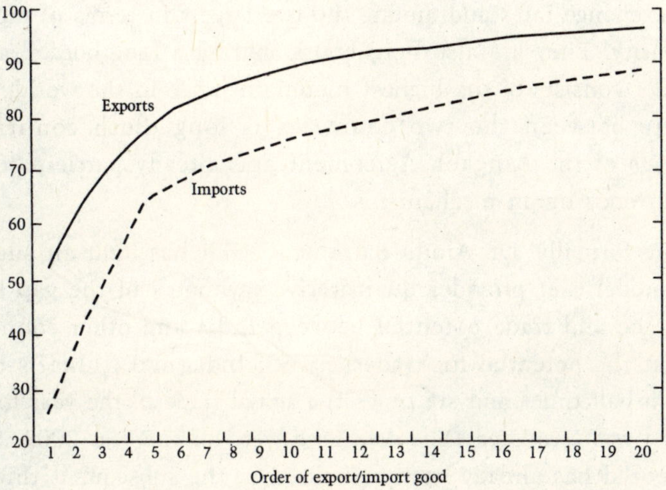

Note: Sorted on year 2004-05.

Source: *www.dgft.delhi.nic.in*, Department of Commerce.

Over time, perhaps during the next 10 years, all countries, including India, may face this fluctuation in intermediate goods trade with China. That is, the net demand for these undifferentiated, intermediate products will at some point be converted to net excess supply turning to net exports. The global economic shock may accelerate this process.

Future Potential

Before examining the potential of India-China trade, it is useful to take stock of the position from another perspective. China's trade with India is less than 1.5 per cent of its trade with the world, whereas India's trade with China is over 6 per cent of its total trade. Consequently, India's exports to China constitute 6.6 per cent of its total exports, whereas they make up only 1.4 per cent of China's imports. China's exports to India account for 1 per cent of its total exports, but constitute 6.2 per cent of India's imports. This is simply a reflection of each country's share of world trade, with India's being about 0.8 per cent and China's about 6.4 per cent (2004-05).

The bilateral trade potential is very high, given the size and economic dynamism of the two economies. Since 1980, China's average growth rate has been the highest, whereas India's has been the eighth or ninth highest. They are among the 10 largest economies in terms of current exchange rates and among the five largest in terms of purchasing power parity. They are also neighbours sharing a long border, although this border consists of the highest mountain range in the world; and the sea route between the two countries is long. Both countries are signatories of the Bangkok Agreement and already participate in the Asian currency union mechanisms.

More formally, Dr. Amita Batra at ICRIER has built an augmented gravity model that provides quantitative estimates of the gap between actual trade and trade potential between India and other countries. It finds that the potential for trade between India and China is between two and a half times and six times the actual trade in the year for which the model was estimated. The data used were for the year 2002. Some of this potential has already been actualised in the subsequent three years to 2005 and is in the process of being realised more fully.

There are also a few other related studies by Batra that have been published as ICRIER working papers and are available on the ICRIER website (*www.icrier.org*). These papers, as well as our analysis for the India-China study group, show the scope for intra-industry trade. Both countries are highly diversified economies with very diversified manufacturing structures. Thus, there is considerable scope for intra-industry trade in intermediate manufactured goods. The share of private consumption in India's GDP is relatively high compared with other emerging economies, whereas that of China is perhaps the lowest in the world. As consumer goods grow in importance, there will also be increasing scope for intra-industry trade in differentiated products and intermediate goods specialisation.There are identifiable differences in export specialisation in the two countries, based on natural resource endowments, skills and policy. The most interesting and important resource-based difference is in textiles. Given the abundance of cotton in India, India's exports are heavily concentrated in cotton textiles and garments, whereas China has a commanding position in textiles and garments based on man-made fibres. An ICRIER study some years ago showed that the two countries' exports were largely non-competing because of this. Among the reasons for this divergence in skill development were a highly rigid labour policy for organised industry, small scale industry reservations, and exorbitant indirect (excise) taxes on man-made fibres in India. One of the indirect consequences of the rigid labour policy has been a greater use of educated labour and higher value-added niche products in India.

There are also differences in skills, because of either-cultural or historical development. In the case of general skills, India has a comparative advantage in the English language and in dealing with multi-ethnic, multi-religious workforces. These strengths could enable a clear advantage in industries such as advertising and entertainment. China has developed a lasting advantage in labour-intensive mass manufacturing, based on the virtual absence of labour laws for the FDI export sectors, the single-party system of government and the organisation and management of the socialist investment system. There are also differences in sector-specific skills. India has developed, over the past half century or more, skills in engineering/automobiles, speciality chemicals and pharmaceuticals. China, by contrast, has developed over the past 25 years skills in consumer electronics, telecommunications and other consumer durables. On the other hand, China and India are similar in that the labour force in each country has strong math and science skills.

The ICRIER studies also identified at the two-digit and six-digit levels a list of commodities with the greatest export potential from India to China and vice versa. Among the former are agriculture and allied products, iron and steel and articles thereof, nuclear reactors, boilers and machinery, man-made steel fibres and man-made filament yarns, organic chemicals and cotton. Among the categories that have potential for exports from China to India are nuclear reactors, boilers and machinery, organic chemicals, silk and electrical and electronic equipment. Nuclear reactors and boilers and machinery appear in both lists and indicate the potential for intra-industry trade.

Barriers and Constraints

To realise the full potential of India-China trade, remaining barriers and constraints have to be relaxed. These include customs rules and procedures, standards, certification and regulatory practices, non-tariff barriers and rules of origin.

Some of the problems that have arisen with respect to customs valuation are: (1) the use of a minimum reference price instead of the World Trade Organisation–sanctioned transaction cost method; (2) a variation of customs valuation across ports, resulting in additional costs to exporters; and (3) a lack of clarity in guidelines and procedures relating to imports for exporters. Though some of these things apply to all trade, there are some changes that may be more acute in a bilateral context that would lead to an increase in India-China trade. Thus, there is a need to evolve a mutual consensus on customs valuation, clarify guidelines, facilitate uniform documentation across ports, and increase the efficiency of handling at ports and customs. An existing mechanism, the India-China Customs Cooperative Group, can be used for this purpose.

To illustrate, variation across ports creates special problems for small exporters. For a large exporter, like the United States to China, these problems are minor; but if you have many small exporters, as we have in India-China trade, these variations create additional costs for both sides. Similarly, there are problems related to imports for exporters. This may be very simple for, as an example, traders in Taiwan Province of China or Hong Kong SAR, but not for those in India. We need more clarity and guidelines.

Also, there are certain problems related to standards, certification, regulatory practices, rules and regulations in terms of national treatment and accessibility. The Chinese language poses a problem for Indian traders, because most Indian trade is in English. It is difficult for them to keep up with the Chinese regulations. This situation creates an extra problem for Indian traders that could be easily remedied if the rules and regulations were published and updated regularly, preferably in English, the language of international commerce.

The certification process, including with respect to sanitary and phytosanitary standards (SPS), also involves delays and high costs. SPS requirements generally exceed what is necessary to protect consumer health. India has a great interest in certain agricultural commodities, the standards for which need clarification. Certain other standards related to commodities such as granite are not available. Harmonisation of technical and agricultural standards would greatly facilitate India-China trade.

Certain non-tariff barriers (NTBs) are also hindering the growth of trade between the two countries. There are problems related to tariff quotas, pre-shipment inspection and definitions of rules of origin. For example, there are NTBs on automotive parts and components and a tariff-quota on agricultural products. These barriers need to be eliminated. A pre-shipment inspection agreement between the two countries could help reduce NTBs and related barriers. Problems relating to rules of origin can be sorted out by agreeing on clear definitions. This in turn could result in smoother movement of goods between the two countries.

Removal of these constraints and barriers in a spirit of cooperation and mutual accommodation will set the stage for a quantum jump in economic cooperation between the two countries.

Next Steps

Going forward, from a global perspective, everybody knows that China has been the fastest growing economy, averaging about 10 per cent for the past 25 to 30 years, but not many people know that India has been the eighth or ninth fastest growing economy over the same period. This is because many people think that India's reforms started in 1992 and that India has been lagging by about a decade. The fact is that India's reforms started around the same time as China's (1980), but its average growth rate has been slower (Virmani, 2005). The East and South-East Asian economies that have grown faster than India during the past 25 years or so are likely to slow during the next decade. India, in contrast, has been on a rising growth rate trend since the reforms of the 1990s. It is therefore likely to be among the five fastest growing economies (if not among the top three) along with China. It will become one of the primary global growth drivers by the end of the decade along with China. During the period 2003 to 2008, it was the fourth highest contributor to world GDP growth after the United States, China and Japan. The possibilities for trade and economic cooperation between China and India will therefore continue to expand.

Once the identified barriers are removed (hopefully in a year or two), we should be in a position to start discussing a comprehensive economic cooperation agreement. Given the high reinvestment, "vent for surplus" approach of the socialist-owned part of China's economy, a free trade agreement is likely to benefit China more than India. So there has to be a tradeoff. I think both sides need to recognise that you cannot have these special agreements unless both sides can balance the gains and losses. There are already some special losses to certain manufacturing sectors such as toys. However, India expects some gains in the services sector. The agreement has to be a comprehensive one that includes trade in both goods and services.

Another area of economic cooperation that is very important for the future of Asia is that Indian and Chinese economic cooperation be embedded in an Asian context. India and China have either framework agreements or ongoing discussions for a Free Trade Agreement/Common Economic Partnership Agreement with the Association of Southeast Asian Nations (ASEAN), Japan and Korea. We have to harmonise these by developing an East Asian community in which ASEAN, China, Japan and India are equal partners. In December 2005, there was a meeting of the East Asian Economic Community, in which both India and China were involved. China's attitude toward Indian inclusion will be closely watched by people in India and Asia as an example of its general approach to hegemonic competition *versus* mutually beneficial cooperation.

References

Batra, Amita (2004). "India's Global Trade Potential: The Gravity Model Approach", *ICRIER Working Paper* No. 151. New Delhi: Indian Council for Research on International Economic Relations. December.

Batra, Amita and Zeba Khan (2005). "Revealed Comparative Advantage: An Analysis for India and China", *ICRIER Working Paper* No. 168. New Delhi: Indian Council for Research on International Economic Relations. August.

Batra, Amita and Arvind Virmani (2004). "Response to East Asian Regionalism and its Impact—The Indian View", Paper presented at the International Conference on *East Asian Regionalism and Its Impact*. Organised by the Institute of Asia-Pacific Studies, Chinese Academy of Social Sciences, Beijing, October 21–22.

———. (2005). "India-China Economic Relations", *Security and Society* 1 (Summer), pp.106–16.

Virmani, Arvind (2005). "Policy Regimes, Growth and Poverty in India: Lessons of Government Failure and Entrepreneurial Success", *ICRIER Working Paper* No.170. New Delhi: Indian Council for Economic Research. October. Available via the Internet: *http://www.icrier.org/WP170GrPov9.pdf*

———. (2006a). "China's Socialist Market Economy: Lessons of Success", *ICRIER Working Paper* No. 178. New Delhi: Indian Council for Research on International Economic Relations. January.

———. (2006b). *Propelling India from Socialist Stagnation to Global Power: Growth Process.* Vol. I. New Delhi: Academic Foundation. forthcoming.

8 Proliferation by Nuclear Weapons States and NNWS NPT Partners

Introduction

In 1964, China carried out its first atmospheric test of an atomic weapon and proudly announced to the world that it had developed atomic weapons. Secret US communications, now declassified, prior to and after the Chinese test clearly predicted that India would react to China's test by taking steps to accelerate its nuclear programme. Elements in the US government even suggested that the US should consider assisting India in this endeavour. Given Indian sensitivities about Chinese occupation of Indian territory in 1962, the Indian Prime Minister authorised theoretical work on the Subterranean Nuclear Explosion for Peaceful Purposes (SNEPP) in November 1964. China's test of a thermonuclear weapon in 1967, clearly accentuated India's insecurity. The non-proliferation treaty was introduced in 1968 and came into effect on 6th March 1970 when the three Nuclear Weapon States (NWS) the USA, the USSR and Great Britain deposited their instruments of ratification. Initially half a dozen non-nuclear weapon States (NNWS) including Germany, Japan, Sweden and India expressed reservations on the treaty.[1] The first three signed the NPT after getting nuclear guarantees from the USA. Such guarantees were refused to India and consequently it did not sign the NPT as a NNWS. Three other NNWS, Israel, Pakistan and Cuba also never signed the NPT.

The nature of the Western dominated discourse began to change in 1971 with the US President Richard Nixon's opening to China, his encouragement to the Chinese leadership to attack India in support of

1. Germany, Japan and India had clear recognisable nuclear threats to their security, while all four countries had nuclear capabilities.

Pakistan and the sending of the nuclear powered aircraft carrier, the Enterprise, to the Indian Ocean to threaten India during the Bangladesh War. China, a NWS under the NPT, refused to accept treaty obligations for over a decade, did not accept IAEA safeguards till 1984 and did not ratify the NPT till 1992. Despite its transfer of nuclear technology to Pakistan and other countries, the non-proliferation crusaders repeatedly discounted the proliferation threat from China.[2]

Three years after Nixon's threat, India carried out an underground nuclear test of a PNE (peaceful nuclear device), justifying the categorisation by reference to the US Ploughshares programme and Russian tests of PNE devices. India did not follow the 1974 test with subsequent tests, nor did it immediately weaponise the device that was tested. Even the research programme was put on hold during 1977-1979, when the government discussed with the US the possibility of signing the NPT. After analysing the Indian research and development programme, the only international violation that the non-proliferation crusaders could discover (and have ever discovered) was the use of spent fuel from a Canadian provided research reactor.[3] Logically, either India carried out a peaceful nuclear explosion in May 1974 and therefore did not violate its agreement with Canada, or it carried out a weapons test and became a nuclear weapons State four years after the ratification of the NPT (by the USA and the USSR) and ten years before China formally acceded to the NPT.[4] No Western non-proliferation expert has gone on record to assert the latter while all have, by classifying the Indian PNE as proliferation activity, asserted that the former is wrong.

The Western countries, their governments and their non-proliferation experts, instead of stemming the leaks in the NPT, focused their attention and ire on India. An elaborate system of denial regimes

2. There was no discussion among other NPT member States or the non-proliferation experts about denying China access to nuclear-missile related technology/equipment/materials until it agreed to (and implemented) its NPT obligations.

3. And use of US/China supplied heavy water to India's indigenously produced commercial heavy water reactors. However, vague, non-specific and totally unsubstantiated allegations continue to be made by the non-proliferation crusaders/ayatollahs till today, to the extent that domestic procurement/production is labelled as proliferation.

4. China's designation as an NWS in the NPT was based on the fact that it had carried out nuclear tests before 1968.

was set up—London Group/Nuclear Suppliers Group, Missile Technology Control Regime, Wassaner Group, Zanger list. In the following decades, every independent, indigenous achievement of India's nuclear and space research complexes was labelled and derided as 'proliferation,' despite the fact that India did not violate any international law that it had accepted as a sovereign country.[5] At the same time Western astigmatism overlooked and even justified European and North American proliferation to Pakistan as legally consistent with these new regimes.

From 1980, Pakistan felt free to train, finance, arm and send religious terrorists across the border into India without fear of retaliatory attacks, while Western media reports constantly regurgitated the bogey of an Indian threat to Pakistan.[6] With every nuclear-missile action of Pakistan justified as a reaction to Indian research achievement, by a slew of Western experts and government spokespersons, the Pakistan military establishment was encouraged and emboldened to continue its clandestine programme.[7] The labelling of Pakistan's transfer of Chinese bomb designs and uranium enrichment technology to Libya, North Korea and Iran, as the private enterprise of Dr. A.Q. Khan, is yet another example of the tacit encouragement of Pakistani proliferation.[8] With the eagle (astigmatic) eyes of non-proliferation crusaders focused on India, Pakistan surreptitiously obtained designs, parts and equipment for uranium enrichment, plutonium generation and extraction, and atomic bombs from NPT weapons States (France, the UK, the USA, China) and NPT non-weapons States (Germany, Netherlands, Switzerland, Canada). In this process these countries continuously violated the spirit and often the letter of the non-proliferation rules and

---

5. Under the UN charter all nation States have the right to voluntarily decide which treaty they will accept/accede to. This is the *quid pro quo* for giving the UNSC the right to initiate military action against States for violations of the UN charter and the treaties that they have voluntarily accepted.

6. I am not aware of any two countries in history with the relative size of India and Pakistan where the smaller country was responsible for killing so many citizens of the larger country without being attacked by the latter.

7. Pakistan was therefore encouraged to either time its own tests to follow such Indian actions or to run to the Chinese after every Indian development, for technology/designs/materials to obtain a counter.

8. Such illogic in the interest of ideology no longer surprises.

regulations they themselves had enacted, on the plea that, "it did not violate the law," or that the specific item, "was not on the restricted/banned list." Occasionally Pakistan was caught, publicly rapped on the knuckles and then let off to pursue its clandestine import programme, on the excuse of more pressing imperatives. Eventually and inevitably it felt emboldened by this indulgence to get into the nuclear import-export business. The chapter redocuments these proliferation activities of Pakistan and its European, Chinese and other collaborators.[9] It suggests that if the ayatollahs had focused on the real problems of proliferation (to and from NPT signatories and among them),[10] Pakistan would still be in approximately the same position as North Korea and Iran are reportedly in and these two NPT signatories would be of little concern. Paradoxically, this would have increased the probability of India capping or rolling back its independent nuclear programme during the Janata governments of 1977-1980 and 1989-1991.

Background and Origins

Zulfikar Ali Bhutto was a passionate believer in nuclear weapons from the late 1950s. Despite being a minister in several governments he was unable to persuade the leaders of Pakistan to initiate a nuclear weapons programme. It was only after the 1970 elections in Pakistan and the formation of Bangladesh that he had the power to order the development of nuclear weapons, which he promptly proceeded to do. Till the 1971 war, the Pakistani scientific establishment recognised clearly that it did not have the economic or scientific capability to build an atomic weapons programme. The separation of East Pakistan into the independent State of Bangladesh and a misunderstanding of the relative role of the Pakistani State and the Indian State created fear of and hatred against the latter. This along with the desire to pay the Indians back was a strong motivating factor in the entire Pakistani elites support for the quest for atomic bombs.

9. Based on country chronologies produced by NTI and other open sources.

10. This is not just a matter of hindsight. Indian security expert K. Subrahmanyam has for decades written about these issues, brought out the real facts and analysed their implications.

Genocide or Perfidy?[11]

The story of the Pakistan's bomb starts from one of the few free and democratic elections in Pakistan, the 1970 election called by President General Yahya Khan. This election resulted in the Awami League of East Pakistan winning a clear majority of 160 seats in the 300 seat house. The leader of the Awami League, Shiekh Mujibur Rehman therefore had the democratic right to form the government. This was such a shock to the ruling West Pakistan elite and to Zulfikar Ali Bhutto, the leader of the party with the largest number of seats in West Pakistan, that it was not difficult for the latter to get the support of the former to thwart the mandate of the elections. On February 22, 1971 the ruling generals of Pakistan took a decision to crush the Awami League and its supporters. President General Yahya Khan reportedly declared at the February conference, "Kill three million of them and the rest will eat out of our hands."[12]

In a March 3, 1971 meeting between Yahya Khan, Z.A. Bhutto and Mujibur Rehman, the latter was offered a compromised solution. This was sought to be done by redefining the government system so that Mujibur Rehman's writ would run only in East Pakistan, while Bhutto and the West Pakistan elite would continue to rule the Western part of the country as well as control all national instruments of power such as the Army. Shiekh Mujibur Rehman, backed by the Bengali citizens of East Pakistan (through a nationwide strike), refused to become a second class leader of Pakistan, restricted to leading what were considered by the elites as second class citizens of Pakistan.

After a month of preparation, the February 22, 1971 decision was implemented with an attack on Dhaka University on March 25. "Within a week, half the population of Dhaka had fled, and at least 30,000 people had been killed. Chittagong, too, had lost half its population."[13] Within a period of 267 days, an estimated 1.5 million people (mostly young men) were killed, about 200,000 women raped and about 10 million

11. This section is based largely on the Wikipedia, supplemented by material in references.

12. Payne, 1973: 50.

13. Payne, 1973: 48.

refugees fled to India, overwhelming that country's resources and spurring the eventual Indian military intervention.[14]

This genocide, carefully hidden from the rest of the world and from the Pakistani public, led inevitably to the creation of Bangladesh.[15] On December 16, 1971, the Indian Army entered Dhaka and more than 93,000 Pakistani soldiers and their abettors surrendered to joint forces (*Mitro Bahini*) and were taken as prisoners of war by the Indian Army, the largest surrender since World War II.

An enquiry commission headed by Justice Hamood-ur-Rahman was set up, but its report was suppressed by Bhutto as it showed the military in poor light. It was leaked out of the country during the tenure of General Musharraf. Among its (supplementary report's) conclusions were the following:

> Para 15. Lt Col. Mansoorul Haq, GSO-I, Division, appearing as Witness No 260, has made detailed and specific allegations as follows:
>
> A Bengali, who was alleged to be a Mukti Bahini or Awami Leaguer, was being sent to Bangladesh—a code name for death without trial, without detailed investigations and without any written order by any authorised authority.

Indiscriminate killing and looting could only serve the cause of the enemies of Pakistan. In the harshness, we lost the support of the silent majority of the people of East Pakistan. The Comilla Cantt. massacre (on 27th/28th of March, 1971) under the orders of CO 53 Field Regiment, Lt. Gen. Yakub Malik, in which 17 Bengali Officers and 915 men were just slain by a flick of one officer's fingers should suffice as an example.

There was a general feeling of hatred against Bengalis amongst the soldiers and officers including Generals. There were verbal instructions to eliminate the Hindus.

When the army moved to clear the rural areas and small towns, it moved in a ruthless manner, destroying, burning and killing.

> Para 17. About the attitude of senior officers in this behalf, Brigadier Iqbalur Rehman Shariff (Witness no. 269), has alleged that during his visit to formations in East Pakistan General Gul Hassan used to ask the soldiers "how many Bengalis have you shot."

---

14. Totten *et al.* (1997), Rummel (1997), Brownmiller (1993). The population of Bangladesh/East Pakistan at the time was about 75 million.

15. All foreign journalists were expelled before March 25, 1971.

> Para 18. The statements appearing in the evidence of Lt. Col. Aziz Ahmed Khan (Witness no 276) who was Commanding Officer 8 Baluch and then CO 86 Mujahid Battalion are also directly relevant. "Brigadier Arbbab also told me to destroy all houses in Joydepur. To a great extent I executed this order. General Niazi visited my unit at Thakurgaon and Bogra. He asked us how many Hindus we had killed. In May, there was an order in writing to kill Hindus. This order was from Brigadier Abdullah Malik of 23 Brigade."
>
> Para 36. .... At the same time there is some evidence to suggest that the words and personal actions of Lt. Gen. Niazi were calculated to encourage the killings and rape.
>
> Para 38. From what we have said in the preceding Paragraphs it is clear that there is substance in the allegations that during and after the military action excesses were indeed committed on the people of East Pakistan,...

"It confirmed the rapes and the killings by the Pakistan Army and their local agents (mostly Jamaati-i-Islami followers) although the figures are far lower than the one quoted by Bangladesh (200,000 women raped, over 3 million people killed). A large section of the intellectual community of Bangladesh were murdered mostly by the Al-Shams and Al-Badr forces, at the instruction of the Pakistani Army.[16] There are many mass graves in Bangladesh and continue to be discovered, such as one in an old well near a mosque in Dhaka discovered in August 1999.[17] The first night of war on Bengalis, which is documented in telegrams from the American Consulate in Dhaka to the United States State Department, saw indiscriminate killings of students of Dhaka University and other civilians."[18]

President Bhutto and the military elite, hid the truth about the election results and its political aftermath from the Pakistani public for decades. Because of the US and Chinese veto at the UN, the atrocities perpetrated by the Pakistani army against its own citizens were never discussed at the UN or investigated by any UN body.[19] Thus, the genocidal actions of the Pakistani Army that were responsible for alienating the population were not only completely hidden from the public, but were ignored or swept under the carpet by even those in the

---

16. Khan, Asadullah (2005). "The loss continues to haunt us" in *The Bangladesh Observer*, December 14.
17. DPA report (1999). "Mass grave found in Bangladesh", in *The Chandigarh Tribune*, August 8.
18. Gandhi, Sajit (2002). "The Tilt: The U.S. and the South Asian Crisis of 1971," National Security Archive Electronic Briefing *Book No*. 79 December 16.
19. An outcome of the Nixon-Mao bonhomie and the role of Pakistan in intermediating the breakthrough in US-China relations and facilitating the Nixon trip to China.

elite who had an inkling of them from their army relatives. Thus, it was easy for the elite to convince itself and the public that the perfidious Indians were solely to blame for the formation of Bangladesh. This fostered a feeling of hatred for India. Added to this was the sense of humiliation at the defeat and surrender of its army. The army and the elites of Pakistan, who were traumatised by the defeat and felt deeply humiliated, both reflected and fostered this hatred to divert the blame from themselves to the 'enemy.' This led the Pakistani Army and elites to formulate a two-pronged strategy against India. One, attain nuclear capability to deter India against any conventional response, and two train and support religious fundamentalists in India to fight against the State. The Bangladesh defeat strengthened the elites in their conclusion that Pakistan needed a nuclear weapon to deter India from any future conventional attack on it.

Motivation and Origins

Zulfikar Ali Bhutto, became President of Pakistan on 20th December 1971. His record, statements and writings since he became a minister in 1958, indicate his obsession with nuclear weapons. "In March 1965, President Ayub Khan, and his Foreign Minister, Z.A. Bhutto met with Chou En-lai in Beijing, a meeting both felt had very positive results and developed Chinese support for Pakistan. It was shortly after this, in mid-1965, that Bhutto stated that, 'If India builds the bomb, we will eat grass or leaves, even go hungry, but we will get one of our own. We have no other choice'."[20] Pakistani Senator Babar has written, "As a minister Bhutto tried to persuade President General Ayub Khan to acquire advanced nuclear technologies. In December 1965 Ayub was on an official visit to the UK. Bhutto planned a meeting of some nuclear experts with him and persuaded Ayub Khan to meet late Munir Ahmed Khan former Chairman of the PAEC who at the time was working in the IAEA. Late Munir Khan had recalled that when he was told that these technologies could eventually place in the hands of Pakistan a nuclear option, the General simply smiled and said that if needed, Pakistan could get it from China."[21] "One of the theses of Bhutto's book *The*

20. Sublette, 2002b.

21. Babar, 2004.

Myth of Independence, finished in 1967 but published in 1969 was the necessity for Pakistan to acquire nuclear weapons to be able to stand against the industrialised States, and against a nuclear armed India." "But Bhutto, who was set on pursuing nuclear weapons, did not have the means to put his views into practice then. That would have to wait until he became Prime Minister."[22] In the book, he had written, "If Pakistan restricts or suspends her nuclear program, it would impose a crippling limitation on the development of Pakistan's science and technology...our problem in its essence, is how to obtain such a weapon in time before the crisis begins."[23]

Consequently, soon after the end of the Bangladesh War, "Zulfikar Ali Bhutto called a meeting on 20th January 1972 with senior Pakistani nuclear scientists to discuss the possibility of embarking on a nuclear weapons program. The meeting was held at the residence of the Punjab Chief Minister Nawab Sadiq Qureshi in Multan. Key invitees included scientists from the Pakistan Institute for Nuclear Science & Technology (PINSTECH), the Pakistan Atomic Energy Commission (PAEC), Quaid-e-Azam University, Islamabad, Government College, Lahore, and the Defence Science & Technology Organization (DESTO). Nobel laureate and former scientific advisor to the Pakistani government Dr. Abdus Salam also attended the meeting. During the meeting, several scientists enthusiastically supported the idea of a nuclear weapons program. Bhutto approved the idea and promised that his government will spare 'no facilities and finances' for a weapons program. He also set a deadline of three years for the scientists to produce a fission device. Toward the end of the meeting, Bhutto announced that Munir Ahmad Khan would replace Dr. Usmani as Chairman of the PAEC."[24]

Two Pakistani nuclear scientists, Dr. Riazuddin and Dr. Masud temporarily working at the International Centre for Theoretical Physics (ICTP), Italy, returned to Pakistan in October 1972 to begin theoretical work on a fission explosive device. The duo was posted to Quaid-e-Azam University and the Pakistan Institute for Nuclear Science and

22. Sublette, 2002b.

23. Bhutto, 1969.

24. Rehman, 1999: 17-18.

Technology (PINSTECH) respectively. As computers were not available, they used the mainframe computers at Quaid-e-Azam University for work related to the theoretical physics of a nuclear explosive device.[25]

"A team of three Pakistani nuclear scientists and engineers, Khalil Qureshi, Zafarullah, and Abdul Majid were sent to the headquarters of the Belgo Nucleaire at Mol in March 1973 to participate in the designing of a pilot nuclear fuel reprocessing facility as well as to gain training in reprocessing spent fuel. Chairman of Pakistan Atomic Energy Commission (PAEC) Dr. Munir Ahmad Khan was in favour of the Belgian pilot reprocessing plant over a British facility on the grounds that it would be difficult for Pakistan to upgrade the downgraded reprocessing plant on offer from the United Kingdom Atomic Energy Agency (UKAEA)."[26]

"By December 1973 the decision was taken by Pakistani scientists to develop an 'implosion' over the 'gun' type of nuclear fission device citing economy in the use of fissile material. Subsequently Dr. Zaman Shaikh, an explosives expert at the Defence Science Laboratories, was assigned the task of developing explosive lenses for the proposed device."[27]

In 1973, Dr. Riazuddin travelled to the International Centre for Theoretical Physics (ICTP), Italy, and from there to the United States to obtain open-source information on the 'Manhattan Project' from the Library of Congress and the National Information Centre, Maryland. After his return from the United States, Riazuddin was inducted into the Pakistan Atomic Energy Commission (PAEC) as member (technical). Dr. Riazuddin later disclosed that he was a member of the team that worked on designs for Pakistan's nuclear explosive device. As he explained, "we were the designers of the bomb, like the tailor who tells you how much of the material is required to stitch a suit. We had to identify the fissile material, whether to use plutonium or...enriched uranium, which method of detonation, which explosive, which type of tampers and lenses to use, how material will be compressed, how shock

25. Rehman, 1999: 38-39.

26. Rehman, 1999: 36-37.

27. Rehman, 1999: 40.

waves will be created, what would be the yield." Riazuddin also disclosed that since Pakistan found it difficult to manufacture beryllium reflectors, the first nuclear explosive device designed by the 'Theoretical Group' used Uranium-238 as a reflector.[28]

Senior Pakistani nuclear scientists Dr. Salam, Munir Ahmad Khan, Dr. Riazuddin, and Hafeez Qureshi convened a meeting on 25th March 1974, with the head of the Pakistan Ordnance Factory at Wah cantonment, Lt. General Qamar Ali Mirza, to set up a plant to manufacture His Majesty's Explosive (HMX) for use in the explosive lenses of the proposed implosion-design fission device. The project was codenamed "Research."[29] In March 1974 the Chairman of Pakistan Atomic Energy Commission (PAEC), Dr. Munir Ahmed Khan constituted a small team of scientists, physicists and engineers to begin work on a nuclear explosive device. The team's office was located at Wah, near Rawalpindi and because of its location came to be referred to as the "Wah Group." The Wah Group began research on conventional explosives used to trigger a nuclear fission device. The original team members included Hafeez Qureshi, head of Radiation and Isotope Applications Division, Pakistan Institute of Science and Technology (PINSTECH) and Dr. Zaman Sheikh, Defense Science and Technology Organisation (DESTO). The group was later expanded to include chemical, mechanical, explosive and precision engineers.[30]

"As soon as he had come to power Bhutto had reached out to the rest of the Islamic world, particularly the nouveau riche oil states of the Middle East, for financial support. During 1973 and 1974 Bhutto held discussions with Libya and other states such as Saudi Arabia to line up financing for a nuclear weapons program. Bhutto and Libya's Colonel Qaddafi finally met and reached an agreement for a Libyan financed Pakistani weapons program in February 1974.[31] In the early seventies billions of dollars also flowed from Iran and Saudi Arabia to Pakistan, most of it for purposes other than the nuclear weapons program, but

28. Rehman, 1999: 39-40.

29. Rehman, 1999: 41.

30. Rehman, 1999: 3-4.

31. Weissman and Krosney; 1981; 59-62.

some of these funds were probably also diverted to support the pursuit of nuclear weapons."[32]

The Pakistan weapons programme was therefore well under way when India carried out its first test of a (peaceful) nuclear explosive device (PNE) on May 18, 1974.[33] Following India's test, Pakistani Prime Minister Zulfikar Ali Bhutto met senior Pakistani officials to discuss the implications of India's nuclear tests. A statement by the Pakistani foreign ministry, released after the meeting, stated that India's pronouncements of peaceful intentions did not satisfy Pakistan's security concerns. The statement also noted that nuclear programmes often incorporate both peaceful and military ends.[34] Next day in a news conference, Pakistani Prime Minister Zulfikar Ali Bhutto indicated that Pakistan will not be threatened by India's 'nuclear blackmail.' He also stated that Pakistan will not alter its current policies.[35] Three weeks later he asserted that India's nuclear programme was designed to intimidate Pakistan and establish "hegemony in the subcontinent" and Pakistan would develop a nuclear programme in response to India's nuclear testing of an atomic device. However, he insisted that Pakistan's programme would be limited to peaceful purposes.[36]

Economic Capability

What was Pakistan's economic and technological capability relative to other countries that have developed a nuclear industry or atomic weapons? An objective measure of inherent capability is essential for judging to what extent the development of nuclear weapons is an indigenous achievement and to what extent it is based on proliferation.

32. Sublette, 2002b.
33. According to P.R. Chari, India's Nuclear Explosion Project was started in 1965, impelled by a trilogy of China-related events—India's traumatic defeat in the 1962 India-China border conflict; China's first nuclear explosion in 1964; and China's support to Pakistan during the Indo-Pak conflict of 1965. Carnegie Endowment for Peace website: *www.ceip.org/Programs/npp/chari2000.htm*
34. Information Bank Abstracts, *New York Times*, in Lexis-Nexis Academic Universe, May 19, 1974, *http://web.lexis-nexis.com/*
35. Information Bank Abstracts, *New York Times*, in Lexis-Nexis Academic Universe, May 20, 1974, *http://web.lexis-nexis.com/*
36. Information Bank Abstracts, *New York Times*, in Lexis-Nexis Academic Universe, June 8, 1974, *http://web.lexis-nexis.com/*

We define nuclear proliferation as either: (a) the breaking of international law by either the source or the destination country or (b) the breaking of the national law of the source country by the destination country.

Virmani (2004) developed a simple measure of the economic and general technical capability of a country. This was used to define an index of relative power VIP^2 where the denominator is the economic and technical capability of the USA.[37] Countries can then be ranked in terms of this index. Table 4.1 shows the index (columns 6 to 9) and the ranking (columns 2 to 5) of various countries from 1980 to 2003. For our current purpose it is more useful to compare the economic/general technical capability of different countries relative to South Africa, a country that was ranked 20th in 2000 and 2003. The reason is that South Africa developed an atomic weapons capability while it was subject to a worldwide embargo that was relatively rigorous (though far from perfect).[38] It can therefore be taken as a reasonable benchmark for the general economic/technological capability needed for indigenous/autonomous development of an atomic weapon. Therefore, the VIP^2 index is recalculated relative to South Africa (instead of the USA) and presented in columns 10 to 13 of Table 4.1.

Destination Countries

Pakistan's economy is ranked around 50th in terms of relative economic/technical capability, over the past 25 years or more. Its relative position has improved very marginally from 51st in 1980 to 48th in 2003. In fact Bangladesh at 50th was ranked higher than Pakistan in 1980 and is only 4 ranks below Pakistan in 2003 at 52nd.[39] Even the Vietnam economy is only a little behind Pakistan today.

Even starker is the comparison with the benchmark, South Africa. In 1980, the Pakistan economy had only 9 per cent of the economic-technological capability of South Africa. As South Africa was on a declining trend at that point while Pakistan was on a rising trend, it can

37. VIP^2 is the Virmani Index of Power Potential.

38. Nazi connections and German help was rumoured to have played a role.

39. Bangladesh/East Pakistan had a longer history of higher education and academic work than West Pakistan, and probably had much greater scientific capability than the latter.

safely be concluded that Pakistan's inherent technological capability was miniscule relative to South Africa during the 1970s. By 1990, the capability of the Pakistan economy had grown to 19 per cent of South Africa's. A decade later it was 29 per cent of South Africa and is still less than 1/3rd of that of South Africa. Besides the declared nuclear weapons States (the US, Russia, the UK, France, China, India), 42 other economies still have a stronger economic and technological base than Pakistan for the development of nuclear weapons.

The contrast with Iran, a country that is currently suspected of trying to attain a nuclear capability is equally striking. Iran's economic-technical capability was 40 per cent of that of South Africa in 1980 (rank 24), 48 per cent in 1990 (rank 32) and 66 per cent in 2000 (rank 31) and is currently more than 80 per cent of that of South Africa (rank 28).[40] It can also be seen from Table 8.1 that countries like Egypt (35 per cent of SA), the Philippines (48 per cent of SA) and Malaysia (48 per cent of SA) always had and still have, greater economic-technological capability than Pakistan. This is also true of 23rd ranked Indonesia (87 per cent of SA) and 25th ranked Turkey (82 per cent of SA) which currently have a higher ranking than the Philippines, though they were ranked lower than the latter in 1980. In 1980, however, Turkey had much closer economic relations with Europe, and particularly Germany, and consequently better access to nuclear technology.

Source Countries

It is also useful to record the relative capability of countries that were the actual or potential sources of clandestine technology transfer for Pakistan. Table 8.2 presents the capabilities of the most advanced countries ordered by their ranking in 1980. Among the important potential sources of technology, equipment and materials during the 70s were the USA, Germany, France, the UK, Canada, the Netherlands and Switzerland. In 1980, Switzerland had only 3.2 per cent of the economic-technological capability of the USA and was ranked 17th, behind South Africa at rank 14th with 4.3 per cent of the US capability. It is also worth noting that India with 3.6 per cent of the US capability was ranked 16th,

40. The variation of GDP with oil prices creates some problems of comparability in the case of oil rich, oil exporting countries like Saudi Arabia, UAE and Iran.

Table 8.1

Inherent Economic and General Technological Capability

1	2	3	4	5	6	7	8	9	10	11	12	13
	Ranking of Power: VIP^2				*Index of Power: VIP^2*				*Relative to South Africa*			
	1980	*1990*	*2000*	*2003*	*1980*	*1990*	*2000*	*2003*	*1980*	*1990*	*2000*	*2003*
South Africa	14	18	20	20	4.3%	3.0%	2.3%	2.3%	100%	100%	100%	100%
Poland		25	21	21		2.0%	2.2%	2.2%		68%	95%	96%
Austria	20	23	22	22	2.4%	2.2%	2.1%	2.0%	57%	74%	93%	88%
Indonesia	36	29	23	23	1.1%	1.6%	2.0%	2.0%	25%	54%	86%	87%
Switzerland	17	20	24	26	3.2%	2.7%	1.9%	1.9%	75%	93%	86%	81%
Turkey	28	26	26	25	1.4%	1.8%	1.9%	1.9%	34%	60%	83%	82%
Thailand	41	33	27	24	0.7%	1.4%	1.7%	1.9%	17%	47%	76%	85%
Norway	26	30	28	30	1.6%	1.5%	1.7%	1.6%	38%	51%	73%	69%
Saudi Arabia	15	27	29	29	4.1%	1.7%	1.6%	1.6%	96%	57%	72%	71%
Hong Kong	39	35	30	32	0.9%	1.3%	1.6%	1.4%	20%	45%	68%	63%
Denmark	23	25	31	33	1.9%	1.6%	1.5%	1.4%	45%	55%	67%	62%
Iran (IIR)	24	32	31	28	1.7%	1.4%	1.5%	1.8%	40%	48%	66%	81%
Greece	22	32	33	31	2.0%	1.4%	1.3%	1.5%	46%	47%	59%	64%
Portugal	32	37	34	35	1.3%	1.3%	1.3%	1.2%	30%	44%	58%	53%
Finland	29	34	35	37	1.3%	1.4%	1.2%	1.1%	31%	46%	51%	50%
Colombia	34	36	36	36	1.2%	1.3%	1.1%	1.2%	29%	45%	50%	51%
Ireland	48	51	37	34	0.4%	0.6%	1.1%	1.4%	11%	19%	49%	61%
Malaysia	46	45	38	39	0.5%	0.6%	1.1%	1.1%	11%	21%	49%	48%
The Philippines	25	38	39	38	1.7%	1.2%	1.1%	1.1%	39%	42%	48%	48%

contd...

contd...

1	2	3	4	5	6	7	8	9	10	11	12	13
	1980	*1990*	*2000*	*2003*	*1980*	*1990*	*2000*	*2003*	*1980*	*1990*	*2000*	*2003*
Israel	40	42	40	42	0.8%	0.8%	1.0%	0.9%	18%	26%	46%	39%
Czech Rep.			41	40			1.0%	1.0%			42%	44%
Singapore	54	55	42	46	0.3%	0.4%	0.8%	0.8%	7%	15%	36%	44%
Hungary	33	40	43	43	1.3%	1.0%	0.8%	0.8%	29%	35%	36%	37%
Egypt (EAR)	43	44	44	44	0.6%	0.7%	0.8%	0.8%	13%	23%	33%	35%
Chile	47	53	45	45	0.5%	0.5%	0.8%	0.8%	11%	16%	33%	34%
Ukraine		16	46	41		3.4%	0.7%	0.9%		116%	32%	41%
Puerto Rico	45	49	47		0.5%	0.6%	0.7%		11%	19%	31%	
Algeria	37	41	48	47	1.0%	0.8%	0.7%	0.7%	23%	28%	30%	31%
Pakistan	51	50	49	48	0.4%	0.6%	0.7%	0.7%	9%	19%	29%	30%
New Zealand	42	46	50	49	0.7%	0.6%	0.6%	0.6%	17%	21%	27%	28%
Venezuela	35	43	51	54	1.1%	0.7%	0.6%	0.4%	25%	25%	25%	18%
Romania		39	52	50		1.0%	0.5%	0.6%		35%	24%	28%
Peru	38	56	53	51	0.9%	0.4%	0.5%	0.5%	20%	15%	21%	21%
Bangladesh	50	60	54	52	0.4%	0.4%	0.4%	0.5%	9%	12%	20%	21%
Vietnam		62	55	53		0.2%	0.4%	0.5%		8%	18%	21%

Source: Virmani (2005) and author's calculations based on WDI, World Bank data on per capita GDP/GDP at PPP.

ahead of both Switzerland and China at 19th position. In fact throughout the 70s and till the mid-1980s, the overall economic and general technical capability of China's economy was inferior to that of India's. It is only during the second half of the 1980s that China overtook India, so that by 1990 it ranked 11th, one position above India at 12th. At that time both had higher capability than the Netherlands.

Because of the extremely rapid growth of China since the mid-1980s, within a decade i.e., by 2000, China's economic-technological capability became 2.5 times that of India and in 2003 it was 2.8 times that of India. Though China's general industrial capabilities were inferior to India's from 1960 to 1980, they are now clearly superior to India's.

Table 8.2

Economic-Technological Capability (VIP²) of Source Countries

	Ranking of Power:VIP²				*Index of Power: VIP²*			
	1980	*1990*	*2000*	*2003*	*1980*	*1990*	*2000*	*2003*
United States	1	1	1	1	100%	100%	100%	100%
Japan	2	2	2	2	33%	36%	30%	28%
Germany	3	3	3	4	24%	22%	19%	18%
France	4	4	5	5	17%	16%	13%	13%
Italy	5	5	7	7	16%	15%	13%	12%
United Kingdom	6	6	6	6	15%	14%	13%	13%
Canada	7	8	8	8	8.9%	8.3%	8.1%	8.0%
Brazil	8	10	11	12	8.8%	6.4%	6.0%	5.7%
Spain	9	9	10	10	6.6%	6.5%	6.4%	6.5%
Mexico	10	13	14	15	4.9%	4.5%	4.6%	4.2%
Netherlands	11	15	17	17	4.5%	4.1%	4.0%	3.9%
Australia	12	14	15	14	4.4%	4.4%	4.6%	4.8%
Argentina	13	22	18	19	4.4%	2.3%	2.7%	2.3%
South Africa	14	18	20	20	4.3%	3.0%	2.3%	2.3%
India	16	12	9	9	3.6%	5.0%	6.8%	7.8%
Switzerland	17	20	24	26	3.2%	2.7%	1.9%	1.9%
Belgium	18	19	19	18	3.2%	2.8%	2.5%	2.3%
China	19	11	4	3	2.7%	6.0%	17%	22%
Austria	20	23	22	22	2.4%	2.2%	2.1%	2.0%
Korea, Rep.	27	17	13	13	1.5%	3.2%	5.0%	5.5%
Russia		7	12	11		13%	5.0%	6.0%

Strategic Technology

As noted in Virmani (2005), strategic technological capability is different from general technological capability, though the latter along with economic strength, provide the foundation on which the former is built. Within a certain range, an obsession with strategic technology and the strong will to acquire it, can result in a relative strategic capability that is much higher than the relative economic strength and general technological capability (as measured by VIP^2). Historically, the USSR/Russia and Maoist China represent such cases. Therefore, even when China's economic strength and general technological capability was inferior to India's (1960 to 1980), its strategic technology and assets were far superior.

Pakistan's relative strategic capability also appears to be above its relative economic strength, though the means adopted were quite different from those of the USSR. Pakistan seems to have learnt from China to use a mixture of diplomatic strategy and covert means to obtain what was otherwise beyond its economic-technological capability.

Foreign Aid and Military Expenditures

The internal economic capabilities of a country can also be supplemented by financial aid received from other countries. This is particularly so if the aid is driven by geopolitical/strategic considerations of the donors. This is patently true of the US and related Western aid to Israel and Egypt (after the Sinai accord and diplomatic recognition). As financial aid is fungible, such aid ostensibly given for economic uplift can allow a country to sustain a higher level of expenditure on building strategic assets, than would otherwise be sustainable. The ratio of financial aid to gross national income (GNI) can be obtained from the *World Development Indicators* of the World Bank and used to rank the large-medium countries. Table 8.3 shows the countries that lie above Pakistan.

Pakistan was the fourth highest recipient of aid in the 1960s and the 10th highest in the 1970s. In 1980, 50 countries had greater economic capability than Pakistan. Of these 50, less than half were developed countries/aid donors, while 23 countries were poor countries/aid recipients. Among the latter, Pakistan was the third highest aid recipient in the 1970s and the fourth highest during the 1980s (Table 8.3). Two countries for which strategic/geopolitical considerations were the prime reason for large aid during both the 1970s and 1980s were Egypt and Israel. Pakistan remained the fourth largest receiver of aid (among this set) in the 1990s though Israel's aid ranking dropped below Pakistan's. Pakistan was therefore, the third most important country from the strategic perspective of the USA/West. This indulgence acted not just as a signal to the military rulers of the country, but also allowed and encouraged it to spend more on strategic assets including the military, than it could sustain on the basis of its own economic capabilities.

Military expenditures, which are a major component of strategic expenditures, can be used as an indicator of the latter. The ratio of military expenditures to total government expenditures is an indication of the government's priorities. We use these to rank all medium-large countries (for which data is available in the *WDI* of the WB) as we have done for economic capabilities and for foreign economic aid received. Table 4.4 shows this ranking for the set of countries that we have been considering. Pakistan is ranked 5th in 1990 and 7th in 2000.[41] This compares with economic ranking of 50th and 49th in 1990 and 2000 respectively. Further, all the countries with higher economic ranking, are ranked much lower than it with respect to military expenditures. Thus, the high level of economic aid received by Pakistan made it possible to spend more on acquisition of strategic assets including military, nuclear and space equipment.

41. For Pakistan, the ratio has been on a declining trend during the 1990s. It was therefore, higher in the past. The military expenditure ranking was probably as high as in the past.

Table 8.3

Foreign Economic Aid Recipients' Ranking in terms of Aid/GNI

	Ranking of Aid Received				*Aid (% of GNI): Decade Average*				
	1960s	*1970s*	*1980s*	*1990s*	*1960s*	*1970s*	*1980s*	*1990s*	*2000s*
United States									
Japan									
Germany									
China		56	45	61		0.0	0.4	0.5	0.1
France									
United Kingdom									
Italy									
Canada									
India	20	33	42	57	2.2	1.2	0.8	0.6	0.3
Spain									
Brazil	36	44	56	77	0.9	0.2	0.1	0.0	0.1
Russia				63				0.4	0.4
Korea, Rep.	5	26	55	84	6.2	1.6	0.1	0.0	0.0
Mexico	47	46	53	75	0.2	0.1	0.1	0.1	0.0
Australia									
Taiwan									
Netherlands									
Argentina	48	48	52	74	0.1	0.1	0.1	0.1	0.1
Belgium									
South Africa				67				0.3	0.4
Poland				37				1.6	0.6
Austria									
Indonesia	9	18	38	42	4.0	2.9	1.2	1.2	1.0
Switzerland									
Sweden									
Turkey	37	40	44	69	0.9	0.5	0.6	0.3	0.1
Thailand	33	36	40	55	1.0	0.8	1.1	0.6	0.1
Norway									
Saudi Arabia	49	53	63	79	0.0	0.0	0.0	0.0	0.0
Hong Kong	45	54	58	81	0.2	0.0	0.0	0.0	0.0
Denmark									
Iran (IIR)		52	62	73		0.0	0.0	0.2	0.1
Greece									

contd...

...contd...

	1960s	*1970s*	*1980s*	*1990s*	*1960s*	*1970s*	*1980s*	*1990s*	*2000s*
Portugal									
Finland									
Colombia	29	35	49	71	1.3	1.0	0.2	0.2	0.6
Ireland									
Malaysia	40	38	43	72	0.7	0.7	0.7	0.2	0.1
The Philippines	38	30	33	34	0.8	1.2	1.7	1.7	0.8
Israel	14	14	21	33	2.8	3.6	4.6	1.8	0.5
Czech Rep.				64				0.4	0.5
Singapore	44	39	51	80	0.2	0.6	0.2	0.0	0.0
Hungary				59				0.5	0.5
Egypt (EAR)	17	3	18	20	2.5	10.4	5.4	5.9	1.3
Chile	25	43	54	68	1.8	0.4	0.1	0.3	0.1
Ukraine				53				0.8	1.2
Puerto Rico									
Algeria	2	31	48	58	8.0	1.2	0.3	0.6	0.4
Pakistan	4	10	25	32	7.0	4.4	2.9	1.9	2.1

Source: World Bank, WDI.

Table 8.4

Ranking of Countries by Ratio of Military to Total Government Expenditures

	Rank		Ratio (%)		VIP² Rank	
	1990	*2000*	*1990*	*2000*	*1990*	*2000*
United States		18		15.6	1	1
Japan	34		6.4		2	2
Germany		67		4.7	3	3
France		57		5.6	4	5
Italy		61		5.3	5	7
United Kingdom		43		6.8	6	6
Russia		13		18.0	7	12
Canada	30	49	7.8	6.0	8	8
Spain		75		3.8	9	10
Brazil	38	60	5.2	5.3	10	11
China					11	4
India	16	21	17.1	14.9	12	9
Mexico	42	79	2.5	3.3	13	14

contd...

...contd...

	1990	2000	1990	2000	1990	2000
Australia		40		7.5	14	15
Netherlands		74		4.0	15	17
Ukraine		26		13.5	16	46
Korea, Rep.	8	23	25.0	14.4	17	13
South Africa	22	62	13.3	5.1	18	20
Belgium		80		3.2	19	19
Switzerland	31	73	7.7	4.2	20	24
Taiwan,China					21	16
Argentina		47		6.2	22	18
Austria		83		2.1	23	22
Sweden		56		5.6	24	25
Poland	37	53	5.6	5.7	25	21
Turkey	9	22	23.1	14.6	26	26
Saudi Arabia					27	29
Denmark		72		4.2	28	31
Indonesia	18	55	15.4	5.7	29	23
Norway		59		5.3	30	28
Iran (IIR)	14	9	18.1	22.4	31	32
Greece		31		10.7	32	33
Thailand		36		8.4	33	27
Finland		77		3.6	34	35
Hong Kong					35	30
Colombia		16		16.2	36	36
Portugal		64		5.1	37	34
The Philippines	29	46	8.1	6.2	38	39
Romania	20	38	13.7	7.8	39	52
Hungary		70		4.3	40	43
Algeria	23	15	12.4	16.5	41	48
Israel		17		16.0	42	40
Venezuela	26	42	9.7	7.1	43	51
Egypt (EAR)	13	27	18.7	12.4	44	44
Malaysia	25	32	11.0	10.5	45	38
New Zealand		78		3.5	46	50
Puerto Rico					49	47
Pakistan	5	7	34.5	23.4	50	49

Source: IMF, Govt. Financial Statistics.

European Foundations

In the decade and a half from the start of Pakistan's weapons programme, it clandestinely obtained from Europe, Canada and the USA, the complete designs, equipment and materials necessary to enrich uranium to weapons grade, extract bomb grade plutonium and manufacture a nuclear explosive device. Despite this, in 1980 Pakistan was still not confident of manufacturing an atomic weapon and testing it successfully, given its economic and general technological capability. The designs and equipment so obtained would remain with Pakistan till they were converted into concrete strategic assets with the direct help of a more economically powerful and technologically capable State with a high degree of strategic capability. One difference between the European and North American supplies to Pakistan was that when they were exposed, the latter lead to prosecution while the former were often ignored on the plea that they were not legally prohibited.

Uranium Enrichment

By a quirk of history, Pakistan's uranium enrichment programme originated in late April-early May 1972 with Pakistani metallurgist Dr. A.Q. Khan taking up a job with the specialised Dutch engineering company—Physical Dynamics Laboratory or FDO at its metallurgical section in the Dutch town of Almelo. FDO was a subsidiary of the Dutch company Verenigde Machine-Fabrieken and was a consultant and subcontractor to Ultra-Centrifuge Nederland (UCN)—the Dutch partner of the tri-national European uranium enrichment centrifuge consortium URENCO for the ultracentrifuge process being developed by Britain, West Germany and the Netherlands to enrich uranium. The Dutch secret service BVD, ran a cursory background check on Khan and granted him a security clearance, "secret inclusive". Elementary principles of security were not, it seems, observed by any part of the URENCO establishment. Routine procedures, such as wearing identification badges marked with the level of clearance appear to have been unknown. Once someone gained access to a part of a facility with one level of clearance, there seem to have been few, if any barriers to moving to higher level areas. The customary practice of checking the security clearance level of a person before signing out classified documents to them appears to have been ignored. Within a week of starting with FDO, A.Q. Khan was sent to the UCN enrichment facility in Almelo, Netherlands, which he visited on 8-9 May.[42] A visit to an external facility would normally require the transmittal of security paperwork to be granted access. This procedure was ignored by both FDO and UCN. Though Khan was not cleared to visit the UCN facility, he did so repeatedly during his employment. In his first two years Khan worked with two early centrifuge designs, the CNOR and SNOR machines.[43]

On 17 September 1974, Abdul Qadeer Khan wrote a letter to Prime Minister Zulfikar Ali Bhutto, through the Pakistani ambassador in Belgium, explaining his expertise in centrifuge-based uranium enrichment technologies at URENCO in Belgium. Khan offered help and urged the prime minister to take the uranium route to a nuclear weapons programme. Bhutto responded favourably to Khan's suggestion and directed the Chairman of the Pakistan Atomic Energy Commission (PAEC), Dr. Munir Ahmad Khan to meet A.Q. Khan.[44] By late 1974, Dr. A.Q. Khan started working with the Pakistani government to help develop plans for setting up an ultracentrifuge uranium enrichment plant. In the fall of 1974, Khan translated secret German documents on a technical breakthrough concerning the ultracentrifuge uranium enrichment process for the FDO. Khan shared this classified information with the Pakistani government.[45]

Dr. Munir Ahmad Khan directed Bashiruddin Mahmood (in October 1974) to prepare a feasibility report on the proposed uranium enrichment programme.[46] After studying the various technical approaches to enriching uranium, Bashiruddin Mahmood recommended (in November 1974) that Pakistan build a uranium enrichment facility based on centrifuge technology. Mahmood's report envisaged the completion of the facility by 1979.[47] On 15 February 1975, Dr. Munir

42. Weissman and Krosney, 1981: 176-177, 178.

43. Sublette, 2002a.

44. Rehman, 1999: 47

45. Weissman and Krosney, 1981: 178.

46. Rehman, 1999: 48.

47. Rehman, 1999: 50.

Ahmed Khan met the Prime Minister Zulfikar Ali Bhutto and sought government's approval for a $450 million nuclear weapons programme that involved among other things, the building of a centrifuge plant for the enrichment of uranium.[48]

Simultaneously, action was initiated for setting up a clandestine nuclear procurement network across Europe so as to beat the various non-proliferation regimes such as the NSG and Wassaner. For this purpose, Pakistani nuclear scientist S.A. Butt was appointed to the Pakistani embassy in the Netherlands in July 1975. Later Butt was shifted to Paris where he became the Pakistani government's chief purchasing agent in Europe for uranium and plutonium enrichment technologies. Butt was one of the scientists who had attended the January 1972 meeting called by Prime Minister Zulfikar Ali Bhutto to discuss the possibility of Pakistan developing a nuclear bomb.[49]

In the fall of 1975, Dr. A.Q. Khan (still at FDO) was asked to translate sensitive documents concerning a German technical breakthrough in the ultracentrifuge uranium enrichment process the G-1 and G-2, from German into Dutch. For this purpose Khan spent 16 days at URENCO's facility in the town of Almelo. Security arrangements at the facility were lax and a colleague later reported seeing Khan making notes at his desk in a foreign script. Khan also used the opportunity to repeatedly tour the Almelo plant.[50] Dr. A.Q. Khan then used S.A. Butt at the Pakistani embassy in Netherlands as a conduit for supplying centrifuge-related technical literature, blueprints, plans for plant design and lists of equipment and material suppliers to the Pakistan Atomic Energy Commission (PAEC).[51] Thus, even though Pakistan did not possess the critical disembodied technology of uranium enrichment, it was now in possession virtually complete knowledge of elements of the technology that could be reduced to pieces of paper.

In late 1975, Pakistan launched Project 706 (according to another source, Project 726) to produce enriched uranium using the centrifuge

48. Rehman, 1999: 50
49. Weissman and Krosney, 1981: 182
50. Weissman and Krosney, 1981: 179-80.
51. Rehman, 1999: 51.

enrichment process.[52] The project involved the construction of a pilot facility at Sihala, to be followed by the construction of an industrial-scale plant housing 10,000 centrifuges at the village of Kahuta. Dr. A.Q. Khan took charge of the new Engineering Research Laboratory (ERL), tasked with designing the centrifuges for the proposed facilities. The Pakistan Atomic Energy Commission (PAEC) led by Dr. Munir Ahmed Khan retained overall charge of the project, while the military's Special Works Commission was asked to help with purchases from abroad and construction of the top-secret facilities.[53]

In August 1975, Pakistan begins buying components for its domestic uranium enrichment programme from European Urenco suppliers. S.A. Butt, a physicist in the Pakistani embassy in Belgium, contacted a Dutch company to obtain high frequency inverters, which are used to control centrifuge motors. Purchases accelerated in the following years and many components were secured from companies in the Netherlands that Khan is familiar with.[54]

In 1976, Pakistan began a major purchasing drive in Western Europe for its uranium enrichment project. During 1976, government agents placed orders with Swiss and Dutch firms. Specific purchases included highly specialised valves for centrifuges (VAT-Switzerland), a gasification and solidification unit to feed uranium hexafluoride gas into centrifuges (CORA Engineering, Switzerland), and 6500 specially hardened steel tubes (Van Doorne Transmissie, Netherlands). Other Dutch manufacturers received orders for large numbers of high strength aluminum and extremely strong martensitic steel, for the crucial centrifuge rotors. Critical support components and sub-systems were purchased from Switzerland (high vacuum valves from Vakuum Apparat Technik of Haag, Switzerland and Germany, vacuum pumps and gas purification equipment from Leybold Heraeus of Hanan, Germany; plus thousands of specially formed aluminum parts).[55] As these items were not explicitly covered under the London Group's 'Nuclear Suppliers

52. For details see Namboodri's article in Subrahmanyam (1981).

53. Weissman and Krosney, 1981: 182; Rehman, 1999: 56.

54. Sublette, 2002b.

55. Sublette, 2002b and Weismann and Krosney, 1981.

List,' the firms treated these as legal exports. Although the Swiss and Dutch governments learned about these purchases and knew that they related to Pakistan's planned centrifuge facility, they consciously chose to stick with a narrow interpretation of nuclear export control regulations and did not interfere with the sales.[56]

The next year in 1977, orders were placed in France for 10,000 metal bellows, whose only use was to stabilise the gas centrifuge rotor. France prohibited the sale, but the company shipped part of order through a subcontractor in Belgium, which did not interfere, along with the dies so that Pakistan could make the bellows themselves.

As part of the acquisition programme Pakistan also attempted to purchase 10-15 tonnes of uranium hexafluoride gas from the West German company Rohstoff-Einfuhr, but this particular attempt proved unsuccessful.[57] This minor obstacle was overcome by November 1976, when Pakistan signed, through a Pakistani textile plant, a $2 million deal with Albrecht Migule, owner of the West German firm CES Kalthof to supply a fluoride plant.[58] By the summer of 1978, the Swiss firm CORA Engineering completed fabrication of a uranium gasification and solidification unit for the Kahuta gas centrifuge uranium enrichment facility. The entire plant was airlifted to Pakistan using chartered C-130 Hercules transport aircraft. CORA Engineering also provided engineers and other technical personnel to help with the post-sales servicing. This was the first of the two gasification and solidification units at Kahuta.[59]

By 1978, ERL at Kahuta reportedly developed a working prototype of P-1 centrifuges, adapted from the German G-1 design Khan worked with at Urenco and enriched uranium for the first time on April 4, 1978.[60]

Frank Allaun, a British Labour Party MP, asked a question in the House of Commons in July 1978, regarding certain components being exported by a British company that would enable Pakistan to build nuclear weapons. Allaun pointed out that the high-frequency electric

56. Weissman and Krosney, 1981: 182-184.

57. Weissman and Krosney, 1981: 218.

58. *Nuclear Fuel* (July 1981), P. 3.

59. Weissman and Krosney, 1981.

60. Sublette, 2002b.

equipment exactly matched the components used by British Nuclear Fuels Ltd. The British company, Emerson Electric Industrial Controls, was a subsidiary of the US firm Emerson Electric.[61] The British government reported back that the items specified in Allaun's question were not included in the British export control list. The order was placed by a firm called Weargate based in Swansea, Wales, which was operated by two Pakistanis.[62] During July to September 1978, the British firm, Emerson Electric Industrial Controls, exported 31 complete inverter systems to Pakistan. The inverter systems can be used to regulate a large number of centrifuge machines in a uranium enrichment plant. The inverters are routed through Weargate Ltd., operated by Abdus Salam and Peter Griffin.[63] By October 1978, the British government changed its mind and imposed tighter export control laws after Frank Allaun revealed that Pakistan had placed further orders with the British company for inverters that could be used in a uranium fuel enrichment plant. The British company was working on 100 more inverters to be supplied to Pakistan when the government imposed further restrictions to stop the export of such components.[64]

The Pakistani nuclear procurement was not, however, limited to Europe, but stretched all the way to North America. In the fall of 1978, a California based firm exported about half-dozen inverters to Pakistan.[65]

In late 1970s and early 1980s, American intelligence officials convinced Dutch authorities on two occasions not to arrest Khan for the purposes of monitoring his activities further.[66]

In early 1979, Indian scientists were reported to have learned from European commercial sources about Pakistan's recent acquisition of large quantities of 'maraging steel,' an extremely hard variety of steel used to make critical components of a gas centrifuge uranium enrichment system. India's pacifist and anti-nuclear weapons Prime

61. Allaun says he received information about the order from "a friend who had a friend."

62. Oberdorfer, Gatier and Schwartz, 1979, *Economist* (14 April); Willis, 1981.

63. Oberdorfer, Gatier and Schwartz, 1979; Weissman and Krosney, 1981: 186.

64. Oberdorfer, Gatier and Schwartz, 1979.

65. Oberdorfer, Gatier and Schwartz, 1979.

66. Broad and Sanger, 2004b.

Minister Morarji Desai therefore wrote a letter to Pakistani President General Zia ul-Haq in mid-February 1979 expressing concern over Pakistan's nuclear weapons programme.[67]

On 6th April 1979, the United States informed Pakistan of its decision to cut off economic and military aid as a result of Pakistan's efforts to secretly build a uranium enrichment facility that can produce weapons grade uranium. The aid cut-off was imposed after the Central Intelligence Agency (CIA) confirmed reports from European intelligence services that Pakistan had acquired most of the equipment needed to operate the plant. The United States also believed that Pakistan's ability to procure the equipment from European companies reinforced the inadequacy of existing export control mechanisms regarding sensitive technology. The US State department officials insisted that the construction of the facility has been continuing for quite some time and revealed that high-level talks had been held between the United States and Pakistan on the issue.[68]

In April 1980, the West German engineering firm CES Kalthof handed over the plans for producing UF6 and UF4 to Pakistan. Pakistan failed to make the final payments for the plants.[69] On July 1, 1980, CES Kalthof admited that it sold Pakistan, equipment for making uranium-hexafluoride (UF), the basic raw material input for producing enriched uranium in the gas centrifuge. Albrecht Migule, the firm's director, however denied a news report in the German magazine *Stern* that the laboratory equipment could be used to make nuclear weapons.[70] On 20 July 1981 the firm was charged for violating West German Foreign Trade Act by shipping a plant capable of producing uranium-hexafluoride to Pakistan. In responding to a Parliamentary question, the German government said that the delivery of the plant required an export licence which would not have been granted by the government. The question regarding the deal was raised in the parliament after a German magazine, *Der Stern* announced that it possesses contracts and other

67. Oberdorfer, 1979.

68. Oberdorfer, 1979, *Xinhua*, 1979, *World Affairs*, 1979.

69. *Nuclear Fuel*, 20 July 1981.

70. *Washington Post*, 1981b.

documents regarding the deals between the German firm and a Pakistani textile company. A spokesperson for the German Economics Ministry said that German authorities have collected enough evidence to charge the German firm with violating the German Foreign Trade Act. The spokesperson said that investigations were being carried out since early 1981 long before the firm's activities were published in *Der Stern*. The outcome of the investigation will determine if the firm will be tried in a court or be handled by tax authorities.[71]

In July 1980, two Pakistan Atomic Energy Commission (PAEC) scientists Anwar Ali and I.A. Bhatty went to Montreal with a list of items needed for a high-speed inverter. Export of inverters is prohibited by the United States and other countries since it is used for spinning gases in a centrifuge for enriching uranium.[72] Over the next two months (July–August) Pakistan bought parts for high speed inverters from American firms like General Electric Co., Westinghouse Electric Corp., RCA Corp. and Motorola Inc. The purchases were made by two small electrical-equipment stores in Montreal. The parts were repackaged and shipped to the Middle East and eventually to Pakistan. The operation was assisted by several highly educated Pakistani expatriates in Canada and the United States. Some of the expatriates are recruited through newspaper advertisements and later persuaded to work for sometime in Pakistan with Dr. Abdul Qadeer Khan. Dr. Khan is in charge of the uranium enrichment programme.[73] At the end of August, Canadian police, acting on a tip from British Customs Service, seized 19 boxes of equipment at the Montreal Mirabel Airport. The boxes were being shipped to Pakistan. The police arrested Abdul Aziz Khan (a Canadian electrical engineer), Salam Elmenyawi (owner of an electrical-equipment store in Montreal) and Mohammad Ahmad (a mechanical engineer working in Quebec). Seized records indicate that 10 other shipments of inverters were sent to Pakistan.[74] The next day Canadian police released Abdul Aziz Khan and followed him to a railroad station where he retrieved a suitcase and several documents. Abdul Aziz Khan then

71. *Nuclear Fuel*, 1981.

72. Fialka, 1984.

73. Fialka, 1984.

74. Fialka, 1984.

shreded the documents, dropped them in a trash can, and proceeded to the airport to catch a flight to Pakistan. He was then rearrested at the airport. The documents, retrieved and pieced together by the Canadian police, included a paper by an American scientist on using high-speed gas centrifuges for uranium enrichment.[75]

In September 1980, US experts confirmed that Pakistan was buying components from Switzerland, the United States, Britain, West Germany and other countries. Pointing to intelligence reports, photographs of construction of the uranium enrichment plant at Kahuta, and statements by the former Prime Minister Zulfikar Ali Bhutto, these experts however believed that Pakistan would need several years to finish the enrichment plant and produce weapons grade uranium for nuclear bombs.[76] In September 1981, Western sources indicated that Pakistan's uranium enrichment plant, located 30 miles southeast of Islamabad at Kahuta, was expected to start operating by the end of this year. The plant uses gas centrifuge technology allegedly stolen from the Netherlands.[77]

On 31st October 1981, a 5,000 lb shipment of zirconium metal worth $153,000 was seized at the Kennedy International Airport prior to its loading onto a passenger plane. Zirconium is used in construction of nuclear reactors and its export requires an export licence. The zirconium shipment wa labelled as mountain-climbing equipment and the passenger accompanying the shipment was Dr. Sarfaz Mir, a retired Pakistani Army officer, and is believed to be a close friend of Pakistan's President Zia ul-Haq. After the seizure of the shipment, US customs officials searched the Pakistan Airlines flight to locate Dr. Mir but were unable to locate him. The Assistant General Manager of Pakistan Airlines said that he will investigate the issue. Agents from the compliance division of the Commerce Department's Office of Export Administration, headed by Sharon R. Connelly, had tracked the shipment from its production plant in Oregon to the Kennedy Airport.

75. Fialka, 1984.

76. Downie, 1980.

77. *Manchester Guardian Weekly*, 6 September 1981.

key parts and manufacture other parts indigenously. The scientists also believed that it would be possible to upgrade the plant indigenously to produce weapons-grade plutonium.[86] For various reasons the UK deal was never consummated.

The first Pakistani facility for plutonium extraction from spent nuclear fuel was a pilot reprocessing facility called the "New Labs" at Pinstech. This facility was a larger and more ambitious project than the original BNFL plan. It was built in the early 1970s by Belgonucléaire and the French corporation Saint-Gobain Techniques Nouvelles (SGN).

The pilot plant was followed by a contract signed with SGN in March 1973 to prepare the basic design for a large-scale (100 tonne) fuel reprocessing plant, considerably more than the (safeguarded) KANUPP power reactor would generate. SGN was the world's chief exporter of reprocessing technology and had previously built military plutonium facilities for France, the secret plutonium plant at Dimona in Israel, and contracted to provide similar plants to Taiwan, South Korea and (later) Iraq. The Chashma plant, as it was known, would have the capability to produce 200 kg of weapons grade plutonium a year, if sufficient fuel were available to feed it.[87] In April 1974, Pakistan signed a contract with France for the design of a nuclear fuel reprocessing plant, to be constructed at Chashma on the banks of Indus river.[88] The initial design contract was followed by one for the final detailed design on 18 October 1974.[89] A contract for the sale of equipment and construction of the nuclear fuel reprocessing plant was signed in March 1976.[90]

On 9th August 1976, the French foreign minister indicated to the US *charge d'affaires* Sam Gammon that France would proceed with the sale of the reprocessing plant and also informed of France's displeasure over the US efforts to hinder the sale of a fuel reprocessing plant to Pakistan. French foreign ministry officials revealed that the sale of the

86. Rehman, 1999: 35-36.
87. Sublette, 2002b and Weissman and Krosney, 1981: 75, 171.
88. *Economist*, 1974.
89. Sublette, 2002b and Weissman and Krosney, 1981: 75, 171.
90. Oberdorfer *et al.*, 1979.

reprocessing plant was approved on 18 March under an agreement reached between France, Pakistan and the International Atomic Energy Agency (IAEA). The French government released a statement indicating that it was in compliance with all international agreements regarding the sale, including an agreement with the IAEA to ensure that the plant is only used for peaceful activities.[91] On 26th August 1976, the French cabinet indicated its intention to proceed with the sale of the nuclear reprocessing plant to Pakistan despite objections raised by the United States.[92] On 13 October 1976, France again reaffirmed its decision to supply Pakistan with the nuclear reprocessing plant despite its recent assertions to prevent the spread of nuclear weapons.[93]

The US State Department withheld nuclear licences for 12 countries including Pakistan. According to the State Department (20th May 1978), the licences were being withheld because of Pakistan's attempts to acquire nuclear fuel reprocessing capacity. The US export licence withheld was for the export of less than one pound of plutonium. The plutonium was intended for a Pakistani research reactor in which the plutonium was to be irradiated with alpha particles.[94]

In October 1978, Pakistan's imprisoned former Prime Minister Zulfikar Ali Bhutto claimed that Pakistan was near to attaining "full nuclear capability" prior to his overthrow in 1977. Bhutto claims that "All we [Pakistanis] needed was the nuclear reprocessing plant." In a 319-page document smuggled out of his prison cell, Mr. Bhutto takes credit for developing Pakistan's nuclear energy programme and indicates that Pakistan only needs a reprocessing facility to attain nuclear capability.[95]

Top US officials in the Carter administration considered Pakistan to be the biggest proliferation threat. US officials pointed (Decemeber 8, 1978) to the document written by deposed Pakistani Prime Minister Zulfikar Ali Bhutto as evidence of Pakistan's intentions to develop a

91. Information Bank Abstracts, *New York Times*, World News Digest, 1976.

92. Information Bank Abstracts, *New York Times*, 26 August 1976.

93. Information Bank Abstracts, *New York Times*, 13 October 1976.

94. O'Toole, 1978.

95. World News Digest, 1978; Benjamin, 1978.

technical assistance for the plutonium reprocessing facility in Pakistan, despite the cancellation of the contract by the French government. Pecqueur wrote, "It is hardly necessary for me to stress the seriousness of the facts, should they be in any way confirmed, as transactions of this kind would call into question the national policy on non-proliferation at the very highest level."[104] Georges Besse in turn wrote to SGN President F.X. Poincet on 31st May 1979, inquiring whether SGN is continuing nuclear-related transfers to Pakistan. In his reply, Poincet denied that SGN is selling any contraband materials to Pakistan. He admitted however that SGN was continuing with limited involvement in relation to "preparation of orders" for some Pakistanis who are still "resident" at SGN. However, Poincet hinted that Pakistan may have gone behind their backs to procure equipment specified in documents supplied by SGN earlier. The nuclear industry's trade journal *Nucleonics Week* alleged that Pakistan has access to 95 per cent of the design plans for the plutonium reprocessing facility and these will likely enable Pakistan to finish the plant despite the termination of French assistance.[105]

Going in to the 80s, Pakistan was still evidently trying to complete the Chashma plant.[106] It is not known that the plant had ever reached operational status (as of 2002), although in the intervening two decades Pakistan presumably could have developed the capabilities to manufacture any components they lacked, and US intelligence agencies believed that they are working on this.[107]

In an interview during the 2nd week of December 1982, Pakistan's President Zia ul-Haq denied the existence of the New Labs reprocessing plant and insisted that "we have no reprocessing facility whatsoever. Pakistani scientists are experimenting with how to reprocess one ounce of plutonium as scientists." US analysts, however, believed that the New Labs reprocessing facility was not (currently) reprocessing plutonium but believed that the facility possessed greater capacity than admitted by Pakistan. US analysts noted that the Chairman of the

104. Weissman and Krosney, 1981: 196.

105. Weissman and Krosney, 1981: 196

106. Weissman and Krosney, 1981; 195-208.

107. Koch and Topping, 1997.

Pakistan Atomic Energy Commission (PAEC) Munir Ahmad Khan had indicated to European scientists that the New Labs facility can reprocess about 6 kg of plutonium. President Zia Ul Haq also stated that the enrichment facility in Kahuta is "a humble, modest program." US sources, however, insisted that the Kahuta facility is built to house 10,000 ultracentrifuges. US intelligence sources also point out that the reprocessing and enrichment facilities are handled by the PAEC and the procurement of equipment and construction of nuclear plants is supervised by the Pakistani military.[108]

NPT Proliferation: Weapon Material

On 9th April 1975, the Director of the US Arms Control and Disarmament Agency (ACDA), Fred C. Ikle, warned that several countries are pursuing efforts to acquire nuclear weapons. He stated that such countries are acquiring the means to produce nuclear weapons under the guise of obtaining nuclear technology for peaceful purposes. Although Ikle did not reveal the names of countries believed to be pursuing nuclear weapons, the *New York Times* claimed that it has learned from "authoritative" sources that the list includes Pakistan, Argentina, Brazil, Libya, Israel, Taiwan and South Korea.[109]

On 3rd January 1980, Michel Pecquer, Director of the French Atomic Commission, denied France's involvement in the sale of Niger-mined uranium to Pakistan and Libya. He also denied reports that uranium shipments from the mines in Niger were stolen. He clarified that the sale of uranium to Libya and Pakistan was made by the government of Niger and involved only those portions of the mines that were controlled by the Niger government. He added that the sale of 258 tonnes of uranium yellow cake to Libya and 110 tonnes to Pakistan was in conformance with IAEA regulations. The sale of uranium to Libya and Pakistan was confirmed by a Niger government spokesperson. The two uranium mines in question were owned by the Niger government, COGEMA—a French company owned by the French Atomic

108. Benjamin (1982). *Washington Post*, 20 December.

109. "Ikle Warns Against Nuclear Spread," Facts on File World News Digest, 12 April 1975; in Lexis-Nexis Academic Universe, 6 February 1975, *http://web.lexis-nexis.com*

"In February 1985, there were reports of Krytron switches used in triggering devices being smuggled to Pakistan from Western sources (Nazr Ahamad Vaid case).[116] In August 1985 there were reports of Pakistan making attempts to purchase flash X-ray devices (used to picture the characteristics of high explosives during detonation) from Sweden.[117] In July 1987 Arshad Pervez was arrested by US customs agents in Philadelphia on charges that he tried to export beryllium and maraging steel to Pakistan. Beryllium is used as neutron reflector in nuclear weapons.[118] Parveez was indicted by a Federal Grand Jury for this act in December 1987."[119]

In January 1987, A.Q. Khan gave an interview to Kuldip Nayyar, an Indian journalist, in which he claimed that "..they (the whole world) told us that Pakistan could never produce the bomb and they doubted my capabilities; but now they know we have done it."[120]

"Two related West German firms provided Pakistan with test quantities of Tritium gas, a tritium purification and storage plant, tritium precursor materials, the design for a reactor that could be used for tritium production, and material and equipment for fabricating fuel for that reactor, including special American made welding lasers."[121]

In early 1996, Great Britain expelled an employee of the Pakistan Embassy in London for attempting to export illegally, specialised laser instruments used in the manufacture of nuclear weapons.[122]

Chinese Weapons Designs

Despite covertly obtaining from Europe, Canada and the USA, industrial scale plants for the manufacture of highly enriched uranium and bomb

116. *New York Times*, February 25, 1985.

117. *Financial Times*, August 17, 1985.

118. *Nucleonics Week*, 1987.

119. *Nucleonics Week*, 1988. The foregoing paragraph is taken from Kargil, 2000: 189-190.

120. *The Observer* (London), March 1, 1987. Kargil, 2000: 191.

121. McDonough/CIEP, 1998, "Pakistan" fn 25; Der Spiegel, 1989, Hibbs, 1989a,b,c,d,e, *News India*, 1989.

122. *Washington Times*, February 1996.

grade plutonium, Pakistan was still not in a position at the end of the 70s, to produce HEU and bomb grade plutonium on a sustained basis without outside help. Nor was it in a position to build and test an atomic bomb and build reliable weapons by itself. It therefore turned to China at the end of 1970s to obtain all the elements needed to put together an atomic bomb. China supplied the designs, the HEU and other material for manufacturing an atomic bomb. As China was not in a position to supply a gas centrifuge plant for enriching uranium (having chosen the diffusion route), Pakistan was forced to change from the uranium to the plutonium route, to put its nuclear capability on a sustained and credible footing. It therefore persuaded China to supply a prototype reactor that would produce spent fuel containing plutonium and a pilot scale plant to extract bomb grade plutonium. It is only after obtaining from China, complete (small scale) un-safeguarded duplicates of all the processes/plants that it had earlier obtained from Europe, the critical missing parts for an atomic bomb and guaranteed-to-be-effective nuclear weapons, did it institute an aggressive policy of large scale training, arming and infiltration of terrorists into India (J&K followed by Kargil and the rest of India).

Chinese Capability[123]

"The Soviet Union basically designed and built the fledgling nuclear industry in China until 1960. In the words of Jonathan Pollack, a prominent China expert, 'In scale and scope Soviet assistance to the Chinese weapons program is without parallel in the history of nuclear proliferation.' Hundreds of Chinese technicians and scientists received training in the USSR and thousands more were trained by soviet technicians in China. On 17 January 1955, just two days after the Chinese leadership decided to develop its own nuclear weapons, the Soviet Union announced that it would assist China with peaceful nuclear energy research, including the supply of a research reactor and a cyclotron (operational in Tuoli, June 1958). Six Sino-Soviet nuclear accords were signed between 1955 and 1958, ranging from joint uranium prospecting to the transfer of Soviet nuclear weapons technology."

123. This sub-section is based largely on Norris *et al.*, 1994: 324, 330; 338, 340.

reportedly reassured Pakistan of support if the war was prolonged.[129] Thus began Pakistan's efforts to persuade China to supply nuclear weapons related technology to it. This effort ended successfully 11 years later.

Zulfikar Ali Bhutto became Pakistan's Prime Minister in 1971 and visited China in 1972, 1974 and May 26-30, 1976. In his memoirs, he wrote (in jail) that, "My single most important achievement, which, I believe, will dominate the portrait of my public life, is an agreement which I arrived at after assiduous and tenacious endeavours, spanning 11 years of negotiations...[130] The agreement of mine concluded in June, 1976, will perhaps be my greatest achievement and contribution to the survival of our people and our nation".[131] Bhutto was in Beijing on June 1, 1976.[132]

General Mirza Aslam Beg was vice chief of army staff in General Zia ul-Haq's military administration, and after Zia's death in a plane crash, was immediately made chief in August 1988. After Zia's death, Beg helped Pakistan to a peaceful transition of power through general elections after which the Pakistan People's Party's (PPP's) Benazir Bhutto became premier. Beg remained a powerful chief of army staff until 1991, a period in which Pakistan developed nuclear weapons. He stated in an interview, "The program that we started in 1976 achieved its purpose in about 12 years' time."

On April 27, 1978, the Marxist People's Democratic Party of Afghanistan (PDPA) overthrew and executed Daoud along with members of his family. Nur Muhammad Taraki, Secretary General of the PDPA, became President of the Revolutionary Council and Prime Minister of the newly established Democratic Republic of Afghanistan. In May

---

129. *http://pakistanspace.tripod.com/65.htm*

130. India-Pakistan War took place 11 years before in 1965. According to the Library of Congress—Country Study, "Iran, Indonesia, and especially China gave political support to Pakistan during the war, thus suggesting new directions in Pakistan that might translate into support for its security concerns. After 1965 China became Pakistan's principal military supplier, providing matériel to all three services in substantial quantity and at attractive prices." *http://lcweb2.loc.gov/cgi-bin/query/r?frd/cstdy:@field(DOCID+pk0152)*

131. *Economist*, 14 July 1979.

132. Kargil, 2000: 185.

1978, up to 400 Soviet military advisers were despatched to Afghanistan. On July 3, 1979, the US President Jimmy Carter signed a directive authorising the CIA to conduct covert propaganda operations against the revolutionary regime. On July 7, 1979, the USSR sent an airborne battalion with crews in response to a request from the Afghan government for such a delivery.

In June-July 1979, sources indicated that Pakistan was attempting to explode a nuclear bomb in October (1979). Pakistan's security forces were reported to be working around Hoshab, a small desert town located 60 miles inland from the Makran coast in southwestern Pakistan. The region is inhospitable and a few nomads living there were reported to have been re-located to different areas. Reliable reports suggested the presence of military construction activity in the area. Experts indicated that Pakistan might test a nuclear bomb in 1979 only if it received sufficient weapons-grade material from another source, since its reprocessing plant and its uranium enrichment plant were still far from operating at full capacity. Experts suspected that source to be China.[133]

Soviet deployment of the 40th Army into Afghanistan started on December 25, 1979. On December 27, 1979, 700 troops, including 54 KGB spetsnaz special forces troops from the Alpha Group and Zenith Group, deposed President Hafizullah Amin. Soviet ground forces entered Afghanistan from the north on December 27 and the Vitebsk parachute division landed at Bagram airport. The invasion transformed the attitude of the USA (Govt., academics, media) and China towards Pakistan and towards each other. "US-China relations entered a 'Golden Age' in the 1980s. Both nations continued to feel threatened by the Soviet Union (what Deng termed the "polar bear") and a new spirit of cooperation marked relations."[134]

Pakistan seemed to have convinced the Chinese that Russia, with the tacit support of India, would break through Afghanistan into the Indian Ocean and thereafter explicitly link up with India. This would

133. *Economist*, 14 July 1979.

134. *Programme Brief* 7(22), The Nixon Center, Washington DC, December 12, 2001, "September 11 and U.S.-China Ties: A Chance for a New Strategic Partnership?" A Nixon Center seminar featuring Richard Solomon. *www.nixoncenter.org/Program%20Briefs/vol7no22Solomon(China).htm*

put China's access to Middle-East oil as well as its ties to Pakistan under risk. China was apparently persuaded that it was therefore, necessary for Pakistan to get nuclear weapons from China to deter both India and the Russians in Afghanistan. This would provide Pakistan with a shield to train jehadis to fight the Soviets in Afghanistan and India in Kashmir. China under Deng Xiaping (1978+), who played a leadership role in China's nuclear weapons programme from its start, was apparently convinced of the need to supply nuclear weapons to Pakistan, just as the USSR had promised to supply to China (but reneged on) 20 years earlier.

Strategic Proliferation

On 12th February 1980, reports indicated that Chinese nuclear experts were assisting Pakistan in its efforts to enrich uranium.[135] On 4th May 1980, Pakistani official sources denounced reports from Kabul and Moscow that President Zia ul-Haq would discuss the question of testing Pakistan's nuclear weapons in China with the Chinese leaders. Sources indicated that Pakistan's nuclear programme was geared towards peaceful purposes and also mentioned that Pakistan had no intention to produce nuclear weapons.[136] Following Pakistani President Zia ul-Haq's conclusion of his visit to China, reports suggested (6-18 May 1980) that the Chinese leaders had promised to permit the testing of Pakistan's nuclear devices on Chinese territory. According to these reports, the tests would be supervised by Chinese and Pakistani scientists.[137]

On 19th August 1982, U.S. Assistant Secretary of State for Oceans and International Environmental and Scientific Affairs, James Malone indicated that one of the factors obstructing the completion of a bilateral nuclear accord between China and the United States was China's relationship with Pakistan regarding nuclear issues. Malone indicated that China supplied Pakistan with material other than fuel-related items. However, he declined to name the specific items. Malone also indicated that the United States was making progress in restricting

---

135. *BBC*, 14 February 1980.

136. Xinhua, 6 May 1980.

137. BBC, 22 May 1980.

the supply of nuclear components to Pakistan's nuclear facilities.[138] On 8th September 1982, the United States placed a hold on bilateral nuclear cooperation with China because of intelligence reports suggesting that China helped Pakistan in its efforts to produce weapons-grade uranium. Some U.S. officials believed that China provided assistance to Pakistan in its efforts to enrich uranium.[139] This was followed on 6th December 1982 by a briefing to the Senate Foreign Relations Committee, in which Reagan administration officials indicated that Pakistan was continuing its nuclear weapons programme. Administration officials informed the Foreign Relations Committee that China is assisting Pakistan to build a nuclear bomb and estimated that Pakistan was about a year away from producing fissile material that could be used to make a bomb.[140]

"By 1982, Pakistan was also subject to sanctions under the reprocessing sanctions provisions of the 1977 Glenn-Symington Amendment. Arms Export Control Act, *op.cit*. These provisions specified that US economic and military aid were to be terminated to any state that imported reprocessing technology (i.e., technology for separating plutonium from spent reactor fuel) after 1977 when the law was enacted. Presumably, this sanction law was triggered by Pakistan's acquisition of equipment to complete a pilot-scale reprocessing plant, known as the "New Labs" at the Pakistan Institute of Nuclear Technology (PINSTECH), and by its continued work on a larger reprocessing plant at Chasma, which France had originally agreed to design and build in the early 1970s."[141]

By 1983 it was known publicly that China supplied complete design of 25 kT nuclear bomb; possibly a Chic-4 design along with enough Highly enriched uranium (HEU) for one or two nuclear weapons.[142] Dr. Samar Mubarakmund, who was responsible for weaponisation of

138. Laufer, 1982.

139. Miller, 1982b; *New York Times* (19 September 1982)

140. Weinraub (1982). *New York Times*, 8 December.

141. McDonough/CIEP, 1998, "Pakistan" fn 11.

142. Milhollin and White, 1991: 17; Millhollin and White, 1991a: C1, C4; Shuey and Kan, 29 September 1995, p.9; Spector and Smith, *Nuclear Ambitions*, pp.101-102. The Chinese design transfer was first reported by *The Financial Times* of August 14, 1984.

Pakistan's capability, said in an interview to a newspaper that, "1983 was an important milestone in the history of Pakistan's nuclear programme, when the first atomic devise was manufactured and tested."[143] A 1983 US State Department analysis of the effort declared that there was "unambiguous evidence that Pakistan is actively pursuing a nuclear weapons development program." The report highlighted Pakistan's progress in key areas of weapons manufacture, its critical dependence on clandestine efforts to procure nuclear equipment from private Western firms, and its receipt of nuclear assistance from China, including assistance "in the area of fissile material production and possibly also nuclear device design."[144]

This was followed by the supply of enough tritium by China to Pakistan, which was used to achieve fusion in hydrogen bombs and boost the yield of atomic bombs, for 10 thermo-nuclear bombs (by 1986).[145] "Pakistan was reported (in 1995) to have conducted a cold test based on Chinese Design—i.e. a fully instrumented test of a dummy weapon, using a core of natural (unenriched) uranium. The event is said to have taken place in September 1986, near Chagai."[146]

It was not till 1985 (or perhaps 1986), however, that Pakistan managed to produce weapons grade uranium (HEU) in its own facilities.[147] Chinese scientists assisted with the production of weapons-grade uranium at Kahuta. The Kahuta lab was centre of Pakistani nuclear weapons research and production facility for weapons-grade fissile material.[148] Pakistan reportedly produced enough "weapons grade uranium for its first nuclear device."[149] "By this time Pakistan was also

---

143. *The Gulf Today*, May 19, 1999.

144. McDonough/CIEP, 1998, Pakistan pp.131-2; US State Dept, 1991.

145. *Asia-Pacific Defense Reporter*, September 1991: 19; Milhollin and White, 1991: 17; Millhollin and White, 1991a: C1, C4; *The Risk Report*, May 1995, p.8; *http://cns.miis.edu/research/india/china/npakpos.htm*

146. McDonough/CIEP, 1998, Hough, 1995: 270.

147. "Pakistan crosses HEU threshold" for Weapons Grade Uranium [McDonough/CIEP, 1998, Pakistan fn13; Smith, 1988. The Pressler Amendment was introduced in 1985 to avoid imposing sanctions on Pakistan.

148. Shuey and Kan, 1995: 9; *Asia Pulse*, 26 March 2003.

149. McDonough/CIEP, 1998, Pakistan fn14; Woodward and Oberdorfer, 1986; Boyd, 1986; Oberdorfer, 1986; Smith, 1988; Woodward, 1986.

believed to have tested the non-nuclear "triggering package" of a nuclear device."[150]

The US government believed that 1987 was the year when Pakistan, for practical purposes, first "possessed" a nuclear explosive device; this has been an issue of some dispute. Some observers (e.g., CIA analyst Richard Barlow) believed that this threshold was crossed by 1987 and that the Reagan and Bush Administrations in 1987, 1988 and 1989 improperly certified that Pakistan did not possess this capability, in order to avoid the imposition of sanctions under the Pressler Amendment.[151] "In late 1989 and early 1990, Pakistan apparently ended this freeze and fabricated cores for several nuclear weapons from pre-existing stocks of weapons-grade uranium."[152]

In 1986 a comprehensive nuclear cooperation agreement was signed between China and Pakistan. Document 18 of the US Department of State, Office of Non-Proliferation and Export Technology, "US Interaction with the PRC Concerning the PRC's Nuclear Relationship with Pakistan," marked secret, whose heavily excised copy was made available on 28 November 1989 provides some information.[153] This heavily excised paper provides some background on the negotiation of the nuclear cooperation agreement although the material relating to its implementation and any specifics on Pakistan is withheld. Whatever this paper may have concluded, the Bush administration determined in the following year that it could not certify that Pakistan was in compliance with Pressler Amendment requirements. In the light of Pakistani decisions to assemble several nuclear cores and an intelligence establishment consensus that this had indeed happened, President Bush withheld the necessary certification, thus triggering a suspension of military and economic aid. Facilitating this decision was the Soviet withdrawal from Afghanistan, which seemingly reduced Pakistan's strategic importance. This action produced an angry reaction in Pakistan where authorities continued the drive towards a nuclear capability.

150. McDonough/CIEP, 1998, Pakistan fn14; Scali, 1985.

151. Hersh, 1993; Reuters, 1993.

152. McDonough/CIEP, 1998, Pakistan p.132

153. Source: State Department FOIA release (D Kux, pp.309-311)

In 1989, the PARR-2 research reactor (27 kW) at Rawalpindi was designed and built with Chinese assistance. It is under IAEA safeguards with no known connection to weapons programme.[154] "China was also believed to have assisted Pakistan with building an un-safeguarded 50-70-MWt plutonium production reactor at Khushab and to have helped Pakistan develop an un-safeguarded plutonium reprocessing facility (for separating plutonium from the Khusab reactors spent fuel) at Chasma that was left unfinished when earlier French assistance was terminated in the late 1970s."[155]

"According to US officials, Pakistan continued work on its 40-MW, unsafeguarded, heavy-water research reactor at Khushab, with Chinese assistance, although Washington was apparently unable to discern the precise nature of this assistance."[156] The Khushab reactor (40-100 MW [?]), built between 1994 and 1996 with Chinese assistance, could produce weapons grade plutonium. The reactor had reportedly gone critical but could not produce power because it lacked the heavy water needed to moderate the chain reaction. Reportedly built with Chinese assistance.[157] During the same period China reportedly reached a deal to supply heavy water to nearby safeguarded Kanupp facility, but the deal was delayed by concerns that the heavy water might be diverted to the Khushab facility (Excess D2O supply has been diverted).[158]

"Reports on the Chasma reprocessing facility in the early 1990s suggested that, it was progressing, but probably still several years from completion. According to an analysis by the CIA quoted in the press, as of April 1996, China was providing technicians and equipment to help finish the facility. According to reports of August 1997, however, US officials believed that, while some Chinese assistance and equipment may have trickled into the Chasma reprocessing project, the reprocessing complex at Chasma "is an empty shell."[159] The

154. *Nucleonics Week*, 9 August 1990, p. 4

155. McDonough/CIEP (1998), p. 50; Gertz, 1996b, Albright *et al.*, 1997: 283.

156. McDonough/CIEP (1998), p. 134; Hibbs, 1996a; Hibbs, 1996b.

157. PTI News Agency(21 May 1996)

158. Hibbs, 1997: 15; Leventhall, 1998.

159. McDonough/CIEP(1998), p 134; Gertz, 1996b; Smith and Lipmann, 1995.

unsafeguarded Chashma plutonium reprocessing facility, can extract weapons-grade plutonium from spent fuel. It is under construction, reportedly near completion. China reportedly provided assistance to the construction of the reprocessing facility.[160]

In 1994-95, China Nuclear Energy Industry Corporation (CNEIC) supplied 5000 ring magnets to the A.Q. Khan Research Lab at Kahuta, to be used in gas centrifuges that can make weapons-grade enriched uranium.[161]

In 1996, special industrial furnace that could be used to melt plutonium or enriched uranium into the shape of a nuclear bomb core, was sold by China to Pakistan, apparently for the Khushab facility.[162] Chinese scientists reportedly were in Pakistan to help install the furnace.[163] The same year China also supplied, high-tech diagnostic equipment, apparently for the Khushab facility.[164] Khushab was apparently the destination of the furnace and diagnostic equipment sold in 1996.[165] In a 1997 report by the Director of Central Intelligence, it stated that China "was the primary source of nuclear-related equipment and technology to Pakistan" during the second half of 1996. (During the Clinton years, *Washington Times* correspondent Bill Gertz published highly damaging communications intercepts on Chinese-Pakistan nuclear transactions in 1996).[166]

"By conservative estimates, Pakistan by 1995 would have been able to deploy about 10 nuclear weapons; by other estimates, the number could have been as high as 15-25. Pakistan's bombs in the basement were presumed credible because of reports that they were based on design supplied by sources in China in the 1980s."[167]

---

160. Gertz, 1996b: A4.
161. Chen, 1996: B6.
162. Schwied, 1996: A11; Smith, 1996c: A38.
163. Schwied, 1996: A11.
164. Gertz, 1996c: A1; Strobel and Gertz, 1996d: A1.
165. Schwied, 1996: A11; Smith, 1996c: A38.
166. Director of Central Intelligence, June 1997 (Gertz, 1999: 206-207.
167. McDonough/CIEP(1998); Gelb, 1984a; Gelb, 1984b; Smith, 1996b; Foreign Report, 1989: 1.

"China's assistance to Pakistan's nuclear program over the last 15 years may have been crucial to Pakistan's nuclear weapons breakthroughs in the 1980s. It is widely believed that in the early 1980s China supplied Pakistan with design information for one of its own earlier atomic weapons, and there has also been speculation that China may have provided Pakistan with enough highly enriched uranium (HEU) for two such weapons."[168]

According to an August 1997 report by the US Arms Control and Disarmament Agency, "Prior to China's [1992] accession [to the NPT], the United States concluded that China had assisted Pakistan in developing nuclear explosives. ...Questions remain about contacts between Chinese entities and elements associated with Pakistan's nuclear weapons program."[169]

On the basis of the history of China's assistance to Pakistan's nuclear weapons and ballistic missile programmes, some observers, especially in India, have come to believe that China perceives Pakistan to be a strategic ally and partner with which it is working to keep India in check. If China does have such an objective, it is doubtful that it will stop all assistance to Pakistan's nuclear and missile programmes—notwithstanding any pledges Beijing may have given the United States.[170]

Pakistani Proliferation[171]

Pakistan "(Khan) acquired the blueprints for the Chinese bomb that was tested in China's fourth nuclear explosion in 1966.[172] In the mid-1980s, Khan, reportedly, began to develop his export network and ordered twice the number of components necessary for the indigenous Pakistani program. This transition from importer to exporter of centrifuge components was, apparently, completely missed by western intelligence

168. McDonough/CIEP(1998), p.50; Gelb, 1984a; Gelb, 1984b; Milhollin and White, 1991a; Albright *et al.*, 1997.

169. McDonough/CIEP(1998), p.50; USacda, 1997: 80.

170. McDonough/CIEP(1998).

171. This section is based largely on CEIP Chronology by Michael Laufer, 2005 and Squassoni, 2004b.

172. Broad and Sanger, 2004b.

services who believe Khan is only working on Pakistan's domestic nuclear weapons programme."[173]

Pakistan's success with its uranium enrichment programme, "was followed by the more advanced design and technologies of the P-2 centrifuge, an adapted version of the German G-2 that can spin twice as fast as the previous P-1 design". Pakistan was "left with an excess inventory of P-1 components and Khan began purchasing additional P-2 components that he would export through many of the same channels he had used to import centrifuge components. Khan made nuclear sales during the mid-1980s to mid-1990s to Iran and offered technologies to Iraq and possibly others."

"From mid-1990s, after initial nuclear transfers to Iran, A.Q. Khan appeared to have expanded his network of customers to include Libya and North Korea. Khan's network was based on a complex structure of international suppliers that shipped components unimpeded by ineffective controls. Details of Libya's acquisition trace the network to Malaysia, Singapore, Turkey, South Africa, Switzerland, South Korea, Dubai, and possibly others. Many details of the sales to Libya have been uncovered since late 2003, when it decided to come clean about its nuclear program. However many aspects of the network remain mysterious, including network sources for some necessary centrifuge components and details about suspected transfers to North Korea."

On February 4, 2004, Dr. Abdul Qadeer Khan, self-styled father of the Pakistani nuclear bomb, appeared on Pakistani television to apologise to his nation. Pakistani officials a few days earlier claimed that Khan provided technology to Iran, Libya and North Korea.[174] Khan's uniqueness lay in his apparent ability to provide "one-stop shopping," what Clary has called a 'Nuclear Walmart'. Khan sold blueprints, components, full centrifuge assemblies; uranium hexafluoride feedstock, and, from some accounts, a nuclear-weapon design.[175] The Pakistan government and all those connected with the government during this proliferation effort routinely denied any knowledge of Pakistan's nuclear

173. Broad *et al.*, 2004.

174. Rhode and Sanger, 2004.

175. Yourish and D'Souza, 2004.

trade, and launched a pro-forma investigation to identify the 'culprits'. Those purportedly investigated by the Pakistan government, on suspicion of involvement in the Nuclear Walmart, "included Mohammed Farooq, who supervised the KRL's contacts with foreign suppliers; Yasin Chohan, a KRL metallurgist; Major Islam ul-Haq, a personal staff officer; Nazeer Ahmed, a KRL director; and Saeed Ahmed, head of centrifuge design. Between 11 and 25 KRL employees were questioned, as well as the generals in charge of KRL security, Generals Beg and Karamat."[176]

Iran

Khan's assistance to Iran in centrifuge uranium-enrichment apparently began in the late 1980s and continued at least until the mid-1990s. Iran told the IAEA its centrifuge enrichment programme began in 1987; Lieutenant General Khalid Kidwai, who briefed journalists on February 1, 2004, on Khan's confession, reportedly stated that cooperation began in 1989 and Khan transferred technology from 1989 to 1991.[177]

Pakistan and Iran were suspected of signing, in 1986 or 1987 a secret agreement on peaceful nuclear cooperation. Allegedly, the deal included a provision for at least six Iranians to be trained in Pakistan at the Institute of Nuclear Science and Technology in Islamabad and the Nuclear Studies Institute. Iranian scientists might also receive centrifuge training at KRL.[178] Khan was suspected of visiting the Iranian reactor at Bushehr in February 1986 and again in January 1987. These early interactions may have led directly to Khan's assistance to Iran, but the content of the visits is unknown.[179] Khan was suspected of having made an offer to Iran in 1987 to provide a package of nuclear technologies, including assistance for the difficult process of casting uranium metal. The price for the package was reported to be from the tens of millions to the hundreds of millions.[180] Khan was believed to

176. Henderson, 2004.

177. New York Times, 2004.

178. Boureston and Ferguson, 2004.

179. Ibid.

180. Sciolino and Sanger, 2005.

make a centrifuge deal with Iran to help build a cascade of 50,000 P-1 centrifuges.[181] In addition, Iran may have received centrifuge drawings through an unknown foreign intermediary around this time.[182]

Khan and his network of international suppliers reportedly began nuclear transfers to Iran in the late 1980s. The period of cooperation is thought to continue through 1995 when P-2 centrifuge components were transferred. The Pakistani government claimed no transfers occurred after the shipments of P-1 components and sub-assemblies from 1989 to 1991.[183] In 1988, Iranian scientists were suspected of having received nuclear training in Pakistan.[184] Iran was suspected of receiving its first centrifuge assemblies and components in 1989. The shipped components were likely older P-1 centrifuge components that Khan no longer had use for in Pakistan. Through 1995, Khan was reported to have shipped over 2000 components and sub-assemblies for P-1, and later P-2, centrifuges to Iran.[185] More advanced components for P-2 centrifuges were suspected to have arrived in Iran in 1994 or 1995. B.S.A. Tahir, a Sri Lankan businessman and Khan's chief lieutenant, told Malaysian police that Iran paid approximately $3 million for these centrifuge parts.[186] An IAEA report stated that Iran received P-2 drawings from "foreign sources" in 1994.[187] Iran had claimed that it received P-2 plans, but no centrifuge components, and tried to develop a carbon-composite rotor on its own, with no success.[188]

Libya

"Assistance to Libya began in the early 1990s and may have continued into 2002. Beyond blueprints, components, full assemblies of centrifuges, and low-enriched uranium, Libya also received—startlingly—a nuclear weapons design. An IAEA report states that in 1997 foreign

181. Broad *et al.*, 2004.
182. Clary, "Dr. Khan's Nuclear WalMart."
183. Congressional Research Service(2005).
184. Weiss, 2005.
185. Kampani, 2004.
186. Sanger, 2004.
187. IAEA, 2004a.
188. IAEA, 2004a & IAEA, 2004b.

manufacturers provided 20 pre-assembled L-1 (equivalent to P-1) centrifuges and components for an additional 200 L-1 centrifuges, including process gas feeding and withdrawal systems, UF6 cylinders, and frequency converters.[189] In both cases, it is clear that Khan provided technology for an advanced centrifuge design (the P-2). Libya received two of the P-2-type centrifuges in 2000 and placed an order for 10,000 more. Libya received two of the P-2-type centrifuges in 2000 and placed an order for 10,000 more."[190] There is no confirmation that the nuclear-weapon design Libya received in 2001 or 2002 is from Pakistan, but some sources have reported that the design contained Chinese text and step-by-step instructions for assembling a vintage 1960s, highly enriched uranium (HEU) implosion device, which could indicate that Khan passed on a design that Pakistan is long rumoured to have received from China.[191]

Khan began to transfer centrifuges and centrifuge components to Libya in 1997. Libya received 20 assembled P-1 centrifuges and components for 200 additional units for a pilot enrichment facility. Khan's network continued to supply with centrifuge components until late 2003.[192] In June 2000, Peter Griffin set up Gulf Technical Industries in Dubai, which serves as a front company for Khan's network. B.S.A. Tahir will use Gulf Technical Industries as one of his front companies to order centrifuge components from Malaysia.[193] In September 2000, Libya received two P-2 centrifuges as demonstrator models and placed an order for components for 10,000 more to build a cascade. Each centrifuge contains around 100 parts, implying approximately 1 million parts total for the entire P-2 centrifuge cascade.[194] In 2001, Libya obtained 1.87 tonnes of uranium hexafluoride, the gas that is used to feed enrichment centrifuges. The amount is consistent with that required for a small pilot enrichment facility.[195] The source of the

189. IAEA, 2004b.

190. IAEA, 2004a & IAEA, 2004b.

191. Broad and Sanger, 2004 and Warrick and Slevin, 2004,

192. Kampani, 2004.

193. Broad *et al.*, 2004.

194. Salama, 2005.

195. Kampani, 2004.

uranium hexafluoride remains uncertain. In 2004, evidence emerged that North Korea might have supplied Libya with the material, which would be the first discovered transfer of nuclear material from North Korea to an A.Q. Khan network recipient. The evidence remains inconclusive, however, and authorities continue to suspect that the uranium hexafluoride came from Pakistan.[196] In December 2001, B.S.A. Tahir signed a $13 million contract with Scuomi Precision Engineering (SCOPE) in Malaysia for 25,000 aluminum centrifuge components. The components would be shipped to front companies in Dubai, including Gulf Technical Industries and SMB Computers. SCOPE representatives later acknowledged manufacturing parts for Tahir, but believed that they would be used in Dubai oil and gas industries.[197] In December 2002, shipments begin from SCOPE of aluminum centrifuge components. Four shipments are believed to have been sent from Malaysia to Dubai before August 2003, en route to Libya.[198]

In late 2001 or early 2002, Libya received the blueprints for nuclear weapons plans. The plans are reported to be of Chinese origin with Chinese notes in the margins. There is reported to be a note on the blueprints that "Munir's bomb would be bigger," possibly a reference to Munir Ahmad Khan of the PAEC, who was in competition with A.Q. Khan to develop a Pakistani bomb.[199]

In October 2003, the German cargo ship BBC China is intercepted en route to Libya with components for 1,000 centrifuges. The parts were manufactured in Malaysia by SCOPE and shipped through Dubai.[200] In December 2003, Libya renounced its nuclear weapons programme and began the process of full disclosure to the IAEA, including the declaration of all foreign procurements.[201] In March 2004, a container aboard the BBC China (the ship that was previously intercepted) arrived in Libya with one additional container of P-2 centrifuge components. Colonel Qaddafi reported the arrival to American intelligence and the

196. Sanger and Broad, 2004.

197. Salama, 2004.

198. Salama, 2004.

199. Broad and Sanger, 2004.

200. Sanger, 1995.

201. Broad and Sanger, 2004.

IAEA. The Libyans warned American officials that not all of the components from Libya's orders had arrived and some might still show up in the future.[202]

North Korea

"During mid-1971 Bhutto approached North Korea in an effort to obtain critically needed weapons. An agreement was quickly reached and on 18 September 1971 the first arms shipment from the DPRK arrived in Karachi. On 9 November 1972, only one day after withdrawing from SEATO, Pakistan announced that it was establishing formal diplomatic relations with the DPRK. Military assistance to Pakistan continued through the late 1970s, with the DPRK providing artillery, multiple rocket launchers, ammunition, and a variety of spare parts."[203]

Whether Khan gave North Korea nuclear-weapon-related technology or equipment is still disputed. US officials and sources close to Khan have said he did; the Pakistani and North Korean governments have denied any technology transfers. Asked by Senator Chuck Hagel (R-NE) what the United States knows about Pakistan's involvement in helping North Korea, Deputy Secretary of State Richard Armitage replied that "we know it's both ways and we know a good bit about a North Korean-Pakistan relationship."[204] One popular theory is that Pakistan bartered uranium-enrichment technology for missile technology from North Korea, but Musharraf has stated that "whatever we bought from North Korea is with money."[205] A Pakistani official involved in Khan's investigation reportedly said North Korea ordered P-1 centrifuge components from 1997 to 2000.[206] Separately, other evidence points to Pakistani nuclear assistance. Reportedly, a competition was encouraged between the plutonium team (PAEC), working towards Chinese-derived nuclear-capable missiles, and the HEU team (KRL), collaborating with

202. Broad and Sanger, 2004.

203. Bermudez, 1998.

204. Richard Armitage, testimony before the Senate Foreign Relations Committee, February 4, 2003.

205. Bokhari *et al.*, 2004 and Squassoni, 2004a.

206. Zaidi, 2004.

North Korea on a Scud derivative.[207] Khan's frequent trips abroad for "legitimate" missile cooperation with North Korea might have provided cover for his nuclear deals.

"Pakistan began missile cooperation with North Korea in 1992. Within Pakistan, KRL is one of the laboratories responsible for missile research and will develop the Ghauri missile with North Korean assistance. This cooperation probably established the connections that Khan could have used to transfer nuclear technologies. However, very little is known about when any nuclear transfers began, what nuclear components might have been obtained by North Korea, and whether or not the Pakistani government was privy to Khan's activities."[208]

"Khan started travelling to North Korea in mid-1990s, where he received technical assistance for the development of the Ghauri missile, an adaptation of the North Korean No Dong design. Khan made at least 13 visits before his public confession in 2004 and is suspected of arranging a barter deal to exchange nuclear and missile technologies, though the details of any nuclear transfers remain unknown. Khan travels with military personnel from KRL. These officials could have helped with the transfer of nuclear technology because programs under the Ministry of Defense were exempt from normal export controls.[209] The military presence at KRL, including personnel who traveled to North Korea, suggests that the Pakistani government might have been aware of Khan's activities. President Musharraf denies this claim.[210] The Pakistani currency reserve crunch in 1996 may have motivated Khan to expand his nuclear network with sales to North Korea. The crisis might have made a barter agreement attractive to Pakistan to avoid defaulting on external debt. Visits of North Korean and Pakistani officials accelerate following the crisis, but it is not known if these meetings include discussions of nuclear transfers or deal exclusively with missile technologies."[211]

207. Broad and Sanger, 2004 and Warrick and Slevin, 2004.

208. Congressional Research Service, 2004.

209. Weiss, 2005.

210. Kampani, 2004.

211. Congressional Research Service, 2004.

Khan is suspected of beginning nuclear transfers to North Korea around 1997, though the dates of the first transfers are highly uncertain.[212] Transfers to North Korea are believed to have continued through 2003, but the Pakistani government claims these transfers ceased in 2001. Over this period, Khan may have supplied North Korea with old and discarded centrifuge and enrichment machines together with sets of drawings, sketches, technical data and depleted uranium hexafluoride.[213] In December 1997, several reports stated that Pakistan's then-Chief of Army Staff General Jehangir Karamat secretly visited Pyongyang.[214] Khan has claimed that Karamat was aware of the deal between Pakistan and North Korea to exchange enrichment assistance for missile technologies (Ibid). Karamat, now Pakistan's Ambassador to the United States, says that this information is incorrect. He says that he never visited North Korea and did not have any knowledge of the proliferation activity.

During the summer of 2001, American spy satellites detected missile components being loaded into a Pakistani cargo plane outside of Pyongyang. Intelligence services assume the cargo to be missile technology traded in direct exchange for nuclear technology, but no hard evidence exists.[215] In April 2003, German authorities intercepted a ship in the Suez Canal with a large cargo of strong aluminum tubing en route to North Korea. The tube specifications suggest that they are intended for use as outer casings for P-2 centrifuges (Ibid).

Others

Khan was, reportedly, approached in the early 1980s by an unknown Arab country (possibly Saudi Arabia or Syria) requesting nuclear assistance.[216] Khan is suspected to have met with a top Syrian official in Beirut in the mid-1990s to offer assistance with a centrifuge enrichment facility.[217]

212. Pinkston, 2002.
213. Clary, "Dr. Khan's Nuclear WalMart."
214. Armstrong, 2004.
215. Sanger, 1995.
216. Clary, "Dr. Khan's Nuclear WalMart."
217. Kampani, 2004.

As far back as the late 1980s, German intelligence investigated potential Pakistani assistance to Iraq, and possibly Iran and North Korea, with processes related to melting uranium.[218]

An Iraqi memo, found during inspections in 1995, indicates that Khan may have offered significant nuclear assistance to Iraq in late 1990. He offered to sell Iraq a nuclear bomb design and guarantee material support from Western Europe for a uranium enrichment programme. Khan stated that any materials needed from Europe could be routed through a company he owned in Dubai and that a meeting with a friendly intermediary could take place in Greece. However, Iraq is believed to have turned down the offer, suspecting it to be a sting and no known follow-ups were made after the 1991 Gulf War. The investigation in the 1990s was inconclusive in its efforts to determine the authenticity of the memo.[219]

In 1991, a German intelligence investigation concluded that Iraq, and possibly Iran and North Korea, obtained uranium-melting information from Pakistan in the late 1980s.[220]

Pakistani Deniability?

"On 5th July 1977, Army General Mohammed Zia ul-Haq launched a coup against Bhutto and took over the government. The military quickly took control of the nuclear weapons program, control it has maintained to the present day—placing Pakistan's nuclear arms outside of the authority of the civilian government (when it has had one)."[221]

"The structure of the nuclear establishment in Pakistan and the key role of the military, as well as long-standing ties between Pakistan and all three countries, raise doubts that Khan acted completely without government knowledge. Pakistan's military is widely believed to control the Pakistani nuclear weapons program. Musharraf has taken pains to clarify that Pakistan established civilian control of the nuclear weapons program (embodied in himself) under the National Command Authority,

218. Congressional Research Service, 2005.

219. Albright and Hinderstein, 2004.

220. Hibbs, 1991 and Hibbs, 2002.

221. Sublette, 2002b.

but until Musharraf steps down as army chief of staff, this distinction may be irrelevant. Moreover, a key feature of Pakistan's export control regulations allows for an explicit exemption for Ministry of Defense agencies, which suggests that weapons programs under military leadership could skirt domestic export control laws."[222]

Khan has alleged that military officials, including former Chiefs of Army Staff (COAS), knew of the transfers. One account claims that equipment to Iran was transferred at the request of the late General Imtiaz Ali between 1988 and 1990.[223] Another states that Musharraf was aware of aid to North Korea, that General Mirza Aslam Beg knew about aid to Iran, and that two other COAS (Generals Jehangir Karamat and Abdul Waheed) knew of aid to North Korea.[224] General Beg for long has had a reputation for being an Islamist and an admirer of the Iranian revolution. Beg officially denied knowledge of aid to Iran, although former Prime Minister Benazir Bhutto said she was approached several times from 1988 to 1990 (the period when Beg was COAS) by military officials and scientists who wanted to export nuclear technology. According to Bhutto, "it certainly was their (scientists') belief that they could earn tons of money if they did this." She asserted that as PM she had established a policy in December 1988 not to export nuclear technology.[225] She also said, however, that "no Pakistani thought Mr. Khan was acting alone". On the other hand, she also said that she did not think it probable that centrifuge parts were exported from Pakistan to Iran from 1994 to 1995 (while she was prime minister), despite revelations of exactly that in a Malaysian police report connected to the Iran investigation. Pinning the blame on individuals is a time-tested and obvious circumvention (*à la* the 1996 provision of Chinese ring magnets to Pakistan, which was not deemed a sanctionable offence).

"Reports of extensive official cooperation between Pakistan and the three countries lend credence to claims that Pakistan's government might have known of transfers. Pakistan reportedly signed a nuclear

222. Srivastava and Gahlaut, 2003.

223. The Times of India, 2004.

224. Lancaster and Khan, 2004.

225. Rohde, 2004 and Fidler, 2004.

cooperation agreement with Iran in 1986, although the terms of that agreement are unknown, and Iranian scientists received training in Pakistan in 1988. Libyan funding of the Pakistani nuclear weapons program in the early years long has been alleged.[226] Pakistan's well-documented missile cooperation with North Korea beginning in the early 1990s may have provided either a convenient excuse for rogue nuclear scientists to ply their trade or sparked the plan for a barter arrangement as Pakistani foreign currency reserves fell dangerously low in 1996."[227]

"Khan reportedly told investigators he hoped to deflect attention from Pakistan's nuclear program and support other Muslim countries (i.e., Iran and Libya) by providing nuclear assistance.[228] In the late 1980s, when cooperation with Iran allegedly began, the argument for deflecting attention from Pakistan could have been plausible, particularly as pressure from the United States grew with each new revelation of Pakistan's nuclear progress."

KRL began in 1987 to publish publicly available technical papers that outline some of the more advanced design features Khan has developed. The papers include information that would normally be classified in the U.S. and Europe and show that KRL is competent in many aspects of centrifuge design and operation. The papers also include specifications for centrifuges with maraging steel that can spin faster than earlier aluminum designs. Later, in 1991, KRL published details on how to etch grooves around the bottom bearing to incorporate lubricants. These technical developments are important for Khan's P-2 centrifuges.[229]

In 1999, Pakistani government released an advertisement of procedures for the export of nuclear equipment and components. The ad lists equipment for sale, including gas centrifuges and magnet baffles for enriching uranium.[230] Other advertisements from KRL are reported to

226. Weissman and Krosney, 1981.

227. Pinkston, 2002.

228. Lancaster and Khan, 2004.

229. Clary, "Dr: Khan's Nuclear WalMart." pp. 176-177.

230. Weiss, 2005.

include an "unsubtle drawing" of a mushroom cloud and vacuum devices that attach to centrifuge casings.[231]

US Interest

The former Dutch Prime Minister Ruud Lubbers has revealed how the CIA protected A.Q. Khan and saved him from going to prison after he was caught stealing secret designs from a Dutch uranium plant in 1975. Mr. Lubbers, who was Minister of Economic Affairs at the time, told a Dutch radio station, *Radio Argus* in a 35-minute programme on Tuesday August 9, 2005, that because of pressure from the CIA no action was taken against Dr. Khan and he was quietly allowed to return to Pakistan. In 1985, Dr. Khan appealed against the judgement and the court ordered a retrial but, according to Mr. Lubbers, Dr. Khan was not put on trial a second time--again because of pressure from the CIA.[232]

"US officials have intimated they knew about Khan's network for several years, and the US government seems to have been quietly working with the Pakistani government to limit the damage from Khan's nuclear network.[233] Shortly after Khan's dismissal in 2001, Deputy Secretary of State Richard Armitage reportedly stated that "people who were employed by the nuclear agency and have retired" could be spreading nuclear technology to other states, including North Korea.[234] Nonetheless, after US intelligence officials leaked the news in 2002 that Pakistani enrichment technology was transferred to North Korea."[235]

Leonard Weiss, a consultant to the Centre for Global Security Research at the Lawrence Livermore National Laboratory and Former Staff Director of the Senate Governmental Affairs Committee, in his testimony stated:

---

231. Sanger, 1995.

232. Broad and Sanger, 2004b; Suroor, Hasan (2005). "How CIA "protected" A.Q. Khan" International, in *The Hindu* of 10th August; Gerard Legebeke, editor-in-chief of the programme in which Mr Lubbers was interviewed, confirmed this to the *The Hindu*. *www.thehindu.com/2005/08/10/stories/2005081000711600.htm*

233. Tenet, 2004, CIA Director.

234. Fidler and Luce, 2001.

235. Robbins, 2002.

Mr. Chairman, one cannot separate the success of the Khan network in the 80s from the policies toward Pakistan pursued by the United States. The Glenn and Symington Amendments were both waived by administrative and Congressional action respectively after the Soviet invasion of Afghanistan. The lifting of sanctions against the Pakistanis coupled with a $3.2 billion aid package sent them the message that they could continue their nuclear weapon acquisition activities with the US government doing little to stand in their way. That message helped embolden Pakistan to widen the Khan network and set off a new round of attempts on their part to get nuclear-related materials and components from other countries, including those with relatively tight export controls like the United States and Canada. In 1981, while the aid package was going through the legislative process, Pakistan attempted to smuggle 5,000 lbs. of zirconium, used for nuclear reactor fuel rods, out of the US. The shipment, marked as "mountaineering equipment", was stopped by US Customs agents. It had no effect on Congressional passage of the aid package. In 1984, a man named Nazir Ahmed Vaid was arrested for illegally attempting to export krytrons, which are used for nuclear triggers. Although the known intended recipient was the Pakistan Atomic Energy Commission, the indictment was rewritten to exclude any mention of the nuclear use of Krytrons. Vaid was permitted to plea bargain to a reduced offense, thus avoiding a jury trial, and a gag order on the case was issued by the judge. He was found guilty of one count of export violation and quietly deported three weeks later.

Although this case had no effect on US aid to Pakistan, it did cause the Congress to pass, in 1985, the Solarz Amendment to the Foreign Assistance Act, which prohibited military and economic assistance to any country that illegally exports or attempts to export US items that would contribute significantly to the ability of that country to make a nuclear explosive device. On the same day the Solarz Amendment was enacted, the Pressler Amendment was signed into law. The Pressler Amendment made continued military assistance to Pakistan contingent on an annual certification by the President that Pakistan did not possess a nuclear explosive device. It also required the President to certify that the US assistance being given to Pakistan would significantly reduce the risk of Pakistan's possession of such a device, but the Reagan Administration ignored this requirement, realising that the clear evidence of Pakistan's ongoing drive for the bomb meant they would have to halt assistance. This misfeasance was explained by falsely claiming that there was no difference in the two requirements in the Pressler Amendment.

Pakistan's nuclear tests in 1998, triggered additional and severe economic sanctions, which were removed via Congressional action in order to prevent what some predicted, would be an economic collapse and serious political instability. The removal of the additional sanctions were unaccompanied by any demand that Pakistan's nuclear activity be cut back. The military embargo on Pakistan lasted until after the 9/11 attack. We seem to have sold our souls to the Pakistanis again, this time to help us with Al Qaeda instead of the Soviets, and I fear we are once again getting the bad end of the deal. Pakistan violated the terms of the sale of F-16s in the 80s when it allowed China to examine the plane, and when it altered the plane's configuration in order to allow the carrying of nuclear warheads. There is no reason to assume the same thing won't happen again. Providing more incentives for Pakistan to make more weapons does not seem to me to make logical sense.[236]

236. Weiss, 2006.

Proliferation Incorporated

Though the so-called A.Q. Khan network was verbally closed down in 2002, Pakistan's international procurement network is, not very surprisingly, alive and well, metamorphosing and evolving in response to the new situation.

"The key to the success of Khan's network was its virtual library of centrifuge designs, detailed manufacturing manuals, and nuclear weapon designs. An important task for investigators is to retrieve as much of this information as possible. Key participants may not yet have been identified out of an estimated total of 50 people who were actively involved in the network. The fact that no prosecutions appear to be planned serves to increase suspicions that the Pakistani government is hiding information about the network's activities, particularly information that could further embarrass itself or its military. The United States has ignored multiple requests from Swiss prosecutors for cooperation that have extended over a year."[237]

"German national police, in March 2006 raided dozens of business locations suspected of being connected with illicit sales of nuclear-related goods in 2004 and 2005 and German authorities are currently prosecuting a number of cases. Some of these are part of Pakistani attempts to rebuild a network for supplying the needs of its own nuclear weapons program. This heightened procurement activity by Pakistani agents has been ongoing since at least 2004. What troubles European investigators, is that Pakistan appears to be buying more nuclear bits and pieces than they need. An explanation, offered privately by several Pakistani officials, is that the newfound nuclear procurement push could be part of an effort to quietly rebuild parts of Islamabad's own uranium enrichment program at KRL in Kahuta if damage was done to the facility in last October's devastating earthquake. Swiss police, say they interrupted a plot in March 2004 to illegally ship 60 tons of specialised aluminium tubes—used for building parts of a centrifuge cascade to enrich uranium—from a Russian supplier through intermediaries in Western Europe and Dubai to Pakistan."[238]

237. Albright, 2006.

238. Koch, 2006.

"In 2004, a South African electronics salesman and former Israeli army major named Asher Karni was arrested for violating export control laws in the illegal shipment of oscilloscopes and spark gap triggers to Pakistan from the US via South Africa. The ultimate destination was a company, headed by Humayun Khan, described by US officials as a front for Pakistan's nuclear weapon program. Humayun Khan, who has been linked with several militant Islamic groups, is still free in Pakistan, while Asher Karni was ultimately convicted and is serving a three year prison sentence. The Guardian of Britain reported (during the week ending 24th May 2006) on the existence of a July, 2005 document prepared by British, French, German, and Belgian intelligence agencies for the European Union, that said the Pakistanis were still shopping in Europe for such things as high-grade aluminum tubing for centrifuges, ring magnets for centrifuge rotors, and machine tools, chemicals, and equipment for producing liquid- and solid-fueled missiles. The document lists 20 Pakistani government offices, laboratories, companies, and trading organizations active in the procurement effort for the bomb program, and hundreds of companies around the world that are said to be involved in some aspect of the production of weapons of mass destruction. An educated guess based on the unclassified literature is that a good part of the network is still intact, and that additions to it are being actively sought."[239]

Reed (2008), a former nuclear weapon designer (1959-1965) and Secretary of the Air Force (1976-77), based on information attributed to Danny Stillman, Director of the Technical Intelligence Division at Los Almos National Laboratory, has written that,

(a) "..extensive hospitality extended to Pakistani nuclear scientists during that same late-1980s time period. ..that cooperation, initiated earlier in the decade, led to a joint nuclear test in China soon after Stillman's departure. (i.e. after April 1990.)

(b) "In 1982, China's premier Deng Xiaping began the transfer of nuclear weapons technology to Pakistan ... Those transfers included blue-prints for the ultra simple CHC-4 design using highly enriched uranium, first tested by China in 1966.

239. Weiss, 2006.

c) "A Pakistani derivative of CHIC-4 apparently was tested in China on 26 May 1990."

These dates can be posited against the previously referred "historical (secret) Pakistan-China nuclear agreement," signed by Z.A. Bhutto in June 1976 and the "success achieved 12 years later" referred to by General Beg, to confirm our analysis of the China-Pakistan proliferation activity.

Henderson (2009) in the *Sunday Times*, quotes a letter from A.Q. Khan stating that, "We put up a centrifuge plant at Hanzhong (250km southwest of Xian)." "The Chinese gave us drawings of the nuclear weapon, gave us 50 kg of enriched uranium, gave us 10 tons of UF6 (natural) and 5 tons of UF6 (3%)." "Probably with the blessings of BB [Benazir Bhutto, who became prime minister in 1988] and [a now-retired general]... General Imtiaz [Benazir's defence adviser, now dead] asked... me to give a set of drawings and some components to the Iranians...The names and addresses of suppliers were also given to the Iranians." "[A now-retired general] took $3 million through me from the N. Koreans and asked me to give some drawings and machines."

Conclusion

Pakistan's economic strength and general technological capabilities are close to those of Bangladesh and below those of 40 other developing countries. They are far below those of South Africa, which acquired nuclear weapons capability while facing global sanctions because of Apartheid. Egypt, Malaysia, Iran, Turkey and Indonesia are among 40 countries with greater economic strengths and general technological capabilities than Pakistan. Given this relative economic weakness, Pakistan was able to acquire nuclear weapons capability because of two reasons. One is its very strong 'will to power' and a fierce determination to acquire nuclear weapons and their delivery systems. This objective overrode virtually any other objective that it had. Second was its willingness and agility in using every possible means (alliances, diplomatic friendship, espionage, untruths) in achieving this objective. The normal rules of international relations or diplomacy did not matter, only the objectives.

A substantial section of the elite in Pakistan has been driven since independence by its antipathy to India. After decades of military rule, much of this elite is either military or has close family ties with persons in the military. The break-up of Pakistan resulting from the Pakistani genocide in Bangladesh and the entry of the Indian army into Bangladesh/East Pakistan turned this antipathy into hatred. The humiliation of the largest military surrender of any army since the Second World War and the refusal of the elite to reveal the military's genocide accentuated this hatred among the general public. This led to a two pronged strategy: Acquire nuclear weapons to deter India's conventional military superiority (and any future nuclear capability) and recruit and train religious minorities in India to foment strife and insurgency.

Pakistan's nuclear weapons programme began immediately after the Bangladesh war, three years before India's test of a nuclear explosive device (PNE). However, it suited Pakistan to have the non-proliferation lobby do the diplomatic heavy lifting for it by linking every Pakistani transgression to the need to counter some specific or general actions of India. Pakistan made full use of the non-proliferation lobby's labelling of each achievement of India's independent (since 1966) nuclear programme as proliferation. Pakistan used this non-proliferation theology to justify its own proliferation activities across the world and to extract weapons technology and materials from countries not so favourably disposed to India.

Pakistan's first real breakthrough came with the employment of Dr. A.Q. Khan by the Dutch company FDO in April-May 1972. Because of the laxity of the Dutch security procedures and its secret service, over the next three and the half years, Dr. Khan obtained copies of the complete and comprehensive design information on the existing and latest/newly designed uranium centrifuge enrichment process. He also obtained comprehensive information on the suppliers of sub-systems, equipment, parts and materials that went into the construction of these centrifuges as well as in running them and producing enriched uranium. Most of these firms were located in the Netherlands, Germany, Switzerland and the UK as the overall project was a trilateral one. While working at the Dutch firm, Dr. Khan passed on these details to the Pakistan government. The Pakistan government set up procurement system in Europe in 1975 under a physicist familiar with Pakistan's weapons plans, with the intention of getting around the NPT and the new restrictions imposed in 1974. The same year Dr. Khan returned to Pakistan and took charge of the construction of the uranium enrichment centrifuge facility. Though he was the overall in charge of the entire centrifuge facility, the operational aspects of clandestine procurement of nuclear equipment and material was supervised by the military.

By the early to mid-1980s, Pakistan had procured from Europe and North America, every single sub-system, part and material needed for the centrifuge plant and for uranium enrichment. Hundreds of companies from Europe and North America, of which 70 from Germany alone, participated in this gigantic proliferation effort as suppliers, intermediaries and trainers. Pakistan obtained in the late 1980s test quantities of tritium gas, tritium purification and storage plants, tritium precursor materials, the design for a reactor that could be used for tritium production, and material and equipment for fabricating fuel for that reactor, including special American made welding lasers from two related West German firms.

In parallel, Pakistan entered into a formal contract with France in 1974 to procure a full scale spent fuel reprocessing/plutonium extraction plant from France. This was at a time when only a commercial power reactor (KANUPP 125MW) had been in operation for two years. US pressure on France forced cancellation of the deal between 1976 and 1978. Design information, equipment and training of technicians, however continued till much later and Pakistan had started construction of the plant by 1979. By the time the flow of designs and equipment tapered off, Pakistan had obtained more than 95 per cent of the complete design for the plutonium extraction plant. Some of the procured equipment was probably diverted to the pilot enrichment plant called the New Lab facility, which was sufficient for the amount of spent fuel generated by the small research reactors.

Pakistan's clandestine procurement efforts were not limited to the generation of bomb grade fissile materials, highly enriched uranium and bomb grade plutonium. It procured uranium from a Niger-French joint venture in Niger. It procured from Turkey, material for explosives needed to detonate a nuclear bomb and routed through Turkey inverters imported from the USA and other material needed to implement a triggering package for the atomic bomb. It procured hollow steel spheres and driver plates needed for the bomb trigger from Argentina and the UK.

Despite this incredibly successful clandestine procurement effort, Pakistan was not able to produce an atomic weapon because the level of the technological capability of its economy and the skills available in the country. It therefore turned to China to fill the gap in these and other areas. A secret agreement was signed with China in 1976 for nuclear cooperation/assistance. Initially, Chinese assistance grew slowly because of the transition from a Maoist regime to the Deng era at the end of the 1970s. The Soviet invasion of Afghanistan in 1978-79 was the turning point, a virtual gift from heaven. Given the fears aroused in the USA and China of USSR's possible thrust to the Indian Ocean, China's leadership was now more amenable to Pakistan's traditional Indian bogey. By 1983 China had supplied complete design of a 25 KT nuclear bomb, possibly a Chic-4 design (from China's fourth test) along with enough highly enriched uranium (HEU) for one or two nuclear weapons. Chinese scientists assisted with the production of weapons-grade uranium at Kahuta. This was followed by the supply of enough tritium, used to achieve fusion in hydrogen bombs and boost the yield of atomic bombs, for 10 thermo-nuclear bombs. China also assisted Pakistan in conducting a cold test based on the Chinese Design, i.e., a fully instrumented test of a dummy weapon, using a core of natural (un-enriched) uranium.

In 1986, a comprehensive nuclear cooperation agreement was signed between China and Pakistan, accelerating the proliferation of technology, skills and equipment to the latter. In pursuance of this agreement, China designed and built the safeguarded PARR-2 research reactor (27 kW) at Rawalpindi. It also assisted Pakistan in building an un-safeguarded 40 to 100 MW research reactor at Khushab to produce weapons grade plutonium and an un-safeguarded plutonium reprocessing facility at Chasma. During the same period, China reportedly reached a deal to supply heavy water to nearby safeguarded Kanupp facility, but the deal was delayed by concerns that the heavy water might be diverted to the Khushab facility (Excess D2O supply has been diverted). This was followed by supply of critical equipment (ring magnets) for the gas centrifuges at the Khan Research Lab (KRL) at Kahuta, special industrial furnace for melting plutonium or enriched uranium into the shape of a nuclear bomb core and high-tech diagnostic equipment. Chinese scientists helped to install the furnace in Pakistan.

With Zia-Ul Haq's and A.Q. Khan's confidence bolstered by the 1986 Sino-Pakistan agreement, the latter started setting up the nuclear and missile trading (import-export) business by signing a supply agreement with Iran. These activities widened and expanded to Libya, North Korea and other countries in step with Chinese strategic support to Pakistan. Despite the deterioration in its economy from 1993, Pakistan felt confident enough to take on the US and European countries who were finally becoming worried about nuclear proliferation from and to NPT signatory states.

Over this entire period of European and Chinese proliferation to Pakistan, the US vacillated between controlling this proliferation and ensuring Pakistan's support for and participation in its own strategic initiatives. Yet another turn in the cycle occured in 2001 with the event of 9/11 and the US need for Pakistan's help in Afghanistan. Pakistan has clearly demonstrated its superior diplomatic skills in turning every event to its advantage. On the basis of history there is a high probability that Pakistan has successfully used this new opportunity to make another quantum jump in its clandestine nuclear weapons and missile procurement programme.

References

Albright, David (2006), "A.Q. Khan Network: The Case is Not Closed", Testimony before the Subcommittee on International Terrorism & Non-proliferation Committee on International Relations, May 25.

Albright, David, Frans Berkhout and William Walker (1997). *Plutonium and Highly Enriched Uranium 1996: World Inventories, Capabilities and Policies* New York: Oxford University Press for Stockholm International Peace Research Institute.

Albright, David and Corey Hinderstein (2004). *Documents Indicate A.Q. Khan Offered Nuclear Weapons Designs to Iraq in 1990: Did He Approach Other Countries?*. Institute for Science and International Security, February 4. *http://www.isis-online.org/publications/southasia/khan_memo.html*

Armstrong, David (2004). "Friend Like This", *New Republic Online*, 18 November.

Asia-Pacific Defence Reporter (1991). "Incidental Intelligence: China Emerging as Third World Weapons Supplier", September.

Associated Press (1979). "International News", in Lexis-Nexis Academic Universe, 26 November. *http://web.lexis-nexis.com/*

———. (1980). "France Denies Uranium Sales", 3 January, International News, in Lexis-Nexis Academic Universe, 3 January. *http://www.lexisnexis.com*

Asia Pulse (2003). "China to Help Set Up Another N-Power Plant at Chashma", 26 March.

Auerbach, Stuart (1980a). "Pakistan Warns Soviets, Afghanistan to Keep Out", *Washington Post*. First Section, A1; in Lexis-Nexis Academic Universe, 16 January. *http://www.lexisnexis.com*

———. (1980b). "Pakistan Seeking US Guarantees in Formal Treaty; Pakistan Asks Formal Treaty to Cement Ties with US", *Washington Post*. First Section, A1; in Lexis-Nexis Academic Universe, 18 January. http:*//www.lexisnexis.com*

Babar, Farhatullah (2004). "Bhutto's Footprints on Nuclear Pakistan", *Pakistan Link*. *www.pakistanlink.com/Commentary/2006/Apr06/14/05.htm*

BBC (1980a). "Pakistan: Increasing Involvement in Alliance with USA and China", *BBC Summary of World Broadcasts*. Part 1. The USSR, C. Afghanistan and Related Topics, SU/6345/C/3, in Lexis-Nexis Academic Universe, 14 February. *http://www.lexisnexis.com*

———. (1980b). "Chinese-Pakistani Military Co-operation: Hegemonism and Expansionism", *BBC Summary of World Broadcasts*, Part 1. The USSR, A. International Affairs, 3. The Far East, SU/6426/A3/1, in Lexis-Nexis Academic Universe, 22 May. *http://www.lexisnexis.com*

———. (1980c). "BBC Says Pakistan Developing Nuclear Bomb", *Associated Press, International News*, in Lexis-Nexis Academic Universe, 16 June. *http://www.lexisnexis.com*

———. (1981). "In Brief: General; Turayki's Remarks about an Islamic Nuclear Bomb", *BBC Summary of World Broadcasts*, Part 4. The Middle East and Africa, A. The Middle East, ME/6798/A/11; in Lexis-Nexis Academic Universe, 11 August. *http://www.lexisnexis.com*

Beg, General Mirza Aslam (n.d.). "Voices From the Whirlwind, Assessing Musharraf's Predicament", Interview to *Frontline*, *www.pbs.org/frontlineworld/stories/pakistan/e.html*

Benjamin, Milton R. (1978). "US Officials View Pakistan as the Leading Threat to Join the Nuclear Club", *Washington Post*, First Section, A16, in Lexis-Nexis Academic Universe, 8 December. *http://web.lexis-nexis.com/*

———. (1982). "India said to Eye Raid on Pakistani A-Plants", *Washington Post*, First Section, A1, in Lexis-Nexis Academic Universe, 20 December. *www.lexis-nexis.com*

Bermudez Jr., Joseph S. (1998). *DPRK: Pakistan Ghauri Missile Cooperation*. May. *http://www.fas.org/news/pakistan/1998/05/ghauri2.htm*; Earlier version was, in *Ballistic Missile Development in the DPRK, Janes Defence Weekly.*

Bhattacharyya, S.K. (1988). *Genocide in East Pakistan/Bangladesh: A Horror Story*. A. Ghosh Publishers.

Bhutto, Zulfikar Ali (1969). *Myth of Independence*. Karachi: Oxford University Press. pp.152-153.

———. (1979). *If I am Assassinated.*

Bokhari, Farhan, Steven Fidler, and Edward Luce (2004). "Pakistan Rejects Nuclear Inspection", *Financial Times*, February 18.

Boureston, Jack and Charles D. Ferguson (2004). "Schooling Iran's Atom Squad", *Bulletin of the Atomic Scientists*, May/June. *http://www.thebulletin.orgarticle.php?art_ofn=mj04boureston*

Boyd, Gerald M. (1986). "Pakistan Denies Developing Bomb", *New York Times*, July 17.

Broad, William J. and David E. Sanger (2004a). "Warhead Blueprints Link Libya Project to Pakistan Figure", *The New York Times*, February 4.

———. (2004b). "The Bomb Merchant: Chasing Dr. Khan", *New York Times*, December 26.

Broad, William J., David E. Sanger and Raymond Bonner (2004). "A Tale of Nuclear Proliferation", *New York Times*, February 12.

Brownmiller, Susan (1993). *Against Our Will: Men, Women and Rape*. Fawcett Books [reprint edition].

Burrows, William E. and Windrem, Robert (1994). *Critical Mass*. Simon and Schuster. pp.362-364.

Burt, Richard (1979a). "Information Bank Abstracts", *New York Times*, p.1, Column 1, in Lexis-Nexis Academic Universe, 7 April. *http://web.lexis-nexis.com/*

———. (1979b). "Information Bank Abstracts", *New York Times*, p.10, Column 3, in Lexis-Nexis Academic Universe, 2 May. *http://web.lexis-nexis.com/*

———. (1979c). "Information Bank Abstracts", *New York Times*, p.8, Column 1; in Lexis-Nexis Academic Universe, 27 May. *http://web.lexis-nexis.com/*

Carnegie Endowment for International Peace (2005). *Issue Brief. Non-Proliferation VIII(8)*. September 7.

Cass, Alain (1982). "Pakistan Denies Giving Pledge on N-Testing", *Financial Times* (London), Section 1, Overseas News, p.3, in Lexis-Nexis Academic Universe, 15 January. *www.lexis-nexis.com*

Chen, Kathy (1996). "Beijing Admits to Sale of Ring Magnets to Pakistan in Bid to Clear US Tension", *Wall Street Journal*, 15 April, p. B6.

Clary, Christopher (2004). "Dr. Khan's Nuclear WalMart", *Disarmament Diplomacy* 76, March/April 2004, The Acronym Institute. *http://www.acronym.org.uk/dd/dd76/76cc.htm*

Coll, Steve (2001). *Ghost Wars: The Secret History of the CIA, Afghanistan, and Bin Laden, from the Soviet Invasion to September 10, 2001*. The Penguin Press.

Congressional Research Service (2004). *Weapons of Mass Destruction: Trade Between North Korea and Pakistan*. Report for Congress, March 11.

———. (2005). *Pakistan's Nuclear Proliferation Activities and the Recommendations of the 9/11 Commission: US Policy Constraints and Options*. Report for Congress, May 24. *http://fpc.state.gov/documents/organization/48792.pdf*

Cooley, John K. (1980). "Qaddafi's Great Aim for Libya is a Nuclear Capability of its Own," *Christian Science Monitor* (Boston): 14, in Lexis-Nexis Academic Universe, 12 November. *http://web.lexis-nexis.com/*

CNS (1999). *China's Nuclear Exports and Assistance to Pakistan*. Center for Nonproliferation Studies, Monterey Institute of International Studies, Monterey, CA. *http://cns.miis.edu/research/india/china/npakpos.htm*

Der Spiegel (1989). "NTG Nuclear Proliferation Case", November 6, translated in *JPRS-TND*, November 29, p. 35.

Director of Central Intelligence (1997). *The Acquisition of Technology Relating to Weapons of Mass Destruction and Advanced Conventional Munitions*, July-December 1996, June.

Downie Jr., Leonard (1980). "US Says Evidence Shows Pakistan Planning A-Bomb", *Washington Post*, First Section, A20, in Lexis-Nexis Academic Universe, 21 September. *http://www.lexisnexis.com*

Economist (1974). "Ban This Bomb-To-Be", World Politics and Current Affairs, International, p.56, 14 April, in Lexis-Nexis Academic Universe, 14 April 1979. *http://web.lexis-nexis.com/*

———. (1979). "Ban this Bomb-To-Be", World Politics and Current Affairs, International, p.56, in Lexis-Nexis Academic Universe, 14 April. *http://web.lexis-nexis.com/*

———. (1979). "Pakistan: A Clue to the Bomb Mystery", World Politics and Current Affairs, International, p.60; in Lexis-Nexis Academic Universe, 14 July. *http://web.lexis-nexis.com/*

Fialka, John J. (1984). "Nuclear Club: Set to Explode?—Nuclear Spread: How Pakistan Secured US Devices in Canada to make Atomic Arms—Despite Proliferation Barriers, Nation will soon have Ability to Produce Bombs—Jitters in India and the West", *Wall Street Journal*, p. 1, in Lexis-Nexis Academic Universe, 26 November. *http://www.lexisnexis.com*

Fialka, John J. and Thomas F. O'Boyle (1989). "West German Firms Admit Supplying Nuclear-Weapons Material to Pakistan", *Wall Street Journal*, April 21.

Fidler, Steven (2004). "Bhutto 'Rejected Request to Sell N-Technology", *Financial Times*, February 24.

Fidler, Steven and Edward Luce (2001). "US Fears North Korea Could Gain Nuclear Capability through Pakistan", *Financial Times*, June 1.

Financial Times (1985). August 17.

Foreign Report (1986). "Pakistan Persists", March 27.

———. (1989). January 12, pp1.

Gelb, Leslie (1984a). "Pakistan Link Perils US-China Nuclear Pact", *New York Times*, June 23.

———. (1984b). "Peking Said to Balk at Nuclear Pledges", *New York Times*, June 23.

Gertz, Bill (1996a). "China Aids Pakistani Plutonium Plant; Facility may Boost Missile Efforts", *The Washington Times*, 5 February.

———. (1996b). "China Aids Pakistani Plutonium Plant; Facility may Boost Missile Efforts", *The Washington Times*, 3 April, p. A4.

———. (1996c). "Beijing Flouts Nuke-Sales Ban", *The Washington Times*, 9 October, p. A1.

———. (1996d). *The Washington Times*, 10 December.

———. (1999). *Betrayal: How the Clinton Administration Undermined American Security* Washington DC: Regnery Pub. pp. 206-207.

Henderson, Simon (1982). "Anxious US could Probe Zia over N-Plans", *Financial Times* (London), Section 1, Overseas News, p. 4, in Lexis-Nexis Academic Universe, 8 December, *www.lexis-nexis.com*

———. (2004). "Link Leaks", *National Review Online*, January 19.

———. (2009). "Investigation: Nuclear Scandal—Dr. Abdul Qadeer Khan", *The Sunday Times*, September 20. *http://www.timesonline.co.uk/tol/news/world/asia/article6839044.ece.*

Hersh, Seymour M. (1993). "On the Nuclear Edge", *The New Yorker*, March 29.

Hibbs, Mark (1989a). "German Firms Exported Tritium Purification Plant to Pakistan", *Nuclear Fuel*, January 5.

———. (1989b). "German Firms Exported Tritium Purification Plant to Pakistan", *Nuclear Fuel*, February 6.

———. (1989c). "US Repeatedly Warned Germany on Nuclear Exports to Pakistan", *Nuclear Fuel*, March 6.

———. (1989d). "German Firms Exports Raise Concern About Pakistan's Nuclear Capabilities", *Nuclear Fuel*, March 6.

———. (1989e). "Prosecutors Link Tritium Plant to Pakistan Weapons Program", *Nuclear Fuel*, May 1.

———. (1991). "Agencies Trace Some Iraqi URENCO Know-How to Pakistan Re-Export", *Nucleonics Week*, November 28, pp. 1, 7-8.

———. (1996a). "China Said Aiding Kahuta Project; US Credits, NPT Status On line", *Nucleonics Week*, 8 February, p. 1.

———. (1996b). "China Challanges US Data Pointing to Pakistani Aid", *Nucleonics Week*, 22 February, p. 3.

———. (1996c). "Pakistan Said Ready to counter Indian Nuclear Tests with its Own", *Nucleonics Week*, 29 February, p. 14.

———. (1997a). "Khusab Reactor said Started, but Lacks Heavy Water Supply", *Nucleonics Week*, 19 June, p. 15.

———. (1997b). "China Accord Would Turn Up US Heat on Pakistani Reactor", *Nucleonics Week*, August 14, p. 8.

———. (2002). "CIA Assessment on DPRK Presumes Massive Outside Help on Centrifuges", *Nuclear Fuel*, November 25.

Hough, Howard (1995). "Pakistan's Nuclear Stand: Confusion of Strategy?", *Janes Intelligence Review*, June, p. 270.

IAEA (2004a). "Implementation of the NPT Safeguards Agreement in the Islamic Republic of Iran", GOV/2004/11, February 24, p. 8 (hereinafter GOV/2004/11 report).

———. (2004b). "Implementation of the NPT Safeguards Agreement of the Socialist People's Libyan Arab Jamahiriya", GOV/2004/12, February 20 (hereinafter GOV/2004/12 report).

Ikle, Fred C. (1975). "Ikle Warns Against Nuclear Spread", Facts on File World News Digest, 12 April, in Lexis-Nexis Academic Universe, 6 February, *http://web.lexis-nexis.com*

Information Bank Abstracts, *New York Times*, 10 August 1976, in Lexis-Nexis Academic Universe, 10 August 1976. *http://web.lexis-nexis.com*

———. *New York Times*, 26 August 1976, in Lexis-Nexis Academic Universe, 26 August 1976. *http://web.lexis-nexis.com*

———. *New York Times*, 13 October 1976, in Lexis-Nexis Academic Universe, 13 October 1976. *http://web.lexis-nexis.com*

Jalal, Hamid and Khalid Hasan (1970). *Awakening the People*. Speeches of Zulfiqar Ali Bhutto 1966-1969. Rawalpindi: Pakistan Publications. p.21 as cited in Zafar Iqbal Cheema, *Pakistan's Nuclear Policies: Attitudes and Postures*, no. 1, p.105.

Kampani, Gaurav (2004). "Proliferation Unbound: Nuclear Tales from Pakistan", Center for Nonproliferation Studies, Monterey Institute of International Studies, February 23. *http://cns.miis.edu/pubs/week/040223.htm*

Kapur, Ashok (1987). *Pakistan's Nuclear Development.* Croon Helm.

Kargil (2000). "From Surprise To Recknoing, The Kargil Committee Report", New Delhi: Sage Publications. December 1999. Kargil Review Committee Report,wastabled to Parliament 23 February, chaired by K. Subrahmanyam.

Koch, Andrew (2006). "A.Q. Khan Network: Case Closed?", Testimony before the Subcommittee on International Terrorism and Non-proliferation, Committee on International Relations, May 25.

Koch, Andrew and Jennifer Topping (1997). "Pakistan's Nuclear Weapons Program: A Status Report", *The Nonproliferation Review*, Spring-Summer, 4(3), Monterey Institute of International Studies. *http://nuclearweaponsarchive.org/pakistanPakRefn.html#Koch97*

Kux, Dennis (n.d.). *The United States and Pakistan*.

Lancaster, John and Kamran Khan (2004). "Musharraf Named in Nuclear Probe", *The Washington Post*, February 3.

Laufer, Rob (1981). "Pakistan's Nuclear Patriarch Faults Homeland's Nuclear Policies", *Nucleonics Week* 22(1): 4, 8 January in Lexis-Nexis Academic Universe, 8 January, *http://www.lexisnexis.com*

———. (1982). "Interview with Malone: Defense Policy and Assessment of 'Hot Spots'", *Nucleonics Week* 23(33): 1, 19 August in Lexis-Nexis Academic Universe, 19 August. *www.lexis-nexis.com*

Leventhall, Paul (1998). "Testimony", by President, Nuclear Control Institute on China Trade Policy, presented to Subcommittee on Telecommunications, Trade and Consumer Protection, Committee on Commerce, US House of Representatives, May 14.

Maitland, Leslie (1981a). "US Studying Foiled Bid to Export a Key Reactor Metal to Pakistan", *New York Times*, Section A, p. 1, Col. 1, Metropolitan Desk, in Lexis-Nexis Academic Universe, 20 November. *http://www.lexisnexis.com*

———. (1981b). "Charges made in Export Case", *New York Times*, Section 2, p. 30, Col. 5, Metropolitan Desk in Lexis-Nexis Academic Universe, 21 November. *http://www.lexisnexis.com*

Manchester Guardian Weekly, 6 September 1981, *The Week*, p. 6, in Lexis-Nexis Academic Universe, 6 September. *http://www.lexisnexis.com*

Mascarenhas, Anthony (1973). *The Rape of Bangladesh*. Vikas Publications.

McDonough, Mark (1998). "Tracking Nuclear Proliferation: A Guide in Maps and Charts", Washington DC: Carnegie Endowment for International Peace. *www.carnegieendowment.org/publications/index.cfm?fa=view&id=125&prog=zgp&proj=znpp*

———. (1998). "Tracking Nuclear Proliferation: Pakistan (chapter 6)", Washington DC: Carnegie Endowment for International Peace. *www.carnegieendowment.org/files/Tracking_Ch06pakistan.pdf*

Milhollin, Gary and Gerard White (1991). "Bombs from Beijing: A Report on China's Nuclear and Missile Exports", Wisconson Project on Nuclear Arms Control, May, p.17. Washington DC.

———. (1991a). "A New China Syndrome: Beijing's Atomic Bazaar", *The Washington Post*, 12 May, p. C1, C4.

Miller, Judith (1981a). "Cranston Sees Iraq as Nuclear Power by '82", *New York Times*, Section A, p. 3, Column 4, Foreign Desk, in Lexis-Nexis Academic Universe, 18 March. *http://www.lexisnexis.com*

———. (1981b). "Reagan Seeking more 'Flexibility' to set Foreign Policy", *New York Times*, 20 March, Section A, p. 6, Column 1, Foreign Desk, in Lexis-Nexis Academic Universe, 20 March. *http://www.lexisnexis.com*

———. (1982a). "US to Tighten Atomic Export Rules", *New York Times*, Section D, p. 1, Col. 3, Financial Desk, in Lexis-Nexis Academic Universe, 25 June. *www.lexis-nexis.com*

———. (1982b). "US is Holding up Peking Atom Talks", *New York Times*, Section 1, Part 1, p. 11, Col. 1, Foreign Desk, in Lexis-Nexis Academic Universe, 19 September. *www.lexis-nexis.com*

Namboodri, P.K.S. in Subrahmanyam (1981). pp.142 -146.

New York Times (1981). "Pakistan Reports US has offered 5-Year Aid Deal", Section A, p.1, Column 5, Foreign Desk, in Lexis-Nexis Academic Universe, 22 April. *http://www.lexisnexis.com*

———. (1982). "Around the World; Papandreou says Turks Build Nuclear Arms", Section A, p.6, Col. 3, Foreign Desk, in Lexis-Nexis Academic Universe, 9 September. *www.lexis-nexis.com*

———. (1985). February 25.

———. (2004). "Key Pakistani is said to Admit Atom Transfers", February 2.

News India (1989). "Germans Sell Nuke Equipment to Pakistan", March 3.

Norris, Robert S., Andrew S. Burrows and Richard W. Fieldhouse (1994). *Nuclear Weapons Databook: British, French and Chinese Nuclear Weapons* Vol. V. Natural Resources Defence Council. Westview Press.

———. (1981). "German Firm Cited in Case Involving Sale of Fluoride Conversion Plant to Pakistan", *Nuclear Fuel* 6(15): 3, in Lexis-Nexis Academic Universe, 20 July. *http://web.lexis-nexis.com*

Nucleonics Week, 18 July 1987.

———. 7 January 1988.

———. 9 August 1990.

O'Toole, Thomas (1978). "Licenses to Ship A-Fuel Delayed For More Review", *Washington Post*, First Section, A7, in Lexis-Nexis Academic Universe, 20 May. *http://web.lexis-nexis.com/*

Oberdorfer, Dan (1979). *Washington Post*. First Section. A1, in Lexis-Nexis Academic Universe, 7 April. *http://web.lexis-nexis.com/*

———. (1981). "US, Pakistan Progressing on New Aid Plan", *Washington Post*, First Section, A1, in Lexis-Nexis Academic Universe, 22 April. *http://www.lexisnexis.com*

———. (1986). "Nuclear Issue Clouds Junejo Visit", *Washington Post*, July 17.

Oberdorfer, Dan, Michael Gatier, and Maralee Schwartz (1979). "Pakistan: The Quest for Atomic Bomb; Problem Discussed by West, Moscow, Peking", *Washington Post*, First Section, A1, in Lexis-Nexis Academic Universe, 27 August. *http://web.lexis-nexis.com*

Palit, Maj Gen (retd) D.K. and P.K.S. Namboodiri (1979). *Pakistan's Islamic Bomb*. New Delhi: Vikas.

Payne, Robert (1973). *Massacre*. Macmillan.

Pinkston, Daniel A. (2002). "When Did WMD Deals between Pyongyang and Islamabad Begin?", *http://cns.mis.edu*

Pollack, Jonathan (1988). "A Chinese Achievement", *Science*, 23 September, p.1691.

PTI News Agency (New Delhi), 21 May 1996; in *BBC Monitoring Service*, 23 May 1996.

Rahman, H. Hamood ur Rahman Commission Report, Supplement. *www.bangla2000.com/Bangladesh/Independence-War/Report-Hamoodur-Rahman/default.shtm*

Reed, Thomas C. (2008). "The Chinese nuclear Tests, 1964-1996," *Physics Today*: 47-54, September.

Rehman, Shahid-ur (1999). "Z.A. Bhutto, A Man in Hurry for the Bomb", *Long Road To Chagai*. Islamabad, Print Wise Publication.

Reuters (1993). quoting former Army Chief Mirza Aslam Beg to this effect. July 25.

Robbins, Carla Anne (2002). "North Korea Got a Little Help from Neighbors—Secret Nuclear Program Tapped Russian Suppliers and Pakistani Know-How", *Wall Street Journal Europe*, October 21; ABC's *This Week*, October 20 (transcript).

Rohde, David (2004). "General Denies Letting Secrets of A-Bomb Out of Pakistan", *The New York Times*, January 27.

Rohde David and David E. Sanger (2004). "Key Pakistani Is Said to Admit Atom Transfers", *The New York Times*, February 2.

Rogal, Kim and William J. Cook and Jane Whitmore (1982). "Worries about the Bomb", *Newsweek*, International, Pakistan, p.50, in Lexis-Nexis Academic Universe, 20 December. *www.lexis-nexis.com*

Rummel, Rudolph J. (1997). *Death By Government.* Transaction Publishers.

———. (1997). "Statistics of Democide: Genocide and Mass Murder Since 1900", Chapter 8, Table 8.1.

Sanger, David E. (1995). "The Khan Network", Conference on South Asia and the Nuclear Future, Stanford University, June 4. *http://iis-db.stanford.edu/evnts/3889/Khan_network-paper.pdf*

———. (2004). "In Face of Report, Iran Acknowledges Buying Nuclear Components", *New York Times*, February 23.

Sanger, David E. and William J. Broad (2004). "Pakistani's Nuclear Earnings: $100 Million", *New York Times*, March 16.

Salama, Sammy (2005). "Companies Reported to Have Sold or Attempted to Sell Libya Gas Centrifuge Components", *Nuclear Threat Initiative*, March.

Scali, John (1985). "Good Morning America", *American Broadcasting Company*, July 11.

Schweid, Barry (1981). "US Asks Turks to Stop Equipment Shipments", Associated Press, Washington Dateline, in Lexis-Nexis Academic Universe, 27 June. *http://www.lexisnexis.com*

———. (1996). "CIA Chief Visits China to Discuss Arms, Terror", *The Washington Times*, 22 October, p. A11.

Sciolino, Elaine and David E. Sanger (2005). "Pressed, Iran Admits It Discussed Acquiring Tools of Nuclear Arms", *New York Times*, February 28.

Shuey, Robert and Shirley A. Kan (1995). "Chinese Missile and Nuclear Proliferation: Issues for Congress", *CRS Issue Brief*, 29 September, p. 9.

Sisson, Richard and Leo E. Rose (1991). *War and Secession: Pakistan, India, and the Creation of Bangladesh.* University of California Press.

Smith, Hedrick (1988). "A Bomb Ticks in Pakistan", *New York Times Magazine*, March 6.

Smith, R. Jeffrey (1992). "Pakistan Can Build One Device, Foreign Official Says", *The Washington Post*, February 7.

———. (1996a). "US Decides to Transfer Weapons that Pakistan Paid for in 1980s", *The Washington Post*, 20 March.

———. (1996b). "US Aides See Troubling Trend in China-Pakistan Nuclear Ties", *The Washington Post*, 1 April.

———. (1996c). "China Sold Nuclear Items Before Vow", *The Washington Post*, 10 October, p. A38.

Smith, R. Jeffrey and Thomas W. Lippman (1995). "Pakistan Is Building Reactor That May Yield Large Quantities of Plutonium", *Washington Post*, April 8.

Spector, Leonard S. (1988). *The Undeclared Bomb*. Cambridge Mass: Ballinger Publishing Co. (pp122ff and notes).

———. (1990). *The Undeclared Bomb: The Spread of Nuclear Weapons, 1987-1988*. Harper Business.

Spector, Leonard S. and Jacqueline R. Smith (1990). *Nuclear Ambitions: The Spread of Nuclear Weapons 1989-1990*. San Francisco: Westview Press.

———. (1991). *Nuclear Ambitions*. Westview Press, Boulder, Co. pp.101-102.

Squassoni, Sharon (2004a). "Weapons of Mass Destruction: Trade Between North Korea and Pakistan", *CRS Report for Congress*, RL 31900, March 11.

———. (2004b). "Closing Pandora's Box: Pakistan's Role in Nuclear Proliferation", *Arms Control Today*, April. *www.armscontrol.org/act/2004_04/Squassoni.asp*

Srivastava, Anupam and Seema Gahlaut (2003). "Curbing Proliferation from Emerging Suppliers: Export Controls in India and Pakistan", *Arms Control Today* 12-16 September.

Strobel, Warren P. and Bill Gertz (1996). "Chinese General Hits Arms Reports", *The Washington Times*, 10 December.

Sublette, Carey (2002a). "Dr. Abdul Qadeer Khan", *Nuclear Weapons Archive*, updated 2nd January. *http://nuclearweaponarchive.org/Pakistan/AQKhan.html*

———. (2002b). "Pakistan's Nuclear Weapons Program: The Beginning", *Nuclear Weapons Archive*, Updated January, 2. *http://nuclearweaponarchive.org/Pakistan/PakOrigin.html*

Subrahmanyam, K. (ed.) (1981). *Nuclear Myths and Realities: India's Dilemma*. New Delhi: ABC Publishing House.

Tenet, George (2004). Speech at Georgetown University, February 5. *www.cia.gov/cia/public_affairs/speeches/index.html*

The Times of India (2004). "Nuke Leak May Cost Pak $3b", *The Times of India Online*, February 5.

Totten, Samuel *et al.* (1997). eds., *Century of Genocide: Eyewitness Accounts and Critical Views.* Garland Reference Library.

US Arms Control and Disarmament Agency, Adherence to and Compliance with Arms Control Agreements, 1997, p.80.

US State Department (1994). *Report to Congress: Update on Progress Toward Regional Non-proliferation in South Asia*. April.

———. (1991). "The Pakistan Nuclear Program", June 23, 1983, Secret/Noforn/Orcon released under the Freedom of Information Act to the National Security Archive, January 17.

US Office of the Secretary of Defense (1996). *Proliferation: Threat and Response*, April, p.38.

———. (1997). *Proliferation: Threat and Response*, November, p.17.

United Press International (1981). "International", in Lexis-Nexis Academic Universe, 11 February. *http://www.lexisnexis.com*

Virmani, Arvind (2004). "Economic Performance, Power Potential and Global Governance: Towards a New International Order", *Working Paper* No.150, ICRIER, December. *www.icrier.org/wp150.pdf*

———. (2005). "Global Power from the 18th to 21st Century: Power Potential (VIP^2), Strategic Assets & Actual Power (VIP)", *ICRIER Working Paper* No. 175, November.

Warrick, Joby and Peter Slevin (2004). "Libyan Arms Designs Traced Back to China", *The Washington Post*, February 15.

Washington Post (1981a). "Saudi Nuclear Pact", *Washington Post*, First Section, Around the World, A22; in Lexis-Nexis Academic Universe, 19 January. *http://www.lexisnexis.com*

———. (1981b). "Sale to Pakistan Questioned", First Section, Around the World, A20, in Lexis-Nexis Academic Universe, 1 July. *http://www.lexisnexis.com*

Washington Times (1996). "Pakistan Nuclear Program at a 'Screwdriver Level", February 20.

Weinraub, Bernard (1982). "Zia tells Reagan He won't Build Atomic Weapon", *New York Times*, Section A, p.1, Col. 5, Foreign Desk, in Lexis-Nexis Academic Universe, 8 December. *www.lexis-nexis.com*

Weintraub, Richard M. and Les Whittington (1980). "Pakistan Said to Receive Nuclear Arms Parts Illegally via Canada", *Washington Post*, First Section, World News, A 37; in Lexis-Nexis Academic Universe, 7 December. *http://www.lexisnexis.com*

Weiss, Leonard (2004). "Pakistan: It's déjà vu all over again", *Bulletin of the Atomic Scientists* 60(03): 52-59, May/June. *www.thebulletin.orgarticle.php?art_ofn= mj04weiss*

———. (2005). "Turning a Blind Eye Again? The Khan Network's History and Lessons for U.S. Policy", *Arms Control Today*, March. *http://www.armscontrol.org/act/2005_03/Weiss.asp*

———. (2006). Testimony on the A.Q. Khan Network before the Subcommittee on International Terrorism and Non-proliferation Committee on International Relations, May 25.

Weissman, Steve & Herbert Krosney (1981). "The Kindly Dr. Khan", *The Islamic Bomb: The Nuclear Threat to Israel and the Middle East.* New York: Times Books.

Wikipedia, *Bangladesh Liberation War.*

Willis, David K (1981). "On the Trail of the A-Bomb Makers; Antinuclear Battle Nears Climax", *Christian Science Monitor* (Boston), p. 1, in Lexis-Nexis Academic Universe, 1 December. *http://web.lexis-nexis.com/*

Woodward, Bob (1986). "Pakistan Reported Near Atom Arms Production", *Washington Post*, November 4.

Woodward, Bob and Don Oberdorfer (1986). "Pakistan A-Project Upsets Superpowers", *Washington Post*, July 15.

World Affairs (1979). "A-Arms Threat Cited," Facts on File World News Digest", *World Affairs*, in Lexis-Nexis Academic Universe, 20 April. *http://web.lexis-nexis.com/*

World News Digest (1976). "US, Pakistan Discuss French A-Plant", Facts on File World News Digest, in Lexis-Nexis Academic Universe, 14 August. *http://web.lexis-nexis.com*

———. (1978). "Bhutto- A-Capability was Near", *Facts on File World News Digest*, Other Nations, Pakistan, in Lexis-Nexis Academic Universe, 20 October. *http://web.lexis-nexis.com/*

Xinhua (1979). "Pakistan Foreign Ministry Spokesman on US Economic Aid Stoppage", Xinhua General Overseas News Service, in Lexis-Nexis Academic Universe, 9 April. *http://web.lexis-nexis.com/*; "US Cuts Aid to Pakistan."

———. (1980). "Moscow's Fabrication About Pakistan's Intended Nuclear Test in China Refuted", Xinhua General Overseas News Service, in Lexis-Nexis Academic Universe, 6 May. *http://www.lexisnexis.com*

Yourish, Karen and Delano D'Souza (2004). "Father of Pakistani Bomb Sold Nuclear Secrets", *Arms Control Today*, March, p.22.

Zaidi, Mubashir (2004). "Scientist Claimed Nuclear Equipment Was Old, Official Says", *The Los Angeles Times*, February 10.

Post Script (September 2008)

Thomas C. Reed, a former nuclear weaponer (1959-1965) and Secretary of the Air Force (1976-77), based on information attributed to Danny Stillman, director of the technical intelligence division at Los Almos National Laboratory, writes in "The Chinese Nuclear Tests, 1964-1996," *Physics Today,* September 2008, pp.47-54, that,

(1) "..extensive hospitality extended to Pakistani nuclear scientists during that same late-1980s time period. ..that cooperation, initiated earlier in the decade, led to a joint nuclear test in China soon after Stillman's departure."(i.e., after April 1990).

(2) "In 1982, China's premier Deng Xiaping began the transfer of nuclear weapons technology to Pakistan ... Those transfers included blue-prints for the ultra simple CHC-4 design using highly enriched uranium, first tested by China in 1966."

(3) "A Pakistani derivative of CHIC-4 apparently was tested in China on 26 May 1990."

These dates can be posited against the previously referred "historical (secret) Pakistan-China nuclear agreement," signed by Z.A. Bhutto in June 1976 and the "success achieved 12 years later" referred to by General Mirza Aslam Beg (page 29).

9 Globalisation, Economic Growth and National Security

Introduction

The focus of this chapter is on the geopolitical system. The world is in the process of moving from an old to a new global system and it is useful to look at some of the projections made in earlier chapters, basically between 2004-2006.[1] The chapter then goes on to look at the new developments since then—there have been quite amazing and unpredictable developments—and see how well the earlier projections have held up.

There is now a clearer discussion on the transition. Earlier papers had focused only on the long-term. Here, the extra part is the transition where the institutions and the implications for India kind of start coming out. It would however be presumptuous for anyone to say that he has got all the answers. The transition is marked by great uncertainty. Some clarity is possible by understanding where the world is coming from and where it is headed. Those two parts will be somewhat similar to those in earlier chapters, but revised and updated using the latest available data. This allows a sharper focus on the 10 years or 15 years which are the period of transition from the old to the new order.

Clearly globalisation is a major driving force and it is there lurking in the background. There is not enough space to bring it out more explicitly.[2] The chapter will explore the implications of the changing global order. How should a country set its objectives and goals for this transition period, which has been assumed to be of the order of 10 or 15 years? The key is to focus on improving the institutions and rules of global security which includes economic, military and other dimensions.

---

1. Virmani (2004), Virmani (2005a, b, c, d, e, f), Virmani (2006a, b).
2. We can take that up in the question session if the things are not very clear about what I say.

Evolution to a New Global Order

So, what is evolution? Is it an evolution of an old order or is it a new global order? Let us start by quoting from the US National Intelligence Committee Forecast which appeared in December 2004. This report used the economic forecasts given in a Goldman Sachs Paper written in October 2003. The NIC (2004) report indicated that China's GDP in US dollars could be second largest by 2020 and India's GDP in US dollars could be third largest by 2035. Virmani (2004b) which was also published in December 2004, showed that the rise of China and India would be much faster than projected by anyone else till then. The author had got an indication of the broad views in the US Intelligence Committee, from a US analyst who was familiar with such US based work, while attending a seminar in Europe around May 2004. The second point that the paper emphasised was that China's GDP at PPP (and this was an outrageous statement at that time), would equal the US by 2015 (Virmani, 2004b).

Unipolar to Tripolar

The power potential, an index (VIPP or VIP^2), was first defined/ used in the same paper. The power potential of China, as measured by this index, was projected to reach 70 per cent of the US by 2035; India's GDP was projected to equal that of the USA at some time after 2035 and the power potential would be about 25 per cent of the USA at that time (in this paper, it was not absolutely clear when that would happen). Virmani (2005a), which came soon after, expounded more clearly on the rise of India saying that it would be the third largest economy by 2015. It forecast that India's GDP would equal that of USA by 2040 and power potential would be 80 per cent of USA by 2050. Similarly, China's power potential would equal USA by 2030-2035 and therefore, a bipolar world would emerge by 2025. This was the big new message of this paper that contrasted sharply with what most international analysts and scholars were saying. It asserted that the global order would move first to a bipolar world and then subsequently to a tripolar world with India coming up by around 2015.

When this paper was presented at seminars, questions were raised about the role of EU (Virmani, 2005d). Recall that Prof. Henry Kissinger

(1994) had written about the EU as a potential great power of the future along with USA, Russia, China and Japan, with India only a distant possibility in sixth place. Subsequently, Virmani (2005e) therefore defined something called a "Virtual State", something like the USSR where decisions regarding external matters, whether it is economic matters or military matters were taken in an unified way. The reasoning was that the EU could not be a power unless it became a virtual State. This chapter will have something more to say on this subsequently.

There were also questions raised about the value of such long term projections. In response, the author had stated one thing that one can be almost sure of: any specific futuristic predictions will turn out to be wrong. Projections, no matter how imperfect are, however essential for any kind of planning. Questions were also raised about the downside risk to the projections particularly for Indian and Chinese economies. Does the projection mean that there are no weaknesses, and that these outcomes would happen automatically? The answer is clearly no. The main weaknesses the author had identified for China were the mercantilist export-FDI oriented policies. Subsequent developments, particularly the global financial and economic crisis has for the first time highlighted this problem for all to see. We believe that China will have to fundamentally change its developmental model if it wants to continue to grow relatively fast and remain among the top three in growth rates. On India's side, the author had identified governance problems, something that everybody is now talking about post-Mumbai. It was specified that the issue of governance was really the issue of the supply of public and quasi-public goods. These are defined as goods which are public in the sense that they cannot be provided in a private market. Such goods and services cannot be sold and bought in the market. They are collective goods. A good example of such a service is the rule of law where the police system, the legal system is common. Defence is a classic example. The author emphasised the rule of law as it is essential for the existence of competitive markets. This is the fundamental flaw which is seen again and again, including the Naxalite controlled districts and most recently in the Mumbai terrorist attacks (Virmani, 2002a, b).

New Developments in 2007 and 2008

There have been a number of new developments in the last few years i.e., since the author's initial projections, so this chapter starts by first presenting these, so readers can judge for themselves the impact of these development by comparing with earlier projections. Four very, significant developments have taken place since then: One, is the oil and energy price boom, which we have just been through and increasingly has the characteristic of a roller coaster. Oil prices rose by 130 per cent till July. Thereafter, they fell by almost that amount. Thereafter, they again started rising and rose above $70 per barrel. The important implication of which is that Russia has come back into the global economic picture. In the author's earlier projections, Russia did not have a prominent role as it has now. Clearly, Russia's comeback has depended on the oil and energy price boom. The fluctuations and trends have been amazing and there are certain implications of that. These will be noted very briefly because they are purely economic stuff that may not be of much interest to non-economists.

The second was a massive change in the PPP estimates by the World Bank/ADB. India and China's GDP, according to this new estimate was 36 per cent lower, reduced with one stroke of the pen. That is a huge change. How does it affect the forecasts? The basis of the book's projections and forecast is the GDP at PPP, which was with one stroke adjusted down by 36 per cent. *Prima facie*, it would appear that everything should go haywire.

The third is the end of the nuclear apartheid and the fourth is the US global financial crisis, its impact on the global economy and big powers. All these factors, with the exception of the ending of nuclear apartheid, a somewhat non-economic factor, have been taken account of in the new projections.

Change in Projections: 2004-05 and 2008

These are summarised in Figures 9.1a and 9.1b which depict the evolution of relative economic size of the major powers (*vis-a-vis* USA) over the 20-year period from 2008 to 2028. This is the relative economic size which is the size of each country relative to the US, which is the benchmark. Recall that by definition, power is always relative (Meerschimer). So, all the numbers, the figures in this chapter will represent the data for the concerned country divided by the data for the US which is the benchmark. One would say that USA is still the sole superpower. Later in the chapter, there is a formal definition of superpower which will show the quantitative basis for this statement.

Figure 9.1a shows that the Chinese economy is now far ahead of the rest of the potential powers; so it is clearly the second largest, and it is projected to equal the US economy in size sometime after 2020 (crossing 100 per cent, that is, US). Initially the Indian economy is smaller than Japan, but equals and exceeds it somewhere around 2012. Thereafter, it breaks away with its size increasing rapidly with the 'magic of compound interest'/or more accurately the compounding effect of growth asserting itself. This is despite the deceleration of growth that is built into these projections. As long the growth rate remains higher than the benchmark US economy's growth rate, the relative size keeps rising.

Figure 9.1a

Relative Economic Size (/USA)—GDP at Purchasing Power Parity

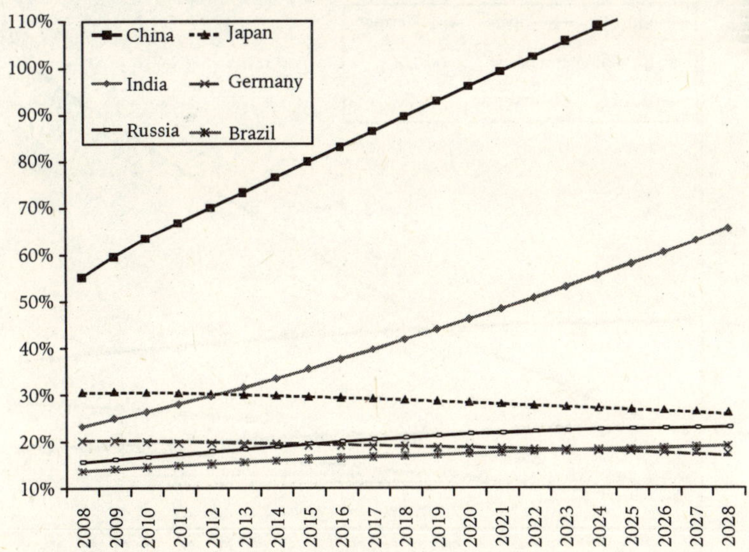

Source: Author's projections based on World Bank, WDI, 2007, 2008.

What is the difference between the latest projections made in 2008 and depicted above, from the projections made in 2004-05? Firstly, the impact of lower GDP-PPP, which as mentioned earlier is minus 36 per cent, results in delayed catch-up. However, this is partly offset by faster growth. The growth which has occurred is actually faster than had been assumed in earlier projections. What does that imply? China will equal the US economy seven years later than projected in the previous papers—around 2022 instead of 2015. There is a similar delay in China equaling the power potential of USA, as visually depicted in a subsequent figure. Second, India becomes the third largest country in terms of relative size in 2012, about six years later than in the earlier projections. India's power potential at the middle of the century (2050) would be about 70 per cent rather than 80 per cent. To summarise, the current projection is completely within the range of possibilities envisaged earlier, despite these huge shocks. Statistically speaking, it is completely within the normal range of errors that characterise virtually all economic variables.

Figure 9.1b

Relative Economic Size (/USA)—GDP at Purchasing Power Parity

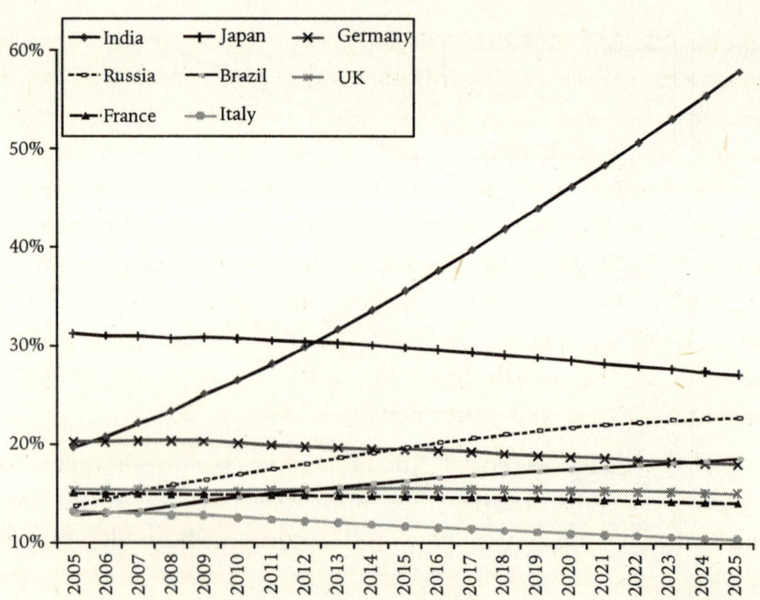

Source: Author's projections based on World Bank, WDI, 2007, 2008.

Here one should again add the answer to the question that was asked many times, "Is this what you are predicting for the future?" The answer is that this is a mean scenario. The actual trajectory may be higher or lower. This in turn means that equivalence occurs some years earlier or later, respectively.

Let us look at the other potential powers such as Germany, Russia and Brazil. As mentioned, the earlier papers, which are reflected in the earlier chapters, had given much less importance to these countries. One major mistake made in the earlier papers, which has been corrected in the current chapter, was to downplay the importance of energy demand-supply imbalances and energy price changes. The earlier papers focused on the effect of energy shortages on countries like China, India and USA that are net oil importers. It was correctly reasoned that all such importers would be affect to varying degrees and consequently, their relative position would change only marginally. This has turned out to be, by and large correct. The mistake was to ignore the effect on oil/commodity exporters like Russia and Brazil. With the experience of the recent oil/energy/commodity price shock, this oversight has now been corrected.

The revision in the commodity and oil price outlook has changed the picture. Recall that Brazil is also a huge commodity producer and exporter. Consequently, towards the end of the period depicted, they become significant global players (Figure 9.1a). Figure 9.1b squeezes the scale and leaves out China so that we can see these countries clearly. This figure shows that in about 20 years, the Russian and Brazilian economies are likely to be larger in size than Germany. Brazil overtakes France and UK by 2012. So, in terms of the current middle powers, if we can call them so, Brazil will be coming up, but only to an extent and substantially due to its natural resource endowment. Russia is somewhere in the middle here. By overtaking Germany by 2015, it becomes fifth in size and power potential.

The reason, for the rise of Russia is quite clear in hindsight, its oil and gas endowments and the price of oil rising due to faster growth of China and increased demand from oil exporters who underprice oil in their own domestic market. Another factor is the non-market power of the oil cartel.

This cartelisation has broader implications in terms of power. It is not a normal market. That are a few key difference between oil and certain energy product and the host of normal manufactured and extracted mineral products. All these products are traded in normal broadly competitive markets. The problem in oil/energy is supplied by a cartel of energy producing and exporting countries (which is much worse than a cartel of firms). There are certain other special characteristics of energy, in that it is a universal intermediate. It is not that it is used in one, two or few industry in relatively small proportions, but is either directly or indirectly an input in virtually every industry and activity. This gives the cartel additional power. This means that power elements beyond pure economics come into the picture here, which Russia is successfully trying to use.

Other Views: US NIC

How does this projection compare with other analysis and views? In November 2008, US NIC (National Intelligence Council) released a new report. This November 2008 report say that, "The eight largest economies in 2025 will be in descending order—the US, China, India, Japan, etc." This is consistent with both the author's earlier projections as well as the revised projections, except that US NIC does not give explicit projections like the author has always given. US NIC also says that, "By 2025, China will have the world's second largest economy and will be a leading military power." Again, this is consistent with our scenario of a bipolar world. After this, however, NIC (2008) goes on and said something quite different: "A global multipolar system is emerging with the rise of China, India and others which will lead to the development of a globalised economy in which China and India play major roles." So, the US NIC believes that China and India will be important but within what looks to them like a multipolar world. Our perspective on this is somewhat different as discussed below.

Global System: Long Term

The evolution of the global system will depend not just on the evolution of the different economies, but on the evolution of power. This section starts by looking at the evolution of power potential over the long term, where the long term is defined as half a century or till

2050. This will help in seeing where the world is coming from and where it is going, and thus put the current period up to 2025/2028 in perspective. The index of power potential, which has been termed VIP^2, has been defined in earlier chapters and in Virmani (2005c) and Virmani (2005e).[3] Figure 9.2 shows that currently and for the next five years or so, there are a number of countries bunched together giving the impression of a multipolar power structure. Within a decade, China pulls away from the crowd, and another two decades later India pulls ahead of the rest. Thus, according to these projections, the global power structure would be transformed within three decades.

Global Powers and Superpower(s)

The index of power potential (VIP^2) can also be used to formally define a potential 'global power'. A 'global power' is defined as a country with a VIP^2 of more than 25 per cent. As the VIP^2 measures power relative to that of the USA, this means that a country with power potential of more than 25 per cent of that of the USA has the potential to exert its power across the world. So, where does this 25 cut-off come from? This is actually the value of the index (VIP^2) for the USSR at its peak of power—as shown in an earlier chapter. It may appear paradoxical that the USSR with less than 25 per cent of US power potential was able to challenge it and convert the world into bipolar. Clearly, there is more to global power and superpower than economic power or power potential.[4] In the globalised world of the 21st century, the relative importance of various elements is changing, as discussed below. A conservative value is used for defining a global power, a VIP^2 that is higher than the one at which the USSR attained global power.

Towards a Tripolar System

Applying this definition of "global power", China is only a few years away from becoming a global power (2010), while India will take another

3. VIPP or VIP^2 or Virmani Index of Power Potential measures the overall economic capability of an economy, including capital, skills and technology. This is then combined with an index of strategic assets and defence capabilities to derive an overall index of power.

4. See Virmani (2005e) for an analysis of the other critical element of power, strategic technology.

two decades (2027) to attain this status (Figure 9.2). Japan has been a global power for a long time and will remain so till 2021. Thus, Japan will cease to have the power potential to be a global power half a decade before India attains this global power potential. The reader must remember, however, that the index measures power potential. To this has to be added, strategic assets or strategic technology, which includes defence assets and technology, to obtain an overall index of actual power (Virmani, 2005e). A 'superpower' is defined as a country with a VIP^2 of 40-50 per cent, less than double the cut-off for a global power. Based on this cut-off value, China will become a potential superpower around 2020 and India around 2040.

The summary picture that emerges is as follows: The past was a unipolar world with the US as sole superpower, whose power peaked in 1999, The future will be a bipolar world by 2020 and a tripolar one by 2040 (Figure 9.2). In between, a situation will be there which the NIC (2008) and others have rightly called a multipolar world. Can anything spoil this simple picture? Some people have talked about the socio-political explosion of 'Communist/Socialist" China, others of the implosion of India. Though nothing can be ruled out, the author is confident that a tripolar world will emerge by the middle of the 21st century as predicted in Virmani (2005a) and Virmani (2006a).

Quadripolar: The Role of EU

The moment one talks about tripolar, the issue of the role and position of the European Union (EU) comes up. In principle, a quadripolar world is possible but for it to happen, the EU has to become a virtual State. In other words, the EU will have to develop unified decision-making with respect to external relations—economic, military etc.—as for example, prevailed in the USSR. Paradoxically, this ideal has receded over the past few years, since the author first addressed this issue, with the EU moving in the opposite direction. A number of country referendums have rejected the EU. The recent global financial crisis saw each member country acting completely independently and focusing on their own national interests, some to the detriment of other member countries. Earlier papers and talks had concluded that the EU had become a virtual State with respect to economics (see previous chapters); since then, response to the financial crisis raises serious doubts about this conclusion if not falsifying it. The EU is a virtual State only with respect to trade and WTO issues. Despite the movement of the EU in a direction opposite to that of a "virtual State", it is not possible to rule out eventual movement in this direction. The degree of uncertainty is so high at present that it is also not possible to make a definite prediction on whether the world will be quadripolar at mid-century.

Figure 9.2

Evolution of Power Potential (VIP²)

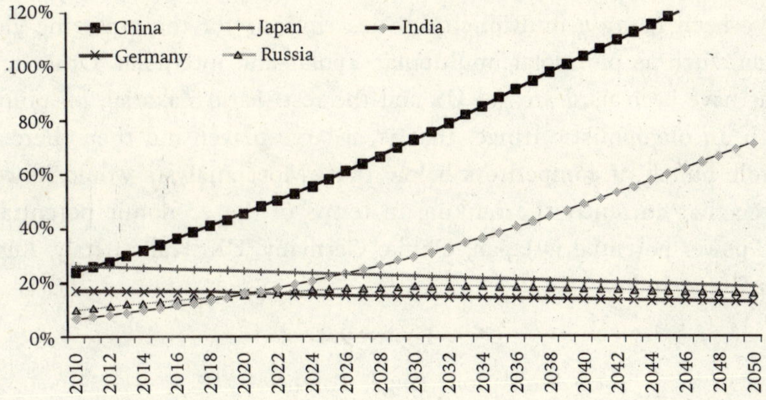

Source: Author's projections based on World Bank, WDI, 2007, 2008.

Global System: Transition Phase

With a picture of the possible evolution of power potential over the long term, the focus of attention shifts to the actions and approaches that need to be adopted over the medium term or during the transition from a unipolar to a tripolar world. Figure 9.3 presents the medium term till 2025 with all potentially significant powers represented. China is now about five years from becoming the second most powerful country in terms of power potential measured by VIP² when its power potential will exceed that of Japan. Japan's power potential will however remain the third highest during the rest of the transition period. According to this data, India's power potential, currently the lowest among the 10 largest economies, is projected to rise rapidly to equal that of Brazil in 2 years, Italy in 5 years, France in 7 years, UK in 9 years and Germany in 12 years. The rising power potential of Russia will remain above India till they both exceed Germany in 2021 when India will simultaneously overtake Russia. According to this data, Brazil's rising power potential will intersect Italy's declining one, to exceed it by the end of the period, but will remain below that of UK and France, who are likely to retain their relative power *vis-à-vis* Germany, the most powerful European country.

We are now ready to analyse this transition phase, a period of 15 to 20 years and draw out the implications. International affairs scholars have been using a multiplicity of descriptions for the emerging global order, such as pluripolar, multipolar, apolar and interpolar. Other terms that have been used are: (a) US and the rest (Farid Zakaria), (b) unipolar with an oligopolistic fringe, that is, a large player and then there is a whole bunch of competitors below that. Most analysts would however agree that currently the ranking in terms of the economic potential or the power potential is Japan, China, Germany, UK, France, Italy, Russia, Brazil and India.

Figure 9.3

Transition: Power Potential VIP[2]

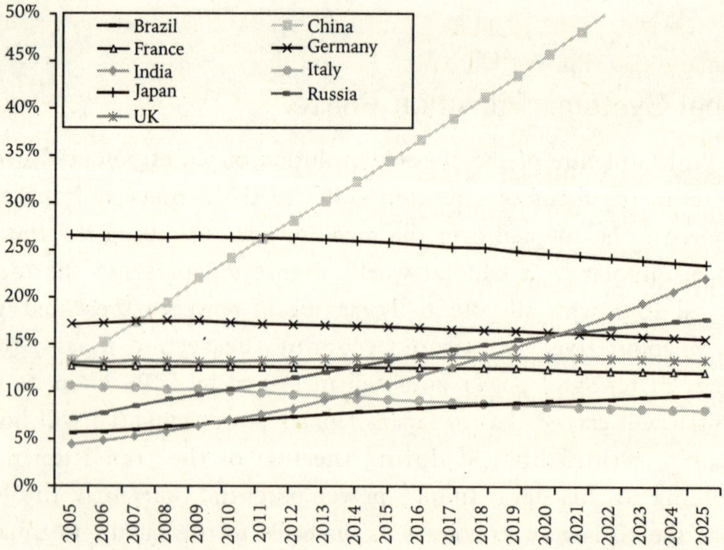

Source: Author's projections based on World Bank, WDI, 2007, 2008.

This is a good point at which to digress briefly and say a little bit about actual power. The index of power potential (VIP^2) is based on economic theory and is an economic concept, but at some point, one has to bring in strategic assets, including a country's strategic military assets, the strategic technology (defence, nuclear, space) into the picture. Virmani (2005e) formally defines an index of power, termed VIP, which is composite of VIP^2 and the strategic assets of the country, including strategic military technology, assets and capability. Unfortunately, it is very difficult to get data on strategic assets and therefore, the author has not been able, so far, to construct this index VIP for all the large powers this.[5]

There are however, a few important implications that can be drawn even without calculating VIP. One is that Russia, because of its legacy of strategic assets, which they developed as the USSR, is actually more powerful than this ordering would suggest. Similarly, China has very determinedly from the days of Mao's nuclear and space deals with the USSR, built up its strategic capability. In contrast, since its defeat in World War II, Japan has turned inwards, shunned the acquisition of strategic capability and consequently comes lower in the power ranking than its rank on VIP^2.

Multipolar: Concentration Index

The first issue to address is the issue of multipolarity raised by many scholars! Ignoring the US, which is at 100 per cent and is not shown in Figure 9.2, the world seems to have some elements of multipolarity. Virmani (2006b) had argued that though the world economy could be described as multipolar, because of the near 'virtual State' nature of EU in terms of trade-WTO and some other issues, the global power structure looked distinctly unipolar with an oligopolistic fringe. The current section applies certain established economic concepts to this issue with the hope of getting more definitive conclusions. The Harfendahl Concentration Index (HCI) is commonly used to measure the concentration of market share among supplier firms in a given industry. This section uses this to measure the concentration of economic size and power potential.

5. In India, VIP is a common abbreviation for Very Important Person. However, countries are not persons, so to keep an allusion to the commonly usage of this abbreviation, the Index was christened Virmani Index of Power.

This can be done, stretching back to the start of the millennium, using Angus Maddison's data and the VIP^2, which had earlier been calculated and presented in Virmani (2005e). Here, we use the data back to 1870-1990 to find out what has been happening to concentration of global power potential, using the VIP^2. On measuring the concentration of power among all countries for which the data is available, it turns out the highest concentration of power occurred in 1950; immediately after World War II. Thereafter, it declined rapidly till 1982 but it has been rising slowly since then. Though the absolute value of the HCI is not important *per se*, it gives an idea of the order of magnitude, by noting that it fell dramatically in 30 years from about 1.0 in 1950 to about 0.07 in 1982. Therefore, the concentration of power potential is increasing since 1980, it remains well below that in the post-war years according to the Maddison GDP data used in the HCI.

The data we have used earlier in the chapter is the World Bank GDP-PPP data, which is available only from 1980 onwards. Use of this data for the top 10 countries (only) produces a slightly different picture. We first calculate the concentration among the 10 largest economies i.e., the concentration in terms of economic size. As shown in Figure 9.4, among the 10 largest countries, economic concentration peaked in 1999 and has been declining since then. Projected forward the concentration reaches a trough in 2014 after which the concentration increases progressively to exceed the 1999 peak by 2030. Thus, the growth of the Chinese and Indian economies, initially serves to disperse power among the large powers as China catches up with the USA, the largest economy (Figure 9.1a) and India catches up with Japan the third (earlier second) largest economy (Figure 9.1b). Subsequently, economic concentration is projected to rise as China's economy rivals and exceeds the USA economy and India's economy does the same *vis-à-vis* Japan's economy (Figure 9.3). What appears to be an unprecedented rise in the concentration of economic activity among the large powers by mid-century, is however, a return to a pre-industrial revolution era, when China and India were the two largest economies by a big margin.[6]

6. Virmani (2006d), Virmani (2007) and Virmani (2008).

Virmani (2005d) and other papers argued that post-war globalisation is leading to a convergence of Asian per capita income to developed country levels. As China and India converge to world average income levels, the population size of these two countries will assert itself. From the start of the millennium (zero) to around 1800, these two countries were both the richest and largest countries in the world. So, the projected future would just be a return to a situation which existed for centuries in the pre-industrial era, before the industrial revolution transformed Europe and USA into high income countries with economies larger than that of India and China.[7]

Figure 9.4

Economic (GDP PPP) Concentration among the 10 Largest Countries (HCI)

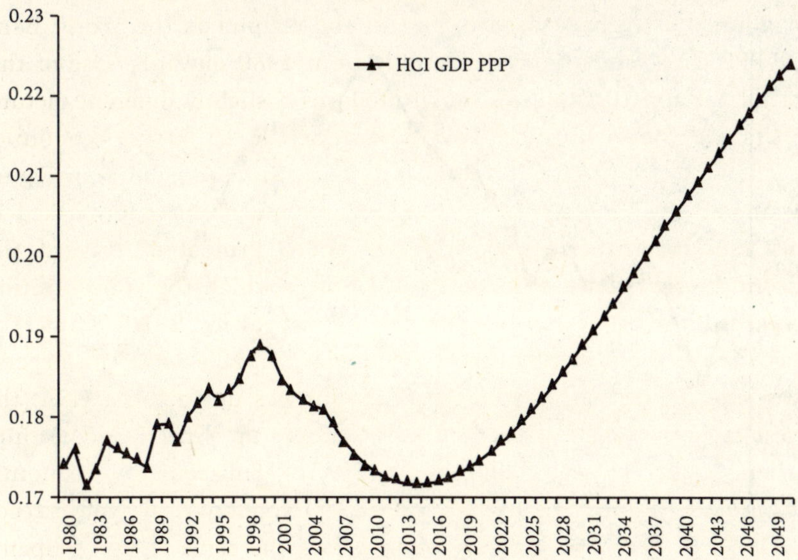

Source: Author's projections based on World Bank, WDI, 2007, 2008.

The measurement and analysis of concentration in terms of VIP², is slightly more complicated for the post-1980 period (using World Bank data). The concentration of power potential (HCI using the VIP²) among the same set of 10 countries (10 largest in terms of size) is shown in

7. Virmani (2006d), Virmani (2007) and Virmani (2008).

Figure 9.5. As in the case of economic concentration, the concentration of power potential is on a rising trend from 1980 to 1999. After peaking in 1999, it trends downwards much more sharply. This pattern suggests that the "Unipolar moment" occurred in 1999. As conventional wisdom classifies the post-war years till 1980-1985 as bipolar, the fact that the HCI is still larger than in any year between 1980 and 1990 is consistent with the view that the world is still unipolar. The HCI is however projected to go below the 1980s trough around 2014. This can be interpreted as being consistent with emerging multipolarity. However, it is also consistent with emerging bipolarity or tripolarity.

Figure 9.5

Concentration (HCI) of Power Potential (VIP²) among the 10 Largest Countries

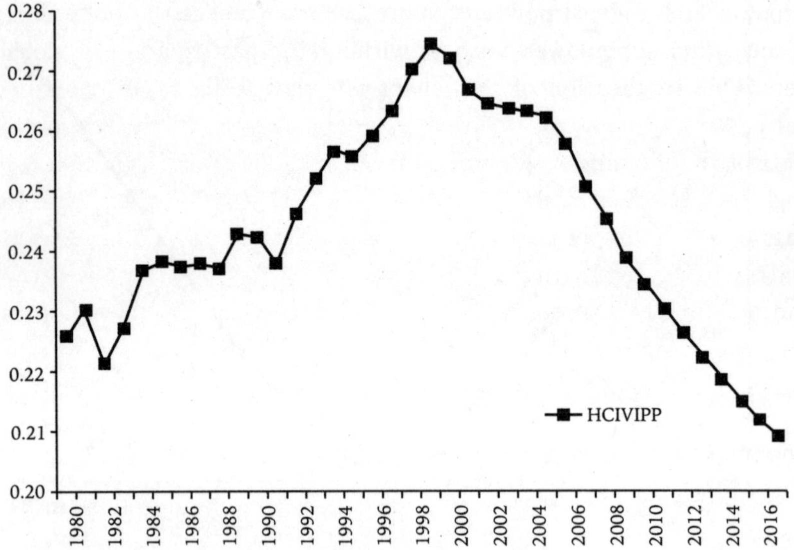

Source: Author's projections based on World Bank, WDI, 2007, 2008.

Global Institutions and Rules

This brings us to the most important part of this chapter—the implications of the evolving global order for national security and international relations. This section explores the implications of this milieu of powers at this point and the rise of China and India. The assertion of power depends on relative power and balance of power, which students of international relations are quite familiar with. But the assertion of power also depends on the constraints imposed by international and national institutions. According to Alfred North who got a Nobel Prize for his work on institutional economics, "Institution" does not mean the physical structure like the UN, but the rules, both formal and informal, under which individuals and organisations operate. By analogy, global institutions are the formal and informal rules under which countries operate in the world. For simplicity, the global organisation such as the UN are encompassed under this overall rubric of global institutions. From this perspective, a key distinction between countries that can be classified as global powers and those that cannot be so classified is that the former helps shape and/or participate in the formulation of global rules. Similarly, the distinction between a superpower and a global power is that the former makes the rules along with any other superpower, with or without the participation of global powers. One implication of this chapter is that India as an emerging global power must aim to influence the formulation and modification of these global rules under which countries operate on the world stage. The global powers help shape the rules, and India must participate in changing the rules of this global game. The second point is that globalisation is changing the factors which underline power, the economic, military and social elements of power. Globalisation is leading to a change in the relative importance of these factors. This is the underlying theme of this section.

Economic Institutions and Rules

Since the classic 19th century balance of power systems of Europe and Germany, which have been widely analysed and depicted in history, there has been a lot of evolution in terms of both economic and social elements. What are these? Let us start with economic elements. As emphasised strongly in Virmani (2004b), economic size and strength is the foundation of a national power. Globalisation of the world economy has resulted an increase in interdependence since the end of the Cold War. This is the first time that every country, except Cuba, North Korea and Myanmar, wants to be part of this global system of trade and financial interdependence. This is a complete change from the so-called bipolar world of the USA-USSR. The USSR and many of its block partners chose to remain completely or partially outside this system. Currently every potential global power, including China and Russia, want to be a part of the global economic system. So, the nature of the rules and institutions of global economic governance are changing. Global trade related issues and problems are now dealt with at and by the WTO. Virtually, all countries want to be a member. Even Russia, which is still not a member, had applied for membership, but recently expressed its desire not to proceed with the process. By and large, however, everybody wants to subject themselves to and be part of this economic system. Members voluntarily accept these rules of trade and competition. As North had said, the rules are not always formal. Even in the UN, WTO etc., the formal rules are not necessarily always the most important. These institutions have informal rules that have evolved over time, and members voluntarily accept these rules in the expectation that they are in their own long term interests.

The only exception, which was mentioned in an earlier section is trade in oil and gas or energy. The oil/gas cartel continues to operate outside the rules of the world trade system with apparently complete impunity. It is an amazing thing. Nobody bothers to haul them up in the WTO. This probably requires some thinking. India is certainly not strong enough to do that, but all large oil importers should certainly be thinking about it. Similarly, there is a voluntarily membership of the World Bank, which deals with aid and social factors. The IMF deals with short-term BOP loans. Though it is called the International Monetary and Financial Organization, it has rarely dealt with other financial issues besides BOP crisies. The recent US-EU global financial crisis exposed the fact that there are big holes in the global financial system. IMF really does not perform the functions which are equivalent to the WTO for global trade. There is no global organisation which deals with capital flows in a manner anywhere comparable to the WTO in terms of trade and competition. These are some of the things that are now being discussed in various fora.

For instance, these issues are currently before the G-20 meeting or the P-20. From India's perspective, it is more important to participate in some way in the formulation of rules of the global financial system. One reason for being considered a power or to become a great power is therefore to be a part of the club which frames the rules. Thus, for instance if a new club emerges to deal with financial issues, India must endeavour to be a part of it. One possibility is a G-4 consisting of the US, EU, China and India, a club that would clearly be in India's interest to bring about, without being inimical in any way to the interests of the other three. The Indian intelligentsia has to think how India can start creating and becoming part of the clubs which shape the rules of the game, so to say, the economic game.

Military Power and Rules

Next, we move to military power and its rules. Earlier sections have given the approximate dates, at which China and India are likely to meet the benchmark for becoming a potential great power and superpower. Superpowers clearly define the rules of the game among themselves. Global powers can influence them if they play their cards well. Military power is an important instrument for enforcement of global rules, whatever they are. Of course, there have been two recent glaring examples of failure of military power, Iraq and Afghanistan. However, even these examples show that the failure was less that of military power *per se* and more of other broader elements of power and the context and competence of its use. Military power also creates a space that allows a global power to act outside the rules. A superpower has the liberty of acting outside the rules. It just invents its own rules. It is not as simple as it sounds, and requires further discussion. But other military powers can also create the space and have done so in the past, to violate the rules of global military action. Pakistan's aggressive militarisation, way beyond its economic size and power potential is a good example.

Two important new elements have come in and become an important part of the canvas of military power and its use. Most people are familiar with the fact that nuclear weapons are game changers. As Mr. K. Subrahmanyam has emphasised, full-fledged war between nuclear weapon States is unthinkable; maybe, that is too strong a word, but clearly it is a game changer. The emergence of alternative instruments of warfare, terrorism, guerrilla warfare, whatever you want to call it is also familiar. Virmani (2006c) gives an indication of Pakistan's strategy of combining nuclear weapons and terrorism (along with incredible diplomacy) to violate global rules and conventions for 25 years. Pakistan's use of these elements is a case study worthy of inclusion in a graduate textbook.

Social-Political Power

The third element, which is new and an important element of post-war globalisation, relates to the issues of human rights. This is an element of power in which there is the greatest philosophical divide. Democratic societies put much more emphasis on individual rights, "The right to life, liberty and the pursuit of happiness,..." as the first democratic Constitution said. In contrast, communist-socialist such as China emphasise collective rights. But leaving this aside, the issue of human and social rights is beginning to shape global rules in a way that has never happened historically. This change is consistent with India's national, social and human development objectives. It must therefore, incorporate into our global objectives and strategy. India must develop a world vision or vision for the world which is consistent with its own ethos, interest in and commitment to democracy. This would intelligently combine national interests with the interests of a wider spectrum of peoples and countries.

Soft power has been widely talked about since it was first proposed by Joseph Nye. Instead of putting this as one of three elements of power, this chapter treats it as a sub-element of socio-political power in a global environment. This is because globalisation is increasing the connect between national elements (economy, security and social) and international elements (economy, military and socio-political). Introduction of a socio-political (social, political) element of power allows us to connect the internal and external elements and thus, bring about a consistency in the narrative of power. When a country takes a global action, it is consistent with the vision that it has been propagating. Thus, Iraq is a failure because there was no consistency between professed vision and the actions taken after the initial military victory. From the perspective of global public opinion clearly, there was what psychologists call dissonance.

If India is to become a global power, its intelligentsia (academics, media, politicians) have to start thinking of this; the perceived consistency of narrative and the credibility and the legitimacy of the use of power. If India is going to use power, for instance to fight the terrorists in either neighbouring country, it has to develop and focus much more on establishing this credibility. There is too little of this propagation; at least it is not very visible or prominent.

In overall power, the will to power (i.e., the will to acquire and use power) is very important. For example, when the nuclear deal was hanging in the balance, Indian political system appeared for a while to be woefully short of any will to power. That has been partly but not wholly corrected.

Globalisation of National Security

Virmani (2006b) argued that, "The changing role of India in the global environment requires a change in the institutional arrangements and approaches that we have for interacting with the current and potential global powers as well as with other countries and regional organizations. Over the next decade or so we have to change our approach from one in which we react to the actions of other more active and hyper active countries to one in which we try to influence the policies of others. We need to bring about a greater conceptual clarity to our foreign policy and revamp our international intelligence capabilities. We also need to ensure that the rise in the 'actual power' of India is commensurate with the rise in 'power potential,' by developing a comprehensive approach to Strategic Technology."

Since then, the Indo-US nuclear deal has been signed and NSG waiver obtained. These and other new issues have arisen to which the chapter returns after looking briefly at the issues raised in the above referenced EPW paper.

Foundation of National Security: Internal Security

"The most fundamental role of the State or the Government that claims to govern it is to provide security of life, limb and property to all its citizens. The State is defined by its monopoly over violence. In return it must provide physical security to all. Only the latter can legitimize the former. The rule of law is a basic foundation of a modern market economy. It is a prerequisite for development and equitable economic growth. A country that cannot ensure the rule of law and public security within its borders cannot become a global power. The writ of the government must be established over the Naxalite dominated interiors of the country and lawlessness (kidnapping and murder industry) eliminated from States/regions of the country where it has become prevalent, because of the abdication of responsibility by the political rulers of these States and the gross failure of governance. Given the limited capabilities of the governments in these States/Regions they must focus on universal provision of the basic public goods (& quasi-public goods) such as police, courts, roads..." (Virmani, 2004a).

The foundation of national security has to be internal security. Post-Mumbai terror attack, the issue of anti-terrorism organisation has returned to centre stage. Having an anti-terrorism organisation(s) is necessary but not sufficient. Unless India corrects its basic system of law and order so that it can protect the innocent and punish the guilty special efforts can only be sustained for a few years, after which they invariably fizzle out or revert to the mean/average quality. The author has been collecting and narrating horrendous stories about law and order for 20 years. The first time such a story came up about two decades ago, he said, well, Bihar has arrived in Delhi. The most recent story is of an average middle class person arrested and kept in jail for six months and released without charges. Though these are mere examples, there are very serious issues underlying them and India cannot have a sustained and sustainable anti-terrorism strategy unless it does something about them. The solutions are well known: The Supreme Court order on police reforms needs to be accepted and acted upon—fine-tuning and correction of anomalies can always follow. The new home minister has started acting on some of these recommendations.

Foreign Policy Constructs and Narative

"If India is to play the 'Balance of Power' game to its advantage the Perspective Planning functions, intellectual effort/output, information/knowledge base and training systems for operational personnel must be re-oriented and strengthened. Similarly, the conceptual basis of our foreign policy approach to our region (S. Asia, E. & S.E. Asia and W. & C. Asia) must be widened and developed with greater sophistication" (Virmani, 2006b).

Foreign policy constructs have to be weaved into a foreign policy narrative that can be understood by engaged citizens and the media. For example, one narrative could be the development of South Asia for all South Asians, an essential element of which is the declaration/creation of South Asia as a terrorism free zone (TFZ). Ideas have power when they can be understood by all. One has to have the words, sentences and paragraphs that express these ideas in simple terms that resonate with the intelligentsia and media of all relevant countries. India has a problem of terrorism. It has to globalise it in some way by thinking of ways to by involve the people, convince the people of other countries and get them to help push these things.

Global Intelligence Capability

"The Subrahmanyam committee long ago recommended the revamping of institutional structures for intelligence collection, integration, analysis and assessment and others have reiterated these recommendations since then. This becomes even more imperative in the changing context. Modern technology must be introduced to upgrade and widen the intelligence network (satellite, internet, radio waves) while strengthening traditional methods of human intelligence (e.g. foreign language training). We must develop an extensive capability for covert action to address asymmetric threats from non-state actors, fundamentalist terrorists, their handlers/ controllers/ motivators/ financiers" (Virmani, 2006b).

This issue is well known, but perhaps needs some re-orientation from domestic to cross-border or global threats.

Strategic Assets and Technology

"Strategic technology and assets [major defence platforms (submarines, fighter aircraft), nuclear and aero space technology, robotics, communication (interception/ eavesdropping), internet (pattern recognition), radar (stealth, ECM)] are critical to India's becoming a

Global power. This requires better planning of procurement and development of strategic technology and an integrated view across different organisations and departments currently engaged in them. Issues like the nature and amount of Offset purchases and the trade-offs between acquisition and development would have to be addressed. Attention has to be given to specialised education and training of scientists and technicians (perhaps in-house) in nuclear, space, oceanic and other technologies. The National Security Council should have a special wing that carries out the planning and monitoring of the development of strategic technology and skills" (Virmani, 2006b).

Post-nuclear apartheid, a comprehensive and non-ideological view has to be taken to accelerate the flow of nuclear technology into India. For instance, the flow of private FDI into the nuclear and other strategic sectors must be facilitated, for the same reasons that Indian policy since 1991 has generally prefered FDI over FII or debt flows. The former brings with it new ideas, skills and managerial capabilities that benefit the whole economy beyond the specific firms. India must also encourage and incentivise the acquisition, adaptation and development of Communication-Interception-Security Technology (CIST) and Remotely piloted aircrafts (Predator).

Defence: Flexible Response

"The nature of the challenge facing India has been evolving over the years. The nature of constraints under which defense and foreign policy operates will also change—some will loosen others will tighten. As open violent wars between major powers becoming increasingly unlikely, those who wish us ill have developed indirect means of undermining our security. We need to increase the range of options available to us to attack the source or fountain head as well as to pay back in the coin that they choose to use or which are more cost effective from our perspective and reduce the potential adversary's benefit-cost ratio. This requires a sharp increase in capability for unconventional warfare and unconventional means of defense. A wider range of options must also be developed and/or enhanced for dealing with asymmetric threats from non-state actors, fundamentalist terrorists, their handlers/ controllers/ motivators/financiers" (Virmani, 2006b).

News reports suggest that former Prime Minister of India, Mr. I.K. Gujral dismantled the limited capacity India had for covert action against non-State actors who have been waging covert warfare against it for decades. This capability must be rebuilt and enhanced to create effective deterrence against terrorist attacks.

Economic Interdependence

"In this age of globalization the size of the market a country offers for other countries' exports is a measure of the (actual or potential) influence it has over them. It is easier to switch most imports from one country to another than to switch exports from an established buyer/country to others.[8] Thus paradoxically, the size of a country's imports is a better measure of its economic power over others than the size of its exports. In some cases the latter can even be a source of dependence and weakness in terms of power relations."[9] "FDI inflows into an economy also the measure the relative attractiveness of an economy.[10] Though the stock of FDI, equity and debt owned by foreigners in an economy denote a mutual dependence of the host and the source country, once invested and to the extent they are difficult to disinvest, the balance of advantage shifts to the host country" (Virmani, 2006b).

An important issue for the future is the role of oil and gas and other energy resources. As already discussed, the cartelisation of petroleum/mineral oil supply by national oil companies/nation states, and the fact that on the demand side it is universal intermediate essential to the functioning of every country, makes it unique. Unlike all other goods and services, it is capable of being used as an instrument

8. Perhaps the only exception is oil imports, where there is an monopoly/oligopoly (OPEC cartel) with a small competitive fringe. It is highly misleading to treat the highly volatile spot and futures markets where most of the these small competitive suppliers operate as the market for oil.

9. This will become clear when the impact of the US-EU financial crises and the consequent global slowdown and trade is clear. I have asserted over the past year that export-led economies such as China will suffer a sharper decline in growth than those with deficits on merchandise trade account such as India. Others in the former category are Japan and Germany.

10. Luxembourg has shown a surge of investment as many European MNCs have shifted their headquarters to it in recent years.

of power. Energy security (oil, gas, uranium) must therefore be an element of our overall national security policy.

International System Objectives

The question to be addressed is what should be India's objectives in the international arena in terms of international security and national security? This has to be done keeping in mind the earlier analysis of this chapter on the need to change global institutions and rules and the cross-border developments over the past few years, including the recent terrorist attacks. The chapter suggests three short term and two medium term objectives. These are by no means exhaustive, and undoubtedly readers will come up with many more suggestions.

Permanent Membership of UNSC

It is the thesis of this chapter that the national and international security are interlinked. Globalisation has and will continue, to result in increasing these linkages. This section therefore starts with the most important institution of global security the UN Security Council (UNSC). Virmani (2004b) suggested that the veto should be based on a voting share that depends on relative power, with a definition of what decisions can be taken with majority and which require super majority. Till such reforms come about, India must aim, as a globally recognised nuclear weapon power, to have veto power as a permanent member of the UNSC.

The UNSC is much more important than some people assert, based on its demonstrated ineffectiveness in many situations of international security. People say, it is a dying club, how does it matter whether you are a permanent member or whether you have a veto or not? What is overlooked by these observers is its informal role as a club where bargaining among permanent members takes place. There are also informal bargains made between permanent and non-permanent members. The formal rules determine whether you are a member or not and the informal rules determine how much of your power you can use to obtain bargains. Thus, it is important for India to aim to become a permanent veto bearing member of the UNSC, if it wants to be able to assert its emerging global power.

Global Anti-Terror Strategy

India needs to develop a national anti-terror strategy that is part and parcel of a global anti-terror strategy and vice-versa. Viewed from another angle, it must help develop a global anti-terror consensus that views its anti-terror strategy as an essential part of fighting global terror.

The anti-terror strategy would include the following elements:

UN Consensus

India had introduced, several years ago, resolution on terrorism. This needs to be pursued in the UN as well as in other forums. India and other democratic countires also need to pursue the development of a globally accepted definition of terror that is consistent with the terrorist problems that they face and the domestic constraints under which the war on terror will have to be fought. The development of a narrative with which thought leaders across the world can empathise, could be helpful in attaining this objective.

As part of this consensus, India could build global public opinion to impose a travel ban and freeze the global financial assets of current and retired members of State intelligent agencies (such as the ISI) associated with terrorists or their activities.

Re-define Aggression and Self-defence

The UNSC definition of aggression and self-defence needs to be modified in the light of the increasing importance of non-State actors and the use of failing States or parts of States as a base for cross-border terrorism. India must aim to change the UN definitions of aggression to include irregular guerrilla warfare, terrorism, etc., and the definition of self-defence to include attacks against them on the territory of such failing States and regions. This requires an identification of conditions under which such counter-attack would be acceptable and the development of markers for identifying cross-border terrorism.

Elimination of Terrorist Networks

Elimination of terror networks was a key objective for India, even before the Mumbai attack, as it has been the target for close to a quarter century. The author has often asked the question, whether there is any case other case in history, of a large country that was so pacifist as to not take any military action against a neighbouring country, that despite being,

(a) 13 per cent to 19 per cent of its size, trained, financed and supported terrorists to attack the larger country, and simultaneously convinced intellectuals and ayatollahs of the great powers that it was constantly under threat? [11]

(b) 6 per cent to 9 per cent of its size, that allows its territory to be used by terrorists of different varieties and persuasion against a neighbour?

It is an amazing situation that is hard to understand unless one concludes that there is something fundamentally wrong in India's conceptualisation and approach and it cannot afford this as a great power.

Access to Strategic Technology

Access to all possible areas of strategic technology must be an important goal. An important area of technology, where a minor apartheid regime still prevails is missile and space technology, which is subject to the missile technology control regime. India must aim to become a member of this club. At a more operational level, it must try and acquire pilotless attack aircraft, communication intercept equipment etc., from those countries that possess such technology.[12]

Objectives: Medium Term

Over the medium term, there are two objectives worth pursuing: The setting up of a new institution for global governance and a new strategic technology club of which India becomes a founder member along with the potential great powers of the 21st century.

---

11. The ratio which was 17 per cent in 1980, rose to a high of 19 per cent in 1992 and has since fallen to 13 per cent.

12. The author thanks Arundhati Ghosh for suggesting this in response to a specific question.

Global Governance Institution

Virmani (2004b) suggested a reform of the United Nations to take account of both current economic and power balance and evolving global socio-political principles such as democratic/human equality (also in Virmani (2006a)).

India has traditionally been hesitant to get involved in global democratic conclaves. This was partly justified when there was clear dissonance between the words and actions of those who proposed these issues. With this dissonance likely to be greatly muted, India as the largest democracy in terms of population and (soon) the third largest in terms of economic size, our approach needs to change. Democratic principles are both globally acceptable and in India's favour. So, Indian's should not feel shy about them. India should conceptualise a system of global governance which is based on some kind of democratic principles. The basic idea is to divide global governance into two components, which have fundamentally different management challenges and therefore require different distribution of global representation. These are global socio-economic development issues and global security (national) issues, corresponding approximately to the current UN General Assembly (and the UN social agencies-WHO etc.) and the UNSC. Voting power in the first must be distributed according democratic principles (all humans are equal and must therefore, have an equal vote), while voting power in the second must be based on relative power, as the key issue is enforcement of rules through exercise of power.

There are two ways to implement the democratic principles. One is through direct election of representatives to the global assembly through individual vote or to let country governments have a vote in proportion to their population. In both cases, there is asymmetry between relatively free democratic countries and relatively controlled dictatorial or oligarchic systems. Democratic countries therefore need to devise a system that adjusts the vote share for the degree of democracy. This requires a system in which an independent and credible rating organisation, rates the degree of democracy—not only must such an agency be independent and unbiased but must be seen to be so across the world. As existing US rating organisations may not be credible, the world needs a global organisation in which all democratic countries are shareholders. The rating (0 to 1 with 1 as perfect democracy) would be used to discount the individual vote or representation in the body that manages global socio-economic developmental objectives.

The other component is global security. The Security Council is the instrument of military power and the use or threat of use of force to enforce the rules. By definition, the veto means that even the weakest member of the veto bearing powers can de-legitimise any action even if the other members support it unanimously. How can countries with completely different amounts of power accept such a rule? A superpower or superpowers will never feel bound by such a ridiculous principle. Thus, the new system must have some kind of proportional vote based on a measure of power, if it is to be both fair and realistic and therefore, credible and sustainable. Thus, it may be reasonable to expect a superpower with less than 50 per cent of the global power to convince a set of countries with more than 50 per cent of the global power that it should be authorised to take certain actions. Conversely, a global power that can convince 25-50 per cent (whether or not it requires a super majority respectively) of the power votes to oppose any action against it would provide acceptable safeguards to the powerful countries to subject themselves to the same global rules. As enforcement of rules through use of military power (or the threat of its use) is an important element of international security decision, a powerful country will not surrender (on a long term basis) its freedom of action, unless its vote is proportional to its power.

Therefore, the international security part of the new global governance organisation must provide for voting shares in proportion to global power (measured for instance by the VIP^2 or VIP). It must define situations which require majority decisions and those that require a super majority (66 per cent or 75 per cent). It must also provide for periodic re-estimation and re-adjustment of voting proportions according to shifts in global power.

Strategic Technology Club

The second one is a new security technology club to supplant NPT, NSG, MTCR etc. Those of you who are familiar with these issues know that, in the existing structure, India has been like a beggar trying to get in, in each club. Why not float an alternative idea which is based on some kind of a global rationale and a global system, taking account of the views of those who are powerful today. For instance, the issue of WMDs, that is on the global table, would have to be addressed.

Conclusion

When the author first projected (in 2004-05) the development of tripolar global power structure by the middle of the 21st century, US foreign affairs journals refused to even consider this possibility seriously. Despite major upheavels in the last few years, including the reduction of India's per capita GDP and GDP at purchasing power parity by 36 per cent virtually at the stroke of the pen (i.e., without a clear and transparent explanation and comparative data on the components of this unprecedented change), it has been shown that the earlier authors projections have changed only marginally. As the author had anticipated, adverse (favourable) changes may delay (accelerate) the achievement of the bipolar and tripolar global power structure, but not derail it. Thus, the dates for these two events have been pushed back by about seven years.

The latest National Intelligence Council (2008) report recognises the eventual emergence of China and India as powers, but still asserts that they will be operating in a multipolar world. This chapter has tried to show that what has been termed a multipolar structure is merely the phase of high uncertainty during the transition between the unipolar structure at the end of the 20th century and the bipolar/tripolar structure that is likely to emerge during the second quarter of the 21st century. However, as Keynes said, "In the long run we are all dead".

The chapter therefore focuses on the transitional phase spanning the remaining years of the first quarter of this century, which can be characterised as multipolar, but also by various other terms that have been used by other scholars. After analysing the nature of this transition phase, it tries to draw out the implication for India, and what it must do to enhance national and international security. Besides traditional measures to enhance national security, it emphasises the need to modify/change the institutions and rules of the global economic, military and socio-political game and to work to set up new institutions that will better serve our national and global security interests.

References

Grevi, Giovanni (2009). "The Interpolar World", *Occasional Paper* No. 79. Paris: EUISS.

Kissinger, Henry (1994). *Diplomacy*. New York: Simon & Schuster.

National Intelligence Council (2004). *Mapping the Global Future, Report of the NIC 2020 Project*. Washington DC. December.

———. (2008). *Global Trends 2025, A Transformed World, Report of the NIC 2025 Project*. Washington DC. November.

Virmani, Arvind (2002a). "A New Development Paradigm: Employment, Entitlement and Empowerment", *Economic and Political Weekly* XXXVII(22): 2145-54 June, 1-7.

———. (2002b). "A New Development Paradigm: Employment, Entitlement and Empowerment", *Global Business Review* 3(2): 222-45, July-December. International Management Institute, SAGE Publications.

———. (2004a). *Accelerating Growth and Poverty Reduction—A Policy Framework for India's Development*. New Delhi: Academic Foundation. January.

———. (2004b). "Economic Performance, Power Potential and Global Governance: Towards a New International Order", *Working Paper* No. 150, ICRIER, December (*www.icrier.org/wp150.pdf*).

———. (2005a). "A Tripolar Century: USA, China and India," *Working Paper* No. 160, ICRIER, March, (*www.icrier.org/wp160.pdf*).

———. (2005b). "China's Socialist Market Economy: Lessons Of Success", ICRIER *Occasional Policy Paper*, April (*http://www.icrier.org/China05_policy7.pdf*).

———. (2005c). "VIP²: A Simple Measure of Nations (Natural) Global Power", ICRIER *Occasional Paper*, July (*http://www.icrier.org/vipp4.pdf*).

———. (2005d). *A Tripolar World, India, China & US*. Lecture delivered at India Habitat Centre on May 18 (*http://www.icrier.org/public/TripolarWrld_IHC5.pdf*).

———. (2005e). "Global Power from the 18th to 21st Century: Power Potential (VIP2), Strategic Assets & Actual Power (VIP)", *Working Paper* No. 175, ICRIER, November. *http://www.icrier.org/WP175VIPP8.pdf*

———. (2005f). "China's Socialist Market Economy: Lessons of Succes", *Working Paper* No. 178, ICRIER, December.

———. (2006a). *Propelling India from Socialist Stagnation to Global Power: Growth Process*, Vol. I (Policy Reform, Vol. II). New Delhi: Academic Foundation.

———. (2006b). "World Economy, Geopolitics and Global Strategy: Indo-US Relations in the 21st Century", *Economic and Political Weekly* XLI(43-44): 4601-12, November 4-10 (*http://www.epw.org.in/showArticles.php?root=2006&leaf=11&filename=10717&filetype=pdf*).

———. (2006c). "Trilateral Nuclear Proliferation: Pakistan's Euro-Chinese Bomb", *IDSA Monograph Series* No. 1. New Delhi: Institute of Defence Studies and Analysis. December.

———. (2006d). *Evolution of World Economy and Global Power: From Unipolar to Tripolar World in Economic Diplomacy*. Editor I.P. Khosla. New Delhi: Konarak Publishers.

———. (2007). "Future Economic Contours of the Asia-Pacific and South Asian Region and their Impact on Global Security Architecture", USI National Security Lecture 2006, in *National Security, Global Strategic Architecture and Information Security, National Security Series, 2006*. New Delhi: KW Publishers Pvt. Ltd.

———. (2008). "The Economic Foundations of National Power: From Multipolar to Tripolar World?", in V.R. Raghavan (ed.), *Economic Growth & National Security*. Chennai: Centre for Security Analysis.

———. (2009). *The Sudoku of India's Growth*. New Delhi: BS Books.

Zakaria, Fareed (2008). *The Post-American World*. Viking Penguin Books.

Index

Q

R

S

Q

R

S

V

W

Z